DIS

A HANDBOOK OF FOOD CRIME

Immoral and illegal practices in the food industry and what to do about them

Edited by Allison Gray and Ronald Hinch

P

First published in Great Britain in 2018 by

Policy Press
University of Bristol
1-9 Old Park Hill
Bristol BS2 8BB
UK
t: +44 (0)117 954 5940
e: pp-info@bristol.ac.uk
www.policypress.co.uk

North American office:
Policy Press
c/o The University of Chicago Press
1427 East 60th Street
Chicago, IL 60637, USA
t: +1 773 702 7700
f: +1 773-702-9756
e:sales@press.uchicago.edu
www.press.uchicago.edu

© Policy Press 2018

British Library Cataloguing in Publication Data
A catalogue record for this book is available from the British Library.

Library of Congress Cataloging-in-Publication Data
A catalog record for this book has been requested.

ISBN 978-1-4473-3601-3 hardcover
ISBN 978-1-4473-3603-7 ePub
ISBN 978-1-4473-3604-4 Mobi
ISBN 978-1-4473-3602-0 ePdf

Cover design by Policy Press
Front cover: image kindly supplied by www.alamy.com
Printed and bound in the United States of America

Contents

CONTENTS

List of tables and figures

Tables

Figures

Notes on contributors

Joseph Yaw Asomah is a PhD candidate at the University of Saskatchewan, Canada. His research interests generally revolve around government accountability, social justice, white-collar and corporate crime, anti-corruption movements and policing.

Stephanie Baran is a PhD student in the Department of Sociology at the University of Wisconsin-Milwaukee, USA. Her research interests include racism, capitalism and feminist theory.

Camilla Barbarossa is Associate Professor in Marketing at Toulouse Business School, Department of Marketing and International Business, France. Her primary research interests are in the field of ethical and pro-environmental consumption. Specifically, she is interested in analysing consumers' adoption of environmentally friendly alternatives, and consumers' cognitive, emotional and behavioural responses to corporate social (ir)responsibility.

Ricardo César Barbosa Júnior is an MA student at the University of Calgary, Canada. His research interests include food sovereignty, urban food activism and the spatiality of contentious politics.

Sue Booth is an academic in the College of Medicine and Public Health at Flinders University, Australia. Her research interests include food security, food charity and alternative food systems.

Hongming Cheng is Professor of Crime, Law and Justice in the Department of Sociology, University of Saskatchewan, Canada. His research focuses on white-collar and corporate crime in the context of globalisation and regional regulatory cooperation. He also studies public attitudes towards the police, land rights, comparative criminology and the sociology of China.

Estevan Leopoldo de Freitas Coca is an Assistant Professor at Londrina State University, Brazil. His research interests include food sovereignty, land reform and territorial development.

Antonia Corini is a PhD researcher at the Doctoral School on the Agro-Food System (Università Cattolica del Sacro Cuore, Italy), where she focuses on food law. Antonia's research interests include food safety, novel foods, official control and food fraud.

John Coveney is a Professor in the College of Nursing and Health Sciences at Flinders University, Australia. His research interests include food policy, food history and food culture and health.

Eileen Davenport holds a BA in Sociology (Exeter), and MA and MPhil degrees in Planning (Nottingham Trent). She is currently an adjunct faculty member the School of Humanitarian Studies and the School of Business at Royal Roads University, Canada. Merging these interests, Eileen will soon embark on research related to how to engage refugees in the fair trade process.

Marcello De Rosa is an Associate Professor in the Department of Economics and Law at the University of Cassino and Southern Lazio, Italy. His research interests include territorial agri-food systems, illegal practices in agro-food systems, rural entrepreneurship and family farm businesses.

Jan Deckers is a Senior Lecturer at Newcastle University in the UK. His research interests focus on bioethical issues.

Sugandhi del Canto is a PhD candidate in the Department of Community Health and Epidemiology, College of Medicine, at the University of Saskatchewan, Canada. Sugandhi's research interests include nutrition, place-based health, mixed-methods research, community-based research, HIV and sexually transmitted infections (STIs), as well as programme and implementation science.

Jinky Leilanie Del Prado-Lu is a Research Professor at the National Institutes of Health at the University of the Phillippines, Manila (UPM), and an Affiliate in the Faculty of the College of Arts and Sciences, UPM. Her research interests include promoting wellbeing through occupational epidemiology and advocacy programmes, especially among vulnerable populations such as farmers.

Rachel Engler-Stringer is an Associate Professor in the Department of Community Health and Epidemiology, College of Medicine, at the University of Saskatchewan, Canada. Her research interests include community food security, food environments and food access, food system sustainability, health promotion and community-based and participatory research.

Amy Fitzgerald is an Associate Professor in the Department of Sociology, Anthropology, and Criminology at the University of Windsor, Canada. She is also a researcher at the Great Lakes Institute for Environmental Research. Amy's research interests are situated at the culture–nature nexus, focusing on the perpetuation of harms by humans against the environment and non-human animals. Her areas of specialisation include green criminology, (critical) animal studies, environmental sociology and gender studies.

Kora Liegh Glatt is an MA student in Sociology at the University of Victoria, Australia. She is currently studying the effects of government regulations on small-scale farmers and the achievement of food sovereignty. Her other interests include Indigenous reconciliation, grassroots social movements and social activism.

Allison Gray is a PhD candidate in Sociology at the University of Windsor, Ontario, Canada. Her research interests intersect around the subject of food, ranging across a variety of sociological and criminological perspectives. She is especially keen in studying issues relating to forms of informal food governance, theoretical concerns surrounding the impact of contemporary food systems on human–nature relationships and the connection of food systems and consumption patterns with green criminology perspectives.

Ronald Hinch is Professor Emeritus in the Faculty of Social Science and Humanities at the University of Ontario Institute of Technology, Canada. His research interests are eclectic, covering many subjects across criminology and sociology, including critical criminology, sexual assault laws, theoretical criminology, policing violence against women, food crime and the study of serial murder.

Richard Hyde is an Associate Professor in the School of Law at the University of Nottingham, UK. He is interested in consumer law in general, and food law in particular, and is particularly interested in the sharing of information between regulators, and the ways that this supports regulatory activity.

Harvey S. James Jr received a PhD in Economics from Washington University in St Louis, USA. He is currently Professor of Applied Economics and Chair of the Department of Agricultural and Applied Economics at the University of Missouri. His research focuses on applied ethics and the economic foundations of trust, ethics and happiness. He has a particular interest in ethical issues affecting smallholder farmers and arising from agricultural contracting and market competition. He is Editor-in-Chief of the journal *Agriculture and Human Values*.

Linnea Laestadius is an Assistant Professor of Public Health Policy and Administration at the University of Wisconsin-Milwaukee, USA. Her research interests focus on the intersection of technology and public health.

Paul Leighton is a Professor in the Department of Sociology, Anthropology, & Criminology at Eastern Michigan University, USA. His research interests include white-collar and corporate crime, as well as how inequalities such as class, race and gender are reflected – and recreated – by the criminal justice system.

Michael A. Long is an Associate Professor at Northumbria University, UK. His research interests include green criminology, political economy and agro-food systems.

Will Low holds a BA and MA from the University of British Columbia and a PhD from the London School of Economics and Political Science (LSE). Trained as an economist, he is currently a professor teaching sustainable business at Royal Roads University, Canada, with a particular interest in sustainable consumption. His research has focused mainly on the fair trade movement, but his most recent project analyses consumption and the production of wild foods through, as an example, alternative food networks, and as a site for transformational learning about sustainability.

Xiaocen Liu is a Post-Doctor of Law at Renmin University of China, and a researcher at the Tencent Research Institute, China. His research interests include the regulation of cybercrime and issues in cybersecurity.

Michael J. Lynch is a Professor at the University of South Florida, USA. His research interests include green criminology, political economy and environmental justice.

Louise Manning is a Senior Lecturer in Food Policy and Management at Harper Adams University, Newport, Shropshire, UK. Her research interests involve issues of integrity in food supply chains in terms of product, processes, data and people. She is also interested in scientific and holistic risk management and wider food governance.

Martha McMahon is an Associate Professor in Sociology at the University of Victoria, Australia. Her current research interests involve the area of food, farming, agri-food governance, food sovereignty, gender and food security, environmental sociology and ecological feminism.

Jan Mei Soon is a Lecturer in Food Safety Management Systems in the Faculty of Health and Wellbeing at the University of Central Lancashire, UK. Her research interests involve food integrity, food control measures, food safety management and risk reduction strategies. She is also interested in halal integrity, allergen risk management, food safety training and education.

Tiziana Pagnani is a PhD student in the Department of Agriculture at the University of Naples 'Federico II', Italy. Tiziana's research interests include illegal practices in the food system, rural development economics, as well as climate change and food security.

Dominique Paturel is a social science researcher at the Institut National de la Recherche Agronomique (INRA). Her research interests include food democracy and issues surrounding the right to sustainable food.

Robert Phillips is a Professor of Management at the University of Richmond, Virginia, USA. His research interests include stakeholder management and business ethics.

Ashley Savage is a Lecturer in Law at the Liverpool Law School, University of Liverpool, UK. Ashley is interested in international cooperation and information sharing in regulation and enforcement, and has a long-standing interest in researching the unauthorised disclosure of official information and whistleblowing.

Judith Schrempf-Stirling is an Associate Professor of Management at the University of Richmond, Virginia, USA. Her research interests include corporate social responsibility, as well as business and human rights.

Juanjuan Sun is a Post-Doctor of Law at Renmin University of China and Researcher at the Center for Coordination and Innovation of Food Safety Governance, China. His research interests involve risk regulation and food law.

Wesley Tourangeu is a Postdoctoral Fellow in the School for Resource and Environmental Studies at Dalhousie University in Halifax, Nova Scotia, Canada. His research interests include agricultural law and policy, green criminology, animal welfare, social and ecological sustainability, agricultural biotechnology, and theories of power and influence.

Ferro Trabalzi is a Lecturer at John Cabot University in Rome, Italy. Ferro's research interests include traditional food networks, urban farming, urban sociology and illegal practices in the food system.

Bernd van der Meulen is a private consultant in food legal affairs and a Professor of Food Law at Wageningen University, Netherlands. His research interests include regulation of food safety, food security and trade at national levels, EU levels, global levels and through private standards.

Reece Walters is Director of the Crime and Justice Centre in the Faculty of Law at Queensland University of Technology, Australia. Reece is interested in studying issues involving eco crime, environmental justice and state and corporate crime.

Rob White is a Professor of Criminology in the School of Social Sciences at the University of Tasmania, Australia. His research interests include green criminology and environmental harm and crime.

Jasmine Yeates is an independent writer and researcher living in Hobart, Australia. Her research interests involve green criminology and innovative justice.

Introduction

Ronald Hinch and Allison Gray

This book is about the food people eat, the conditions under which it is produced and what is done to it before it is bought and consumed. It is about the way food is regulated, poorly regulated or in need of regulation. It involves questions of governance, how problems involving foodstuffs and food processes are enforced, ineffectively enforced or not enforced at all. From this perspective, this book encompasses an understanding of food crimes and harms beyond legalistic anthropocentric definitions. This entails a critical contextualisation of humanity's relationship to food, and questions many phenomena, including the role of speciesism and social inequalities among various actors within the food industry, the commodification of food and the greenwashing of its marketing, and the consequences of changing agricultural techniques and food technologies on humans, non-human animals and the environment. Above all else, this book is about *food crime*.

While the study of the legal regulation of food has been subjected to prolonged study by sociologists and legal experts for more than a century (see Paulus, 1974), and there were some references to food crime in the literature in purely legal contexts (see Ponting, 2005), Hazel Croall (2007) was the first to attempt to offer a broader concept of food crime that was not confined to legal definitions. She defined 'food crime' as a range of crimes involved in producing, distributing and selling foodstuffs. Food crime includes a wide range of offences:

> ... involving economic and physical harms, issues of personal
> safety and health, and many different kinds of frauds, from
> the evasion of subsidies and quotas and the avoidance of

revenue, to food adulteration and misrepresentation through written and pictorial indications, the quality and contents of food. (Croall, 2007, p 207)

Since then, articles on food crime have been published in various journals or included as chapters or sections within edited books focused on green criminology, environmental crime, corporate crime, rural crime or similar topics (see, for example, Beirne and South, 2007; White, 2009; Sollund, 2015; Donnermeyer, 2016). However, in none of these was food crime made the primary focus – which is the objective of this book.

A criminological study of food necessitates a combination of criminology, sociology, anthropology, legal studies, political science, geography and other social sciences through an interdisciplinary marriage founded on matters involving food. The multiplicity of issues, concerns and questions are significant to everyone and everything involved in food production and consumption. This allows comprehensive theorising and research on the complex relations between humans (farmers, consumers, food manufacturers, food corporations and such), animals (livestock or wild), technologies (chemicals, machinery, biotechnologies and such) and environments (soil, water, air, urban, rural and such), based around issues of food safety, population wellbeing and environmental health across varying concerns involving sustenance, diet or nutrition. In other words, the study of food crime matters to anyone who eats!

Some of these multifaceted relationships are organised by a multitude of policies, laws, regulations and rules – both formal and informal – while others, which arguably ought to be, are not. This (lack of) legal organisation within the food system is the key area of analysis and criticism for researchers in food crime, who may hold concerns or raise questions relating to issues of morality, ethics, social justice, harm, deviance, criminality or legality. The more critical scholars are engaged in investigating how these forms of governance (laws, policies, regulations and rules) frequently fail to provide either safe food for consumers or safe working conditions for agricultural workers, while allowing corporate enterprises, in the form of agribusinesses, to promote their interests.

Section I, *Thinking about food crime*, provides a theoretical overview of food crime and how it is conceptualised. This includes questioning the constitutive understandings of food crimes and harms and the consequences of shifting away from illegally defined intentional (in) actions by rational but deviant individuals, to broader structural and cultural patterns of harms with both direct and indirect victimisation and by both intentional and unintentional (in)actions from individuals, organisations, corporations and so on. In the first chapter, Allison Gray outlines a food crime perspective for the criminological study of food. In doing so, she provides an overview of the concept of food crime and its theoretical positioning, contextualised in current epistemological and ontological issues involving the contemporary study of food. Martha McMahon and Kora Liegh Glatt, in Chapter 2, comment on how cheapened food systems are organised by agri-food safety governance interwoven with neoliberal technologies of individual liability. Through a feminist perspective, they argue that the biopolitical ways in which societies are protected from food crimes and harms are problematic themselves, characterised by slow violence and harm committed without an identifiable individual criminal. In Chapter 3, Marcello De Rosa, Ferro Trabalzi and Tiziana Pagnani comment on the social construction of illegality and legality as applied to food production, specifically involving the case of buffalo mozzarella in southern Italy. Given that organised crime characterises the area, they propose the 'Evil Trinity' model to explain the normalisation and institutionalisation of illegal behaviour in food production.

Section II concerns issues relating to *Farming and food production*. It addresses food crime issues associated with the production stage of the food system, specifically targeting farm-level concerns. It begins with Chapter 4 on farm decision-making and the controversies that result from mixing economic pressures and farming ethics. Harvey S. James Jr argues that farmers' ethical actions are constantly pressured by contemporary farming economics and agricultural laws and contracts, especially in terms of potential harming of humans, non-human animals and the environment. In Chapter 5, Ronald Hinch examines the long history of the use of slave labour in cocoa production, illustrating the context and extent of the use of slavery in that industry. Through this case study, Hinch points to the myriad of ways different actors within food systems appropriate such food crimes and harms, including the passivity of governments. Jinky Leilanie del Pradu-Lu continues in Chapter 6 with an assessment of the regulation and consequences involved in the use of pesticides on the farm, with a focus on their impact on farming communities, farmers and farm workers. She argues that contemporary agriculture is an ironic situation: society is dependent on farmers to provide food and nourish populations, yet participating in such agricultural work makes farmers uniquely vulnerable to illness, disease and bodily harm.

Section III shifts the focus to *Processing, marketing and accessing food*. It discusses various problems associated with what is done to food, how consumers access food and how laws, regulations and discourses enable these problems. In Chapter 7, Judith Schrempf-Sterling and Robert Phillips discuss the regulation and enforcement of marketing policies of food companies and their consequences on the wellbeing and health of the general population. More specifically, they argue that the harm associated with the global epidemic of obesity must be rectified by broadening the emphasis on responsibilising consumers for food decisions, to actively involving governments and food corporations. Louise Manning and Jan Mei Soon, in Chapter 8, analyse the impact of regulations, or lack thereof, dealing with food fraud, specifically the adulteration of food. They argue that current controls and countermeasures are insufficient to protect populations from adulterated foodstuffs, and propose additional risk-based measures. The section concludes with Chapter 9, where Sugandhi del Canto and Rachel Engler-Stringer assess the prevalence of food deserts, the politics of food access and the role of restrictive covenants in constructing and maintaining unjust food provision by corporate grocery retailers. They argue that governments must actively limit these regulations, as well as help develop alternative food channels, in order to help rectify food and nutrition deserts.

The subject matter for Section IV is *Corporate food and food safety*. Agribusiness has become a global enterprise. This concentration of food corporations has a significant impact on foodstuffs and food processes, in terms of safety, nutrition and justice. Due to the international characteristic of many food companies, there are a myriad of legal policies and regulatory bodies that are involved in food systems. These connections can be positive, but also enable forms of organised crime. In Chapter 10, Antonia Corini and Bernd van der Meulen begin this section with an analysis of the governance of food systems and corporate self-regulation associated with the horsemeat scandal in Europe. They argue that to combat food fraud, private schemes are a promising tool. Paul Leighton follows in Chapter 11 with an assessment of how the state facilitates corporate food crimes and harms with a case study description of a deadly *Salmonella* outbreak associated with the Peanut Corporation of America. He argues that the conviction and sentencing outcomes of the case do not signify that justice has been accomplished. In Chapter 12, Joseph Yaw Asomah and Hongming Cheng argue that the state, the food industry and globalisation processes drive what they term 'cheap capitalism' – a conceptual framework to explain the negative consequences of profit maximisation on food safety.

In Section V, *Food trade and movement*, attention is transferred to issues related to the (global) transportation of foodstuffs and how to deal with this in the case of food crimes and harms. In Chapter 13, Amy Fitzgerald and Wesley Tourangeau comment on the illegal and harmful treatment of farmed animals during transportation. Through a case study of Ontario's 'pig trial', they argue the food crime involved is not due to livestock tampering by the defendant, but associated with the (in)actions of the state and food industry. Richard Hyde and Ashley Savage, in Chapter 14, follow this discussion with an examination of cross-border information-sharing networks responding to food crimes and harms. They argue that while there are weaknesses in the current regulatory networks, they are essential tools in dealing with various food crime. Chapter 15 concludes this section with an assessment by Will Low and Eileen Davenport of the fair trade movement and how laws, labels and ethical considerations impact agricultural labour within fair trade movements. They argue that the fair trade label cannot be a solution itself for macro-level food crime, but is a practical alternative for food producers fighting the state of hegemonic 'free trade'.

Section VI, *Technologies and food*, assesses the intersection of science and technologies with food laws, regulations and food crimes and harms. The relationship between technology and food crime is not straightforward, as some technologies benefit food safety, nutrition and ethics, while others produce more risk, harms and crimes, sometimes simultaneously. In Chapter 16, Reece Walters begins this section with an overview of the knowledge politics involved in regulating genetically modified organisms (GMOs). He takes a political economy perspective to argue that the way knowledge is constructed about GMOs by state and corporate actors has significant impacts on the global food politics of power and profit. In Chapter 17, Juanjuan Sun and Xiaocen Liu provide an overview of issues involved in the regulation of novel foods. They argue that the creation of new food materials and food products in China, such as aloe vera and lean meat powder, produces unique technological risks in terms of food safety, and facilitates criminal and harmful opportunities in the food system, especially given the contemporary tendency for the deregulation of entrepreneurialism. Linnea Laestadius, Jan Deckers and Stephanie Baran, in Chapter 18, assess the crimes and harms associated with meat and livestock technologies, or what they term 'carnist technologies'. They argue that technologies that aim to respond to the growing demand for food, and animal-based foods in particular, are advocated with promises to remedy some troubles, but actually facilitate many other crimes and harms.

Green food is the focus for Section VII. This section targets the connection between foodstuffs and food systems and environmental harms and crimes. In particular, it involves discussions of issues related to climate change, the regulation of food waste and sustainable diets. Rob White and Jasmine Yeates, in Chapter 19, comment on the connections between food production and climate change. Specifically, they argue that profit-oriented food production contributes to carbon emission-based climate change, and the consequential natural resource degradation further harms agricultural systems, contributes to famine and produces climate-induced migrations. In Chapter 20, Michael A. Long and Michael J. Lynch assess the lack of regulation with respect to food waste, and its ethical, social and ecological consequences. They comment on potential helpful responses to food waste, but argue that its level in neoliberal global food systems, and its non-regulation, can be considered criminal. Estevan Leopoldo de Freitas Coca and Ricardo César Barbosa Júnior, in Chapter 21, show how food has become increasingly 'mercantilised' as a commodity, and offer an assessment of how local food programmes in schools in Brazil and Canada attempt to resist this trend through various sustainable practices. They argue that while some programmes only alter food consumption patterns, better options go beyond consumption to recognise the pedagogical potential of food and utilise schools as spaces for producing food, too.

The final section, Section VIII on *Questioning and consuming food*, deals with the impact of food crimes and harms on consumers and consumption patterns, as well as evaluations of food movements in responding to food crime and food harms. In Chapter 22, Sue Booth, John Coveney and Dominique Paturel comment on the potential of food democracy movements in responding to food crime. They argue that participatory 'counter-crimes', or democratic forms of resistance to food crimes and harms, offer some hope in re-making a just food system. Camilla Barbarossa, in Chapter 23, discusses consumer reactions to food scandals. She argues that there are multiple influences on how consumers attribute blame in reaction to food crimes and harms, and that food companies should seek to understand these in order to mitigate consumers' negative responses to future food scandals. In the concluding chapter, Allison Gray comments on the forms of resistance to food crimes and harms, including corporate cooptation of food movements that facilitates the prioritisation of 'food choice' and the responsibilisation of individual consumers. She argues that while it is regulators who are defined as the 'food cops', food corporations actively police what people eat, and are thus key facilitators of food crime.

No single collection of articles could illustrate all of the concerns and issues relevant for the study of food crime. Nonetheless, this collection brings together some key research examining issues related to the way food is grown, produced, marketed and regulated in various parts of the world. Food and food quality are not just local issues, but also embody global concern. As such, future research needs to be directed towards the complex relationship between food producers, food processors and the corporate domination of the food industry, as well as the role international regulatory agencies and governments play in mediating the interests of all actors and organisations involved. Turning a criminological gaze on the conditions under which food is (un)regulated and (poorly) enforced, this book encompasses a range of discussions on the problematic conditions under which food (dis)connects with humanity and its consequences on public health and wellbeing, non-human animals and the environment, often simultaneously. All of this is done in the hope that the future of food is less criminal and more palatable.

References

Beirne, P. and South, N. (eds) (2007) *Issues in green criminology: Confronting harms against environments, human and other animals*, Portland, OR: Willan Publishing.

Croall, H. (2007) 'Food crime', in P. Beirne and N. South (eds) *Issues in green criminology: Confronting harms against environments, human and other animals*, Portland, OR: Willan Publishing, pp 206–29.

Donnermeyer, J.F. (2016) *The Routledge handbook of rural criminology*, New York: Routledge.

Paulus, I. (1974) *The search for pure food: A sociology of legislation in Britain*, London: Martin Robertson.

Ponting, J. (2005) 'Food crime and food safety: Trading in bushmeat – Is new legislation needed?', *Journal of Criminal Law*, vol 69, no 1, pp 42–9.

Sollund, R.A. (ed) (2015) *Green harms and crimes: Critical criminology in a changing world*, Basingstoke: Palgrave Macmillan.

White, R. (2009) *Environmental crime: A reader*, Portland, OR: Willan Publishing.

Section I
Thinking about food crime

1

A food crime perspective

Allison Gray

Introduction

The subject of food is simultaneously ubiquitous and routine. Spanning roles of biological nourishment, cultural representations, technological innovations, religious proceedings, medical components, social occasions and personal tastes and pleasures, food surrounds and intertwines the myriad of human existences and ways of life. Yet individuals' experiences with food remain habitual, mundane, regular and perhaps increasingly void or withdrawn. The importance of food, in all its roles, cannot be understated. Food decisions and practices figuratively and literally invade the very being of humanity, having deliberate and unintentional global implications on every measure of public welfare, individual wellbeing and environmental health, impacting both human and non-human animals and environments in the present and the future.

Thus, it is quite easy to justify concern for food and food systems, especially when there are problems ranging from global agricultural land grabbing, to horsemeat scandals and mad cow disease, to ineffective corporate self-regulation of food safety, to the harmful transport conditions of livestock, to the consequences of food patent laws, to the impact of contemporary food systems on climate change and the over-responsibilisation of the rational and ethical consumer – to name just a few. These concerns extend across the processes of food production, processing, marketing, distribution, disposal and consumption, across decisions about growing and harvesting, agricultural labour, levels of food safety, effective labelling, the use of different and new technologies, the consequences of food processes on peoples and environments, and questions of the role and regulation of the individuals, private corporations and public governments involved in all of these issues.

The purpose of this chapter is to provide a perspective on the ways in which harmful practices with negative consequences are involved along the food chain, anywhere from agricultural inputs to individuals' digestive systems. More specifically, this chapter assesses the decisions, practices, organisations, omissions or other ways actors engage in society, which involve illegal, criminal, harmful, unjust, unethical or immoral food-related issues, and broadly defines them as *food crimes*. This may include situations of law-making or law-breaking, suspect or ineffective enforcement or the lack thereof, harms resulting from insufficient or absent regulation, or philosophical and pragmatic questions of corruption, deviance, justice and erroneousness. Such a perspective – a *food crime perspective* – intertwines various disciplines and multiple theories in encompassing a critical perspective that problematises many of the glitches among and within food systems beyond their comprehension as unlucky errors, rare events or necessary risks. In this sociological fashion, a food crime perspective involves researching patterns of deviance, harm and crime concerning foodstuffs and food processes, along with critically questioning events within their social systems and contexts.

An introduction to a food crime perspective will be presented in three sections in this chapter. The first involves a note on some epistemological and ontological concerns regarding the study of food and humanity's relation to food. This is followed by an overview of some key theoretical views in common with food crimes and their explanation. The third section presents the brief history and the origin of the concept of food crime, including a discussion of why it is important to think criminologically about food and to develop a food crime perspective.

Studying food, eating food

Food is a subject of scholarly inquiry that can no longer be defined as emerging, but rather, as present – albeit the development of this field of inquiry is not experienced globally (Belasco, 2008), and nor has the seriousness of food as a field of inquiry been accepted throughout history (Nestle and McIntosh, 2010). The importance of food spreads across worlds of research and lifestyles, of sciences and societies, of cultures and natures. Consequently, food is a platform where epistemological and ontological questions are central, where thinking about food crime – and food more generally – involves critical considerations of processes of knowing and studying food, as well as humanity's relationship with foodstuffs and systems. With this in mind, there are two points of discussion that are crucial in thinking about food crime: first, the multi- and transdisciplinarity of food studies and corresponding problems, and second, the current literal and figurative rift between humans and food.

There is little disagreement with the argument that the study of food is necessarily multidisciplinary. This 'intrinsic multidisciplinarity' is both the wonder and the challenge in studying food (Smith et al, 2010). The advantages are fairly clear – providing a larger and deeper picture of the role of foodstuffs and food processes within the human–nature relationship, expanding the scope of knowledge and working to balance the strengths and weaknesses of varying paradigms and disciplines. Similarly, as a subject of study, food facilitates the integration of theory and application (Long, 2002). However, food studies needs to go beyond inter- and multidisciplinarity, which combines or unites various viewpoints and disciplines, towards transdisciplinarity, which broadens the fusion to non-academic perspectives (Koç et al, 2012a). Such an ability to effectively blend academic and tangible knowledge has Smith and colleagues (2010) arguing that studying food enables the use of both the pen and the knife, which provides truly potent and exciting research. As the discipline of green criminology has experienced, cross-discipline cooperation has been both sought and essential, particularly in regards to the operationalisation of crimes and harms that depend on biological, geological and social scientists.

Yet there are institutional barriers that impede the holistic study of food matters, where the social sciences examine food pathways and cultures, nutritional sciences focus on the contents and health impacts of foods, and culinary or vocational schools provide training on the uses of food (Hamada et al, 2015). Such segregation can be deconstructive, as Wilk (2012, p 474) argues that 'no discipline can accommodate the meal as a whole, and the proliferation of new and hybrid interdisciplines furthers this fragmentation, rather than putting the fragments back together.' If food crime is to enter academia as a multi- and transdisciplinary object of study, it will not escape these evaluations.

A way to minimise these criticisms and anxieties for the criminological study of food is to identify the subject of food as a boundary object. Star and Griesemer (1989; Star, 2010) developed the idea of a boundary object to help conceptualise the process of cooperation in the absence of consensus. Essentially, a boundary object is something that simultaneously holds an active common identity, which is both plastic and robust, and successfully overlaps social worlds through communicative channels of translation. This means that boundary objects are able to preserve intricacy for some actors while providing simplified information for others, as Shackley and Wynne (1996) exemplify in collaborations between scientists and policy-makers on matters involving climate change. Boundary objects are not always successful, as Eden (2011) argues, demonstrating that food labels are illustrations of translation between producers and consumers, with limited effect on consumers' knowledge about food safety and nutrition. Nonetheless, conceptualising food crime as a boundary object can help enable transdisciplinary collective work, while avoiding the assumption that any understanding of a concept can be universally accepted.

Related to ways of understanding food, it is also important to note the contemporary reality of the global food system. Irrespective of history, food production and consumption functions reside at the most intense and dominant nexus of humanity and nature (Kareiva et al, 2007; Wittman, 2009; Sbicca, 2014). Grocery shopping, chopping, cooking and eating are some of the customary ways in which the majority of individuals interact with food. However, in modern Western nations, even these exchanges are simplifying to practices such as manoeuvring through a drive-thru and turning on a microwave. This distance or rift between people and food is evident as:

> ... people in many parts of the world are sitting down to meals with less idea than ever before about where the food in front of them was grown, the conditions under which it was cultivated, reared and processed, what chemicals in contains, who is making the decisions or how it was distributed, much less anything about the broader social and environmental implications of the system through which they get their food. (Weis, 2007, p 45)

As part of broader developments of the invisibilisation of nature, this human–food distance is the key organising principle of modern life (Worthy, 2013), through both physical and informational 'distancing'

(Kneen, 1995). In North America, the food – and edible food-like products – on the typical plate travel from farm to plate over thousands of kilometres (Clapp, 2012), effectively becoming (re)understood as 'food from nowhere' (McMichael, 2004). The implications being that 'the groceries we buy are mostly produced in distant places, by people we don't know, using processes that we know little about and have little or no control over' (Worthy, 2013, p 31). Such changes have led Rinella (2005, p 12) to argue that 'human history is just a long story of depersonalization of food production.'

Critical researchers argue that such 'food alienation' is exacerbated by the current global industrialised neoliberal food system (Princen, 1997, 2002; Wittman et al, 2010; Clapp, 2015; Leguizamón, 2016). This argument is based on the transition of foodstuffs from being sources of sustenance and nourishment to their (inappropriate) reformulation as marketised products and commodities – a process that has led some to define food as a 'fictitious commodity' (Polanyi, 1957; McClintock, 2010). In current societies (of the Global North), where the proportion of active farmers makes up a small fraction of the entire population, it is common to witness average consumers having very limited knowledge and experience with food production and what is in packaged or frozen foods and restaurant meals. Testing current generations of American children on their food knowledge has shown that a significant number are unable to identify or name many fruits, vegetables, grains and the plants that grow them, yet can cite numerous (corporate) brands of food and food-like products (see Oliver, 2010).

The consequences of this disconnection on (the potential for) food crimes are numerous and grim. For instance, the problem is displayed as one of insufficient knowledge, thus the solution is that individuals – as rational consumers – must be provided with (more) information. This is the role of food labels, such as Fairtrade emblems, which aim to 'lift the veil' that is obscuring the recognition of the social relationships involving food production and its consequences (Hudson and Hudson, 2003). If the majority of individuals are relying on the contents displayed on food packaging as their main knowledge about food, this places these individuals in incredibly vulnerable positions, subject to the bias of food corporations and limited to information about foodstuffs that the state deems valuable. This, of course, constrains the agency individual consumers experience, and 'undermines our capacity for making decisions about this key determinant of our lives and our economies' (Wittman et al, 2010, p 5). With humanity's relationship to food persistently reliant on minimally labelled, over-packaged products available on grocery store shelves, the abundance of social harms accompanying the production practices of such foodstuffs are disguised or completely hidden. In other words, when food is predominately or solely equated with marketised commodities, and communication about food production is minimised to food product tags and barcodes, the complex social decisions, practices and networks involved in food systems remain largely mysterious and the (potential) encompassing negative consequences and social harms covert and unsolved.

Conceptualising harm and crime

The theoretical position exercised within a food crime perspective is critical and open to constitutive assessment. Largely guided by the thinking of related (sub-)disciplines of critical criminology, green criminology, corporate criminology and victimology, a food crime perspective continually questions the concepts of crime and harm, and the consequences that such epistemologies have on broader notions of wellbeing and social justice throughout food systems. This section opens the discussion on how to situate a food crime perspective within debates concerning the conceptualisation of crimes and harms.

Criminology was built on positivistic models of legally defined criminality, while more recent history of the discipline is filled with questions targeting the concept of crime itself. Most criminologists understand and define the crime concept as involving a balancing act between narrow legalistic classifications and broader forms of deviation (Lanier and Henry, 2001). The discipline's mainstream focus on the former as 'true' definitions of crime is targeted by advocates of the social harm approach, including Hillyard and Tombs (2007), who posit that the concept of crime is socially constructed, and as such the concept has no ontological reality. Essentially, the social harm approach extends 'beyond criminology' and legality to recognise the social acts (or omissions) that represent immoral, deviant or unjust behaviour that is threatening to public health and safety, or has negative consequences on either human or non-human victims, including environmental harms. Social harms must be understood as socially mediated and context-dependent (Tifft and Sullivan, 2001; Pemberton, 2007; Lasslett, 2010). The focus on the content of crime, the criminality of marginalised populations, actuarial crime control enforcement and the responsibilisation of securitised individuals, while overlooking an understanding of crime as socially constructed and ignoring the broader experiences of marginalised populations, is a harm in itself deflecting attention from significant harms, if not excluding them altogether (Hillyard and Tombs, 2004; Tombs and Hillyard, 2004).

The social harm approach has been directly criticised for the (potential) vagueness associated with the concept of harm, especially in comparison to criminal conduct as represented through legal codes. The objective concept of legally defined crime, for Tappan (2001), enables the stability and dependability of justice, while broader ambiguous terms, like social harm, are exceptionally prone to ethical biases and vulnerable to unsolicited interventions or cooptation (see also Pemberton, 2007). This defence of order is problematic for Schwendinger and Schwendinger (2001, p 89), who question:

> ... isn't it time to raise serious questions about the assumptions underlying the definition of the field of criminology when a man who steals a paltry sum can be called a criminal while agents of the State can, with impunity, legally reward men who destroy food so that price levels can be maintained while a sizeable portion of the population suffers from malnutrition. Our nation is confronted with a grave moral crisis which is reflected above all in the technocratic "benign neglect" shown in the unwillingness to recognize the criminal character of great social injuries inflicted on heretofore powerless people, merely because these injuries are not defined in the legal code.

Similar responses argue against the championing of the law within criminological perspectives. For instance, Milovanovic and Henry (2001) reason that the law is often harmful through both its denial of certain harms and the legitimisation of the relations of power that produce other harms; as 'a second order of harm production' (2001, p 172), they label the law itself as a crime. Pemberton (2004, 2007) also problematises the law as privileging a moral hierarchy during the allocation of (criminal) responsibility, where intentional acts triumph over unintentional or indifferent acts, even though the latter are frequently more harmful.

While there are concerns about the conceptualisation and (mis) use of the concept, a food crime perspective greatly benefits from the inclusion of a social harm approach within its framework. It is not an either-or debate between the concepts or crime and harm, but a pragmatic utilisation of a social harm approach to allow the analysis of the relationship and intersectionality between crimes and harms

(Gordon, 2004; Pemberton, 2007). Thus criminology is not to be abandoned, as Hillyard and Tombs (2007) argue, but it must move away from privileging law so that there is no need to choose to represent social problems as either crimes or harms. Or, as Passas (2005) puts it, there is a need to also recognise activities that are 'lawful but awful'.

Given this re-thinking, it becomes much easier to understand how other (sub-)disciplines can be involved in a food crime perspective. The influence of (state-)corporate criminology, green criminology and (radical) victimology continue to provide critical analyses of conceptualisations of crime as well as the actors involved in criminal events. Such research involves the application of a criminological perspective to the harmful behaviour of corporations and white-collar criminals (Sutherland, 1949; Braithwaite, 1984), and broadening the range of victims as well as questioning how victimhood is experienced (Quinney, 1972; Dignan, 2004), including an extension to non-human animals and the environment (Lynch, 1990; Beirne and South, 2007) and the corporate colonisation of nature (South, 2007; White, 2011). Taken together, this area scrutinises the social events involving both crimes and harms, generally and specifically, committed by both the powerful and the marginalised, by both corporations and individuals, which inflicts intersectional harm on a variety of human, animal and environmental victims.

Taking a social harm approach to food crime is necessary (Croall, 2012) and valuable for multiple reasons. First, it allows recognition of harms over time. Harms are not single, isolated events, but have repercussions beyond the acts themselves, often impacting future generations (Dorling, 2004). This is crucial to food harms and crimes, as while food systems are large dynamic networks grounded in historical and socio-political relationships, contemporary humanity is fundamentally dependent on food systems for its continued survival and ability to thrive well into the future. Essentially, there is a need to be future-oriented when making important decisions about food production and consumption patterns, or else they may not be a future at all. Second, by understanding food crimes as including unintentional activities and moral indifference, Pemberton (2007) argues that such harm is both enabled and facilitated by social and physical distance between actors − a prevalent characteristic throughout the Global North, as previously explained as the human−food rift. The longer and more complex the food chain grows, the less visible it is and the greater the potential for harms. Third, a social harm approach to food crime enables cross-cultural and cross-nations comparisons, as well as understanding in stateless societies (Tifft and Sullivan, 2001). This is the reality of contemporary global food systems, burdened by unsuccessful attempts of international regulation disconnected from food existences, where the 'global governance of food and agriculture is fragmented and incoherent' (Clapp and Cohen, 2009, p 6).

A food crime perspective

As this book highlights, the detrimental practices and negative consequences of criminal and harmful events involving food systems are many and significant. There has been important recent attention to these subjects more generally, both inside and outside of academia. Multiple books showcase and argue for the various intersections between contemporary food systems and an array of problems: Sinclair's (1965) *The jungle*, Lappé's (1982) *Diet for a small planet*, Mintz's (1986) *Sweetness and power*, Schlosser's (2001) *Fast food nation*, Pollan's (2009) *The omnivore's dilemma*, Belasco's (2007) *Appetite for change*, Patel's (2008) *Stuffed and starved*, Lawrence's (2008) *Eat your heart out*, Hauter's (2012) *Foodopoly* and many others.

However, the discipline of criminology has largely ignored the intersections of food, harms and crime. It was only quite recently that Hazel Croall defined food crime as the 'many crimes that are involved in the production, distribution and selling of basic foodstuffs' (2007, p 206). Otherwise, the topic of food has been investigated occasionally in association with green criminological (see, for example, White, 2003, 2011; Walters, 2006, 2011; Croall, 2013), (state-)corporate criminological (see, for example, Fitzgerald, 2010; Croall, 2012; Cheng, 2012; Gray and Hinch, 2015) and legal–political perspectives (see, for example, Paulus, 1974; Nally, 2011). The lack of unified attention, especially compared to topics involving inter-personal criminality, should not be equated with an insignificance of food harms and crimes, as evidenced in the many deaths of individuals across varying cases involving contaminated sources of water, meat and milk (Pennington, 2003; see, for example, Snider, 2003; Hatt and Hatt, 2012; Ghazi-Tegrani and Pontell, 2015). However, these accounts are merely the tip of the iceberg, focusing on individualised and medicalised understandings of wellbeing, ignoring the abundance of crimes and harms that proliferate across social, cultural, political, economic and industrial patterns involved within the range of food production and consumption processes more generally beyond mortality statistics.

Given the complexity and sophistication of contemporary global food systems, as well as the (potential) negative impact that they (may) have if problems are overlooked or facilitated, there is a role for the subject of food within (critical) criminology. There is a need for a food crime perspective. This involves subjecting what is common to food studies – 'the web of relations, processes, structures, and institutional arrangements that cover human interaction with nature and other humans involving the production, distribution, preparation, consumption, and disposal of food' (Koç et al, 2012b, p xii) – with an evaluation of the (lack of) criminal, legal and regulatory organisation, and the insufficient, ineffective or lack of enforcement, which surrounds the social harms produced within systems of food production, processing, marketing, distribution, selling, consumption and disposal, victimising (often simultaneously) humans, animals and the environment.

A food crime perspective weds the constitutive mindset of a social harm approach with the matters of (critical) criminology. Some food crimes and harms are criminally defined illegal events (the use of agricultural slave labour, or the intentional adulteration of food), some are defined as directly or indirectly harmful (targeted food marketing, or the influence on climate change), and some are defined as unethical, immoral or unjust (food deserts in vulnerable communities, or the use of humane slaughter techniques to justify livestock murder). Many are a mixture of all of such constructions: food harm events are both directly illegal and indirectly harmful, food crimes are also socially harmful or unjust, and unethical food practices ought to be criminalised. This is why a food crime perspective cannot abandon the discipline of criminology, because there is still a role for laws, regulations and forms of governance in understanding, minimising and resolving food crimes and harms, whether it involves using the law as a standard for food production processes, strengthening regulations of food processing and marketing to facilitate public health goals or utilising a combination of forms of governance to manage food systems. However, a food crime perspective must seek to deconstruct the privileged status of the law and recognise the role that various policies have in constructing and enabling harms. Such reflexivity is noted by Cohen (1988) as the need for 'new criminology' to recognise both the object of criminology – crime – and the subject of criminology – criminologists – as fundamentally constitutive and actively (re-)constructing.

Criminology can also benefit from the existence of a food crime perspective. Grounding research in the material and practical social events along the global food chain, inquiries aim to develop a 'criminological imagination' (Young, 2011). This is accomplished by locating problems in structural contexts and histories – by analysing the habits of farmers and farm workers, the practices of food processers, the choices of food marketers and food corporations, the systems of food trade, the application of technologies to food, the environmental consequences and the decisions of consumers, within the global industrialised neoliberal food systems, in cooperation with other fields and disciplines. Additionally, shifting attention away from anthropocentric legalism, a food crime perspective embraces an eco-centric perspective, decentring humanity and including the experiences of other species, plants and environments into considerations of harms and crimes. Finally, criminology is currently labelled as irrelevant to social policy, despite the magnitude of (published) research (Austin, 2003). This lack of attention threatens to uphold the (profit-based) self-interests of food corporations and industries, while neglecting more collective public and environmental health interests. Through the pursuit of 'deviant knowledge' (Walters, 2003) and the critical questioning of criminological knowledge, food crime as a subject of criminology, argues Croall (2012), can help make criminology relevant today.

References

Austin, J. (2003) 'Why criminology is irrelevant', *Criminology & Public Policy*, vol 2, no 3, pp 557–64.

Beirne, P. and South, N. (eds) (2007) *Issues in green criminology: Confronting harms against environments, humanity, and other animals*, Portland, OR: Willan.

Belasco, W.J. (2007) *Appetite for change: How the counterculture took on the food industry*, Ithaca, NY: Cornell University Press.

Belasco, W.J. (2008) *Food: The key concepts*, New York: Bloomsbury Publishing.

Braithwaite, J. (1984) *Corporate crime in the pharmaceutical industry*, London: Routledge Kegan Paul Books.

Cheng, H. (2012) 'Cheap capitalism: A sociological study of food crime in China', *The British Journal of Criminology*, vol 52, no 2, pp 254–73.

Clapp, J. (2012) *Food*, Cambridge: Polity Press.

Clapp, J. (2015) 'Distant agricultural landscapes', *Sustainability Science*, vol 10, no 2, pp 305–17.

Clapp, J. and Cohen, M. J. (2009) 'Introduction', in J. Clapp and M. J. Cohen (eds) *The global food crisis: Governance challenges and opportunities*, Ontario, Canada: Wilfred Laurier University Press, pp 1–12.

Cohen, S. (1988) *Against criminology*, New Brunswick, NJ: Transaction Books.

Croall, H. (2007) 'Food crime: A green criminology perspective', in P. Beirne and N. South (eds) *Issues in green criminology: Confronting harms against environments, humanity, and other animals*, Portland, OR: Willan Publishing, pp 206–29.

Croall, H. (2012) 'Food, crime, harm and regulation', *Criminal Justice Matters*, vol 90, no 1, pp 16–17.

Croall, H. (2013) 'Food crime: A green criminological perspective', in N. South and A. Brisman (eds) *Routledge international handbook of green criminology*, New York: Routledge, pp 167–83.

Dignan, J. (2004) *Understanding victims and restorative justice*, Maidenhead: Open University Press.

Dorling, D. (2004) 'Prime suspect in Britain', in P. Hillyard, C. Pantazis, S. Tombs, and D. Gordon (eds) *Beyond criminology: Taking harm seriously*, London: Pluto Press, pp 178–91.

Eden, S. (2011) 'Food labels as boundary objects', *Public Understanding of Science*, vol 20, no 2, pp 179–94.

Fitzgerald, A. (2010) 'The "underdog" as "ideal victim"? The attribution of victimhood in the 2007 pet food recall', *International review of victimology*, vol 17, no 2, pp 131–57.

Ghazi-Tegrani, A.K. and Pontell, H.N. (2015) 'Corporate crime and state legitimacy: The 2008 Chinese melamine milk scandal', *Crime, Law and Social Change*, vol 63, pp 247–67.

Gordon, D. (2004) 'Poverty, death and disease', in P. Hillyard and S. Tombs (eds) *Beyond criminology: Taking harm seriously*, London: Pluto Press, pp 251–66.

Gray, A. and Hinch, R. (2015) 'Agribusiness, governments and food crime: A critical perspective', in R. Sollund (ed) *Green harms and crimes: Critical criminology in a changing world*, Basingstoke: Palgrave Macmillan, pp 97–116.

Hamada, S., Wilk, R., Logan, A., Minard, S. and Trubek, A. (2015) 'The future of food studies', *An International Journal of Multidisciplinary Research*, vol 18, no 1, pp 167–86.

Hatt, K. and Hatt, K. (2012) 'Neoliberalizing food safety and the 2008 Canadian listeriosis outbreak', *Agriculture and Human Values*, vol 29, no 1, pp 17–28.

Hauter, W. (2012) *Foodopoly: The battle over the future of food and farming in America*, New York: The New Press.

Hillyard, P. and Tombs, S. (2004) 'Beyond criminology?', in P. Hillyard and S. Tombs (eds) *Beyond criminology: Taking harm seriously*, London: Pluto Press, pp 10–29.

Hillyard, P. and Tombs, S. (2007) 'From "crime" to social harm?', *Crime, Law and Social Change*, vol 48, pp 9–25.

Hudson, I. and Hudson, M. (2003) 'Removing the veil? Commodity fetishism, fair trade, and the environment', *Organization and Environment*, vol 16, no 4, pp 413–30.

Kareiva, P., Watts, S., Mcdonald, R. and Boucher, T. (2007) 'Domesticated nature: Shaping landscapes and ecosystems for human welfare', *Science*, vol 316, no 5833, pp 1866–9.

Kneen, B. (1995) *From land to mouth: Understanding the food system* (2nd edn), Toronto: NC Press.

Koç, M., Sumner, J. and Winson, A. (eds) (2012b) *Critical perspectives in food studies*, Ontario, Canada: Oxford University Press.

Koç, M., MacRae, R., Noack, A.M. and Üstündağ, Ö.G. (2012a) 'What is food studies? Characterizing an emerging academic field through the eyes of Canadian scholars', in M. Koç, J. Sumner and A. Winson (eds) *Critical perspective in food studies*, Ontario, Canada: Oxford University Press, pp 4–15.

Lanier, M.M. and Henry, S. (2001) 'Crime in context: The scope of the problem', in S. Henry and M.M. Lanier (eds) *What is crime: Controversies over the nature of crime and what to do about it*, New York: Rowman & Littlefield Publishers, pp 1–18.

Lappé, F.M. (1982) *Diet for a small planet*, New York: Ballantine Books.

Lasslett, K. (2010) 'Crime or social harm? A dialectical perspective', *Crime, Law and Social Change*, vol 54, pp 1–19.

Lawrence, F. (2008) *Eat your heart out: Why the food business is bad for the planet and your health*, New York: Penguin Books.

Leguizamón, A. (2016) 'Disappearing nature? Agribusiness, biotechnology and distance in Argentine soybean production', *The Journal of Peasant Studies*, vol 43, no 2, pp 313–30.

Long, L. (2002) 'Food studies: Interdisciplinary buffet and main course', *Appetite*, vol 38, pp 81–2.

Lynch, M. (1990) 'The greening of criminology: A perspective for the 1990s', *The Critical Criminologist*, vol 2, pp 11–12.

McClintock, N. (2010) 'Why farm the city? Theorizing urban agriculture through a lens of metabolic rift', *Cambridge Journal of Regions*, vol 3, no 2, pp 191–207.

McMichael, P. (2004) 'Biotechnology and food security: Profiting on insecurity', in L. Beneria and S. Bisnath (eds) *Global tensions: Challenges and opportunities in the world economy*, New York: Routledge, pp 137–54.

Milovanovic, D. and Henry, S. (2001) 'Constitutive definition of crime: Power as harm', in S. Henry and M.M. Lanier (eds) *What is crime? Controversies over the nature of crime and what to do about it*, New York: Rowman & Littlefield Publishers, pp 165–78.

Mintz, S.W. (1986) *Sweetness and power: The place of sugar in modern history*, New York: Penguin Books.

Nally, D.P. (2011) *Human encumbrances: Political violence and the great Irish famine*, Indiana, IN: University of Notre Dame Press.

Nestle, M. and McIntosh, W.A. (2010) 'Writing the food studies movement', *Food, Culture & Society*, vol 13, no 2, pp 159–68.

Oliver, J. (2010) *Jamie Oliver's food revolution*, American Broadcasting Company.

Passas, N. (2005) 'Lawful but awful: "Legal corporate crimes"', *Journal of Socio-Economics*, vol 34, pp 771–86.

Patel, R.C. (2008) *Stuffed and starved: The hidden battle for the world food system*, Brooklyn: NY: Melville House.

Paulus, I. (1974) *The search for pure food: A sociology of legislation in Britain*, London: Martin Robertson.

Pemberton, S. (2004) 'A theory of moral indifference: Understanding the production of harm by capitalist society', in P. Hillyard, C. Pantazis, S. Tombs and D. Gordon (eds) *Beyond criminology: Taking harm seriously*, London: Pluto Press, pp 67-83.

Pemberton, S. (2007) 'Social harm future(s): Exploring the potential of the social harm approach', *Crime, Law and Social Change*, vol 48, pp 27–41.

Pennington, T.H. (2003) *When food kills: BSE, E. coli, and disaster science*, Oxford: Oxford University Press.

Polanyi, K. (1957 [1944]) *The great transformation: The political and economic origins of our time*, Boston, MA: Beacon Press.

Pollan, M. (2009) *The omnivore's dilemma: A natural history of four meals*, New York: Penguin Press.

Princen, T. (1997) 'The shading and distancing of commerce: When internalization is not enough', *Ecological Economics*, vol 20, no 3, pp 235–53.

Princen, T. (2002) 'Distancing: Consumption and the severing of feedback', in T. Princen, M. Maniates and K. Conca (eds) *Confronting consumption*, Cambridge, MA: MIT Press, pp 103–32.

Quinney, R. (1972) 'Who is the victim?', *Criminology*, vol 10, pp 314–23.

Rinella, S. (2005) *The scavenger's guide to haute cuisine*, New York: Miramax Books.

Sbicca, J. (2014) 'The need to feed: Urban metabolic struggles of actually existing radical projects', *Critical Sociology*, vol 40, no 6, pp 817–34.

Schlosser, E. (2001) *Fast food nation: The dark side of the all-American meal*, Boston, MA: Houghton Mifflin.

Schwendinger, H., and Schwendinger, J. (2001) 'Defenders of order or guardians of human rights?' in S. Henry and M.M. Lanier (eds) *What is crime? Controversies over the nature of crime and what to do about it*, New York: Rowman & Littlefield Publishers, pp 65–100.

Shackley, S. and Wynne, B. (1996) 'Representing uncertainty in global climate change science and policy: Boundary-ordering devices and authority', *Science, Technology & Human Values*, vol 21, no 3, pp 275–302.

Sinclair, U. (1965) *The jungle*, Harmondsworth: Penguin Classics.

Smith, A., Pilcher, J.M. and Goldstein, D. (2010) 'Food scholarship and food writing', *Food, Culture & Society*, vol 13, no 3, p 319.

Snider, L. (2003) 'Captured by neo-liberalism: Regulation and risk in Walkerton, Ontario', *Risk Management*, vol 5, no 2, pp 17–27.

South, N. (2007) 'The "corporate colonization of nature": Bio-prospecting, bio-piracy and the development of green criminology', in P. Beirne and N. South (eds) *Issues in green criminology: Confronting harms against environments, humanity, and other animals*, Portland, OR: Willan Publishing, pp 230–47.

Star, S.L. (2010) 'This is not a boundary object: Reflections on the origin of a concept', *Science, Technology, & Human Values*, vol 35, no 5, pp 601–17.

Star, S.L. and Griesemer, J.R. (1989) 'Institutional ecology, "translations" and boundary objects: Amateurs and professionals in Berkeley's Museum of Vertebrate Zoology, 1907–39', *Social Studies of Science*, vol 19, no 3, pp 387–420.

Sutherland, E. (1949) *White collar crime*, New York: Holt, Rinehart & Winston.

Tappan, P.W. (2001) 'Who is the criminal?' in S. Henry and M.M. Lanier (eds) *What is crime? Controversies over the nature of crime and what to do about it*, New York: Rowman & Littlefield Publishers, pp 27–36.

Tifft, L.L. and Sullivan, D.C. (2001) 'A needs-based, social harms definition of crime', in S. Henry and M.M. Lanier (eds) *What is crime? Controversies over the nature of crime and what to do about it*, New York: Rowman & Littlefield Publishers, pp 179–206.

Tombs, S. and Hillyard. P. (2004) 'Towards a political economy of harm: States, corporations and the production of inequality', in P. Hillyard and S. Tombs (eds) *Beyond criminology: Taking harm seriously*, London: Pluto Press, pp 30–54.

Walters, R. (2003) *Deviant knowledge: Criminology, politics and policy*, Cullompton: Willan Publishing.

Walters, R. (2006) 'Crime, bio-agriculture and the exploitation of hunger', *British Journal of Criminology*, vol 46, no 1, pp 26–45.

Walters, R. (2011) *Eco-crime and genetically modified food*, Abingdon: Routledge.

Weis. T. (2007) *The global food economy: The battle for the future of farming*, London: Zed Books.

White, R. (2003) 'Environmental issues and the criminological imagination', *Theoretical Criminology*, vol 7, no 4, pp 483–506.

White, R. (2011) *Transnational environmental crime: Toward an eco-global criminology*, London: Routledge.

Wilk, R. (2012) 'The limits of discipline: Towards interdisciplinary food studies', *Physiology & Behavior*, vol 107, no 4, pp 471–5.

Wittman, H. (2009) 'Reworking the metabolic rift: La Via Campesina, agrarian citizenship, and food sovereignty', *The Journal of Peasant Studies*, vol 36, no 4, pp 805–26.

Wittman, H., Desmarais, A.A. and Weibe, N. (eds) (2010) *Food sovereignty: Reconnecting food, nature and community*, Halifax: Fernwood Publishing.

Worthy, K. (2013) *Invisible nature: Healing the destructive divide between people and the environment*, New York: Prometheus Books.

Young, J. (2011) *The criminological imagination*, Cambridge: Polity Press.

2

Food crime without criminals: Agri-food safety governance as a protection racket for dominant political and economic interest

Martha McMahon and Kora Liegh Glatt

Introduction

> We need every organic operator to speak up and let the government know we do not support the Safe Food for Canadians Regulations as it's currently proposed. (COG, 2017)

Like many Irish country women, mother used the words 'it's a crime' to describe particular kinds of bad things. These were bad things that unjustifiably harmed someone or something in a significant way, but were not against the law. Transgressions that were crimes in the eyes of the justice system did not need mother to name them as such. Such crimes called for remedy, but she had only her words. It is with this colloquial community sense of crime that this discussion of food crimes and the shadow sides of 'agri-food safety governance' is situated.

Unlike the justice system's concept of crime, 'colloquial crimes' do not necessarily involve an identifiable criminal or individual agent. The case against agri-food safety governance will enlist new feminist materialisms that offer innovative ways of thinking about safety in terms of the often 'unpredictable and unwanted actions and exchanges between human bodies, nonhuman creatures, ecological systems, chemical agents, and other actors' (Alaimo, 2010, p 2). This conceptual assistance is invaluable for ensuring future food is safe and also good. These new ontologies embody a post-human turn in that they collapse the radical distinction between society and nature, subject and object, humanity and matter. Alaimo offers the concept of trans-corporeality to theorise 'interchanges and interconnections between various bodily natures ... of human corporeality with the more-than-human world and the often-invisible material flows and forces between people, nature, places, political and economic systems' (2010, p 9). As a concept, trans-corporeality shifts understandings of agri-food safety governance away from individual health toward understanding human health as inseparable from the 'health' of the eco-system and the more-than-human. Policies that pursue individual human health or food safety in isolation from the entanglements of people, natures, things and institutions are misguided. Much agri-food safety governance operates within outdated modernist human/nature stuff framings – framings that now threaten earthly survival in the Anthropocene (Haraway, 2008).

Yet agri-food safety is so intuitively sensible. Timid interjections at meetings with food safety and agri-food governance regulatory authorities, at farmers' market meetings or food security round tables are often met with discomfort, if not hostility. One knows how this will go. If one tries to explore the implications of our policies and rules for the goals of good health, food security (not to mention food sovereignty), global justice, the environment and climate change mitigation, biodiversity or animal welfare, one is silenced with the discursive invocation of a dead child caused by the (hypothetical) breaking of such rules by someone at the farmers' market. Some ask 'what if a child got sick or died?', some lapse into silence, while others probe 'who would dare risk causing a child to die?' These discourses hang in the air and close down discussion in all sorts of ways. Then someone at the meeting will invoke liability. The conversation ends.

The argument here is not one against agri-food safety governance. It is one in favour of different, more contextually, socially and ecologically adaptive and better kinds of governance that embody diverse understandings of the relationships between people and nature embodied in food and where food is recognised as an assemblage of biological, ecological, cultural, material and political economic relationships.

Agri-food safety governance promises to protect. This promise has been a key masculinist organising trope, particularly of the modern state. War, militarism and policing are some ways in which the state is associated with masculinist motifs of protection. Even the welfare state, despite being called a nanny state by Margaret Thatcher, is more accurately characterised as paternalistic protection. The protections of the welfare state have been replaced by the robust individualism of a neoliberalising state that is masculinist in quite different ways (Fraser, 2013). Feminist analysis (Young, 2003b) inspires questions of whether an appeal to justice and care, rather than protection, would provide an effective, different and/or better organising logic for the public sphere and approach to protecting food and keeping people safe. The right to good food for all, not food safety primarily for the privileged, would be central to such governance, and would enhance the wellbeing of food-insecure people.

A case for better rules

McMahon's (2011) research looked at the harmful consequences for local farmers and local food security following changes in Canadian provincial public agri-food safety governance around meat production. In practice, much contemporary agri-food governance is actually private in that the policies and regulations are created and/or made effective by corporations or networks of corporate food retailers. The state often models public governance on such programmes. Public and private governance are not as different as might seem. Both are now typically neoliberal and HACCP (hazard analysis and critical control points) approaches. One carries the weight of law. The other carries the weight of economic power. Both sources of governance operate as part of the technologies of rule. The former technology hails individuals as consumers, and the latter, as citizens.

The changes to agri-food governance harmed small-scale farming while enabling a more globalising food system (McMahon, 2011). Women farmers in particular seemed affected. Dunn (2003) identified a similar pattern in the European Union (EU), although without a gendered perspective. She found that the introduction of EU food safety standards drove restructuring – namely, consolidation and concentration – of the Polish pork sector by posing barriers to market entry for smaller agribusinesses and processors. Ana Larsen (2009) found an analogous marginalisation and destruction of subsistence provisioning from EU biosecurity policies when they were introduced in Slovenia. Similarly, DeLind and Howard (2008) wrote of the harm to small-scale US agri-food operations when new food safety programmes were introduced. There are examples of traditional or localised ways of food provisioning and trading being rendered illegal by new agri-food safety policies: street hawkers in India, raw milk in Columbia, nomadic herders having their traditional pathways and practices deemed dangerous, if not illegal, and heritage pigs in Michigan declared invasive species and their owners guilty of a felony. New agri-food standards such as organic or fairtrade governance, however, can also provide opportunities for some small-scale producers, to enter global retail chains and new markets. In practice, the benefits typically revert to the larger operations.

Drawing on the methodology of institutional ethnography (Smith, 1999), this chapter's focus is not the ideas, values or experiences of the farmers affected by agri-food governance. Rather, this chapter reflects on the ways in which farmers' lives are organised by food safety governance. In institutional ethnography the problematic is not the problem understood as an informant, whether farmer or local food activist group might explain it, but the broader social and economic institutionalised relations that organise the experiences relayed.

It is difficult to theorise harms done in the name of the public good such as the 'crimes' of high modernity identified by James Scott (1998). Scott's highly acclaimed work was criticised for carrying a subtext of libertarian justification for free market non-regulation. That is not where the analysis in this chapter is going, and neither was Scott's work. For Scott, much of the harm came from the often coercive imposition of top-down change and from ignoring the complexity of local situations and knowledge. A critique of top-down state-centric regulation does not necessarily imply a case for deregulation or private voluntary regulation. Some mistakenly see private agri-food safety governance as bottom-up in terms of being market or consumer-driven. It is probably more accurate to see it as driven by the need to maintain consumer trust at a distance in 'food-from-nowhere' (see Chapter 1, this volume). Concern displayed for the welfare of the 'consumer' functions ideologically in a retail industry that proclaims consumer sovereignty. Consumer diets sustained through the dominant food system are generally unhealthy and associated with increasing rates of chronic disease and obesity. For Winson (2013), food production is now so far removed from real food that food has become 'pseudo-food'. Clearly not everyone is being well fed or kept safe. People need to be protected from food frauds and foodborne disease, but they also need to be protected from much of what passes for protection.

From individual liability to political responsibility

One of the harms from dominant kinds of agri-food safety governance is the barrier they present to sustainable farming and ways of food provisioning that are better adapted to a more ecological and socially just future, especially in the context of 'unsafe' climate change (MacIntyre et al, 2009). The rationale offered for contemporary forms of agri-food safety governance is typically health, but trade, integration of supply chains, market share, managerial priorities and offloading liability offer more convincing explanations of a great deal that happens in public and private agri-food governance (McMahon, 2011). Agri-food safety governance has become interwoven with the technologies of governance central to the neoliberalisation of the food economy.

Conventional approaches to public agri-food safety governance are framed within what feminist political theorist Iris Marion Young (2003a) calls a liability model of responsibility. This liability model has limited usefulness for addressing institutional, structural or systemic causes of harm such as those to health, social justice, animals and ecology resulting from the dominant food system (see McMahon, 2013). Ways of assigning responsibility and liability in modern societies typically come from legal reasoning about guilt or fault for a harm inflicted, Young explains. This is a 'fault model', where responsibility is attributed to an agent (including corporate entities) who can be shown to be causally connected to the harm and thus deemed responsible, allowing for mitigating circumstances. For example, under a concept of strict liability, even if there were no intention to harm, responsibility and liability can still be assigned. This legal convention encouraged the introduction of new kinds of agri-food safety governance, focusing more on process than outcome, and allowing the avoidance of culpability if 'due diligence' could be shown. This is not unreasonable – HACCP-derived programmes focus on the documentable process of managing risks by regulating the process. If due diligence is observed, then there is limited or no liability, even if there is harm. Conversely, a liability or a crime can be committed simply by not following a proper process. In other words, there can be crime against the approved ordering of things.

What remains constant between the older and modernised versions of agri-food safety governance is that both are still driven by individualistic understandings of liability. The farmer (or whomever) is liable for transgressing the proper order of processes. This holds even when well-established traditional processes do not result in harm, or in more harm than the new institutionally approved approach. Traditional ways of producing food can become illegal for little reason other than violating the proscribed process. These processes can be culturally or geographically or ecologically inappropriate, almost impossible to observe, or they may even be prohibitively expensive. To violate or ignore these new processes when they are state-sanctioned constitutes a crime. The small-scale farmer who refused to hand over her rare breeds of sheep to be slaughtered for a disease they did not have but were implicated in a 'trace back' or 'stamp-out' slaughter policy could thus become a criminal by regulatory fiat (see Shropshire Sheep, 2017). She struggled to protect her sheep and the rare genetics of the breed while regulatory authorities struggled to protect the industry and the authority of the state. It was a very sad story of actors framed as heroes/heroines and villains. The sheep ended up dead – protection policies, not disease or nature, killed them.

Drawing on Smith (1999) it can be seen that textually mediated protocols and policies of agri-food safety provide the social licence and technologies to extra-local relations of ruling to reconfigure people's everyday lives. For Smith, ruling relations are forms of bureaucracy, administration, management, professional organisation and the media, and also include the complex of discourses, scientific, technical and cultural, that intersect, interpenetrate and coordinate the multiple sites of ruling. They are embodied in the text-mediated and text-based systems of 'communication', 'knowledge', 'information', regulation', 'control now central to the organization of everyday life' (Smith, 1999, p 77). In food, relationships to nature have been 'rationally' reconfigured: the hallmark of modernity and the nation-state.

Young's (2003a) concept of political responsibility offers a way of thinking about responsibility for outcomes that flow from institutionally organised processes that unwittingly produce or reproduce harm. Young's approach avoids the limitations of the liability model of harm and remedy: responsibility becomes the political responsibility to create alternative institutions as the real remedy. This would meld real food safety protection with social justice. This has become one of the goals of some alternative food activism.

Slow violence

Nixon's (2011) concept of slow violence analytically connects agri-food safety governance and crime. It enables the appreciation of how some pernicious harms done to individuals and communities remain invisible within justice systems, untheorised in the social sciences and un-addressed in life. Slow violence explains how the harms that come through the processes of a bureaucratic state, corporations or organisations are real violence and this should not be discursively sanitised by words like 'this is our policy' or 'for your protection'. It is the kind of violence so clearly documented in James Scott's (1998) book *Seeing like a state*. Slow violence typically occurs gradually and out of sight with a kind of delayed destruction that is spread over time and space. It can be symbolic violence, it can violate dignity, it can physically harm, it can lead to death. More often than not it is not viewed as violence at all. Lives are violated. But no individual criminals are identifiable. No one can be charged. Yet ways of life and kinds of people are disappeared.

Biosecurity protocols, HACCP, traceability, Good Agricultural Practices (GAP) and other policy objects now function among small-scale farming and food producers like trailing parts of discursive comets that Morton (2013) calls 'hyperobjects'. Hyperobjects are entities of such vast temporal and spatial dimensions that they defeat traditional ideas about what a thing is in the first place. The 'thing' used to be food, better understood as an assemblage or network of social and ecological relationships than as a thing. Agri-food safety reduces the symbolic and material complexities of food to a potential liability-carrying 'thing' whose risks need to be globally managed. Hyperobjects function like dense black holes into which too much is absorbed and into which it is easy to be sucked. Such discursive hyperobjects put unbearable strains on normal ways of reasoning, Morton explains. In the risk society of late modernity (Beck, 1992), hyper-danger objects abound. Fear of disease from new and mysterious things external to the body coming into the body, or threats to the integrity to the body-politic by alien terrorists, seems to now function as hyperobjects making the slow violence associated with security regimes of protection invisible and/or acceptable.

Protection has long been central to the biopolitics of modernity. Protection becomes more important when trust is fragile in a world with little or no understanding of a common good, where if Beck's (1992) understanding of risk society is correct, the distribution of environmental bads (and goods) has replaced the distribution of material goods as a focus of public concern, anxiety and conflict. Anxieties about food, according to Lavin (2015), have become proxies for concerns about wider process such as globalisation.

Consuming politics: intimate entanglements of nature, culture and political economy

Contemporary forms of agri-food safety governance play a major legitimating role in the dominant food system. They reassure 'safety', yet many new food safety technologies are unnecessary on health and safety grounds because there are other ways of ensuring that food is safe. Perversely these arrangements now threaten to defeat the goals of promoting and protecting health. This is the dystopian side of modernity of which Beck speaks. Contemporary forms of public and private agri-food safety governance exchange limited safety in the present for increased precariousness in the future. Apart from health problems in the present, the agri-food system is a major contribution to climate change emissions and a very unhealthy future. Agri-food safety governance serves the interests of the dominant food system. It works ideologically to supress questioning. It works politically to foreclose the possibility of change. It works economically in facilitating market access primarily for large-scale producers or agri-food corporations while marginalising others from the market. Rather than enabling competition, it enables large-scale economic actors to gain monopoly status. This is how slow violence works: harm done without an identifiable, individual criminal. Is it analytically adequate to see these harms simply as the unintended outcomes of established, but now outdated, ways of doing things?

Boundary protections

Eating is among the most intimate relationship among (human) animals and the environment. The society/nature boundary-transgressive nature of food may help explain the intense anxiety associated with food safety issues in contrast to far scarier ecological health issues such as climate change. Feminist scholars offer boundary transgressive paradigms that challenge not just nature/culture divides, but also the animate/inanimate. These paradigms recognise the agency and subjectivity of creatures, things and stuff. The work of feminist scholars is at the forefront in attempting to engage the epistemological and ontological challenges prefigured by the boundary-transgressing nature of food and its ability to disrupt the dichotomies of nature and culture. Such work is deeply biopolitical as it disrupts the authority of the privileged knower, who is typically drawn from among the already privileged. It disrupts exclusionary claims to be privileged subjects whether of rights or entitlements (to food, protection or individual choice) by recognising the subjectivity of many others, including the 'more-than-human'. It is biopolitical not just because it recognises the different authorities of marginalised voices and Indigenous knowledges, but because it demonstrates the various ways of being part of nature and of understanding human/nature entanglements, and how these entanglements uphold different kinds of socio-economic-political orders. Ways of knowing and interacting with the more-than-human are political, not least in how colonisation works through nature rather than simply on nature (Moore, 2015). The deployment of dominant scientific food and agri-knowledge in contemporary society intertwines food safety, power and security regimes. There are numerous examples of farmers being held captive by seed markets controlled by a handful of corporations enabled by agri-knowledge governance regimes. One can recognise impulses to democratise agri-food knowledge in the growing practice of seed saving and local seedy Saturday community markets, for example, and in the increasingly important role of citizen scientists around food and environmental issues. One can also find support for such efforts from within some elements of government. Food is biopolitical.

For Douglas (2003), food rules and ideas about what is safe and unsafe to eat are more matters of culture than nature. This is not to say botulism poisoning is not fatal, but that food rules and agri-food governance are complex and cannot be reduced to issues of safety. From the realist traditions of veterinary medicine and public health, Waltner-Toews (2009) takes seriously the suffering and death caused by foodborne disease, whether involving salmonellosis, campylobacteriosis, listeriosis or *E. coli*. However, he, too, calls for boundary-transgressive understandings of the links between disease and food. Such new eco-health approaches, he concludes, must abandon simple causal links between bacteria and disease that frame current food safety thinking. Instead, he argues to extend the understanding of food safety to the implicated networks of disease and health including cheap food policies, land use, global trade, poverty, economic inequity and climate change (see Chapters 12, 14 and 19, this volume). The public health evidence seems to support Waltner-Toews: food-related health problems are understood to be approaching public health crises levels. In addition, malnourishment, hunger and poverty stalk much of the world's small-scale farmers in the Global South and the number of farmers in the Global North is rapidly declining. Why, then, do outdated practices and so much agri-food safety governance seem to coincidentally extend the economic reach of corporate agri-food actors? This is literally biopolitics.

People whose livelihoods are deeply entangled with nature in the production of food are now being globally regulated in new ways. They are being pushed and pulled into what Moore (2015) calls the global ecology of capitalist relations of cheap food. However, because their work and lives are already locally pre-organised by their relationships with nature, this creates unending contradictions and irrationalities. Their lives and work are being reorganised in the service of protecting and promoting the wellbeing of some abstract population of consumers, not the more parochial and traditionally intergenerational occupation of feeding families, neighbours and community. These are very different relationships with time, space, place and others, whether human or more-than-human. Nomadic herders find their ancient pathways caught up in biosecurity policies that seem to have been inspired by mad cow disease in the UK, for example. These developments are biopolitical because new agri-food safety governance reframes the complex meanings of living with livestock or growing food into a national, if not a global, market project. They are biopolitical because the management of the boundaries and relationships between nature and culture is central to the protection of the dominant economic agri-food order and the neoliberalised economy of the nation-state. For Moore, it is important to understand capitalism as a world ecology that joins capital accumulation, power and nature in dialectical unity. Contemporary agri-food governance is part of the governance technologies by which nature and food are made cheap. It is part of a world ecology (Moore, 2015), a way of reorganising nature, in which the modern and modernising state is deeply implicated (Parenti, 2015), and agri-food safety is indeed biopolitical.

To serve and protect whom?

Moving from biopolitics to Foucault's concept of biopolitics one can see how since the 19th century human conduct became increasingly managed by calculated and administrative means focused around the welfare of the population rather than coercion, albeit experienced as slow violence. Protection and a kind of universalising conception of population(s) (rather than people) is at its very heart. In agri-food safety governance it is 'the consumer' who calls out the trope of protection. The population – whose welfare is to be advanced through the managing of life – is an abstract, homogenising whole made available primarily through the data-making technologies of knowing such as census, statistics and social and market research. The particularities of everyday life, of individuals and their places are lost in what Scott (1998) calls the 'gaze of seeing like a state' and what Smith (1999) calls the textually mediated world of 'the relations of ruling'. The textually managed abstractions of the national and the global obtain priority over the complexities of the local and the particularities of animals' lives, of plants, crops and farmers, the histories, relationships to time and place, particularities that all become irrelevant. In a world of biopolitics, sheep become an industry to be well managed for the good of the economy that is conflated with the good of the nation. The national and global are conflated with a kind of universal good that is threatened by the local and the particular.

The concept of biopolitics teaches that the will to govern is inseparable from the will to improve the welfare of the population. Not surprisingly, 'experts' emerge almost everywhere to direct those improvements – including the 'food police' (see Chapter 24, this volume). Foucault created the term 'governmentality' to capture the distinctiveness of the rationality of governments animated by the will to improve, to be accomplished through an almost exhaustive range of actions and strategies so that the right things are done in the right way at the right time in the right place to make life better. The implicit utopianism along with the promise to protect the population makes resistance to such governmentalities by small-scale farmers or raw milk activists or others who are marginal seem perverse. Where, then, if anywhere, is the crime?

If biopolitics is, as Tania Murray Li (2010) puts it, about 'making live', what, then, about the biopolitics of 'letting die'? What happens when governance enhances the lives of one subset of the population while others are abandoned, let die or disappear? Li argues that there are over a billion 'surplus' population in whose lives no state has an interest in 'making live'. Many are small-scale farmers dispossessed by the neoliberalisation of agriculture – to become migrant non-citizens. These unsafe lives fall outside the boundaries with which agri-food governance concerns itself. Playing on the concept of biopolitics these are people, Li argues, 'who are simply "let die"'.

Back to biopolitics

Moore (2015) pulls this chapter's analysis from biopolitics back to biopolitics. Capitalism, historically and currently, does not simply work on nature but works through nature. Since the 16th century the biopolitics of food and agriculture that made food and nature 'cheap' have been central to the trajectories of power and economics and the development of capitalism. Capitalism constantly re-configures agriculture to produce more and more cheap calories with less and less labour power, but not with less nature. If the cost of industrial wages can be kept low, it helps keep profits up. Food is not cheap – it is food *made* cheap. For Moore and others, historically this pseudo productivity has only been possible by combining technological and organisational advances with the relentless appropriation of 'free' or cheap soil/land, energy, water and cheap non-industrial labour. Cheap food/nature has historically been accomplished by the dispossession of Indigenous peoples, by the extraction of soil's fertility and the externalisation of real social and ecological costs. Now there are no more frontiers from which to appropriate cheap nature. Agri-food safety governance is a central actor in a world in which food and nature are made cheap. As such, this governance is party, not simply to a kind of food fraud, but also to theft.

In addition, agri-food safety governance co-produces the problems it claims to solve. The logic and ethics of mass slaughter to solve biosecurity problems are partly functions of industrial production organised in massive poultry barns, for example, but also of the increased transportation of livestock and food in globalised supply chains. Its horror evokes little by way of horrified responses. Sometimes it is open trade borders or a state's disease-free trade status (Nerlich, 2004), not human or animal health, that animates governance responses. There are real risks in the word. Food will always be a kind of biopolitics, but safety can be 'done' differently, even eco-democratically, and surely it must be done without the mass slaughter of and misery of animals. One might ask what bodies need to be protected?

Conclusion

Moore's insight that a capitalist food system works through nature not on nature shifted the initial argument from one about unintended consequences of institutional arrangements and biopolitics to recognising agri-food safety governance as ruthlessly biopolitical.

Some may mistakenly believe that the problems stem from the shift from public to private agri-food governance. Parenti (2015) rejects an easy public/private distinction by arguing that the state plays a central role here because it actually manages nature for capital. Both public and private agri-food safety governance manage the most intimate of nature–society networks: food. Whereas private governance relies on the market to govern, the state is unique in that it has privileged access to law. Both increasingly organise the delivery of cheapened nature to the food consumer. That does sound like a bit of a racket.

It may seem counter-intuitive, but the market is a modern way of accomplishing agri-food governance: it organises, disciplines, orders and reorders, calls into being and disappears people and things. It does not do this by simple competition, as citizens are misleadingly told, but rather through creating 'games' of winners and losers (Dean, 2017). Despite a rhetoric of deregulation, the state and its regulatory legal powers, even in the context of neoliberalisation, plays a pivotal role. The market is not really a market in the common-sense use of the term. The 'rules of the game' are stacked against some. Colonisation, slavery, plantations, enclosure and other overt forms of coercion were earlier strategies for organising the delivery of cheap nature and cheap food. Participation in a market that disadvantages the powerless is less bloody, albeit characterised by slow violence. Agri-food safety governance disciplines and reorganises the work of small-scale farmers, street traders, artisan food produces, nomadic herders and the like for a newly conceptualised abstract market. Food that does not fit the 'standards' is deemed unacceptable by retailers and their agents or made illegal by the state. When once farmers, artisanal food produces or street vendors could use traditional local practices to feed their families and neighbours, they may find this now becomes a crime, and/or consumers are made afraid of food that is not in clamshells. Contemporary agri-food governance helps make food and nature cheap while making the world unsafe. Women, including mother, would have called that 'a crime'.

The imagined 'community' to be protected in national policies and in the food safety programmes of favourite grocery retailers embraces a narrow notion of community in which many are disenfranchised or marginalised. An imagined community, different than the nation–state or the 'consumer', would reframe understanding and challenge the dominant food system on behalf of the excluded. Yes, agri-food safety governance may protect. But like protection rackets, they protect those who are part of the in-group and willing to pay up. Others are left unprotected and vulnerable. While the privileged may feel confident that their green beans are 'safe', the marginalised are left vulnerable to poverty, garbage food, hunger, inequality and insecurities, and increasingly the vagrancies of climate change. In time things will become riskier as the externalities of poverty, poor health or climate change start to be internalised, even in the worlds of the privileged.

The questions of what food is to be kept safe and for whom unpacks both the narrow parochialism and the misleading universalism of food safety talk (see McMahon, 2013). These questions bring issues of justice, global public health and the nature of governance into the heart of food safety discussions. In what Fraser (2010) calls a post-Westphalian political-economic order, one can no longer politically or ethically implicitly assume that only citizens of a territorial state count as subjects of food safety governance, nor can one invoke the false universalism of 'the consumer'. Far from substituting a single global 'who' for the Westphalian 'who', Fraser explains, governance principles should avoid homogenising a 'one-size-fits-all' framing of governance. In the contemporary world, she continues, people are subject to a plurality of different governance structures, some local, some national, some regional, and some global. Therefore, there needs to be a variety of different frames for different issues that can mark out a plurality of 'who's' for different purposes (Fraser, 2010).

What would new food safety governance look like? Feminist theorists have particularly valuable contributions to make in the thinking of governance in the context of diversity and the complexities of power. Their work would encourage a look beyond the limitations of the liability model towards creating diverse institutional arrangements for safe, just and ecological food systems that are responsive to the complexities of power, difference, capacities and context, rather than a globalised food safe system that privileges the few. Feminist theorists also aim to recognise that governance in a post-Westphalian order can no longer legitimate itself by reference to the inhabitants of a particular state or the falsely universalising referent of 'the consumer'. Thinking about good safety governance can start with the simple questions: 'what food is to be kept safe and for whom?' But it needs to go beyond that to engage the new feminist ontologies that recognise food's central entanglements of nature and culture that co-produce each other. The profound theoretical shifts with new configurations of matter in a post-humanist and post-consumer era call for the abandonment of the qualitative distinctions between nature and human that underwrites both concepts of disease and agri-food safety. This has far-reaching socioeconomic and political implications. Protecting an outdated political-economic ontological order is a dangerous protection racket. To continue to do so is surely a crime?

References

Alaimo, S. (2010) *Bodily natures: Science, environment, and the material self*, Indiana, IN: Indiana University Press.

Beck, U. (1992) *Risk society: Towards a new modernity*, vol 17, London: Sage.

COG (Canadian Organic Growers) (2017) (https://madmimi.com/p/447ee9/preview).

Dean, J. (2017) *Neoliberalism and its contradictions* (www.academia.edu/1145526/Neoliberalism_and_its_contradictions).

DeLind, L.B. and Howard, P.H. (2008) 'Safe at any scale? Food scares, food regulation, and scaled alternatives', *Agriculture and Human Values*, vol 25, no 3, pp 301–17.

Douglas, M. (2003) *Purity and danger: An analysis of concepts of pollution and taboo*, Abingdon: Routledge.

Dunn, E.C. (2003) 'Trojan pig: paradoxes of food safety regulation', *Environment and Planning A*, vol 35, no 8, pp 1493–511.

Fraser, N. (2010) 'Who counts? Dilemmas of justice in a postWestphalian world', *Antipode*, vol 41, s1, pp 281–97.

Fraser, N. (2013) *Fortunes of feminism: From state-managed capitalism to neoliberal crisis*, New York: Verso Books.

Haraway, D. (2008) 'Companion species, mis-recognition, and queer worlding', in M.J. Hird and N. Giffney (eds) *Queering the non/human*, Abingdon: Routledge, pp xxiii–xxvi.

Larsen, A.F. (2009) 'Semi-subsistence producers and biosecurity in the Slovenian Alps', *Sociologia Ruralis*, vol 49, no 4, pp 330–43.

Lavin, C. (2015) *Eating anxiety: The perils of food politics*, Minneapolis, MN: University of Minnesota Press.

Li, T.M. (2010) 'To make live or let die? Rural dispossession and the protection of surplus populations', *Antipode*, vol 41, s1, pp 66–93.

MacIntyre, B.D., Herren, H.R., Wakhunga, J. and R. Watson, R. (eds) (2009) *Global report*, International Assessment of Agricultural Knowledge, Science and Technology for Development, IAASTD, Washington, DC: Island Press.

McMahon, M. (2011) 'Standard fare or fairer standards: Feminist reflections on agri-food governance', *Agriculture and Human Values*, vol 28, no 3, pp 401–12.

McMahon, M. (2013) 'What food is to be kept safe and for whom? Food-safety governance in an unsafe food system', *Laws*, vol 2, no 4, pp 401–27.

Moore, J.W. (2015) *Capitalism in the web of life: Ecology and the accumulation of capital*, New York: Verso Books.

Morton, T. (2013) *Hyperobjects: Philosophy and ecology after the end of the world*, Minneapolis, MN: University of Minnesota Press.

Nerlich, B. (2004) 'War on foot and mouth disease in the UK, 2001: Towards a cultural understanding of agriculture', *Agriculture and Human Values*, vol 21, no 1, pp 15–25.

Nixon, R. (2011) *Slow violence and the environmentalism of the poor*, Cambridge, MA: Harvard University Press.

Parenti, C. (2015) 'The 2013 ANTIPODE AAG lecture: The environment making state: Territory, nature, and value', *Antipode*, vol 47, no 4, pp 829–48.

Scott, J.C. (1998) *Seeing like a state: How certain schemes to improve the human condition have failed*, New Haven, CT: Yale University Press.

Shropshire Sheep (2017) 'Farmed and dangerous?', Blog (http://shropshiresheep.org/farmedanddangerous/).

Smith, D.E. (1999) *Writing the social: Critique, theory, and investigations*, Toronto, Canada: University of Toronto Press.

Waltner-Toews, D. (2009) 'Food, global environmental change and health: EcoHealth to the rescue?', *McGill Journal of Medicine: MJM*, vol 12, no 1, p 85.

Winson, A. (2013) *The industrial diet*, Vancouver, BC: University of British Columbia Press.

Young, I.M. (2003a) 'From guilt to solidarity', *Dissent*, Spring (www.dissentmagazine.org/article/from-guilt-to-solidarity).

Young, I. (2003b) 'Feminist reactions to the contemporary security regime', *Hypatia*, vol 18, no 1, pp 223–31.

3

The social construction of illegality within local food systems

Marcello De Rosa, Ferro Trabalzi and Tiziana Pagnani

Introduction

This chapter discusses the institutionalisation of illegality within a community of food producers in territories where the presence of organised crime is both historical and endemic. The economy and its processes have been mostly analysed from the point of view of consensus and conflict theories, which understand illegality as an aberration of an otherwise legal system of production and exchange. To understand illegality apart from legality – in opposition to, parallel with, or intertwined with – limits the possibility of the state being able or willing to enforce the law. In territories where organised crime is a fact of life, illegality is a *modus operandi on the economic scene*, neither in opposition nor an alternative to the legal economy, but simply the most viable and efficient collective system of rules given the prevalent system of power in the territory.

Organised (corporate) crime imposes purposeful order on a territory. Rather than re-appropriate resources, the goal of organised crime is to change the ways populations think, distorting the collective perceptions to believe that being ruled by clans is good, efficient and rational. The lower the level of cultural hegemony exerted by organised crime on a territory, the less questioning there is of the difference between legal and illegal behaviour. This chapter argues that the historical presence of organised crime in the political, social, economic and institutional fabric of a territory contributes to a blurring of this difference, to a point where the population in general, and entrepreneurs in particular, do not consider legal and illegal behaviours as oppositional. Rather, behaviours are understood as alternatives along a fluid legal–illegal continuum. The relative positioning along the continuum is never casual or arbitrary, but obeys socially constructed conventions and institutionalised processes.

This chapter provides a conceptual model, the *Evil Trinity*, which proposes three dynamic forces behind the institutionalisation of illegality: territoriality, institutions and entrepreneurship. Examples from a case study approach are discussed (Yin, 2009; Smith and McElwee, 2013), with the support of participant observation, and structured and semi-structured interviews (Aoyama et al, 2010). Drawing on previous research by De Rosa and Trabalzi (2016), integrated with more recent findings, the conceptual model is applied to a typical Italian cheese – buffalo mozzarella DOP – the quality of which is strictly linked to the area of production through protected designation of origin labelling. In combination with documentary methods (Scott, 2006) and internet-mediated techniques research (Hewson, 2003), the case studies are reported according to a 'farm to fork' perspective that allows the pinpointing of illegal behaviours along the entire supply chain of the product.

What is food crime?

According to the National Food Crime Unit based in the UK (FSA, 2016, p 9), food crime is 'dishonesty relating to the production or supply of food, that is either complex or likely to be seriously detrimental to consumers, businesses or the overall public interest.' Within this context, food fraud specifically is defined as an activity 'intended for personal gain or to cause loss to another party.' Judging from the most recent food scandals ranging from meat to fish and from wine to honey, illegality in the food system is widespread throughout the European Union (EU).

The possibility of food products with dubious origins, made in ways and with ingredients that pose a risk to the health of populations, vilify the efforts of many honest producers, states and non-governmental organisations (NGOs) that devotedly invest in food crime prevention and enforcement. In particular, food fraud is a matter of cunning artistry, as those who operate illegally excogitate new ways to trick enforcement authorities. In the face of such an uneven battle, thinking and writing about food crime is a few steps behind. The ways in which food crimes are formally classified show a mode of thinking that reflects an outdated mode of thinking. For example, the separation of fraud and crime appears to be more semantic than factual because law enforcement officials on the ground often face single criminals or isolated dishonest producers who are rigging the system for their own benefit, but established systems of illegality that have ramifications that are not easy to map. Perpetrators only play a small role in such systems; although relevant, the cause of food crime is linked into large, complex and dynamic social networks in which different actors (from veterinarians to distributors to sellers) participate with different responsibilities for the crimes committed. Where does the crime start? In the cow shed, where water is added to the batch of milk that is directed to the cheese house for processing? At the independent laboratory, where the technician who analyses the batch of milk declares it absent of water? At the cheese house, where a dishonest cheese maker knowingly processes milk extracted from brucellosis-infected cows? Or is it at the veterinarian office, where the doctor signs the health bill for the herd, declaring it immune from the virus? Food fraud occurs at any point in the food process, so focusing just on one actor, rather than the whole network, limits our understanding of food crime and efforts to mitigate or dissolve it.

This network perspective (encompassing from farm to fork) helps expand the discussion on food crime and illegality within food systems. In other words, confining food crime to the technical aspect of production or on single phases without considering the whole production network obscures the fact that food fraud is committed throughout the food chain, and not all are necessarily related to the product. From this perspective the conventional discrimination between legal and illegal becomes problematic because practices can overlap in their definition as legal, illegal or criminal. This chapter analyses food fraud in terms of a network with different levels: geographic, institutional and individual. Using this analytic triad – the Evil Trinity – it is possible to observe legal, illegal and criminal behaviours as variations of the same processes of production located along a legal–illegal continuum.

The Evil Trinity: territoriality, institutions and entrepreneurship

To understand entrepreneurial behaviours and aptitudes that seem to escape logic or the rule of law, context matters. In its multiple declinations (social, cultural, geo-historical, institutional, economic), 'context' provides opportunities and sets boundaries to action that shapes and is shaped by individual and collective action (Simpeh, 2011; Welter, 2011). Territories, institutions and entrepreneurs are the three main axes used in this chapter to frame the issue of the social construction of illegality. Building on Storper's (1997) Holy Trinity of technology, organisation and territory used to explain regional, uneven development, a concept of an Evil Trinity is proposed to explain the nature of social relationships and of the origins of the economic imaginary of entrepreneurs. The model shares with the Holy Trinity the idea that the ways people interact with each other (formally, informally, face-to-face, mediated, in the absence or presence of mutual trust) shape the overall nature of industrial systems and their propensity to learn, innovate and connect more generally. Such a framework, founded in a constructivist and cultural perspective, transforms industrial systems and communities of producers in socio-cultural ensembles governed by conventions: systems of action. The main difference between the trinities involves the centrality given to the territory under observation. The focus on locality permits the problematisation of the conventional antagonistic division between a legal and illegal system of rules. In areas where clans are hegemonic, for example, in the coastal areas of southern Italy, where agricultural production is most developed and so are local food systems, the conventions behind processes and practices of production show that a clear boundary between legal and illegal is not always easy to discern. This theoretical boundary is substituted with a continuum where individual behaviours range indifferently from legality to criminality. The next sections focus on describing each one of these dimensions and their role in shaping the approach towards legality and illegality in food production.

Territoriality

The centrality of the 'territory' of social and economic life has been recognised in the literature for some time (Delaney, 2005; Paasi, 2008). The economy in the age of global production and exchange has dual implications. On the one hand, it has weakened, relatively speaking, the power of the nation-state as a regulatory entity, while on the other hand, it has re-evaluated sub-national spaces as the fundamental spatial dimension in the contemporary economic environment (Storper, 1997). The hegemonising role played by big firms notwithstanding, the contemporary global economy is far from being placeless. The standard picture of globalisation leading toward a 'McWorld' is countered by an alternative paradigm that argues that the knowledge necessary to make the economy spin at a global level is place-specific. Indeed, place-based human relations are the fundamental resources in contemporary capitalism, a key ingredient for the level of coordination necessary to compete on a global scale. Therefore the region, and more generally, territoriality, is an active agent able to shape the quality of social relations and vice versa (Harvey, 1989; Soja, 1989; Lefebvre, 1991 [1974]). All this highlights a simple but fundamental truth: ways of behaving in the economic scene are embedded and rooted in place, and therefore differ from place to place (Simpeh, 2011; Welter, 2011). Borrowing from the language of economic geography, it is possible to imagine the territorial nature and quality of entrepreneurship being structured around a series of local 'cultural' specificities, each with its own 'politics' that interact with each other in a continuous, self-reinforcing loop. This may lead towards virtuous effects of innovation, competitiveness and development, or alternatively, vicious effects with associated convoluted and detrimental effects on the territory (Storper, 1997).

The so-called 'reflexive' turn is important because it helps to get rid of the old structure-conduct problematic, opening economic analysis to research based less on political analysis and more on concrete, observable and meaningful practices connected to market efficiency. On the other hand, the scenarios that result from this new conceptual pragmatism end with another set of arbitrary dichotomies: vicious–virtuous, innovation–stagnation and legal–illegal. These do not necessarily represent the everyday reality of entrepreneurs in territories controlled and managed by the logic of organised crime. From the point of view of an entrepreneur operating in such areas, the limits of heterodox approaches seem to involve the idea of legal exchange being the base of the economic system. However, in certain areas people consider illegality part of the game and accept it even if they understand the amorality of the system. Rather than having absolute validity, legality in areas controlled by organised crime betrays historical and geographical specificity, that is, its contingent nature.

The image of the self-reinforcing loop helps introduce another dimension of the territory relevant to analyse the social construction of illegality: the notion of proximity (Patel and Pavitt, 1994; Sternberg, 1999). Proximity identifies face-to-face, informal, intricate relational networks that tie groups of firms operating in a limited space, and thus is useful in studying the social construction of illegality. Rallet and Torre (2004; see also Torre and Rallet, 2005) overlap geographical proximity with organisational proximity, including the dynamics of social interaction. The resulting image showcases forms of organisation as structured around two territorial logics: a *logic of belonging* defined by a shared set of routines and practices in the process of production, and a *logic of similarity* marked by a tacitly shared system of representations, beliefs and knowledge by members of an organisation (Torre and Beuret, 2012). According to Kebir and Torre (2013), organisational proximity can be based on forms of collaboration that have no moral or ethical motivations. For example, 'Mafia organisations often feed on both the logic of similarity (ethnic origins) and on the logic of belonging (strong connection within a network of actors), which can be considered immoral ethically' (Kebir and Torre, 2013, p 10).

This is a relevant aspect of the question related to food crime in Italy, where the agri-food sector is characterised by the presence of numerous territorialised agri-food systems producing common local products. The geographical traits of the 'Made in Italy' products feeds the risk of fraud due to the higher probability of the joining of geographical and organisational proximity – a sort of 'spillover effect' of illegality on territorial bases. Thus territorial proximity becomes a fundamental element for analysing the transition from legal to illegal constructions within territorialised agri-food systems. Accelerating this move is a question of other driving forces: institutional selection and entrepreneurial orientation and learning.

Institutions

Part of the economic identity of territories is the way people operate on the market scene. Some territories are characterised by mutual trust and a tendency to cooperate at different institutional and geographical levels, while others show the opposite. Numerous studies have analysed the role of institutional factors, endogenous to the territory, to explain regional, cultural specificities and differences. Such research sheds light on a relevant strand of institutional literature that may be of help in interpreting the social construction of illegality: original institutional economics (OIE). This perspective argues that the institutionalisation of illegality within localised food production systems may be explored through an evolutionary analysis of informal institutions of an economic nature (Veblen, 1899; Parada, 2001).

What are institutions? According to OIE, institutions are 'settled habits of thought common to the generality of men' (Veblen, 1909, p 234). The institutional perspective adopted here suggests that if institutions are assimilated to the culture of the people, these institutions set the boundaries and shape forms of actions (Hamilton, 1932; Young, 1996; Hodgson, 2004). From this perspective, the theme of illegality can be analysed from two points of view: illegality as a norm, and illegality as an institution. Veblen (1899, p 118) posits that 'the situation of today shapes the institutions of tomorrow through a selective, coercive process, by acting upon human beings' habitual view of things.' This emphasis on the process of selection exemplifies a fertile research strategy to investigate the institutionalisation of illegality. Against this background, OIE appears particularly effective for two reasons:

- First, one of the characteristic topics of OIE is the analysis of the role of conventions, informal institutions and power structures in conditioning economic processes and performance. In this respect, the proposed perspective may be useful in differentiating the relational modes in the local system capable of generating institutional selection, moving the local system along the continuum.
- Second, closely related to the first, an OIE perspective is context-based. It references the concept of typification (Stanfield, 1999) to address the determination of the characteristics of individuals operating in a particular social context.

Read in the perspective of food criminality, institutional selection is at work when legal institutions are systematically replaced by illegal ones, involving circular feedback from institutions to individuals and vice versa. Recalling a recent contribution by Geoffrey Hodgson (2006), De Rosa and Trabalzi (2016) posit that a 'reconstitutive downward effect' may change human behaviour by creating new perceptions and dispositions within individuals, thus giving rise to processes of institutional selection. At the same time, the opposite idea of 'upward causation', where it is possible for individuals to change institutions, is widely accepted. In many agri-food territorial systems of Italy, characterised by endemic, organised crime, the consequence of the interaction between positive and negative instincts has been systematically detrimental to positive ones. This process has also involved entrepreneurial aptitudes, which is the third key driving force towards the renegade side of the economy.

Entrepreneurship

As Dickson and Weaver (2008) point out, entrepreneurial orientation is strongly affected by the institutional environment. This is particularly true in cases of illegal entrepreneurial behaviour, and illegality has been acquiring growing attention in the literature on entrepreneurship (McElwee and Smith, 2015). According to Gray (2002, p 61), the entrepreneur is an individual 'who manages a business, with the intention of expanding that business and with the leadership and the managerial capabilities for achieving their goals.' Similarly, entrepreneurial orientation is a strategic decision-making process aiming at enacting a firm's organisational purpose and consequently supporting its competitiveness (Wang, 2008). However, as Baumol (1990) points out, decision-making may respond to a constructive or destructive orientation, or, as argued here, both. More precisely, McElwee and colleagues (2011, p 50) make reference to the term of 'value extracting' (in opposition to 'value creation') to describe entrepreneurial processes aimed at enriching the individual but impoverishing society: 'value extracting entrepreneurship occurs outside of and seeks to delegitimise established legislative structures and ethical mores.' Therefore, entrepreneurship doesn't always work for the common good or in respect to the law.

By making specific reference to Baumol's work on productive, unproductive and destructive entrepreneurship, Smith and McElwee (2013) classify a typology of entrepreneurship along an illegal–legal continuum, ranging in order from organised crime, white-collar crime, illicit, immoral, amoral and moral behaviours. The first two types are classified as illegal and destructive entrepreneurship, the third (illegal) and fourth (legal) types as unproductive entrepreneurship, and the final two types as legal productive entrepreneurship. The following section uses this conceptualisation as a platform in which to help understand food crimes and harms along a similar legal–illegal continuum.

Moving along the legal–illegal continuum

The juxtaposition between legal and illegal entrepreneurship and the transition from one type to the other has been depicted by Webb and colleagues (2009) within illegal economies. Against this background, actors (from individual entrepreneurs to large groups) recognise and exploit opportunities through illegal but legitimate activities – a dynamic that parallels Baumol's (1990) progressive transition toward unproductive and destructive entrepreneurship. The illegal side of an economy is then perceived as opposite to the legal one, and is marked by emerging destructive entrepreneurial aptitudes.

A slightly different interpretation is provided by De Rosa and Trabalzi (2016), who don't share the dichotomic approach of legal and illegal economies belonging to fundamentally different systems and/or mentalities. Instead, they propose a single economic process, a continuum, with legality on the one hand and illegality (or renegade) at the opposite side (see Figure 3.1). Along the continuum, people can and do move from one side to the other at the same time, and indeed, within the same production processes. In other words, it is possible to observe, as De Rosa and Trabalzi have in their research on typical food products in southern Italy, that producers may be legal or respectful of the law in one phase of production (for example, during the purchasing of agricultural inputs, such as buffalo milk) and illegal in others (for example, employing workers without a contract). This overlapping of legal and illegal can also occur when food products or agricultural inputs are illegally produced but legally processed. This is the case for milk producers who use hormones and other prohibited substances to extract more milk from their cows and then sell their product to cheese makers who later process it in a legal manner. The way people behave in particular segments along the continuum can be ascribed to the prevalent system of power in place within the territory, which influences the process of institutional selection in favour of certain types of behaviour rather than others.

Figure 3.1: The economy continuum

Illegal economy   Legal economy
(Criminal food processes)   (Permitted food processes)

To exemplify the movement along the continuum, several case studies were analysed that follow the production of a common Italian cheese with governmental certification concerning a protected designation of origin: buffalo mozzarella DOP. Research tends to analyse territories controlled by organised crime where the state has tremendous difficulties imposing its order and rules. Such weakness of the state combined with the strength of organised criminal organisations has historically conditioned economic life in certain regions of southern Italy. Nonetheless, numerous examples witness the presence of many cheese producers passionately manufacturing this product by following the procedural guidelines specified in the code of practice (Case Study 1, CS_1 hereafter). Many producers treat their buffalo with respect, safeguarding animal welfare. Some don't use oxytocin during milking or give antibiotics to their animals. To get the Protected Designation of Origin (PDO) certification, milk and cheese producers must comply with the code of practice, which rules the way of producing mozzarella (CS_2). Compliance with the code generally means higher costs of production, which (should) then bring about higher final premium prices at the consumer level. This argument links to the Holy Trinity, where entrepreneurial attitudes, local conventions of production and territory play a relevant role in granting a product of excellence that may be identified as a food ambassador for the territory. Many honest producers act along this logic of productive entrepreneurship. In recognition of the significant proportion of honest producers, (potentially) powerful initiatives have been carried out by the producers' consortium to prevent illegal actions. In 2012 an ethical code was approved, which states that every year breeders and cheese makers are obliged to produce an anti-mafia certificate as a 'legal brand' to be exhibited, which helps confirm that the buffalo mozzarella has been produced according to a legal standard. More recently, the consortium has signed a new procedure for intensifying greater controls to grant high-quality standards. Nonetheless, many case studies showcase how the realities of buffalo mozzarella production have disappointed such regulation expectations.

Unfortunately, the reputation of buffalo mozzarella is at risk due to frequent cases of illegality. On this track between legal and illegal are some manufacturers that decide to buy milk from other producers because they are unable to fulfil the demand for the quantity of milk required (CS_3). In this case, processors buying buffalo milk from other companies doesn't constitute a crime, but this behaviour is perceived as criminal because it is not always possible to ensure the quality of the milk. Reliability is a significant concern in food production, as consumers are unable to ascertain many characteristics of food products during purchasing, consumption and post-consumption, and must therefore rely on the word of manufacturers.

The price–cost squeeze represents an important factor influencing illegal, entrepreneurial behaviour. In numerous cases farmers dispose of all male calves and any female calves that do not have the required characteristics for milk production (CS_4) – male buffalo calves are disposed of because there is no market for buffalo meat. The police have responded to calls made by individuals who have discovered the carcasses of male calves disposed of along rivers and canals and other rural areas. In other cases, manufacturers produce their product in a completely legal way, but declare lower production outputs, in order to reduce their share to the consortium, which also reduces production costs (CS_5).

It is often the case that milk producers decide to stretch out their milk quantity through the addition of frozen buffalo milk, water or milk from other mammals (CS_6). Due to the involvement of the highest managerial spheres in this mixing of buffalo milk with water, in 2010 the Italian Ministry of Agriculture put the consortium under temporary receivership for the legal protection of the product. This typical white-collar crime (Smith and McElwee, 2013) provides an example of a 'thus do they all' attitude to produce a common food through fraudulent actions – practices that are contrary to the rules of production, but that do not cause any (known) health damage to populations.

Illegality also involves exploiting farm workers, especially those of Indian and Pakistani descent. Similar to Hinch's (2018) discussion of illegal agricultural labour and its harmful consequences (see Chapter 5, this volume), these individuals are employed on farms with no grants and no insurance; they are 'invisible' workers (CS_{7a}). Over the years, a new phenomenon linked to this exploitation has been emerging, known as *caporalato* (CS_{7b}). In the past, supervisors were responsible for recruiting labourers and transporting them from the collection point to the workplace and vice versa. In the last few years, these supervisors (*caporales*) have obtained more power, and such illegal practices, and their harmful consequences, have become increasingly widespread in the various spheres of the everyday life of agricultural workers. Immigrant workers depend on the *caporale* for an employment salary, to get a green card for displacement, for necessary goods and for food and shelter, all of which is provided at highly increased prices and is of poor quality. This organisation is frequently managed by organised crime, and thus such cases exemplify the renegade side of the economy.

In 2013 the police discovered discovered a criminal association aimed at food sophistication through various illegal practices (CS_8). These included the use of cow milk or water to produce buffalo mozzarella, systems of breeding that paid no concern to animal welfare, and the illegal provision of massive doses of vaccines aiming at hiding brucellosis throughout the buffalo herds. A more recent scandal, revealed in 2016, confirms such a 'systemic perspective' of the transition towards the renegade side of the economy. These frauds involve the involve the coordination and cooperation of breeders or dairies as well as certification bodies governing agri-food quality (Cinotti, 2016). According to wiretappings, inspectors from the certification body warned breeders in advance to 'agree the documentation for the analysis of both milk and farm's production data' (CS_9). Another case emerged in February 2017, with the discovery of old milk that had been 'regenerated' with caustic soda by a large firm with a yearly turnover of €8 million (CS_{10}). A dependent declared that he was in charge of "adding caustic soda in the milk in order to reduce the level of acidity", without knowing that this additive increases the bacterial charge and, consequently, damages consumers' health. All of these cases showcase a fast-moving trend towards the renegade side of economy (see Figure 3.2).

Figure 3.2: Case study positioning along the continuum

CS_1 CS_2 CS_3 CS_4 CS_5 CS_6 CS_{7a} CS_{7b} CS_8 CS_9 CS_{10}

Legal   Renegade

Discussion and conclusion

This chapter has explored the multidimensional aspects contributing to the social construction of food criminality. Reference to the legal–illegal (or renegade) continuum has permitted consideration of legality as neither in opposition with nor an alternative to illegality, but has enabled an understanding of the contemporary existence of both the legal and illegal to emerge in the case of buffalo mozzarella production in southern Italy. Case study analysis has shown that illegal behaviour, when it happens and how it happens, responds to specific local conventions that are the products of institutional selection. The growing number of related food harms and crimes synthesise the propensity to share new ways of (illegally) doing things in an entrepreneurial manner.

The conception of the Evil Trinity provides grounding for the Darwinian process of institutional selection, selecting the worst, not the best (Dosi and Winter, 2002). This approach shows how the institutionalisation of illegality takes on territorial characteristics that cannot exist in the same, similar forms everywhere. Consequently, the institutional selection environment might be conceptualised as a complexity of competing legitimisation processes at different levels bringing about emergent properties. As pointed out by O'Hara (2002), these emergent properties are marked by the presence of Veblen's (1899) 'negative instincts', as pecuniary instincts and rapacious conduct, which prevail through time. Additionally, this process is marked by the presence of new reference groups, such as organised criminals, and within a territorial context, local entrepreneurs receive messages of new prevailing cultural systems that satisfy their entrepreneurial profiles. Thus, illegality becomes an efficient and rational answer to the existing hegemonic system of power.

The influential presence of organised crime, through mechanisms of organisational proximity, creates and generates the process of institutional selection boosting a sort of entrepreneurial fluidity, converging towards mafia entrepreneurship. As pointed out by De Rosa and Trabalzi (2016, p 310), 'institutional transition is realised through mechanisms of both downward and upward effects: on the one hand, the "everyone does it" logic conditions individual attitudes, and on the other hand, illegal behaviour of individuals such as organised criminals may influence and force entrepreneurship to operate illegally.' Therefore, the contemporary presence of the three pillars of the Evil Trinity boosting the move towards illegality makes it difficult to imagine a U-turn in the short term. A new process of institutional selection is necessary, where new emergent properties may bring about new organisational proximity and new productive entrepreneurial behaviour. This is what is required to preserve the dignity and honesty of many hard-working rural entrepreneurs.

References

Aoyama, Y., Murphy, J.T. and Hanson, S. (2010) *Key concepts in economic geography*, London: Sage.

Baumol, W. (1990) 'Entrepreneurship: Productive, unproductive and destructive', *Journal of Political Economy*, vol 98, no 5, pp 893–921.

Cinotti, E. (2016) 'Mozzarella di bufala nel caos, controlli concordati e false certificazioni', *Il Salvagente* (www.testmagazine.it/2016/05/09/mozzarella-di-bufala-nel-caos-controlli-concordati-e-false-certificazioni/8306/).

Coldiretti-Eurispes (2015) Agromafie, 3 Rapporto sui crimini agroalimentari in Italia, Roma, Eurispes.

Delaney, D. (2005) *Territory: A short introduction*, Malden, MA: Blackwell.

De Rosa, M. and Trabalzi, F. (2016) 'Everybody does it, or how illegality is socially constructed in a southern Italian food network', *Journal of Rural Studies*, vol 45, pp 303–11.

Dickson, P.H. and Weaver, K.M. (2008) 'The role of the institutional environment in determining firm orientations towards entrepreneurial behaviour', *International Entrepreneurship and Management Journal*, vol 4, no 4, pp 467–83.

Dosi, G. and Winter, S. G. (2002) 'Interpreting economic change: evolution, structures and games', in M. Augier and J. March (eds) *The economics of choice, change and organisations: Essays in memory of Richard M. Cyert*, Cheltenham: Edward Elgar, pp 337–53.

FSA (Food Standards Agency) (2016) *Food crime*, Annual strategic assessment, National Food Crime Unit.

Gray, C. (2002) 'Entrepreneurship, resistance to change and growth in small firms', *Journal of Small Business and Enterprise Development*, vol 9, no 1, pp 61–72.

Hamilton, W.H. (1932) 'Institutions', in E. Seligman and A. Johnson (eds) *Encyclopedia of social sciences*, New York: Macmillan, pp 560–95.

Harvey, D. (1989) *The condition of postmodernity*, Oxford: Wiley Blackwell.

Hewson, C. (2003) 'Conducting research on the Internet', *The Psychologist*, vol 16, no 6, pp 290–3.

Hodgson, G.M. (2004) *The evolution of institutional economics: Agency, structure and Darwinism in American institutionalism*, New York: Routledge.

Hodgson, G.M. (2006) 'What are institutions?', *Journal of Economic Issues*, vol XL, pp 1–25.

Kebir, L. and Torre, A. (2013) 'Geographical proximity and new short supply food chains', in L. Lazzeretti (ed) *Creative industries and innovation in Europe: Concepts, measures, and comparative case studies*, New York: Routledge, pp 328–54.

Lefebvre, H. (1991 [1974]) *The production of space* (translated by D. Nicholson-Smith), Oxford: Basil Blackwell.

McElwee, G. and Smith, R. (2015) *Criminal entrepreneurship*, London: Emerald.

McElwee, G., Smith, R. and Somerville, P. (2011) 'Theorising illegal rural enterprise: Is anyone at it?', *International Journal of Rural Criminology*, vol 1, no 1, pp 40–62.

O'Hara, P.H. (2002) 'The contemporary relevance of Thorstein Veblen's Institutional-Evolutionary Political Economy', *History of Economics Review*, vol 35, pp 78–103.

Paasi, A. (2008) 'Territory', in J. Agnew, K. Mitchell, and G. Toal (eds) *A companion to political geography*, Malden, MA: Blackwell, pp 109–22.

Parada, J.J. (2001) 'Original institutional economics: An agenda for the 21st century?', *Oeconomicus*, vol V, pp 46–60.

Patel, P. and Pavit, K. (1991) 'Larger firms in the production of world's technology: An important case of "non-globalization"', *Journal of International Business Studies*, vol 22, no 1, pp 35–54.

Rallet A. and Torre, A. (2004) 'Proximité et localisation', *Économie Rurale*, vol 284, pp 5–41.

Scott, G. (2006) *Documentary research*, London: Sage.

Simpeh, K. (2011) 'Entrepreneurship theories and empirical research: A summary view of literature', *European Journal of Business Management*, vol 3, pp 19.

Smith, R. and McElwee, G. (2013) 'The embeddedness of illegal entrepreneurship in a closed ethnic community', *International Journal of Business and Globalization*, vol 11, no 1, pp 45–62.

Soja, E. (1989) *Postmodern geographies: The reassertion of space in critical social theory*, London: Verso Press.

Stanfield, J.R. (1999) 'The scope, method and the significance of original institutional economics', *Journal of Economics Issues*, vol XXXIII, no 2, pp 231–55.

Sternberg, R. (1999) 'Innovative linkages and proximity: Empirical results from recent survey of small and medium sized firm in German regions', *Regional Studies*, vol 33, pp 529–40.

Storper, M. (1997) *The regional world*, New York: Guilford Press.

Torre, A. and Beuret, J.E. (2012) *Proximités territoriales*, Paris: Economica.

Torre, A. and Rallet, A. (2005) 'Proximity and localization', *Regional Studies*, vol 39, no 1, pp 47–59.

Veblen, T. (1899) *The theory of leisure class*, New Brunswick, NJ: Transaction Publishers.

Veblen, T. (1909) *The place of science in modern civilisation and other essays*, New Brunswick, NJ: Transaction Publishers.

Wang, C.L. (2008) 'Entrepreneurial orientation, learning orientation and firm performance', *Entrepreneurship Theory and Practice*, vol 32, no 4, pp 635–56.

Webb, J.W., Tihanyi, L., Ireland, R.D. and Sirmon, D.G. (2009) 'You say illegal, I say legitimate: Entrepreneurship in the informal economy', *Academy of Management Review*, vol 34, pp 492–510

Welter, F. (2011) 'Contextualizing entrepreneurship. Conceptual challenges and ways forward', *Entrepreneurship Theory and Practice*, vol 35, no 1, pp 165–84.

Yin, R.K. (2009) *Case study research: Design and methods*, Thousand Oaks, CA: Sage Publications

Young, H.P. (1996) 'The economics of convention', *Journal of Economic Perspectives*, vol 10, no 2, pp 105–22.

Section II
Farming and food production

4

Ethical challenges facing farm managers

Harvey S. James Jr

Introduction

Understanding managerial decision-making is difficult. Understanding farmers' decision-making is also difficult, but is complicated by the fact that farm management decisions are affected by and contribute to unique environmental uncertainties. In this context, 'environment' can be interpreted literally. What farmers do is affected by the physical environment, including the quality of the soil, weather conditions and drought, as well as how farmer actions affect the environment, for instance, through environmental degradation and climate change.

Like managers in other businesses, farmers make investment decisions, such as what and how much to plant, based on expectations of future market conditions. Farmers have to consider competition from other farmers, many of whom happen to be their neighbours. They must negotiate deals with seed, chemical and other farm input suppliers, and contract with buyers of their crops and livestock. They need to understand complex government regulatory and tax requirements, many of which are unique to agriculture. Farmers must also contend with evolving social norms and expectations about what farmers do and how they fit into the fabric of society.

Like business owners who face ethical challenges in the decisions they make, farmers are not immune to ethical pressures and problems. However, the complex combination of environmental, market, regulatory, personal and social forces impacting on farmers can create significant and unique pressures on them, pressures that can translate into major ethical and legal lapses and result in food crimes. These ethical challenges of farming are manifested in the activities and decisions of farmers that violate moral and ethical standards of right and wrong.

What are the ethical challenges that farmers face? Where and how do they arise? To what extent are they similar to and different from the ethical challenges that non-farming business professionals face? While it is not possible to answer adequately all of these questions, this chapter provides a general overview of the conditions that affect the propensity of business professionals to engage in unethical conduct, and relates them to the ethical challenges that farmers face. It also presents a typology of ethical challenges in agriculture and a discussion of unique fault lines – that is, pressures and constraints — existing in farming that can lead to food crimes perpetuated by farmers.

Background

Unethical behaviour means doing things that one knows, feels or believes to be wrong, that a vast majority of people agree is wrong, or that causes harm to others (Armstrong, 1977). Obvious examples would be lying, cheating and stealing. More subtle cases involve exploiting others so that a gain one receives comes at the expense of others, and using others as a means to an end. The literature exploring the causes, consequences and cures of ethical dilemmas arising in business and from managerial decision-making is huge. At the risk of oversimplifying the content of this literature, managerial ethics is based on two fundamental pillars or general approaches for understanding the root causes of unethical decision-making and where to look for solutions to solve them. The two general approaches relate to (1) moral character and (2) environmental context. This characterisation is sometimes expressed as the problem of 'bad apples' and 'bad barrels.'

In the 'bad apples' perspective, moral character refers to the dispositional characteristics of people, such as their ability to recognise ethical problems, to make ethical judgements and to behave ethically (Rest, 1986). Recognising ethical challenges is a particularly important consideration when studying the ethical behaviour of people. Some people may not realise they are facing an ethical challenge, while others may not realise they have cognitive blinders keeping them from being aware of the ethical challenges they face (Bazerman and Chugh, 2006). Also relevant is a person's ability and willingness to feel guilt and shame when they do something or are about to do something wrong. Listening to one's conscience or gut feelings can be an effective way of navigating through ethical challenges.

In the 'bad barrels' perspective, environmental context refers to the opportunities, incentives and sanctions that people face, as well as the rules, laws and social norms that exist. Whereas moral character focuses on the inward aspects of people, environmental context points to external conditions and circumstances. For example, organisational climate and culture can have a powerful effect on the ethical judgements and behaviours of individuals (James, 2000; Martin and Cullen, 2006). Social cues that people receive about what is appropriate, and observations of the actions of others, can also affect ethical decision-making. For example, in their study of farmer ethics, James and Hendrickson (2008, p 349) found 'that the more frequently a farmer reports observing an unethical action, the more accepting he is of it.'

There is an extensive literature examining the question of whether unethical decision-making is the result of 'bad apples' or 'bad barrels' (see, for instance, Treviño and Youngblood, 1990; Ashkanasy et al, 2006). The general assessment is that unethical behaviour is a combination of both. That is, the interaction of moral character and environmental context define the extent to which ethical dilemmas pose a challenge for people and society. For example, some people have high moral qualities and great integrity so that even the most pressing incentives for unethical behaviour will not push them to do things they know, feel or believe to be wrong. Other people seem to be prone to engage in unethical behaviour regardless of the incentives that exist promoting virtuous behaviour.

It is difficult to generalise about the moral character of individuals, although scholars have identified some interesting patterns. For example, experiments by Bartels and Pizarro (2011) showed that people who consistently adopt utilitarian solutions to moral dilemmas are more likely than others to have indications of psychopathic personalities or to feel that life is meaningless. In this context, a utilitarian solution might be allowing harm to occur to a few and using a few as a means to an end in order to benefit a greater number of people. There is more consensus among scholars about the influence and role of environmental context and external incentives and disincentives, although even here there are healthy debates within the literature.

For example, most cases of unethical behaviour in business can be traced back to some form of perverse incentive that promoted rather than discouraged the particular behaviour in question. For example, O'Hara (2016, p 5) describes how market incentives combined with complex accounting rules made financial decision-makers 'prone to overlook ethical dimensions' of the decisions they made, and ultimately resulted in the housing financial and subprime mortgage crisis in 2007. Experimental research shows that people will often rationalise unethical conduct when there is a financial or other gain for doing so (see, for instance, Mazar et al, 2008).

However, there is a debate about which incentives are primary and whether laws, rules and other sources of incentives can be properly changed. Since incentives work, they can be used to promote ethical conduct, but there is a debate about which kinds of codes, rules and incentives are effective. For example, some scholars argue that corporate codes of ethics and statements about appropriate ethical behaviour often have little effect on actual ethical conduct (Cleek and Leonard, 1998), while others claim that they do work (McCabe et al, 1996). Additionally, because incentives influence behaviour, questions arise about the appropriateness of using them to affect ethical change. There are two perspectives. The first is that incentives are ethically innocuous, so that they can and ought to be used to promote ethical conduct; the second is that incentives are a form of power and can exploit vulnerabilities in others and, as such, are inappropriate for promoting ethical conduct (Grant, 2006). Related here is the belief that for behaviour to be ethical it must be properly motivated. In other words, some people argue that behaviour cannot be defined as ethical if it is motivated by incentives.

In order to make sense of this confluence of dimensions, perspectives and factors relating to ethical conduct, researchers have developed many theories of ethical conduct. Some of the most prominent theories include Ferrell and Gresham's (1985) contingency framework for ethical decision-making, Treviño's (1986) person-situation interactionist model, Hunt and Vitell's (1986) descriptive general theory of marketing ethics, Jones' (1991) issue–contingent model and Ajzen's (1991) theory of planned behaviour. Each of these theories presumes that decision-makers are rational. In these theories, people behave ethically or unethically after completing a cognitive process of evaluation. In contrast to the cognitive approaches, some scholars have proposed non-rational explanations for ethical decision-making and behaviour. For example, Haidt (2001) argues that moral judgements are made intuitively, and that moral reasoning occurs after-the-fact as people attempt to rationalise or explain their behaviour. A related literature argues that ethical decision-making relates to emotional and psychological considerations. For example, Barnes et al (2011) show that a lack of sleep increases cognitive fatigue and emotional distress, leading to a reduction in one's ability to exercise self-control and make ethical decisions.

Gino (2015) provides a useful organising framework for understanding the extensive literature on why people engage in unethical behaviour. There are three main steps or stages in ethical decision-making (see Figure 4.1).

Figure 4.1: Ethical behaviour framework

Ethical awareness ➔ Ethical judgement ➔ Ethical behaviour

Ethical awareness is recognising that a situation involves ethical concerns. Ethical judgement is being able to determine what is right or appropriate. Ethical behaviour is following through with what is judged as right or appropriate. Within this context, streams of research divide in understanding unintentional versus intentional, unethical behaviour. The former focuses on the ethical awareness stage of decision-making and the latter focuses somewhat equally on making ethical judgements and behaving ethically.

The farming context

According to James (2003), there are two general types of ethical challenges that farmers face. The first focuses on perplexing ethical questions about what is the right thing to do, that is, problems in which there is not a general consensus as to the right course of action. The second focuses on behaviour and the encouragement of people to do the right thing. Here there tends to be a general consensus of what is right, but people have incentives or pressures to violate the consensus norms. There is considerable research examining ethical challenges of the first type in agriculture. For example, Thompson (2015) provides an accessible summary of the ethical controversies about food and agricultural production, much of which relates to uncertainties about what farmers should or should not be doing (for example, whether to plant genetically modified crops, or whether and how to consider animal welfare in livestock production). In contrast, there is limited research examining the ethical challenges of the second type, that is, of the ethical behaviour of farmers and other participants in the agri-food industry. A few papers can be considered applications of more general business ethics problems, such as Maloni and Brown (2006) on corporate social responsibility, and Nuttavuthisit and Thøgersen (2015) on consumer trust, but very little research reflects the unique and varied contexts of agricultural and food production and consumption. However, what research exists tells a consistent story. For example, surveys by Knorr (1991) and Rappaport and Himschoot (1994) show that farmers believe the ethical standards and the conduct of other farmers have deteriorated over time, and that 'their own ethical standards have also deteriorated' (Knorr, 1991, p 11). According to James (2005), some farmers engage in activities that they know to be unethical because they believe such behaviour is in their interest.

James and Hendrickson (2008) provide a comprehensive examination of farmer ethics, focusing in particular on the relationship between the pressures farmers feel and their ethics. They surveyed farmers to assess their perspectives regarding a variety of ethically questionable farming practices and activities. Examples of the scenarios they presented to farmers include: when a farmer tells buyers his crops are organic, even though some chemical fertilisers and pesticides were used; when a farmer continues using a herbicide, even though traces of it have begun to show up in the wells in his community; when a farmer plants only part of a field and later suffers crop damage, but files a crop insurance claim on the entire field; or when a rancher claims business depreciation on a pickup truck used primarily by other members of his family. James and Hendrickson show that there are three broad categories of ethical problems farmers face: (1) actions that cause harm or potential harm to others, the environment and non-human animals; (2) actions that are defined as wrong by law, contract or agreement; and (3) actions that are inappropriate for other reasons. They also show that there is a correlation between how frequently farmers perceive unethical conduct in other farmers and their tolerance of certain types of unethical practices. Specifically, farmers who believe that other farmers are engaging in activities that are wrong by contract or agreement have a greater tolerance of such practices themselves. This correlation does not exist for 'harmful' ethical problems.

Fault lines

Because context (that is, 'bad barrels') influences the ethical behaviour of people, we can draw conclusions about the *potential* for ethical challenges that farmers face by considering conditions with the farming sector that can or have been shown to produce fault lines or areas of concern. Pressures and constraints are particularly relevant. A pressure is a thing that strongly influences a person into doing something, and a constraint is a thing that limits what a person can do. Stated more simply, a pressure 'pushes' while a constraint 'pulls'. Research has demonstrated that pressures and constraints affect one's propensity to engage in unethical behaviour. For example, Rest's (1986) moral development framework and Treviño's (1986) person–situation interactionist model posits 'that personal costs and other pressures will have an impact on individual moral behaviour' (Treviño, 1986, p 614), a finding supported empirically by Staw and Szwajkowski (1975) for organisational pressure and by Bohns et al (2014) for social pressure. In the case of farming, James and Hendrickson (2008) show that there is a positive correlation between the intensity of pressures that farmers feel and their willingness to accept as tolerable activities that are wrong because they cause harm or because they are defined as inappropriate. Similarly, Hendrickson and James (2005) show how constraints farmers face contribute to enhanced incentives for unethical behaviour. Important pressures and constraints affecting farmers include (1) increasing production costs and land prices; (2) rising debt and worsening financial health; (3) more stringent government rules and regulations; and (4) reduced options for producing and marketing agricultural products.

First, land prices are important in agriculture because they are tied to production costs. For instance, in order to increase the size of a farm, farmers can either buy more land or enter into rental agreements with landowners. Increasing land prices makes the purchasing of land more difficult and is tied to rising land rental rates. Land prices also create pressures on farmers to increase agricultural production. One scholar noted that when land prices are rising, 'growers face pressure to maximise production in order to make a living' (Stuart, 2009, p 56). Average farm real estate values per acre for land and buildings in the continental US more than doubled between 1970 and 2016, from US$505 to more than US$1,200 per acre, holding constant the effect of inflation (USDA, 2017). While land prices have fluctuated during this time period, since the early 1990s there has been a clear and steady increase in land prices. The increase in land prices points to the potential for greater financial pressures on farmers as well as pressures to increase agricultural production, both of which can induce some farmers to lower their ethical standards in their farm management decision-making.

Second, while the financial stability of agricultural producers has always been variable and often chaotic, a study by agricultural economists reveals a trend for a relative worsening of farm income, wealth and financial health. As noted by Patrick et al (2016, p 1):

> Over a five-year period beginning in 2009, the US farm sector's income grew rapidly. However, after years of strong farm sector performance, the US Department of Agriculture (USDA) estimates net farm income declined in 2014 and projects continued declines in 2015 and 2016, returning to levels last observed in 2002, after adjusting for inflation. The continued drop in farm sector income is expected to place downward pressure on farm asset values, which had appreciated during the previous several years. The resulting drop in liquidity from multiple years of lower income is also expected to increase the need for sector borrowing relative to the 2009-2013 period. As a result, the USDA predicts a decline in sector equity and an increase in leverage, which signals the potential building of financial stress within the farm sector.

Financial stress within the farm sector translates into financial stress for individual farmers, especially those whose debt obligations are rising even as farm incomes decline. Farmers facing financial pressure and rising debts might be tempted to engage in practices that are ethically questionable.

Third, a common complaint by farmers is that government rules and regulations are increasing and, as a result, making it more difficult for them to manage their farm operations. For example, during a meeting of the US Senate Committee on Agriculture, Forestry and Nutrition in 2016, policy-makers observed that 'Falling commodity prices have been a primary concern for farmers and ranchers across the country, but the rising number of federal regulations are also weighing on the ag economy' (DTNPF, 2016). Obtaining an objective assessment of government regulations is difficult because of the complexity of regulations and the lack of consensus on how to measure regulatory growth. For instance, some scholars use the number of pages published in the Federal Register, which is the official repository of new regulations and rules, as a measure of regulatory reach (see, for instance, https://cei.org/10KC). An interesting measure of the restrictive nature of governmental regulations is the number of restrictive words in those regulations. According to Al-Ubaydli and

McLaughlin (2017, p 112), restrictive words, such as 'shall', 'must', 'may not', 'prohibited' and 'required' 'are likely to indicate binding constraints' in government regulations. The number of these restrictive words in federal regulations between 1970 and 2014 relating to crop production and livestock agriculture has more than doubled over this time period. If restrictive words are a reasonable proxy for the extent of government rules and regulations, then there is a trend of increasing governmental constraints and requirements on US farmers. James and Hendrickson (2008, p 355) found that farmers who believed 'it would be impossible to make a living if farmers followed all government rules and regulations' were more likely to rationalise unethical conduct than farmers who do not hold these beliefs.

Fourth, scholars have documented the increasing industrialisation, concentration and globalisation of agriculture since the mid-1950s. Virtually every sector of the agri-food system has become more concentrated over time. For example, in 1990 four-firm concentration ratios, or combined market shares of the four largest firms in the industry, were 69 per cent for beef slaughter, 45 per cent for pork slaughter and 45 per cent for broiler slaughter, and in 2011 the ratios increased to 82, 63 and 53 per cent, respectively (see Hendrickson et al, 2014). Understanding industry concentration is important because it creates unique constraints on agricultural producers. According to Hendrickson and James (2005, p 283), industry concentration 'limits or inhibits' the choice, options or kinds of decisions that farmers can make as well as 'compels or obliges' the choices of farmers 'by forcing them into the kinds of decisions that they otherwise would not have chosen for ethical or other reasons.' The implication is that farmers may be required to make ethical trade-offs when making farm management decisions, which can, in turn, result in an erosion of farmer ethics.

Important manifestations of ethical problems by farmers and food producers

While there have always been challenges to agricultural production, the pressures and constraints outlined above suggest that the current environment within which farmers make farm management decisions might be particularly difficult for encouraging ethical behaviour. For this reason it is helpful to consider problems that might be of particular ethical concern for farmers.

One problem is that farmers may be pressured into engaging in activities that they know, feel or believe to be wrong, which is one definition of unethical behaviour, as noted previously. James and Hendrickson (2008) show how specific pressures and constraints tied to financial wellbeing can influence farmers to rationalise unethical conduct. A related problem occurs when pressures and constraints compel farmers to engage in activities that they firmly believe are wrong but that are not generally considered to be wrong. An example is provided by Stuart (2009). In her analysis, many farmers in California have a strong desire to utilise sound land, environmental and conservation management practices, such as maintaining wildlife buffers or using non-chemical fertilisers. However, a growing emphasis on food safety standards by the consuming public, commodity groups and third party certifiers places farmers in a dilemma of having to choose food safety over environmental quality. For example, because outbreaks of *E. coli O157:H7* can be tied to cattle faeces, Stuart shows how agricultural producers are required to remove buffer zones in order to eliminate any animal presence on farm fields, even though 'only 0–1% of wildlife associated with natural environments are known to carry *E. coli O157:H7*' (2009, p 58). There is not only a resulting deterioration of environmental quality, but also a problem that goes beyond just a dilemma between competing priorities. Because some farmers genuinely believe that adopting the enhanced food safety measures is the wrong thing to do, by being required to do so, they are being forced to engage in farm management practices they believe are wrong. In other words, pressures and constraints for enhanced food quality create real 'personal conflicts and ethical dilemmas' for farmers (Stuart, 2009, p 65).

Another problem resulting from the pressures and constraints illustrated here is that some farmers may engage in activities that cause harm, particularly to the environment and animals. For example, in the case of crop farming, it has long been known that fertiliser use by farmers in the central states of the US has created a problem of hypoxia, or the depletion of oxygen in the water, in the Gulf of Mexico (see Rabalais et al, 2001). In the case of animal farming, there is increasing evidence that the growth of CAFOs (concentrated animal feeding operations) specifically and livestock production generally are 'one of three most significant contributors to environmental problems', leading to increased greenhouse gas emissions, land degradation, water pollution, and increased health problems because of the concentration of animal waste such farm operations produce (Ilea, 2009, p 164). Both of these problems can be tied to the incentives and pressures farmers face to increase the size of their farming operations.

Pressures and constraints have also been linked to cases of degraded animal welfare and even animal cruelty, as demonstrated in the study of Danish farmers by Andrade and Anneberg (2014). Pressures they consider include 'financial trouble, technological break down, family problems, stress and a growing concern among the farmers towards the governmental control in farm animal production' (2014, p 103). As examples, they find that farmers with multiple cases of documented animal neglect have significantly higher rates of personal debt and of operating farms with financial losses than farmers with only minor or no evidence of animal neglect. They conclude that animal neglect and cruelty are not linked to large-scale agriculture, but rather to 'severe financial difficulties, divorce and [even] psychiatric problems', or, in other words, the pressures and constraints that the farmers face.

The case of animal wellbeing is important because there is a growing consensus among consumers for an improvement in the welfare of farm animals (Verbeke, 2009; McKendree et al, 2014; You et al, 2014). In other words, consumers are increasingly interested in ensuring that animals are treated well while being raised on farms, even if they are willing to consume animals and their by-products or otherwise use animals for human benefits. Consumers also show increasing support for legislative efforts to regulate farm animal production practices, such as laws restricting the use of gestation crates in hog production (Tonsor et al, 2009) and conventional laying cages for egg production (Mench et al, 2011). But the implication for farmer decision-making is clear – any intentional efforts to harm farm animals is considered ethical and, in some cases, also illegal, which explains why news stories of farmer mistreatment of farm animals or undercover videos taken by animals rights groups are usually prominent news stories (see, for instance, PRN, 2012; AP, 2015).

Conclusion

Food crimes can arise from any aspect of the agri-food system. While farmers are often perceived by consumers as exhibiting 'ethically praiseworthy conduct and ... likely to base action and decision on ethical principles' (Thompson, 1998, p 95), they also face important and unique pressures and constraints that can result in their engaging in unethical behaviour. Such behaviour can be manifested as actions that cause harm to individuals, animals or the environment, as well as actions that are defined as wrong by society. A particularly important food crime is when farmers face pressures and constraints to engage in activities they know or believe to be wrong or that violate their ethical standards. Pressures and constraints are ubiquitous, although a carefully defined policy can mitigate some problems. Recognising potential fault lines as well as where problems occur and why they affect the ethical behaviour of farmers is therefore a necessary step in improving our understanding of food crimes.

References

Ajzen, I. (1991) 'The theory of planned behaviour', *Organizational Behaviour and Human Decision Processes*, vol 50, pp 179–211.

Al-Ubaydli, O. and McLaughlin, P.A. (2017) 'RegData: A numerical database on industry-specific regulations for all United States industries and federal regulations, 1997-2012', *Regulation & Governance*, vol 11, no 1, pp 109–23.

Andrade, S.B. and Anneberg, I. (2014) 'Farmers under pressure: Analysis of the social conditions of cases of animal neglect', *Journal of Agricultural and Environmental Ethics*, vol 27, no 1, pp 103–26.

AP (Associated Press) (2015) 'Farm worker accused of "maliciously" killing 4 chickens', AP Newswires, 10 December.

Armstrong, J.S. (1977) 'Social irresponsibility in management', *Journal of Business Research*, vol 5, no 3, pp 185–213.

Ashkanasy, N.M., Windsor, C.A. and Treviño, L.K. (2006) 'Bad apples in bad barrels revisited: Cognitive moral development, just world beliefs, rewards, and ethical decision-making', *Business Ethics Quarterly*, vol 16, no 4, pp 449–73.

Barnes, C.M., Schaubroeck, J., Huth, M. and Ghumman, S. (2011) 'Lack of sleep and unethical conduct', *Organizational Behaviour and Human Decision Processes*, vol 115, no 2, pp 169–80.

Bartels, D.M. and Pizarro, D.A. (2011) 'The mismeasure of morals: Antisocial personality traits predict utilitarian responses to moral dilemmas', *Cognition*, vol 121, no 1, pp 154–61.

Bazerman, M.H. and Chugh, D. (2006) 'Decisions without blinders', *Harvard Business Review*, vol 84, no 1, pp 88–97.

Bohns, V.K., Roghanizad, M.M. and Xu, A.Z. (2014) 'Underestimating our influence over other's unethical behaviour and decisions', *Personality and Social Psychology Bulletin*, vol 40, no 3, pp 384–62.

Cleek, M.A. and Leonard, S.L. (1998) 'Can corporate codes of ethics influence behaviour?', *Journal of Business Ethics*, vol 17, no 6, pp 619–30.

DTNPF (DTN/The Progressive Farmer) (2016) 'Ag economy rocky: Some Senators cite government regulations as concern for Ag', 21 September (www.dtnpf.com/agriculture/web/ag/news/world-policy/article/2016/09/21/senators-cite-government-regulations).

Ferrell, O.C. and Gresham, L.G. (1985) 'A contingency framework for understanding ethical decision making in marketing', *Journal of Marketing*, vol 49, no 3, pp 87–96.

Gino, F. (2015) 'Understanding ordinary unethical behaviour: why people who value morality act immorally', *Current Opinion in Behavioural Sciences*, vol 3, June, pp 101–11.

Grant, R.W. (2006) 'Ethics and incentives: A political approach', *American Political Science Review*, vol 100, no 1, pp 29–39.

Haidt, J. (2001) 'The emotional dog and its rational tail: A social intuitionist approach to moral judgment', *Psychological Review*, vol 108, no 4, pp 814–34.

Hendrickson, M.K. and James, H.S. Jr (2005) 'The ethics of constrained choice: How the industrialization of agriculture impacts farming and farmer behaviour', *Journal of Agricultural and Environmental Ethics*, vol 18, pp 269–91.

Hendrickson, M.K., James, H.S. Jr and Heffernan, W.D. (2014) 'Vertical integration and concentration in US agriculture', in P.B. Thompson and D.M. Kaplan (eds) *Encyclopedia of food and agricultural ethics*, Dordrecht, Netherlands: Springer, pp 1799–806.

Hunt, S.D. and Vitell, S. (1986) 'A general theory of marketing ethics', *Journal of Macromarketing*, vol 6, no 1, pp 5–16.

Ilea, R.C. (2009) 'Intensive livestock farming: Global trends, increased environmental concerns, and ethical solutions', *Journal of Agricultural and Environmental Ethics*, vol 22, no 2, pp 153–67.

James, H.S., Jr (2000) 'Reinforcing ethical decision making through organizational structure', *Journal of Business Ethics*, vol 28, pp 43–58.

James, H.S. Jr (2003) 'On finding solutions to ethical problems in agriculture', *Journal of Agricultural and Environmental Ethics*, vol 16, no 5, pp 439–57.

James, H.S. Jr (2005) 'The ethical challenges in farming: a report on conversations with Missouri corn and soybean producers', *Journal of Agricultural Safety and Health*, vol 11, pp 239–48.

James, H.S. Jr and Hendrickson, M.K. (2008) 'Perceived economic pressures and farmer ethics', *Agricultural Economics*, vol 38, no 3, pp 349–61.

Jones, T.M. (1991) 'Ethical decision-making in organizations: An issue-contingent model', *Academy of Management Review*, vol 16, no 2, pp 366–95.

Knorr, B. (1991) 'Ethics. The American farmer', *Farm Future*, pp 10–13.

Maloni, M.J. and Brown, M.E. (2006) 'Corporate social responsibility in the supply chain: An application in the food industry', *Journal of Business Ethics*, vol 68, no 1, pp 35–52.

Martin, K.D. and Cullen, J.B. (2006) 'Continuities and extensions of ethical climate theory: A meta-analytic review', *Journal of Business Ethics*, vol 69, pp 175–94.

Mazar, N., Amir, O. and Ariely, D. (2008) 'The dishonesty of honest people: A theory of self-concept maintenance', *Journal of Marketing Research*, vol 45, December, pp 633–44.

McCabe, D.L., Trevino, L.K. and Butterfield, K.D. (1996) 'The influence of collegiate and corporate codes of conduct on ethics-related behaviour in the workplace', *Business Ethics Quarterly*, vol 6, no 4, pp 461–76.

McKendree, M.G.S., Croney, C.C. and Widmar, N.J.O. (2014) 'Effects of demographic factors and information sources on United States consumer perceptions of animal welfare', *Journal of Animal Science*, vol 92, pp 3161–73.

Mench, J.A., Sumner, D.A. and Rosen-Molina, J.T. (2011) 'Sustainability of egg production in the United States – The policy and market context', *Poultry Science*, vol 90, no 1, pp 229–40.

Nuttavuthisit, K. and Thøgersen, J. (2015) 'The importance of consumer trust for the emergence of a market for green products: The case of organic food', *Journal of Business Ethics*, vol 140, no 2, pp 323–37.

O'Hara, M. (2016) *Something for nothing: Arbitrage and ethics on Wall Street*, New York: W.W. Norton & Company.

Patrick, K., Kuhns, R. and Borchers, A. (2016) 'Recent trends in US farm income, wealth, and financial health', *Choices*, vol 31, no 1, pp 1–8.

PRN (PR Newswire) (2012) 'Whistleblowing expose reveals cruelty at Iowa pig breeding factory farm and Hormel supplier', *PR Newswire*, 15 February.

Rabalais, N.N., Turner, R.E. and Wiseman, W.J. Jr (2001) 'Hypoxia in the Gulf of Mexico', *Journal of Environmental Quality*, vol30, pp 320–9.

Rappaport, A. and Himschoot, R.A. (1994) 'Ethics perceptions of American farmers: An empirical analysis', *Journal of Business Ethics*, vol 13, no 10, pp 795–802.

Rest, J.R. (1986) *Moral development: Advances in research and theory*, New York: Praeger.

Staw, B.M. and Szwajkowski, E.W. (1975) 'The scarcity-munificence component of organizational environments and the commission of illegal acts', *Administrative Science Quarterly*, vol 20, pp 345–54.

Stuart, D. (2009) 'Constrained choice and ethical dilemmas in land management: Environmental quality and food safety in California agriculture', *Journal of Agricultural and Environmental Ethics*, vol 22, no 1, pp 53–71.

Thompson, P.B. (1998) *Agricultural ethics: Research, teaching, and public policy*, Ames, IA: Iowa State University Press.

Thompson, P.B. (2015) *From field to fork: Food ethics for everyone*, New York: Oxford University Press.

Tonsor, G.T., Wolf, C. and Olynk, N. (2009) 'Consumer voting and demand behaviour regarding swine gestation crates', *Food Policy*, vol 34, no 6, pp 492–8.

Treviño, L.K. (1986) 'Ethical decision-making in organizations: A person-situation interactionist model', *Academy of Management Review*, vol 11, no 3, pp 601–17.

Treviño, L.K. and Youngblood, S.A. (1990) 'Bad apples in bad barrels: A causal analysis of ethical decision-making behaviour', *Journal of Applied Psychology*, vol 75, no 4, pp 378–85.

USDA (United States Department of Agriculture) (2017) *Quick stats*, Washington, DC: USDA NASS (https://quickstats.nass.usda.gov/).

Verbeke, W. (2009) 'Stakeholder, citizen and consumer interests in farm animal welfare', *Animal Welfare*, vol 18, pp 325–33.

You, X., Li, Y., Zhang, M., Yan, H. and Zhao, R. (2014) 'A survey of Chinese citizens' perceptions on farm animal welfare', *PLOS ONE*, vol 9, no 10, e109177.

5

Chocolate, slavery, forced labour, child labour and the state

Ronald Hinch

Introduction

The history of cocoa production is filled with tales of slavery, forced labour, illegal child labour and a great deal of deception. Efforts to eliminate these forms of labour abuse have met with varying degrees of success. The cocoa and chocolate industries, as well as governments, have been successful in diverting attention away from these abuses. The objective of this chapter is to review the history of slave and forced labour in the cocoa industry, including forced labour and illegal child labour, to illustrate how governments often collaborate with the cocoa industry to create and perpetuate these abuses. This collaboration creates illusory restrictions on forced labour that allow slavery to persist. Slavery in the cocoa industray is a serious form of food crime affecting hundreds of thousands of people (Walk Free Foundation, 2016).

To illustrate the ways in which governments and the cocoa industry have interacted, their relationship is assessed from the time of the arrival of the Europeans in the Americas to contemporary times. The first section focuses on the consequences of the European invasion and the conquest of the Americas after the arrival of Cristoforo Colombo (also known as Christopher Columbus) in 1492. The second section is concerned with attempts to either embarrass chocolate makers to stop buying slave-produced cocoa, or to convince cocoa-producing nations to voluntarily put an end to the use of slave labour. The third section is focused on potential ways to reduce or elimate slavery and forced labour in the cocoa industry.

Origins of the problem

When Colombo arrived in the Americas, cocoa production was well established. Colombo did not think much of it as a potential trade product. It was not until somtime after 1585, after Hernando Cortez introduced it to Spain, that it began to emerge as a trade commodity (Coe and Coe, 2007). Its ascendency as one of the world's favourite food treats coincided with an increase in the use of slave labour, as well as a major change in the source of slave labour.

Slavery was common in pre-Columbian America (Coe and Coe, 2007). Pre-Columbian slaves were prisoners of war, convicted criminals, debtors or indentured servants, and sometimes orphaned children (McLoughlin, 1974; Coe, 2010). Anyone who had been sold into slavery, including indentured servants, could work off their debt and regain their freedom. Slave status was not hereditary and the children of slaves were born free.

The Europeans, including the Spanish, Portuguese, French, English and Dutch, had intended from the start of their colonisation of the Americas to enslave at least some of the local population to provide labour for their colonial enterprises. Not only did the Spanish intend to enslave the local populations, they also imported slaves from Africa (Yeager, 1995). The first African slaves in the Spanish colonies arrived in around 1501. The Spanish utilised two distinct forms of slavery. The first was the *encomienda*, the system they applied to indigenous people. The second was chattel slavery, the system they applied to slaves imported from Africa. The *encomienda* was a softer form of slavery for those enslaved, but was a more restrictive form of slavery for those who enslaved them. Slaves could not be owned, meaning that they could not be bought, sold or even rented, nor could they be inherited or forcerd to relocate. These restrictions made it more difficult for their masters to make a profit. It was used because it allowed access to a cheap local labour supply negating the high cost of importing labour from elsewhere. Masters could also continue to convert the local populations to Christianity in the belief that their converted capitives would endure their capitivity in anticipation of a better life in heaven (Yeager, 1995). Alternatively, chattel slaves could be owned and thus bought, sold, rented and relocated at the will of the owner. Harsh punishments, including death, could also be imposed for misbehaviour.

Slavery was a major commercial enterprise wherever the Europeans made contact with non-European, non-Christian cultures (Raiswel, 1997; Love, 2007). It even received the blessing of the Catholic Church. The Third Lateran Council of 1179 authourised the enslavement of Islamic peoples, then known as Saracens. Later Popes would expand the slave pool to any non-Christian (Maxwell, 1975; Raiswel, 1997; Love, 2007). Both Spain and Portugal were granted permission to engage in the slave trade. Both governments, as well as other European governments, provided the legal framework granting the right to engage in the slave trade to various state enterprises engaged in building colonial enterprises. The Portuguese were among the first to import slaves to Europe from Africa in around 1442. Thus, by the time the Europeans arrived in the Americas, the religious and legal bases for slavery were well established, as was the slave trade itself.

Not everyone was comfortable with all aspects of slavery in the Americas. Some of the colonisers were resistent to slavery from the beginning. Despite the many papal bulls encouraging slavery for non-Christian people, there were some within the Catholic church who were opposed to it (Maxwell, 1975: Yeager, 1995). Branding the enslavement of the indigenous peoples as 'sinful' and 'unjust', some Catholic clergy in Spain's American colonies openly campaigned against the enslavement, including *encomienda*, of the the local population that they wanted to convert to Christianity (MacNutt, 1909; Wagner and Parish, 1967). They petitioned King Carlos V who agreed to outlaw the practice in 1530. He promptly overturned the ban two years later on the pretext that the indigenous peoples themselves had practised slavery long before the arrival of the Spanish (Maxwell, 1975). However, after Pope Nicholas V issued a papal bull in 1542 that once again authorised the enslavment of non-Christians, but disallowed the enslavement of indigenous Americans, Carlos again outlawed the enslavement of indigenous peoples who had become Christian (Maxwell, 1975). The Pope hoped that the efforts of the clergy in the Americas to convert the native populations to Catholicism would promote the interests of the Church. Since Carlos was subject to the authority of the Pope he complied with the papal bull. Consequently, the colonisers turned to reliance on chattel slavery and began importing more slaves from Africa (Wagner and Parish, 1967).

For close to 300 years after indigenous populations were set free in Spainish colonies, slave traders, slave owners and other governments around the world vigourously defended the slave trade. During this time governments continued to create and enhance the legal basis for slavery. It was not until the 19th century that abolitionists marshalled sufficient forces to make the abolitionist movement a worldwide movement. The results were mixed. The United Kingdom abolished the slave trade in 1807 and the ownership of slaves in 1838 (Brown, 2007; Pettigrew, 2007). France abolished slavery in 1794, reintroduced it in 1802, and abolished it again in 1818. The Ottoman Empire abolished the slavery of Caucasians in 1830, and all forms of slavery in 1890 when it signed the Brussels Conference Act (Allain, 2008). It was not until 1926 that a League of Nations' treaty, the *Slavery Convention,* called on all nations to abolish the slave trade. The last country to formally abolish slavery was Mauritania in 1981.

Nonetheless, slavery persists despite legal condemnation, and it survives for several reasons:

- There is a high demand for cheap labour.
- Marginalised peoples have little or no other economic resources and may lack the ability to escape it. There are weak or ineffective laws administered by either weak or corrupt governments.

Examination of some specific examples of attempts to abolish slavery in the cocoa industry in the 19th and 20th centuries illustrate how the formal abolition of slavery did not mean the end of slavery.

The appearance of abolition

This section reviews two key moments in the struggle to abolish slavery in the cocoa industry. The first deals with attempts in the UK to convince chocolate producers to end dependence on cocoa produced by slave labour. The second focuses on the state of forced labour in contemporary Côte d'Ivoire. Both instances illustrate the extent to which modern slavery persists in the cocoa industry.

One of the most famous attempts to embarrass a major chocolate manufacturer to put an end to their reliance on slave labour centred on a slander trial initiated by Cadbury Brothers, a major chocolate company in England. Cadbury attempted to use the courts to defend itself from the accusation that they were hypocrites for denouncing slavery while profiting from it. Before discussing the Cadbury lawsuit, it is important to examine some of the history of slavery in the UK that contributed to the creation of this situation.

The legal status of slavery in the UK and its colonies was unclear prior to 1672 (Mtubani, 1983). It existed alongside other forms of forced labour, including serfdom and indentured service. As early as 1569, a British court ruled that English Common Law did not recognise slavery (Mtubani, 1983). In the one hundred years that followed, other court decisions offered conflicting decisions. Some declared that UK law permitted slavery while others said it was unlawful. Parliament also granted Royal Charters that included the right to buy and sell slaves to various British companies engaged in colonising the world. For example, the Royal African Company (RAC) obtained a charter from Charles II in 1672 granting the company a monopoly over the English slave trade in colonies controlled by the RAC (Brown, 2007).

From 1690 until the 1800s, the British Parliament engaged in frequent debates regarding provisions of the RAC Charter and the slave trade (Brown, 2007; Pettigrew, 2007). The RAC sought to protect its monopoly while other business interests attempted to break the monopoly so that they could legally enter the slave trade. Parliament debated whether it was in the interests of the state to maintain the RAC's monopoly or to allow other commercial interests to participate in the slave trade. The interests of the state became clear during the Seven Years War when the UK expanded not only its colonial empire, but also the slave trading rights of the RAC (now known as the Company of Merchants), giving it control of the slave trade in Senegal and several other colonies. In doing so, the UK clearly established its interests in maintaining and profiting from the slave trade, both in terms of the slave trade itself and the profits to be made in related industries such as shipbuilding and the production of various goods needed to trade for slaves (Richardson, 2007; Nunn, 2008).

When the UK finally outlawed slavery, it did so in stages. First, in 1772, a British court ruled in the case of *Somerset v Stewart* that there was no basis in English common law for slave ownership in the UK (Usherwood, 1981). This decision effectively brought an end to slavery in the UK. However, it did not end British involvement in the slave trade, as slavery was still permitted in the colonies. It was not until passage of the Slave Trade Act 1807 that the *buying and selling* of slaves became illegal. Slave *ownership* was still allowed. It was not until the passage of the Slavery Abolition Act 1833 that slave ownership was abolished – albeit this occurred in stages allowing some slave ownership until 1840.

There is no mistaking that the movement to abolish slavery received significant energy from those forces arguing for its immorality (Short, 2009). As Richardson (2007) and Tannenbaum (1946) have argued, the moral arguments put forward by William Wilberforce in England and others around the globe were powerful contributions in the war against slavery. While the debate still rages over whether economic factors or moral arguments were more important in the formal abolition of slavery, there is no doubt that moral arguments played a significant role.

As previously noted, the first noteable event in modern history to embarass a company into ending its reliance on slavery came in 1909. In 1909, Cadbury Brothers, the makers of Cadbury chocolate, filed a libel suit against the British liberal newspaper *The Standard*. Cadbury alleged that *The Standard* had wrongfully called Cadbury 'hypocrites'. The accusations against Cadbury's focused on three key issues:

- Cadbury profited from the use of raw cocoa imported from Portuguese slave colonies in Africa, while also belonging to organisations dedicated to the abolition of slavery (The Anti-Slavery Society and the Aborigines' Protection Society);
- Cadbury used its control over the conservative newspaper *The Daily Mail* to denounce the British government for using Chinese coolies (indentured workers) to help rebuild South Africa after the Second Boar War ended in 1902; and
- Cadbury refused to participate in a boycott of cocoa from Portuguese colonies until after they conducted their own prolonged investigation into labour practices, the purpose of which was to delay joining the boycott until after the price of cocoa came down (Dellheim, 1987; Satre, 2005; Hasian, 2008).

Cadbury defended itself by arguing that its interests in the Portuguese colonies were purely humanitarian. They were deeply concerned with the plight of all their workers, as evidenced by their humanitarian work and their involvement in the anti-slavery movement at home and abroad, including the Portuguese colonies. They also claimed to be trying to convince other companies to stop buying cocoa from the Portuguese. After a lengthy trial, the jury agreed that Cadbury had been defamed, but it awarded damages of just one farthing. Such a small penalty is known as contemptuous damages (Satre, 2005). This signified that the jury decided that the wrong committed by *The Standard* against Cadbury was insignificant since, while Cadbury was involved in the anti-slave movement, it did knowingly profit from slave-produced cocoa.

This case illustrates that while it was illegal to either own or trade in slaves in the UK, it was legal to import the products of slavery. During the peak of the anti-slavery campaign, and despite popular sentiment favouring anti-slavery, the British government refused to take action. It argued that it would not interfere in another colonial power's business, given that no colonial power's hands were clean (Paviakis, 2010), an explicit recognition that all colonial powers were either involved in the slave trade or were reliant on slave labour in their colonies. The failure to ban the importation of goods produced by slave labour allowed Cadbury and other chocolate manufacturers, including Rowntree's and Fry's, the freedom to import from wherever they chose. The government had provided an escape clause and the chocolate manufacturers took advantage, demonstrating that economic interests outweighed morality in this instance.

The second notable attempt to end contemporary slavery is more recent. As a common experience across Africa, slavery was part of life in Côte d'Ivoire long before the arrival of Europeans. Thus, when the cocoa industry was established in Côte d'Ivoire in 1905 (Coe and Coe, 2007), slave labour was utilised and remains in use to this day. However, the 21st-century form of slavery in Côte d'Ivoire exists as *forced labour*. The International Labour Organization (ILO) defines *forced or compulsory labour* as 'all work or service that is exacted from any person under the menace of any penalty and for which the said person has not offered himself voluntarily' (ILO, 2008). The word 'slavery' is not used, but the ILO makes it clear that these are *slave-like* conditions: workers are not free to leave, and are subject to whatever punishment the employer chooses to enforce for rule violations. The work is also hazardous, often involving spraying coca trees with pesticides without protection or training, and long hours of work without food or rest (Manzo, 2005; Off, 2006; SPHTM, 2015).

Recent estimates suggest that there are approximately 450,000 cocoa farms in Côte d'Ivoire, and half of its population depends on cocoa for an income (Ellenbogen, 2004). Survey data shows that 40 per cent of all children in Côte d'Ivoire work in the agricultural sector, with 23 per cent of children under the age of 18 (some as young as five) working in the cocoa sector (SPHTM, 2015). Many of these children are the children of the farmers who own small farms. Among the children who do not work on family-owned cocoa plantations, only about 5 per cent are paid (SPHTM, 2015). There are an estimated 144,000 slaves in Côte d'Ivoire, a significant number of whom are children (Walk Free Foundation, 2016). Everyone involved in creating these estimates agrees that it is difficult to arrive at definitive numbers. Researchers comment that it is often difficult and dangerous to conduct the research, especially in the remote areas where a significant amount of cocoa is grown. For example, one journalist had to leave Côte d'Ivoire fearful that threats to her life were real, given the disappearance of another journalist engaged in similar research (Off, 2006).

Ivorian law prohibits children under 13 from any kind of work. It also limits the work performed by children aged 14 through to 17 to light, non-hazardous work (SPHTM, 2015). Thus, while these children are forbidden from doing any hazardous work, a large number of them work in cocoa production, the working conditions of which meet the ILO's definition of *forced labour* and 'the worst forms of child labour' (ILO, 2008).

Côte d'Ivoire has endured ongoing political instability since 2000. It was very prosperous during the 1970s when its two major export products, coffee and cocoa, were in high global demand and the country was politically stable. By the mid-1990s demand for these products waned, the economy grew weaker, and the standard of living dropped substantially (Kouadio, 2009). The resultant poverty and political strife among the multi-ethnic population led to the First Ivorian Civil War, 2002–05. The war left the country with an even weaker economy and divided into a largely rebel Muslim north and a largely Christian government-controlled south (Chirot, 2006; Kouadio, 2009). The 2010 general election, viewed by the United Nations (UN) as a triumph of democracy with an 80 per cent electoral turnout, did not resolve the situation (Bassett, 2011). Despite the large turnout, the election was disputed. Old rivalries resurfaced and Côte d'Ivoire broke out into a second civil war with similar ethnic and political divisions that had produced the first war.

Amid the political turmoil, numerous media sources began publishing stories about the use of child slave labour in Côte d'Ivoire, generating widespread public concern (Ould et al, 2004). It was guesstimated in 2002 that there were 109,000 children working in what was described as the 'worst forms of child labor' (Bureau of Democracy, Human Rights, and Labor, 2006). Subsequent research suggested the number of children under the age of 18 working in cocoa growing regions increased by 440,000 from 2008 to 2014, accompanied by an increase in the number of children doing hazardous work in cocoa production. The number of boys working in hazardous conditions climbed by 40 per cent, while the number of girls climbed by 20 per cent (SPHTM, 2015).

Political turmoil in the country makes progress difficult. Nonetheless, the Ivorian government has undertaken a number of commitments since 2002 to limit the amount of both forced and child labour. Both the Ivorian and Ghanaian governments committed themselves, and encouraged local community-based efforts, to implement the Harkin-Engel Protocol (the Cocoa Protocol) (Bertrand and de Buhr, 2015), although they did not make producer participation in the programme mandatory. The Protocol itself was an attempt by two US senators to get the private sector to voluntarily end their dependence on cocoa produced by forced labour through several goals:

- devoting resources to reduce forced child labour;
- creating an advisory board to oversee implementation of the Protocol by October 2001;
- creating an action plan by 2002 to eliminate the worst forms of child labour, including a means for enforcement; and
- creating a non-profit foundation to address the worst forms of child labour in the cocoa supply chain by 2002.

None of these timelines were met. The advisory board was established and then abandoned in 2006 over a funding dispute. This led to an extension (until 2007) that once again was not met. The industry never established enforcement procedures that would ensure success.

In 2006, the US Congress contracted researchers at Tulane University, New Orleans, to conduct research on child labour in Côte d'Ivoire and Ghana. The objective was to assess the extent of forced labour in both countries, and to assess the abilities of governments and the private sector, via participation in community development projects, to fulfil the objectives of the Protocol (Bertrand and de Buhr, 2015). The resultant research reports show mixed results (PCIDTT, 2011; SPHTM, 2015). On the one hand, there has been a reduction in the hours worked by children, and more children are receiving some form of education. On the other hand, only a small number of the cocoa producers participate in the programme, and the total number of children working in the cocoa sector has actually *increased*, not decreased, including continued work in hazardous conditions (PCIDTT, 2011; Bertrand and de Buhr, 2015; SPHTM, 2015).

There are a significant number of people still working in slavery and slave-like conditions in both countries. Estimates suggest there are 144,000 slaves in Côte d'Ivoire and 103,000 in Ghana, as well as hundreds of thousands in Nigeria, the Democratic Republic of the Congo, Cameroon and Mali (Walk Free Foundation, 2016). While not all slaves work in the cocoa sector, and not all workers in this sector are slaves, both Ghana and Côte d'Ivoire are listed among those countries still using child and forced labour in cocoa production (Bureau of International Labor Affairs, 2014). Slavery persists in these areas because the governments are either unwilling or unable to take effective action to stop it, often fearing that if they do it would damage already weakened economies. Major cocoa buyers also continue to buy cocoa from Côte d'Ivoire.

What to do

There have been a number of efforts to get cocoa producers and chocolate makers to reduce their reliance on slavery, forced labour and child labour. For example, both the Fairtrade movement (Fairtrade International, 2014) and the Rainforest Alliance (2017) have established mechanisms for onsite overview and enforcement of their mandates to support cocoa growers and their workers, improve farming techniques and put an end to forced labour. Fairtrade International's mandate requires that cocoa producers are paid above what non-Fairtrade buyers pay for raw cocoa, workers are to be paid above the rate paid to other workers on farms not certified as Fairtrade, and farmers should use sustainable farming practices. A portion of the premium paid for cocoa must also go to community development projects such as improving educational programmes. In 2014, Fairtrade International reported that more than 1.4 million farmers and workers were involved in 1,210 'producer' organisations across 74 countries. They also reported that they had entered into agreements with some of the world's largest chocolate companies, including Mars and Ferrero, as well as German, Swiss and Japanese chocolate makers, to increase the amount of Fairtrade cocoa they buy (Fairtrade International, 2014). Similarly, the Rainforest Alliance, which has won favour with some major chocolate producers, is attempting to ensure that farmers receive a fair price for their cocoa, and that workers receive the statutory minimum wage paid in each producing country. Both have established certification and enforcement programmes.

Both have also been subject to criticism for lack of enforcement and for not being the ethical traders they claim to be (Jaffee, 2007; Griffiths, 2012). It has been suggested that the certification process is cost-prohibitive. The amount of money farmers need to pay for certification is often beyond their capacity, and thus some farmers do not seek it. It is also not clear exactly how much of the retail price paid by the consumer actually goes to farmers and farm workers, and how much is absorbed by others along the supply chain. With specific reference to Fairtrade, even though a premium price is paid for the product, the farmer must deduct the cost of certification and the cost of operating the cooperative structures required by these programmes

(Nelson and Pound, 2009; Cramer et al, 2014). As a result, the gains derived from the premium price are absorbed by higher costs. Indeed, wages for farm workers may actually be lower than wages paid to workers on non-Fairtrade farms. There is also concern that the motives for some private enterprise companies to be involved in these programmes may be disingenuous. They may be more interested in making themselves appear to be socially conscious so that consumers will ignore the fact that the bulk of their products are not certified and may contain products associated with slavery, forced and child labour (Blowfield and Dolan, 2001; Jaffee, 2007).

With specific reference to the Rainforest Alliance, Jaffee (2007) argues that the enforcement mechanism amounts to *greenwashing*, the practice of making it appear as though the company is environmentally friendly but actually spending very little effort or money on environmental protection. Other critics have suggested that cocoa production in Ghana using Rainforest Alliance standards is not as profitable as farming using more traditional methods (Gockowski et al, 2013). If this is accurate, it is unlikely that farmers and farm workers will derive significant benefit from certification and compliance. For a more thorough assessment of the pros and cons of Fairtrade, see Chapter 15 in this volume by Will Low and Eileen Davenport.

Discussion

The Rainforest Alliance, the Fairtrade movement and the attempt to implement the provisions of the Harkin-Engel Protocol are all attempting to do what governments have not done. Governments have either directly participated in the creation and enforcement of regulations that permit forced labour, or have neglected the harmful existence of the problem. They have also turned a blind eye to the illegal use of child labour. While virtually all governments ban slavery, and what the ILO calls the 'worst forms of child labour', both persist. Many governments also knowingly permit the importation of the products of forced and child labour.

The 1926 *Slavery Convention* by the League of Nations was a reaffirmation of the intent to abolish slavery and the slave trade. It specified that the nations were obligated 'to prevent forced labour from developing into conditions analogous to slavery' and 'to adopt all appropriate measures with a view to preventing and suppressing the embarkation, disembarkation and transport of slaves in their territorial waters and upon all vessels flying their respective flags' (League of

Nations, 1926). The Convention was hardly a success. Several nations refused to acknowledge it or refused to accept that they had any form of forced labour in their country. Individual nations were also allowed to exempt certain territories, and the definition of slavery was too vague to be enforced, as were the timelines for abolition that were defined using words like 'as soon as possible' and 'progressively' (Miers, 1998).

While the Convention remains active, it has been ineffective. For this reason, and in response to growing global public concern over slavery, individual nations have begun to enact their own revised anti-slavery laws in the early 2000s. For example, in 2015 the UK passed the Modern Slavery Act, the US passed both the Trade Facilitation and Trade Enforcement Act (HR 644) 2015 and the Justice for Victims of Trafficking Act of 2015, and the European Union (EU) passed its Directive 2011/36/EU in 2011. These laws expressly forbid the importation of products produced by forced or slave labour. It is too early to assess what impact these new laws will have. For example, the Trade Facilitation and Trade Enforcement Act doesn't provide specific measures to ensure slave-produced products don't enter the US; rather, it calls for the US Customs and Border Protection Agency to report on steps it has taken to ensure that slave-produced products don't enter the US. The Act itself was created to block a loophole in previous US legislation that allowed imports of such products if US producers were otherwise unable to meet the demand for the product. In other words, if the only available source of a certain product is one that utilises slave labour in its production, it is allowed to be imported.

Conclusion

It is doubtful if slavery, forced and illegal child labour can be curtailed without enforcement of laws that are already on the books. What is needed is a willingness to do so. Far too often governments have either provided legislative approval of slavery, or left it to the private sector to find a solution. As illustrated, the Cadbury case, the Harkin-Engel Protocol and the work of groups like Fairtrade International and the Rainforest Alliance are all dependant on a private sector that has historically defended and relied on forced labour to provide cheap cocoa. Without the effective enforcement of regulations, governments become facilitators of forced labour, and thus become part of the problem and not the solution.

References

Allain, J. (2008) 'Nineteenth century law of the sea and the British abolition of the Atlantic slave trade', *British Yearbook of International Law*, vol 1, no 78, pp 342–88.

Bassett, T.J. (2011) 'Winning coalition, sore loser: Côte d'Ivoire's 2010 presidential elections', *African Affairs*, vol 110, no 440, pp 469–79.

Bertrand, W. and de Buhr, E. (2015) 'Trade, development and child labor: Regulation and law in the case of child', *Law and Development Review*, vol 8, no 2, pp 503–21.

Blowfield, M. and Dolan, C. (2001) 'Outsourcing governance: Fairtrade's message for C21 global governance', *Corporate Governance: The International Journal of Business in Society*, vol 10, no 4, pp 484–500.

Brown, C.L. (2007) 'The British government and the slave trade: Early parliamentary enquiries', in S. Farrell, M. Unwin and J. Walvin (eds) *The British slave trade: Abolition, parliament and people*, Edinburgh: Edinburgh University Press, pp 27–41.

Bureau of Democracy, Human Rights, and Labor (2006) 'Côte d'Ivoire' (www.state.gov/j/drl/rls/hrrpt/2005/61565.htm).

Bureau of International Labor Affairs (2014) *List of goods produced by child labor or forced labor*, Washington, DC: United States Department of Labor.

Chirot, D. (2006) 'The debacle in Côte d'Ivoire', *Journal of Democracy*, vol 17, no 2, pp 63–7.

Coe, M.D. (2010) *The Maya*, 8th edn, London: Thames & Hudson, Ltd.

Coe, S.D. and Coe, M.D. (2007) *The true history of chocolate*, 2nd edn, London: Thames & Hudson Books.

Cramer, C., Johnston, D., Oya, C. and Sender, J. (2014) *Fairtrade, employment and poverty reduction in Ethiopia and Uganda*, London: SOAS, University of London, for the Department for International Development.

Dellheim, C. (1987) 'The creation of a company culture: Cadburys, 1861–1931', *The American Historical Review*, vol 92, no 1, pp 13–44.

Ellenbogen, M. (2004) 'Can the Tariff Act combat endemic child labour abuses? The case of Côte d'Ivorie', *Texas Law Review*, vol 82, no 5, pp 1315–47.

Fairtrade International (2014) *Strong producers: Strong future. Annual report 2013–2014*, Bonn, Germany: Fairtrade International (www.fairtrade. net/fileadmin/user_upload/content/2009/resources/2013-14_ AnnualReport_FairtradeIntl_web.pdf).

Gockowski, J., Afari-Sefia, V., Sarpong, D.B., Oseri-Asare, Y.B. and Agyeman, N.F. (2013) 'Improving the productivity and income of Ghanaian cocoa farmers while maintaining environmental services: what role for certification?', *International Journal of Agricultural Sustainability*, vol 11, no 4, pp 331–46.

Griffiths, P. (2012) 'Ethical objections to Fairtrade', *Journal of Business Ethics*, vol 23, no 2, pp 277–89.

Hasian, M. (2008) 'Critical memories of crafted virtues: The Cadbury chocolate scandals, mediated reputations, and modern globalized slavery', *Journal of Communication Inquiry*, vol 32, no 3, pp 249–70.

ILO (International Labour Organization) (2008) *Fighting human trafficking: The forced labour dimensions*, ILO Background Paper (www.ilo.org/sapfl/Events/ILOevents/WCMS_090236/lang--en/index.htm).

Jaffee, D. (2007) *Brewing justice: Fair trade coffee, sustainability, and survival*, Berkeley, CA: University of California Press.

Kouadio, B.K. (2009) 'From stability to insurgency: The root and proximate causes of the September 2002 civil war in Côte d'Ivoire', Unpublished doctoral thesis, Miami, FL: Florida International University.

League of Nations (1926) *Slavery Convention* (www.ohchr.org/EN/ProfessionalInterest/Pages/SlaveryConvention.aspx).

Love, D.A. (2007) *The color of law on the Pope, paternalism and purifying the savages* (https://zcomm.org/znetarticle/the-color-of-law-on-the-pope-paternalism-and-purifying-the-savages-by-david-a-love/).

MacNutt, F.A. (1909) *Bartholomew de Las Casas: His life, apostolate, and writings* (www.gutenberg.org/files/23466/23466-pdf.pdf?session_id=52fa37e4284966b20293fc4797093d2ad830360).

Manzo, K. (2005) 'Modern slavery, global capitalism and deproletarianisation in West Africa', *Review of African Political Economy*, vol 32, no 106, pp 521–34.

Maxwell, J.F. (1975) *Slavery and the Catholic Church*, Chichester and London: Barry Rose Publishers (http://anthonyflood.com/maxwellslaverycatholicchurch.pdf).

McLoughlin, W.G. (1974) 'Red Indians, black slavery and white racism: America's slaveholding Indians', *American Quarterly*, vol 36, no 4, pp 367–85.

Miers, S. (1998) 'Slavery and the slave trade as international issues 1890–1939', *Slavery and Abolition*, vol 19, no 2, pp 16–37.

Mtubani, V.C.D. (1983) 'African slaves and English law', *Journal of African Studies*, vol 3, no 2, pp 71–5.

Nelson, V. and Pound, B. (2009) *The last ten years: A comprehensive review of the literature on the impact of fair trade*, London: Natural Resources Institute, University of Greenwich.

Nunn, N. (2008) 'The long-term effects of Africa's slave trades', *The Quarterly Journal of Economics*, vol 123, no 1, pp 139–76.

Off, C. (2006) *Bitter chocolate*, Toronto, Canada: Random House Canada.

Ould, D., Jordan, C., Reynolds, R. and Loftin, L. (2004) *The cocoa industry in West Africa: A history of exploitation*, London: Anti-Slavery International (www.antislavery.org/wp-content/uploads/2017/01/1_cocoa_report_2004.pdf)

Paviakis, D. (2010) 'The development of British overseas humanitarianism and the Congo reform campaign', *Journal of Colonialism and Colonial History*, vol 11, no 1.

PCIDTT (Prayson Centre for International Development and Technology Transfer) (2011) *Oversight of private and public initiatives to eliminate the worst form of child labour in the cocoa sector:* Côte d'Ivoire and Ghana, New Orleans, LA: Tulane University.

Pettigrew, W.A. (2007) 'Parliament and the escalation of the slave trade, 1690–1714', in S. Farrell, M. Unwin and J. Walvin (eds) *The British slave trade: Abolition, parliament and people*, Edinburgh: Edinburgh University Press, pp 12–26.

Rainforest Alliance (2017) *Working with you to rebalance the planet* (www.rainforest-alliance.org/about).

Raiswel, R. (1997) 'The papal bulls of Eugene IV', in J.P. Rodriquez (ed) *The historical encylopedia of world slavery*, Santa Barbara, CA: ABC-CLIO, pp 260–1.

Richardson, D. (2007) 'The ending of the British slave trade in 1807: The economic context', in S. Farrell, M. Unwin and J. Walvin (eds) *The British slave trade: Abolition, parliament and people*, Edinburgh: Edinburgh University Press, pp 127–40.

Satre, L.J. (2005) *Chocolate on trial*, Athens, OH: Ohio University Press.

Short, E. (2009) 'William Wilberforce and the fight for life', *Human Life Review*, vol 35, no 3, pp 80–97.

SPHTM (School of Public Health and Tropical Medicine) (2015) *Survey research on child labour in West African cocoa growing areas*, New Orleans, LA: Tulane University.

Tannenbaum, F. (1946) *Slave and citizen: The Negro in the Americas*, New York: Vintage Books.

Walk Free Foundation (2016) *The Global Slavery Index*, Broadway Nedlands, Australia: The Minderoo Foundation.

Usherwood, S. (1981) 'The black must be discharged – The abolitionists' debt to Lord Mansfield', *History Today*, vol 31, no 3, pp 40–5.

Wagner, H.R. and Parish, H.R. (1967) *The life and writings of Bartolome de las Casas*, Albuquerque, NM: University of New Mexico Press.

Yeager, T.J. (1995) 'Encomienda or slavery? The Spanish crown's choice of labor organization in the sixteenth century', *The Journal of Economic History*, vol 55, no 4, pp 842–84.

6

Impact of hazardous substances and pesticides on farmers and farming communities

Jinky Leilanie Del Prado-Lu

Introduction

There is an estimated 1.3 billion people in the global agricultural sector, representing one in three of all workers, and about 40 per cent of the global workforce (ILO, 2015a). In developing countries, agriculture remains the biggest employer of the rural poor, and is one of the largest contributors to national economic revenues. However, agriculture is also one of the most hazardous industries worldwide, exposing farmers to both fatal and non-fatal diseases and injuries. Agricultural workers are exposed to the weather, close contact with animals and plants, extensive use of chemical and biological products, difficult working postures and lengthy hours, as well as hazardous agricultural tools and machinery (Del Prado-Lu, 2011). The entire farming community is often affected since farming is a household economy, and extended families reside within the broader farm premises (NIOSH, 2013).

The International Labour Organization (ILO, 2015b) has reported that at least 170,000 agricultural workers and farmers die annually, representing twice the fatality rate in other sectors of the labour economy (ILO, 2015b). Due to the difficulty of access to areas of investigation, absence of social and health statistics and the difficulty in establishing the epidemiology of disease causation, there is considerable under-reporting of statistics. Hence, actual occupational risks are greater than what is actually reported.

Farmers are among the occupational groups that suffer the most from health risks as they are usually unprotected, poorly covered for health insurance, and experience more barriers in accessing healthcare services and programmes (Holden and Jacobson, 2013; IBON, 2017). Addressing the long-term impact of structural factors on the health of certain population groups is an ongoing challenge. There are multiple means of harm involving farming lifestyles, including physical (for example, sun radiation or noise), chemical (for example, dusts or fertilisers), biological (for example, bacteria or parasites) and ergonomic (for example, musculoskeletal disorders or injuries). However, exposure to pesticides in particular has been shown to cause adverse health effects among farmers (ILO, 2015a).

This chapter on the health risks of farmers and farming communities is essential in exploring further the phenomenon of food crime. The production of agricultural products and food crops is inimical to the health and safety of those who produce them. This is an ironic situation, where the providers of agricultural crops – farmers – become vulnerable, ill, injured, disabled or even die in the process of agricultural production. This is compounded by the lack of social and health protection for the farmers, and the absence of institutional support for farming in many developing countries despite the importance of farming and food production. This chapter pursues a food crime perspective (see Chapter 1, this volume) in analysing the ways in which agricultural practices, as unnecessarily hazardous and significantly unregulated, harm farmers and farming communities. In other words, there are structural patterns of harm, authenticated by corporate action and government inaction, which endanger the safety and wellbeing of farmers whom global populations are dependent on for sustenance and health.

This chapter aims to review the adverse health and safety risks of food production practices on farmers and farming communities, with particular attention on pesticide-related harms. The first part of the chapter outlines the vast array of harms impacting farmers and farming communities. The latter part provides a case study of farming communities in Benguet in the Philippines, and the impact of pesticide-related illnesses. The chapter concludes with an outline of policy recommendations and a final summary.

Adverse health and safety risks in farming and food production

Farmers are exposed to hazards, or a combination of hazards, that affect their health and safety. Hazards are defined as the presence of a material or condition that has the potential for causing loss or harm, whereas risk is a combination of the severity of consequences and likelihood of occurrence of undesired outcomes (Johnson, 2000). Pesticides are one of the more common sources of harm used in the agricultural system. A pesticide is any substance or mixture of substances intended for preventing, destroying, repelling or mitigating any insects, rodents, nematodes, fungi, weeds or any other forms of life declared to be pests; and any substance or mixture of substances intended for use as a plant regulator, defoliant or desiccant. Organochlorine (OC) pesticides are used successfully in controlling a number of diseases, such as malaria and typhus, but were banned and restricted after the 1960s in most of the technologically advanced countries. Synthetic insecticides that were introduced from the 1960s to the 1980s include organophosphates (OP), carbamates and pyrethroids, which contributed greatly to pest control and agricultural output (Aktar et al, 2009). However, pesticides are non-selective and may also harm humans, animals and the environment indirectly or unintentionally.

The health and environmental impacts of pesticide exposure affect farming communities, and sometimes negate the economic advantages of its use. Studies have correlated the extent of direct and indirect pesticide exposure to health hazards such as increased mortality, dermal contamination, a depression in cholinesterase levels, and both foetal abnormalities and spontaneous abortion among pregnant women (Ostrea et al, 2008). It is discouraging that even with some knowledge of the health risks, many farmers perceive that crop productivity outweighs the health risks associated with pesticide use. Some campaigns and programmes have been implemented to respond to the risks contributed by pesticides, such as organic farming and integrated pesticide management, although these alternative methods are yet to be sustained on a long-term basis.

Bodily health risks in farming communities

The adverse health effects of pesticide exposure have been documented worldwide. Chemical hazards among farmers are primarily attributed to pesticides that may cause direct injuries and fatalities, from burns, respiratory illness or poisoning to the workers and the surrounding community. Pesticide exposure has been associated with prostate cancer (van Maele-Fabry and Willens, 2003), adverse consequences for human reproduction and survival (Peiris-John and Wickremasinghe, 2008), reproductive disorders (Bretveld et al, 2008) and neurologic functioning (Keifer and Firestone, 2007).

Due to their underdeveloped detoxification function, behavioural patterns and environmental interactions, children in farming communities are the most affected age group. According to the US Environmental Protection Agency (EPA, 2013), poison control centres answer 3.6 million calls each year, with children younger than six making up about half of the cases (Keifer and Firestone, 2007). In rural Asia, pesticide self-poisoning is the most common form of suicide, accounting for 60 per cent of all suicide-related deaths (Tirado et al, 2008). Children who play for longer hours outdoors in a farming community and who play in irrigation water with pesticide residues have lower gross motor, fine motor, visual motor and problem-solving skills (Cohen, 2007). And the near proximity of the farmers' houses to farming areas poses an increased risk of pesticide contamination because of spraying drifts.

Some congenital abnormalities and pregnancy disorders are associated with pesticides, such as microcephaly, mental retardation, clubfoot, hydatidiform mole and ectopic pregnancy (Bretveld et al, 2008). Ethnographic reports of children among farmworkers in California suggested a relationship between air quality and childhood asthma, and that pregnant women were also at risk of affecting their foetuses due to pesticide exposure (Schwartz et al, 2015). Maternal or paternal pesticide exposure before and any time after conception also increased the risk of childhood leukaemia and orofacial clefts in their children (Romitti et al, 2007). In another study, gastroschisis among infants of women aged 20 and above was more likely to occur after exposure to multiple pesticides pre- and post-conception, after controlling for maternal and infant risk factors (Kielb et al, 2014). Infertility has also been found among married male farmworkers, and higher among farmworkers' families (such as wives experiencing stillbirths and abortions) compared to rates in the general population (Neghab et al, 2014). Similar findings were established by Berton and colleagues (2014) on the exposure of mothers and foetuses to OP pesticides, pyrethroids and carbamates, as well as by Guo and colleagues (2014) on prenatal exposure to OC pesticides. The prevalence of males in the agricultural sector also increases the occurrences of male-related health problems caused by pesticide exposure – in some studies, pesticide exposure affected the reproductive functioning of single male farmers, with pesticide use causing disruption in semen quality and lower testosterone levels (Peiris-John and Wickremasinghe, 2008).

In more severe instances, tremors, abdominal cramps, excessive urination, bradycardia, staggering gait, pinpoint pupils and hypotension may be observed (Boiko et al, 2005). Pesticide poisoning has biologic correlates, including contact with OP pesticides that terminates the action of the acetylcholine neurotransmitter, producing delayed and irreversible neuromuscular effects usually seen in extremities (Keifer and Firestone, 2007). A group of researchers who have collated evidence over the last decade (2002–12) on the effect of OPs found a positive dose–response relationship between OP and neurodevelopment among children that manifested in cognitive memory deficits, behavioural attention deficits in toddlers and abnormal reflexes (Muñoz-Quezada et al, 2013). This is corroborated by a study of school children in Spain, where the biological metabolites of pesticide concentration in the body increased with vegetable consumption with high pesticide residues and the residential use of pesticides (Roca et al, 2014). The neurodevelopment of farmers is also affected by pesticide exposure which affects suicidal ideation, which was found to be associated with the occupation of farming, particularly the effect of pesticide use among male, Korean farmers (Kim et al, 2014).

Reports of pesticide-related dermatoses are increasing as a result of exposure through skin contact. These include allergic or irritant contact dermatitis, and rare clinical forms such as urticaria, erythema multiforme, ashy dermatosis, parakeratosis variegata and porphyria cutanea tarda, chloracne, nail and hair disorder (Boiko et al, 2005). Likewise, dermal symptoms are a common health problem among those who are exposed to pesticides through dermal contact. The dermal contamination from pesticides has been reported to be statistically correlated with physical contact with branches or any part of the vegetable during certain agricultural tasks such as harvesting, pruning, thinning, cutting or sorting (Baldi et al, 2014). Pesticides can also vaporise into the air and affect the larger community.

Respiratory symptoms due to pesticide contact have also been widely documented. Senthilselvan and colleagues (1992) found a significant association between carbamate exposure and prevalence of asthma among non-asthmatic farmers, and lower mean lung function among those with asthma. Qaqisha and colleqagues (2016) found a link between chromosomal aberration and occupational exposure to pesticides among a group of Jordanian farmers, where farmers occupationally exposed to pesticides and insecticide were 13.5 times more likely to have an increased risk of developing noise hearing loss. Aside from lymphoma, a large prospective cohort in France suggests a possible link between agricultural activity and bladder cancer with an exposure–response relationship with duration of work (Lemarchand et al, 2016). Prostate cancer rates are also common among farmers (Lemarchand et al, 2016).

The two main groups of biological agents to which farmers are exposed are allergenic or toxic agents forming bioaerosols, and agents causing zoonoses and other infectious diseases. Workers in agriculture and their families are exposed to both. Bioaerosols are particles of organic dust and/or droplets suspended in the air, such as viruses, bacteria, endotoxin, fungi, particles of faeces, bodies of mites and insects, and the hair, faeces and urine of birds and mammals. These often induce disorders of the respiratory system and the skin (Rim and Lim, 2014). The common respiratory diseases associated with dust exposure in farming are organic dust toxic syndrome (ODTS) and Farmer's lung. ODTS is a common respiratory illness with symptoms of temporary influenza-like illness due to the toxicity induced by inhaled materials such as grain kernel fragments, bits of insects, bacteria, fungal spores, moulds or chemical residues (Seifert et al, 2003). Farmers' lung, less common than ODTS, is a type of hypersensitivity pneumonitis that is an inflammatory lung disease caused by severe or prolonged exposure to inhaled biologic dusts. Schlünssen and colleagues (2015) showed the prevalence of allergic sensitisation inducing an airway disease due to bovine allergens in the residence of the farmers.

In humans, pesticides are absorbed through all routes of entry, and can produce both acute and chronic effects. Common acute effects include vomiting, diarrhoea, cough, seizures, changes in the sensorium, headache and skin irritation or itchiness. Chronic effects include endocrine disruption, hypertension, neuropathies, cancer, bone marrow effects, skin lesions and cytogenetic or immunotoxic effects (Panganiban, 2006). Lu (2012) found that among eggplant (aubergine) farmers, the most common health problems – itchiness of the skin, redness of the eyes (29.3%), muscle pains (27.6%) and headaches (27.6%) – were related to farmers' pesticide exposure. Cheng and Bersamina (1994) also found that farmers in Benguet in the Philippines exposed to pesticides manifested adverse health such as itchy, dry skin, red eyes, abdominal pain, muscle cramps, body malaise and discoloured nails.

Pesticides used in the Philippines are primarily OPs, carbamates and pyrethroids (Del Prado-Lu, 2010). Most of the chemicals commonly available in the Philippines and in Asia are classified by the World

Health Organization (WHO) as extremely hazardous (category I and II), and are either banned or restricted for use in the developed world (Pingali et al, 1994). In a study conducted in Region VIII, Phillipines, the top common manifestations among rice farmers in the following descending order were chest pain and back pain, elevated blood pressure and paleness, blurring of vision, body weakening and numbness, skin lesions and/or thickening, bronchial asthma or chronic cough, colds, wheezing, nail destruction and/or pitting, and difficulty of breathing. These symptoms are also consistent with the use of OPs, carbamates and acetamides, which are the pesticides the farmers used most frequently (Cheng and Bersamina, 1994).

Harmful effects and associations of pesticides on humans documented in the Philippines, aside from the direct manifestations, include:

- Parkinson's disease: In a descriptive study in Negros Oriental, in the Philippines, Parkinson's disease was evaluated for its potential relationship with environmental and occupational exposure. It was reported that 69 per cent of cases had consumed well water and 23 per cent of cases had drunk well water near the use of pesticides (Lennon and Diputado, 1995).
- Chromosomal disorders: In a retrospective study by Padilla and colleagues (2009), the most common reason for referral for chromosomal analyses done at the National Institutes of Health from 1991 to 2007 was that of cytogenetic effects due to environmental toxins such as pesticides (2,264 out of 8,391 samples). This suggests that chromosomal disorders may be associated with pesticide exposure.
- Pregnancy abnormalities: A literature review by Nagami (2009) reports adverse outcomes of pesticide exposure including birth defect, spontaneous abortion, stillbirth, preterm delivery and low birth weight. Specific malformations, such as anencephaly, were noted to be significantly related to pesticide exposure. Hypospadias and cryptorchidism were also found to be significantly associated with various kinds of pesticides.
- Hearing loss in infants: In a cohort of pregnant women exposed to pesticides, it was noted that there is a 1.4 per cent risk of hearing loss with exposure to Propoxur, 6.25 per cent risk with Cypermethrin exposure and 6.25 per cent risk with Pretilachlor exposure (Chiong et al, 2012).

The aforementioned data in the international landscape have shown that globally, farmers and farming communities are exposed to a multitude of adverse working conditions and various occupational hazards. These environments and working conditions have significant negative impacts on the health of these populations, with statistically significant differences in comparison to non-farming communities. How do such patterns exemplify food crimes and harms? The global food system and its agricultural practices are increasingly reliant on pesticides. This is not simply due to the stresses of feeding larger and larger populations with decreasing agricultural land that is continually overworked and depleted of essential minerals. Rather, a small oligopoly of chemical companies manages the world's supply of pesticides, fungicides and insecticides, enforcing power through lobbying of governments and international trade organisations. This comes at the expense of concern for the health and safety of farmers and farming communities. In other words, global agriculture is organised around an economy built from the (over)use of harmful chemicals, which unfairly victimises vulnerable populations of humans, and negatively impacts non-human animals and environments.

A case study of pesticide-related illnesses among farmers in the Philippines

A study of farmers in Benguet, the largest vegetable-producing area in the Philippines, targeted 534 farmers in order to assess the health effects of pesticide exposure (Del Prado-Lu, 2014). There are about 27,500 farms in Benguet covering 30,000 hectares of agricultural land. The province is known as the 'salad bowl' of the Philippines, with its major crops consisting of tubers, roots and bulbs, and leafy vegetables, stems and flowers (BAS, 2016). This study used an interviewer-guided questionnaire, a physical health assessment and a laboratory test for complete blood count including red blood cell cholinesterase for possible OP and carbamate poisoning. The health assessment looked at the farmers' general body as well as their eyes, ears, noses, throats, respiratory systems and skin. The study showed that almost half (47.9%) of the farmers were working as agricultural workers, 23.7% as agricultural pesticide applicators/mixers or loaders, 12% as growers and 8.8% were housewives who assisted in farming. Approximately 20% of the households have children aged 13–15 who assisted adult family members on the farm. Among the married women respondents, there were 938 full-term pregnancies, where 6.1% ended in spontaneous abortion. Reported congenital abnormalities and pregnancy disorders included microcephaly, mental retardation, clubfoot, hydatidiform mole and ectopic pregnancy.

Pesticide exposure

The duration of pesticide use and exposure can pose a risk factor in chronic and long-term health effects. In Benguet, the most commonly used pesticides are Tamaron (36.1%), Dithane (34.1%), Sumicidine (29.0%), Selecron (24.9%) and Lannate (15.2%). Tamaron, the most commonly used, has an active ingredient of methamidophos, an OP pesticide. Occupational exposures account for most pesticide exposures (84.8%), affecting respiratory (69.94%), dermal (50.7%) and ocular (27.7%) systems. Pesticide exposure usually occurs during agricultural activities such as application (39.6%), mixing (23.7%), loading pesticides into the sprayer (21.1%) and field re-entry (6.0%). Based on a multi-response survey on areas where exposure to pesticide occurred, 53.6% of farmers said that exposure mainly occurs on the farm or in the field areas, 32.7% in rural gardens and 6% in their homes. Farmers use pesticides from three to six hours per day (51.2%), one to two days weekly (86.8%), and three to four weeks per month (82.3%), using insecticides (86.1%), fungicides (65.9%) and herbicides (37.5%).

Occupational and environmental health assessment

Among the surveyed farmers, 49% complained of being sick due to farm work. Of those who got ill, 69.8% receive no medical attention. As for common respiratory symptoms, farmers often complained of coughing (39.4%), difficulty breathing (15.6%), breathlessness (14.9%) and having pulmonary secretions (13.3%). For cardiovascular symptoms, the most common complaints were chest pain (38.2%), palpitations (25.3%) and arrhythmias (11.4%). For skin problems, 30.1% complained of itchiness, 13.9% of sweating, 12.9% of skin rashes and 5.6% of skin bruisability.

The farmers also underwent physical examinations to determine any health problems associated with pesticide exposure. Results show that 90.5% of the farmers presented a normal respiratory rate, while 7% have an increased respiratory rate or tachypnoea, and 2.5% showed decreased respirations or bradypnoea. Additionally, 40.9% were diagnosed with an abnormal physical health assessment result, 4.6%

presented with problems in their neurological functioning, and less than 10% of the farmers exhibited abnormal laboratory results. The assessment showed that the following abnormalities were manifested among the farmers: ear symptoms (22.5%), eye symptoms (20.8%), neck problems (13.7%), abdominal complaints (10.2%) and dermal problems (8.8%). Blood samples were also taken from the farmers. Out of 534 blood samples, 8.4% were found to have abnormal creatinine values, 10.5% had abnormal white blood cell counts, 29.2% showed abnormal haemoglobin values and 5.3% were found to have abnormal platelet counts.

Policy recommendations

Given the data on pesticide poisoning and related health effects, the challenge is to lessen pesticide use in agriculture, and to understand the health impacts on productivity and income for farming communities. As a case in point, Pingali et al (1994) investigated the health effect trade-offs and the income losses due to non-use of pesticides. Pesticide use is prevalent among farmers to boost agricultural productivity. It is often hypothesised that non-use or reduced use of pesticides may adversely affect farm income. On the contrary, the researchers showed that pesticide use has a negative impact on farmers' health, and farmers' health has a positive impact on productivity. They concluded that there is a net social gain from the reduction of insecticide use in rice production in the Philippines through an economic analysis of the production from a farm-level survey integrated with health data collected from the same farmers. They noted that farmers are not only exposed to acute pesticide-related illnesses, but also to chronic illnesses due to prolonged exposure to pesticides, which increase the costs to health, and offset income and profit in the long run (Pingali et al, 1994).

Certain regulatory frameworks and legislative agendas should be pursued, particularly regarding pesticide regulation. Subscribing to the recommendations in the study by Matthews and colleagues (2011) on their assessment of the 142 member states of the WHO in regard to regulation of public health pesticides, there are certain key areas that could be adopted for policy consideration in the Philippines:

• There should be legislation and regulatory frameworks governing agricultural pesticides, including their registration in the market and access to information about their qualities.

- Legislation should include the essential aspects of labelling, storage, transport and disposal of pesticides.
- Registration guidelines of pesticides should be reviewed by external and objective organisations, and include a more comprehensive assessment of their toxicity levels and active ingredients based on internal studies. Additionally, there should be benchmarking with international standards.
- Regulatory guidelines and policies on pesticides should be strictly enforced, backed up by adequate human resources, processes and tools for monitoring and enforcing corrective actions.
- National databases should include information on the production and trade of pesticides, as well as data on poisoning incidents and reported health manifestations of pesticide poisoning.

Research strategies could start with identifying populations at risk along each exposure route. This may include estimating the health outcomes that the farmers experienced or could experience in the future, identifying the health outcome information available, analysing the areas where there were gaps in agency responsibilities, where exposure sources were adequately identified, where new data flows were available, and where improvements could have been effected through inter-agency cooperation. Based on such a framework, there is a need to estimate the burden of mortality and morbidity among farmers who are identified to be among the poorest. Health cost analysis can be estimated where necessary interventions and strategies are in place, such as early detection and treatment of diseases. Above all, measures to prevent ill health among farming communities must be in place. In this approach, the social determinants of health, and in particular, the occupational health risks of farmers, should be addressed in order to achieve the highest level of health and wellbeing, so that farms can become even more productive.

Based on the data on health risks presented in this chapter, it is clear that such a lack of regulation of agricultural pesticide use leads to direct harmful effects for farmers and farming communities. These individuals develop lung diseases, cancers and severe respiratory and dermatologic conditions while carrying out their agricultural activities, and hence, their right to healthy working conditions and to health itself is violated by food production systems. Hence, the global food system itself, corroborated by the lack of regulation and social safety nets, is producing significant health and socioeconomical harms against farmers and farming communities. To prevent or at least mitigate these harms, researchers and policy-makers must develop a 'criminological imagination' (Young, 2011) within a 'food crime perspective' (see Chapter 1, this volume), in order to recognise pesticide-related exposure as causing structural-level harm to food production populations. In light of the abundance of intersectional harms involved in food production, rather than responsibilising individual farmers for misusing pesticides, or rural citizens for being too close to sprayed fields, among other examples, efforts must target the broader patterns of harms. While it is important to work toward Matthews and colleagues' (2011) policy recommendations in combating the *direct* harms on the health of farmers and farming communities, longer-term goals must also recognise the political economy of agriculture and the indirect harms on the overall wellbeing of humanity and its environment.

Conclusion

This chapter has demonstrated that agricultural occupational hazards and pesticide exposures affect the health of farmers and farming communities directly, as well as the health of non-farming populations, non-human animals, and nature more indirectly due to the persistence and spread of pesticides in open environments. There are multiple hazards and risks associated with agricultural chemicals, with little or no protection from regulatory institutions and enforcement organisations. Legislation, policy and compliance must come hand in hand with ensuring good agricultural practices including the regulation of banned and restricted pesticides. This puts forward a paradigm shift in the food production systems from deregulation that favours market forces over national government regulation, from the massive commercialisation of food products using chemicals and genetic engineering to more ecological and healthy food production systems. In other words, a shift is needed from the concept of food supply to food security. There should be a conscious and concerted consideration within institutional frameworks to include the ecological, health and social implications of the overall food production systems. In crafting policies and programmes involving the entire cycle and process of food production, careful consideration should be applied to the farm level in order to afford protection for farmers and farming communities, while they fulfil the crucial responsibility of supplying populations with nourishing food.

References

Aktar. M.W., Sengupta, D. and Chowdhury, A. (2009) 'Impact of pesticide use in agriculture: Their benefits and hazards', *Interdisciplinary Toxicology*, vol 2, no 1, pp 1–12.

Baldi, I., Lebailly, P., Bouvier, G., Rondeau, V., Kientz-Bouchart, V., Canal-Raffin, M. and Garrigou, A. (2014) 'Levels and determinants of pesticide exposure in re-entry workers in vineyards: Results of the PESTEXPO study', *Environmental Research*, vol 132, pp 360–9.

BAS (Bureau of Agricultural Statistics) (2016) 'Crop statistics' (www.bas.gov.ph).

Berton, T., Mayhoub, F., Chardon, K., Duca, RC., Lestremau, F., Bach, V. and Tack, K. (2014) 'Development of an analytical strategy based on LC–MS/MS for the measurement of different classes of pesticides and theirs metabolites in meconium: Application and characterisation of foetal exposure in France', *Environmental Research*, vol 132, pp 311–20.

Boiko, P., Keifer, M., Furman, J., Weyrauch, K. and Hanks, C. (2005) *Cholinesterase monitoring for agricultural pesticide handlers: Guidelines for health care providers in Washington State*, Washington State, Washington, DC: Department of Labor and Industries.

Bretveld, R.W., Hooiveld, M., Zielhuis, G.A., Pellegrino, A., van Rooij, I.A. and Roeleveld, N. (2008) 'Reproductive disorders among male and female greenhouse workers', *Reproductive Toxicology*, vol 25, no 1, pp 107–14.

Cheng, C. and Bersamina, K.V. (1994) *Pesticides: Its hazardous effects on Benguet vegetable farmers*, Baguio City: Unique Printing.

Chiong, C.M., Ostrea, E.M., Llanes, E.G.D., Uy, E.T.V., Reyes, A.L., Cruz, T.L.I.G. and Quintos, M.R.T. (2012) 'Auditory brainstem response latencies of infants and maternal exposure to environmental toxic product', *Acta Medica Philippina*, vol 46, no 3, pp 5–10.

Cohen, M., (2007) 'Environmental toxins and health--the health impact of pesticides', *Australian Family Physician*, vol 36, no 12, pp 1002–4.

Del Prado-Lu, J.L. (2010) 'Multi-pesticide residue assessment of agricultural soil and water in major farming areas in Benguet, Philippines', *Archives of Environmental Contamination and Toxicology*, doi:10.100/00244-90-9748-5.

Del Prado-Lu, J.L. (2011) 'Occupational safety of vegetable farmers in Benguet', *International Journal of Occupational Safety and Ergonomics*, vol 4, pp 445–53.

Del Prado-Lu, J.L. (2012) 'Farmers' exposure to pesticides and pesticide residues in soils and crops grown in Benguet, Philippines', *Philippine Journal of Crop Science (PJCS)*, vol 36, no 3, pp 41-9.

Del Prado-Lu, J.L. (2014) 'Insecticide residues in soil, water, eggplant fruits and farmers' health effects due to exposures to pesticide', *Environmental Health and Preventive Medicine*, vol 20, no 1, pp 53–62.

EPA (Environmental Protection Agency) (2013) 'Prevent poisonings in your home' (www.epa.gov/safepestcontrol/food-and-pesticides).

Guo, H., Jin, Y., Cheng, Y., Leaderer, B., Lin, S., Holford, T.R. et al (2014) 'Prenatal exposure to organochlorine pesticides and infant birth weight in China', *Chemosphere*, doi:10.1016/j. chemosphere.2014.02.017.

Holden, W.N. and Jacobson, D. (2013) *Mining and natural hazard vulnerability in the Philippines: Digging to development or digging to disaster?*, London: Anthem Press.

IBON (2017) 'Food producers poorer, hungry three years after Yolanda', January, Manila: IBON Networks (http://ibon.org).

ILO (International Labour Organization) (2015a) 'Agriculture; plantations; other rural sectors' (www.ilo.org).

ILO (2015b) 'Occupational safety and health in the mining (coal and other mining) sector' (www.ilo.org).

Johnson, R. (2000) 'Risk management by risk magnitudes – Unwin Company Integrated Risk Management' (www.unwin-co.com/files/ RiskMgtByRiskMags,1998.pdf).

Keifer M.C. and Firestone, J. (2007) 'Neurotoxicity of pesticides', *Journal of Agromedicine*, vol 12, no 1, pp 17–25.

Kielb, C., Lin, S., Herdt-Losavio M., Bell, E., Chapman, B., Rocheleau, C.M., et al (2014) 'Maternal periconceptional occupational exposure to pesticides and selected musculoskeletal birth defects', *International Journal of Hygiene and Environmental Health*, vol 217, no 2–3, pp 248–54.

Kim, J., Shin, J. and Lee, W. (2014) 'Suicidal ideation and occupational pesticide exposure among male farmers', *Environmental Research*, vol 128, pp 52–6.

Lemarchand, C., Tual, S., Boulanger, M., Levêque-Morlais, N., Perrier, S., Clin, B., et al (2016) 'Prostate cancer risk among French farmers in the AGRICAN cohort', *Scandinavian Journal of Work, Environment, & Health*, vol 42, no 2, pp 144–52.

Lennon, J.L. and Diputado, B.V. (1995) 'A descriptive epidemiology of Parkinson's disease and environmental exposure in Negros Oriental, Philippines', *Philippine Journal of Internal Medicine*, vol 33, no 6, pp 205–9.

Matthews, G., Zaim, M., Yadav, R., Soares, A., Hii, J., Ameneshewa, B., et al (2011) 'Status of legislation and regulatory control of public health pesticides in countries endemic with or at risk of major vector-borne diseases', *Environmental Health Perspectives*, vol 119, no 11, pp 1517–22.

Muñoz-Quezada, M.T., Lucero, B.A., Barr, D.B., Steenland, K., Levy, K., Ryan, P.B., et al (2013) 'Neurodevelopmental effects in children associated with exposure to organophosphate pesticides: A systematic review', *NeuroToxicology*, vol 39, pp 158–68.

Nagami, H. (2009) 'Pesticide exposure and pregnancy outcome: a literature review', *Journal of the Japanese Association of Rural Medicine*, vol 57, no 5, pp 681–97.

Neghab, M., Momenbella-Fard, M., Naziaghdam, R., Salahshour, N., Kazemi, M. and Alipour, H. (2014) 'The effects of exposure to pesticides on the fecundity status of farm workers resident in a rural region of Fars province, southern Iran', *Asian Pacific Journal of Tropical Biomedicine*, vol 4, no 4, pp 324–8.

NIOSH (National Institute for Occupational Safety and Health) (2013) 'NIOSH workplace safety and health topics' (www.cdc.gov/niosh)

Ostrea, E.M. Jr, Bielawski, D.M., Posecion, N.C. Jr, Corrion, M., Villanueva-Uy, E., Jin, Y., Janisse, J.J. and Ager, J.W. (2008) 'A comparison of infant hair, cord blood and meconium analysis to detect fetal exposure to environmental pesticides', *Environmental Research*, vol 106, no 2, pp 277–83.

Padilla, C.D., de la Paz, E.M., Cadag, N.S., Salonga, E.A.G. and Chiong, M.A.D. (2009) 'A review of the results of chromosomal analyses done at the National Institutes of Health from 1991 to 2007', *Acta Medica Philippina*, vol 43, no 1, pp 4–6.

Panganiban, L.C. (2006) 'Health impact of pesticides and genetically modified organisms', Proceedings from the UPCM Centennial Grand Scientific Symposium.

Peiris-John, R.J. and Wickremasinghe, R. (2008) 'Impact of low-level exposure to organophosphates on human reproduction and survival', *Transactions of the Royal Society of Tropical Medicine and Hygiene*, vol 102, no 3, pp 239–45.

Pingali, P.L., Marquez, C.B. and Palis, F.G. (1994) 'Pesticides and Philippine rice farmer health: A medical and economic analysis', *American Journal of Agricultural Economics*, vol 76, no 3, pp 587–92.

Qaqisha, B.M., Al-Dalahmahb, O., Al-Motassemc, Y., Battaha, A. and Said, S. (2016) 'Occupational exposure to pesticides and occurrence of the chromosomal translocation t(14;18) among farmers in Jordan', *Toxicology Reports*, pp 225–9.

Rim, K.T. and Lim, C.H. (2014) 'Biologically hazardous agents at work and efforts to protect workers' health: A review of recent reports', *Safety and Health at Work*, vol 5, pp 43–52.

Roca, M., Marco, A.M., Ferré, J., Pérez, R. and Yusà, V. (2014) 'Biomonitoring exposure assessment to contemporary pesticides in a school children population of Spain', *Environmental Research*, vol 131, pp 77–85.

Romitti, P.A., Herring, A.M., Dennis, L.K. and Wong-Gibbons, D.L. (2007) 'Meta-analysis: Pesticides and orofacial clefts', *Cleft Palate-Craniofacial Journal*, vol 44, no 4, pp 358–65.

Schlünssen, V., Basinas, I., Zahradnik, E., Elholma, G., Wouters, L. and Kromhout, H. (2015) 'Exposure levels, determinants and IgE mediated sensitization to bovine allergens among Danish farmers and non-farmers', *International Journal of Hygiene and Environmental Health*, pp 265–72.

Schwartz, N., von Glascoe, A., Torres, V., Ramos, L. and Soria-Delgado, C. (2015) 'Where they (live, work and) spray: Pesticide exposure, childhood asthma and environmental justice among Mexican-American farmworkers', *Health & Place*, vol 32, pp 83–92.

Seifert, S., von Essen, S., Jacobitz, K. and Crouch, R. (2003) 'Organic dust toxic syndrome: A review', *Journal of Toxicology: Clinical Toxicology*, pp 185–93.

Sethilselvan, A., McDuffee, H.H. and Dosman, J.A. (1992) 'Association of asthma with use of pesticides. Results of a cross-sectional survey of farmers', *The American Review of Respiratory Disease*, vol 146, no 4, pp 84–7.

Tirado, R., Englande, A.J., Promakasikorn, L. and Novotny, V. (2008) 'Technical Note 03/2008 GRL-TN-03-2008', Greenpeace Research Laboratories.

van Maele-Fabry, G. and Willens, S.L. (2003) 'Occupation related pesticide exposure and cancer of the prostate: A meta-analyses', *Occupational and Environmental Medicine*, vol 60, pp 634–42.

Young, J. (2011) *The criminological imagination*, Cambridge: Polity Press.

Section III
Processing, marketing and accessing food

7

Agency and responsibility: The case of the food industry and obesity

Judith Schrempf-Stirling and Robert Phillips

Introduction

The World Health Organization (WHO, 2004, 2011) and US Centers for Disease Control and Prevention (CDC, 2010) refer to obesity as an epidemic. The health consequences of obesity are severe, including increased risks of stroke and type-2 diabetes. Two-thirds of the US population is overweight or obese, and obesity is the leading cause of preventable death (Haomiao and Lubetkin, 2010). While there is agreement on the dangers and consequences of obesity, there exists a robust discussion on what exactly causes obesity. Candidates include portion sizes, aggressive marketing, ignorance about ingredients and their effects, government subsidies, sedentary lifestyles, or a lack of alternatives. Closely linked to this discussion of causes is a debate about responsibility.

The term 'responsibility' has its roots in 18th and 19th-century political and legal spheres (Feinberg, 1970; Fletcher, 1999). Given the legal foundations of the term, it comes as no surprise that responsibility has mainly been interpreted as a retrospective concept. Retrospective responsibility refers to an actor's past actions and the resulting outcomes (Miller, 2001). The retrospective interpretation of responsibility aims at punishment of the perpetrator for harm caused and at compensation for the victim (Feinberg, 1970; Fletcher, 1999). Central to the retrospective approach to responsibility is the identification of the offender or wrongdoer and assigning responsibility:

> Once we know that a crime – described as wrongdoing or wrongful conduct – has occurred, the next question: Who did it? Who is responsible? The inquiry requires us to localize the crime in the person or a particular offender. The "attribution" captures the idea of bringing home the crime to the offender and holding the offender responsible for the crime. (Fletcher, 1999, p 81)

The challenge regarding food crimes in general, and obesity more specifically, is that obesity is the result of many actions by a variety of actors such as governments, businesses and consumers. This chapter introduces a more nuanced approach informed by recent work in philosophy addressing questions of complex responsibility and agency. Because questions of agency are complicated by the number and diversity of actors across global value chains, responsibility needs to be understood as shared and interactive. How does each main player in the obesity epidemic – the members of the value chain: *governments, corporations* and *consumers* – encourage, limit or circumvent consumer agency and consumers' capacity to make responsible food choices? What can each of the three main players do to support and improve consumer agency going forward? The responsibility of corporations and government for addressing the obesity challenge derives from three key elements: consumers' lack of *awareness* and *alternatives* as well as the possibility of *addictive* (or addiction-like) tendencies toward unhealthy food ingredients such as salt, sugar and fat. An analysis of the actions and interactions of these elements, and the actor-members of the value chain, helps make sense of the impact of each on the allocation of shared responsibility.

This chapter begins with elaborating an understanding of shared responsibility based on a connection to the problem and capacity to contribute to solutions. This is followed by an overview of the challenges in assigning responsibility for complex issues, using obesity as a key example of these challenges with a discussion of the current activities of the three main actors and their impact on consumer agency. Finally, how the three actors can – and should – share responsibility for addressing the obesity epidemic is considered.

Elements of agency: awareness, alternatives and addiction

Generally speaking, individuals are responsible for their own actions and the consequences of those actions. This personal responsibility is, however, a function of agency – an actor's capacity to act. Individuals are responsible and accountable for their actions and consequences when they are able to exercise agency and free will. Very broadly speaking, freedom is the absence of external constraints (Watson, 2004). Free will and agency refer to voluntary actions in which the individual is not forced, pressured or unduly influenced by external forces. When considering complex challenges such as the obesity epidemic, there are three mitigating influences on relative freedom of choice: the level of knowledge (*awareness*), the number and quality of available *alternatives*, and physical or psychological compulsion (defined here as *addiction*).

The first precondition of agency is full knowledge concerning the elements of the decision. While not a matter of omniscience, a fully free choice includes (but is not necessarily limited to) awareness of the current state of scientific knowledge as well as a probabilistic sense of what the choice is likely to entail into the foreseeable future. Relatedly, the second precondition of agency is the availability (and knowledge of) alternatives. In order for an action to be considered free and voluntary, the actor must, *ex ante*, have had at least two viable alternative courses of action. At the most basic, this can be a choice between action and inaction. If an actor could have, without negative penalty, chosen to *not* take an action, then that action is *ceteris paribus,* freely taken. Beyond this, the greater the number of reasonable and actionable alternatives, the more freely chosen the action is said to be.

Finally, the choice may not be entirely free due to the possible influence of some physical or psychological compulsion internal to the actor. Addiction is used here to describe natural addictions (such as to sugar and salt) as well as other forms of compulsion leading to addiction-resembling behaviour such as cravings or impairment in behavioural control. Specific to obesity, Gearhardt and colleagues (2009) developed the 'Yale Food Addiction Scale' to help understand the more compulsive elements of diets. While there are a myriad other bases for asserting and questioning the relative freedom of any given choice or action, awareness, alternatives and addiction are the bases that arise most commonly in discussions of obesity and, hence, the ones that are examined here.

The case of obesity

The precise causes of obesity remain unclear. In general, weight gain results from a calorie imbalance and is influenced by an interaction of genetic, metabolic, behavioural, environmental, sociocultural and socioeconomic factors (Malik et al, 2006). While diet and other behaviours are subject to some individual control, genetic and metabolic factors are significantly less so. Notably, however, the genetic profile of the population has not changed enough to be a substantial cause for the dramatic rise in obesity. Instead, 'the large increase in ... [obesity] must reflect major changes in non-genetic factors' (Hill and Trowbridge, 1997, p 571).

Given the many factors and actors that influence obesity, allocation of responsibility presents a complex challenge. There are a myriad of individuals and groups with roles to play, and many of these groups overlap in membership and interact functionally. What can each of the three main actors (consumers, corporations and governments) in the obesity epidemic do that limits or circumvents consumer agency? And what can each of the three main players do to support and improve consumer agency and clarify responsibility? Table 7.1 provides an overview of how the three actors influence elements of consumer agency (awareness, alternatives and addiction). The next section elaborates in detail the cells of the matrix.

Table 7.1: Actor-agency matrix

	Awareness	Alternatives	Addiction
Consumer	Economy of time Scientific understanding	Taste Affordability Access Convenience	Visual cues Natural addiction
Corporation	Industry-funded science and advocacy Marketing and communications 'Leanwashing' Branding and labelling	Allocation of Research and Development (R&D), and product development	'Bliss point' Portion sizes (Potentially) addictive ingredients (sugar, salt, caffeine ...)
Government	Labelling of prepackaged foods Marketing/advertising regulations Exercise campaigns	Farm policy subsidies Tax policy School lunch policy	Portion size control

Consumers' limitation to their own agency

Awareness of food and obesity is influenced, at a minimum, by limitations in time and scientific understanding. Consumers often lack the time to acquire nutrition information when buying food. However, even if consumers had time to acquire all the information regarding their food – and even if this were possible given the nature of trade secrets in the food business – they might not be able to make complete sense out of it. Consumers often lack the scientific knowledge to understand, for example, the differences between saturated and unsaturated fat, the meaning of transfats or the effects of sodium on health. These issues merely scratch the surface of the scientific complexity of today's food processing. Wansink and Huckabee (2005) show how consumers can be overwhelmed by nutrition information. Karnani, McFerran and Mukhopadhyay (2014) point to the power of mistaken 'lay theories' concerning the relative influence of diet, exercise and genetics as factors contributing to obesity. Conflicting studies evaluating the effects of certain ingredients or food types on consumer health are not always helpful in promoting consumer understanding. Even as consumers gain information, difficulties remain for typical consumers to adjudicate diverging scientific findings and make judgements based on often complex and esoteric considerations. This is not to say, however, that consumers have no role in becoming as informed as possible. Consumer agency and responsibility is a function of their capacity to acquire and process information relevant to food choices. Where this capacity is higher, consumers bear greater responsibility.

Consumer choice between alternatives is influenced by taste, affordability, access and convenience. While taste preferences differ among consumers, most share a tendency to buy tasty food, and at present, what counts as tasty corresponds closely with high levels of salt, fat and sugar. Although weaker, perhaps, than the other limits on consumer agency, taste substantially constrains the (apparent) viability of alternatives. Affordability also tends to limit alternatives. Many of the same tasty items described above are also the cheapest source of caloric energy. Finally, convenience can substantially tip the scales in favour of fast or processed foods. For some people, convenience connotes a luxury – access to fast sources of caloric energy leaving discretionary room in the schedule. For others, speed is essential to the effective functioning of their lives. Fresh ingredients simply take more time to prepare and clean up after, and this is time that a single parent rushing between multiple jobs may not have.

Finally, consumers' food choices are influenced by the addictive qualities of certain ingredients and visual cues. For example, humans are highly attracted to sugar as a source of quick energy and pleasure-inducing taste, and have tendencies to act compulsively toward other substances as well, such as caffeine. Another important psychological tendency involves visual cues and portion sizes. Consumers establish an expectation of the quantity they intend to eat such as cleaning the plate or eating half a portion (Raghubir and Krishna, 1999). Wansink, Painter and North (2005) compared the consumption of food between participants who received a normal-sized bowl and participants who received a self-refilling bowl – unbeknownst to the subjects the bowl refilled through a hole in the bottom of the bowl. Participants who received the self-refilling bowl consumed 73 per cent more compared to the control group with a normal bowl, underestimated the amount of calories consumed, and did not feel significantly more sated than the control group. The reliance on visual cues is automatic. Portion sizes and other visual cues play tricks on the mind leading to compulsion-driven behaviours. How, then, do each of the three main responsible actors contribute to the increase or decrease in these elements of agency? The next sections spell this out in greater detail.

Corporation and consumer agency

Corporations influence awareness and the extent of knowledge about food through activities including funding science and advocacy groups, re-framing, marketing and branding and labelling. First, while some research shows the dangers of fat-, salt- and sugar-laden food, research funded by food and beverage corporations de-emphasises unfavourable results for the food industry (Lesser et al, 2007). Second, corporations influence consumer awareness through their external and in-store marketing. Corporate advertising budgets can amount to several billion dollars (US) per year: fast-food corporations spend over US$4 billion yearly on advertisements and TV advertisement of fast-food restaurants rarely includes healthier food choices (Harris et al, 2010). While advertisement of other problematic food groups such as cereals, candy (sweets) or snacks has decreased, advertising of fast-food products has increased in recent years (Harris et al, 2010).

Corporations also influence awareness levels by re-framing the obesity epidemic. In some marketing campaigns, corporations support a more active lifestyle as a substitute, rather than a complement, for healthier food choices. While these are positive initiatives, corporations refer less frequently to alternative actions such as changing eating habits (Karnani et al, 2014). Finally, corporations influence consumer awareness of food and ingredients through their branding and labelling strategies. Kellogg, for example, changed the name of its leading brands from 'Sugar Frosted Flakes' to 'Frosted Flakes' and from 'Sugar Smacks' to 'Honey Smacks' when the critique on the high amount of sugar increased. This is not to say that food companies must eschew marketing. However, these activities illustrate how companies can decrease consumer awareness of potentially unhealthy food.

The presentation of alternatives is perhaps the most obvious area where food companies can affect consumer agency. The availability of healthier alternatives on menus and store shelves makes consumer choice relatively more autonomous. Notably, this is also the area where corporations have perhaps the least range of choice themselves. Due to space constraints on menus and shelves, executives are faced with the brute fact that consumers very often choose the less healthy one – even when health information is relatively available and understandable. This, then, leads not only to stock-outs for these more popular items, but to the healthier options spoiling. There is, at least to some degree, a tension between the agency-improving provision of healthy alternatives and the history of unpopularity of these alternatives. Besides, corporations influence food alternatives directly through their allocation of resources to research and product development. Efforts to create chemical substitutes for the harmful ingredients have not always ended profitably or pleasantly (for example, Olestra, Saccharin). Even products with reduced caloric content face criticism. Some corporations are investing in potential substitutes for saturated fat, but this research is still in its infancy (Moss, 2013).

Finally, food producers have been accused of using consumers' natural addiction to sugar and salt to their advantage. While corporations add certain ingredients like sugar, salt, fat and caffeine for flavouring, they are also said to add them to processed food because it makes consumers want more (Moss, 2013). Food processors have added caffeine to products such as soft drinks, energy drinks, potato chips, jelly beans or candy bars putatively for flavour enhancement (Brownell and Warner, 2009). Griffiths and Vernotica (2000, p 732) concluded 'the high rates of consumption of caffeinated soft drinks more likely reflect the mood-altering and physical dependence-producing effects of caffeine as a central nervous system-active drug than its subtle effects as a flavoring agent.' In addition, current corporate practice includes the optimisation of food ingredients (especially the mixture of salt, sugar and fat) to reach the so-called 'bliss point' – 'the precise amount of sweetness – no more, no less – that makes food and drink most enjoyable' (Moss, 2013, p 47). This bliss point evokes almost the same satisfaction received from some recreational drugs. At the same time, the optimal mix of ingredients can also undermine consumers' feeling of satiety. This is achieved through 'vanishing caloric density' (Moss, 2013). Food melts so quickly in the mouth that the brain does not notice any calories, leading consumers to eat more. Examples of food with vanishing caloric density are popcorn or potato chips. Vanishing caloric density coupled with people's natural tendency to rely on visual cues instead of their stomach leads to a tendency to overeat. The natural addiction to sugar and other created addictions are vulnerabilities that are beyond consumers' control. Thus, there lies more responsibility on business and governments to support consumer agency and to decrease the potential addictive effects of food and certain ingredients.

Governments and consumer agency

Like the previous actors, governments influence consumer awareness, availability of food alternatives and availability of addictive ingredients. Governments affect awareness through labelling, advertising regulations and exercising campaigns. First, governments play a prominent role in the dissemination of accurate, complete, useful and actionable information. Several governments started labelling initiatives. For example, the UK introduced the 'food traffic light' in 2006 (FSA, 2007). Finland had such a high rate of cardiovascular disease that the government decided to introduce labels for products with a high salt content. The initiative was successful and Finland's salt consumption reduced significantly (Moss, 2013). New York City has been a leader in food-related regulation, most recently introducing a salt shaker label for restaurant items with high sodium. Second, governments influence consumer awareness through their marketing and advertising regulations. Norway banned the advertisement of unhealthy food to children under 16. Ireland banned television advertisements for sweet and fast-food products, and banned the use of celebrities in advertisements for junk food targeted at children (Flanagan, 2013). The US Federal Trade Commission recently finalised voluntary guidelines regarding the advertisement of junk food to children, and recommends that food advertisements should only include food that meets nutritional standards (Nestle, 2002, 2011). Finally, governments raise awareness through exercise campaigns and similar initiatives. The US launched a 'Let's Move' campaign in 2010, and Germany introduced a similar national anti-obesity action plan that includes educating Germans about nutrition and encouraging them to engage in more physical exercise.

Governmental policies also have an effect on the set of food alternatives. Farm subsidy policies affect what is produced and in what quantity. This then influences the relative affordability of different kinds of food which, in turn, affects the affordability and economic viability of certain agricultural products and foods derived from them. US farm subsidy policies have led to an increase in corn production, as well as high-fructose corn syrup, which some have criticised as contributing to the rise in obesity (Bray et al, 2004). Second, governments can influence the availability and affordability of alternatives through tax policies. In 2016, the UK announced a new tax on sugary drinks scheduled to take effect in 2018, with the estimated £520 million in first-year proceeds going to school sports programmes. Giesen and colleagues (2011, p 389) examined the effect of tax on high-calorie foods, and concluded that 'a tax of ≥ 25% on high-calorie foods may decrease the demand for calories and could be a good policy measure to decrease the prevalence of obesity.' Such taxes can function as an incentive for consumers to abstain from buying certain products, thereby reducing unhealthy alternatives. This also has the effect of making unhealthy food more expensive, and healthier options more viable alternatives in the marketplace. Finally, some governments have introduced policies to improve the food served in schools. The US Healthy Hunger-Free Kids Act, for example, aims at adjusting school lunch offerings to include healthy alternatives for children. The German anti-obesity plan includes actions to improve the food in firm and school cafeterias.

Despite the natural compulsions toward sugar and salt, there is no explicit regulation of these as addictive ingredients. While there are no direct regulations, other regulations can have an impact on food addiction. New York's Mayor Bloomberg, for example, introduced a ban of big soda cups in restaurants. The goal of such bans is to control portion sizes and the concomitant psychological influences described previously.

Shared responsibility for obesity

This description of how consumer behaviour, corporate operations and governmental actions influence consumer agency illustrates the connections each actor has to the obesity epidemic, and the capacity of each actor to have an influence. Prior work has described the limitations of a retrospective approach to responsibility for consumption-related issues. Such issues cannot be addressed with a classic notion of responsibility that builds on causality, absolution of others, retrospective argumentation, static background conditions and a community-cosmopolitan focus. Schrempf-Stirling (2014) proposes a social connection model to corporate responsibility, and illustrates this alternative model of responsibility using obesity. This chapter extends this work by elaborating on how the network of actors can take responsibility together to re-establish consumers' agency. This section examines what consumers, governments and business can do to meet these responsibilities, as well as demonstrating the dynamism involved in rising to these capacities.

Awareness

Awareness is influenced by the time that consumers have to inform themselves about food-related issues, and by their education and ability to understand the available information. Consumers' share of responsibility involves investing reasonable time to acquire the necessary information to make conscious food choices. However, this might have its limits as consumers depend on others to provide them with the information in a clear and reasonable way. If the information is not immediately available, consumers' responsibility includes proactively demanding it.

Thus, consumers depend on corporations to provide information on food and ingredients. The argument that it is unrealistic for consumers to know as much about their food as those who produce food does not suggest that there is nothing that those producers can do to increase awareness among consumers. A clear first cut at the problem is for producers to avoid *mis*representation of information to consumers. In an experiment, over a third of consumers in a restaurant with nutrition information believed they were eating fewer calories than they actually did because other cues, such as healthy labels, misled them (Wansink and Huckabee, 2005). Consumers can be overwhelmed by nutrition tables and lack time to read and understand them. Instead, they focus more on labels such as 'low fat' or 'light.' Corporate responsibility regarding awareness goes beyond simply providing information; it involves providing information in an understandable way and avoiding any misrepresentations.

In addition to the black boxes on the sides of manufactured foods, a growing number of restaurants are providing nutritional information on their menus. However, it is possible for producers to provide too much data, thereby drowning the informational value. The key becomes providing the right bits of data that are most relevant to consumers, and providing it in ways that are comparable across products and across companies. The more consumers know, the more responsibility for their choices shifts from producers to consumers.

Governments can aid the process of providing the right information with a particular emphasis on protecting vulnerable populations. Often thought of in terms of minors, children are not the only groups who are vulnerable to potentially addictive food. Much of the research cited above suggests that consumers are *all* vulnerable. Simply because consumers are aware of the manipulative capacities of marketing techniques and the addictive qualities of certain ingredients does not necessarily mean they are immune to their agency-reducing effects.

Obviously, when it comes to awareness, the actions of consumers, corporations and governments influence each other. This illustrates the shared and interdependent responsibility aspects of agency. When governments provide some baseline as to what type of food information should be shared by corporations in what type of format, corporations will react and comply. This, then, provides consumers (ideally) with better awareness of food-related issues. This is not to say that there is a clear sequence of governments acting first and introducing rigid regulation that corporations then have to follow. Established discussions in corporate social responsibility stress that corporations have a (moral) responsibility to go beyond legal requirements and to take responsibility for issues to which they are connected (Schrempf-Stirling, 2014). Once information is available in an understandable way, it is the consumers' responsibility to use this information to make responsible food choices. Consumers can only take responsibility after other actors fulfil their obligations to support choice and agency. *Ceteris paribus*, well-informed consumers are seen as more responsible for their own decisions, with concomitant reductions in responsibility for the other actors. So, corporations' share of responsibility includes the provision of information which, in turn, reduces corporations' responsibility for obesity as they increase consumer agency for food choices. Responsibility at that moment shifts to consumers, who are then able to make more informed food choices.

Alternatives

Consumers' economic position and taste preferences can limit the set of available food alternatives. While consumers are responsible for efficiently managing their own budgets (including the food component), this is not without problems. What if there really are no affordable, healthier food options? The constraints facing consumers in food deserts (see Chapter 9, this volume), subsisting on limited budgets, underscore the need for a more nuanced understanding of shared responsibility that is sensitive to the structural challenges that mitigate consumers' responsibility.

Competitive pressures limit corporations' capacity to make and sell healthy alternatives. Often such pressures are the result of collective action problems, and the food business is extraordinarily competitive. Companies that would like to offer healthier options face the prospect that their competitors will see this as an opportunity to steal shelf space and market share. If healthier ingredients are more expensive, making healthier foods will put manufacturers at a cost disadvantage due to collective action and challenges associated with being the first companies to make these changes. Actors willing to neglect their responsibilities present competitive challenges for the entire industry.

Research and Development (R&D) efforts could also result in healthier, more economically viable, alternatives as well. Some fast-food restaurants, for example, stopped using transfats due to risks of coronary heart disease. However, in some cases, companies only stopped using transfats where such use was legally forbidden, and continue using it where such legislation does not exist.

Government regulations can help reduce potential competitive disadvantages by making it less disadvantageous to provide healthier alternatives (see the regulation on transfats) in addition to subsidy, tax and school policies. Taxes on unhealthy food that would be borne by consumers could be one way to direct consumers to different food options. Governments should also re-evaluate their subsidy policies to examine unintended consequences in food production. While introducing targeted food taxes for consumers is one way to motivate alternative food options, changing subsidy policies could push the food industry to rethink its current research and production activities. Financial incentives could motivate additional research on tastier recipes. As above, where governments and corporations work together to provide healthier food alternatives while mitigating the competitive disadvantages of doing so, consumers bear concomitantly greater responsibility for their choices.

Addiction

Given the addictive potential of specific food ingredients, consumers are restricted in their capacity to contribute to a solution. As discussed by Watson (2004), addiction makes taking responsibility difficult, if not impossible – individuals are controlled by their compulsion. In such cases, other actors have the remedial responsibility to take extra care for consumers and to avoid the exploitation of consumer addiction.

While no one can be blamed for a natural addiction, it might be morally problematic if someone uses such urges for their own advantages. Food corporations are said to design foods in ways that maximise the addiction potential so that consumers buy more of their product. In processed food in particular, high levels of salt 'have been creating a desire for salt where none existed before' (Moss, 2013, p 439).

Some corporations, such as Nestlé, have already started to reduce the amount of sugar in some of its products while maintaining taste (Moss, 2013). Other food producers have reduced portion sizes to support consumers in resisting visual cues. Reducing portion sizes will support consumers in moving from compulsive agents to stronger agents who can be held more responsible for their actions. If a consumer intentionally buys two 12-ounce soft drinks, then this decision is not driven by the visual cues present in a single 24-ounce drink cup. Where corporations voluntarily reduce portion sizes, or governments introduce portion size controls, more responsibility shifts back to the consumer, who is then less vulnerable to the visual cues trap. Portion control does not stop consumers from ordering multiple portions. With less exposure to addictive substances, limiting visual cues that call for overeating, and other inhibitors of choice and agency, consumers would (again, *ceteris paribus*) shoulder relatively more responsibility for their food choices.

Conclusion

While this book highlights various examples of how consumers are negatively affected by harmful practices along the food value chain, including food safety scandals (see Chapter 23, this volume), this chapter has elaborated on three fundamental elements that significantly influence agency in the context of food decisions: *awareness* and knowledge, the presence of *alternatives*, and *addictive* or addiction-like tendencies of human physiology and psychology. This chapter has also discussed examples of how the individual actions of consumers, corporations and governments relate to harmful, unjust and unethical food-related issues. As argued, under current conditions consumers do not have full agency to take full responsibility for obesity. Instead, corporations and governments play an active role in restoring consumer agency to make responsible food choices.

There is a sense in which consumers will never be in a position of informational parity with producers. This applies to the obesity case, but can also apply to other societal issues. This does not imply, however, that a measure of responsibility cannot be transferred from producers to consumers. Where there is more information, less vulnerability and a greater number of alternatives from which to choose, consumers should be considered, to that same degree, as having made a free choice. And, to that same degree, corporations and producers bear less responsibility for the obesity epidemic (or other societal issues). More corporate and governmental responsibility leads to a greater share of responsibility for consumers, thereby creating precisely the conditions many corporate spokespeople wish to see prevail. Responsibility can be given away by taking one's share.

References

Bray, G.A., Nielsen, S.J. and Popkin, B.M. (2004) 'Consumption of high-fructose corn syrup in beverages may play a role in the epidemic of obesity', *The American Journal of Clinical Nutrition*, vol 79, no 4, pp 537–43.

Brownell, K.D. and Warner, K.E. (2009) 'The perils of ignoring history: Big tobacco played dirty and millions died. How similar is big food?', *The Milbank Quarterly*, vol 87, no 1, pp 259–94.

CDC (Centers for Disease Control and Prevention) (2010) *Obesity rises among adults* (www.cdc.gov/vitalsigns/pdf/2010-08-vitalsigns.pdf).

Feinberg, J. (1970) *Doing and deserving: Essays in the theory of responsibility*, Princeton, NJ: Princeton University Press.

Flanagan, P. (2013) 'Junk food adverts to be banned from children's television'. *Irish Mirror*, 4 June (www.irishmirror.ie/news/irish-news/junk-food-adverts-banned-childrens-1931533).

Fletcher, G. (1999) *Basic concepts of criminal law*, Oxford: Oxford University Press.

FSA (Food Standards Agency) (2007) 'Food. Using traffic lights to make healthier choices', London: FSA (www.food.gov.uk/multimedia/pdfs/publication/foodtrafficlight1107.pdf).

Gearhardt, A.N., Corbin, W.R. and Brownell, K.D. (2009) 'Preliminary validation of the Yale food addiction scale', *Appetite*, vol 52, no 2, pp 430–6.

Giesen, J.C., Payne, C.R., Havermans, R.C. and Jansen, A. (2011) 'Exploring how calorie information and taxes on high-calorie foods influence lunch decisions', *The American Journal of Clinical Nutrition*, vol 93, no 4, pp 689–94.

Griffiths, R.R. and Vernotica, E.M. (2000) 'Is caffeine a floring agent in cola soft drinks?', *Archives of Family Medicine*, vol 9, pp 727–34.

Haomiao, J. and Lubetkin, E.I. (2010) 'Trends in quality-adjusted life-years lost contributed by smoking and obesity. Does the burden of obesity overweigh the burden of smoking?', *American Journal of Preventive Medicine*, vol 20, no 10, pp 1–7.

Harris, J.L, Schwartz, M.B. and Brownell, K.D. (2010) *Fast food F.A.C.T.S.: Food advertising to children and teens score*, Yale Rudd Center for Food Policy and Obesity.

Hill, J.O. and Trowbridge, F.L. (1997) 'Childhood obesity: Future directions and research priorities', *Pediatrics*, vol 101, no 3, pp 570–4.

Karnani, A., McFerran, B. and Mukhopadhyay, A. (2014) 'Leanwashing: A hidden factor in the obesity crisis', *California Management Review*, vol 56, no 4, pp 5–30.

Lesser, L., Ebbeling, C.B., Goozner, M., Wypij, D. and Ludwig, D.S. (2007) 'Relationship between funding source and conclusion among nutrition-related scientific articles', *PLoS Medicine*, vol 4, no 5, pp 41–6.

Malik, V.S., Schulze, M.B. and Hu, F.B. (2006) 'Intake of sugar-sweetened beverages and weight gain: A systematic review', *American Journal of Clinical Nutrition*, vol 8, no 2, pp 274–88.

Miller, D. (2001) 'Distributing responsibilities', *The Journal of Political Philosophy*, vol 9, no 4, pp 453–71.

Moss, M. (2013) *Salt sugar fat: How the food giants hooked us*, New York: Random House.

Nestle, M. (2002) *Food politics*, Berkeley, CA: University of California Press.

Nestle, M. (2011) 'New federal guidelines regulate junk food ads for kids', *The Atlantic*, 29 April (www.theatlantic.com/health/archive/2011/04/new-federal-guidelines-regulate-junk-food-ads-for-kids/238053/).

Raghubir, P. and Krishna, A. (1999) 'Vital dimensions in volume perception: Can the eye fool the stomach?', *Journal of Market Research*, vol 36, pp 313–26.

Schrempf-Stirling, J. (2014) 'A social connection approach to corporate responsibility: The case of the fast-food industry and obesity', *Business & Society*, vol 53, no 2, pp 300–32.

Wansink, B. and Huckabee, M. (2005) 'De-marketing obesity', *California Management Review*, vol 47, no 4, pp 6–18.

Wansink, B., Painter, J.E. and North, J. (2005) 'Bottomless bowls: Why visual cues of portion size may influence intake', *Obesity Research*, vol 13, no 1, pp 93–100.

Watson, G. (2004) *Agency and answerability*, Oxford: Oxford University Press.

WHO (World Health Organization) (2004) *Obesity: Preventing and managing the global epidemic*, Geneva: WHO.

WHO (2009) *Obesity and overweight*, Geneva: WHO (www.who.int/dietphysicalactivity/publications/facts/obesity/en/).

WHO (2011) 'Obesity and overweight', Fact sheet No 311, Geneva: WHO (www.who.int/mediacentre/factsheets/fs311/en/index.html).

8

The value of product sampling in mitigating food adulteration

Louise Manning and Jan Mei Soon

Introduction

Food fraud operates at many levels, for example, at global, national and/or a localised level, and spans both urban and rural criminality (Manning et al, 2016). Fraudulent activity occurs if there is recognition that there is an opportunity to make money or, alternatively, avoid loss (Schuchter and Levi, 2015, citing Coleman, 1987). Food fraud can arise in terms of the integrity of the food item, the processes used and/or the people employed or the associated data (Manning, 2016). The UK's Food Standards Agency (FSA) states that food fraud is: 'deliberately placing food on the market, for financial gain, with the intention of deceiving the consumer' (Elliott Review, 2014). Collectively, food fraud encompasses the deliberate and intentional substitution, addition, tampering or misrepresentation of food, food ingredients or food packaging; or false or misleading statements made about a product for economic gain (see Spink and Moyer, 2011a, b; Grundy et al, 2012). Further definitions have been synthesised (see Table 8.1), and these all focus on fraudulent activity and motivation in terms of deliberate intent.

Table 8.1: Definitions of food fraud

Food fraud	Source
A collective term that is driven by economic gain and encompasses the deliberate substitution, addition, tampering or misrepresentation of food, food ingredients or food packaging, or false or misleading statements made about a product	Spink and Moyer (2011a, b)
Deliberately placing food on the market, for financial gain, with the intention of deceiving the consumer	Elliott Review (2014)
Deliberate quality and/or safety problems caused by intentional behaviour of food business operators (FBOs) to gain economic profit	Tähkäpää et al (2015)
The deliberate intent to deceive, motivated by the prospect of financial gain	Hines and Murphy (2016)
The deliberate alteration of food, where a food ingredient is included for economic gain	Charlebois et al (2016)
An intentional act with motivation for economic gain	Spink et al (2015)
The intentional misrepresentation of fact by one person solely, or acting on behalf of an organisation, in order to encourage another individual erroneously to part with something of intrinsic value	Manning (2016)

The foods most vulnerable to food fraud include (see WHO, 2008):

- Foods of high value, where substituting an alternative ingredient in the food can provide significant financial gain.
- Foods associated with an ideological grouping, whereby adulteration of that food can be seen as an ideological or ethnic challenge to that group itself.
- Foods produced, manufactured and stored in readily accessible or poorly supervised areas, or where staff who are working in those areas have little awareness of the potential for food crime.
- Foods susceptible to tampering or interference where this can go undetected by the inspection and testing routinely undertaken in the food supply chain.
- Widely disseminated or distributed foods with complex interactions in the supply chain.

Similarly, a number of drivers exist that can influence the potential for food fraud: market competition and resource scarcity, power imbalance, inadequate governance, lack of sanctions and low probability of discovery, rapid development of systems, logistics and technology, data swamping and opacity (Charlebois et al, 2016; Manning, 2016; Manning et al, 2016; Marvin et al, 2016). Indeed, fraudulent practices may well go undetected by regulatory authorities and also senior management within food companies. The aim of this chapter is to consider food fraud, and specifically, food adulteration, to provide a comment on the reported prevalence of the incidence of food adulteration, and to critique the use of procedural and policy-driven countermeasures and product sampling as a countermeasure to minimise, or where possible, eliminate, food adulteration risk. This chapter looks specifically at product adulteration within the wider context of food crime (see Chapter 1, this volume) and wider notions of food supply fraud, which have such a multiplicity of motivations, outcomes and potential victims that it would be difficult to examine and critique all aspects in a single book chapter.

Adulteration

Adulteration is the specifically motivated, intentional replacement of an ingredient for economic or ideological gain (Manning and Soon, 2016, citing Lipp, 2011), and is an emerging global topic that is becoming a focus of industry, agencies and researchers (Spink et al, 2015; Black et al, 2016). Concerns over adulteration are nothing new, especially the potential of such practices to not only affect food quality, but also to cause harm (Bansal et al, 2015). The US Federal Food, Drug, and Cosmetic Act Section 342 defines adulterated food as food that bears or contains: 'any poisonous or deleterious substance which may render it injurious to health; but in case the substance is not an added substance such food shall not be considered adulterated under this clause if the quantity of such substance in such food does not ordinarily render it injurious to health.' However, the definition does not distinguish explicitly between intentional or unintentional inclusion (Manning and Soon, 2016). The US Food & Drug Administration (FDA) determine Economically Motivated Adulteration (EMA) as 'the fraudulent, intentional substitution or addition of a substance in a product for the purpose of increasing the apparent value of the product or reducing the cost of its production', that is, for economic gain (Lutter, 2009). In the food safety literature, a food hazard has been defined as 'a biological, chemical, or physical agent in, or condition of, food with the potential to cause an adverse health effect' (CAC, 2003, p 5; Wallace et al, 2011, p 65). However, current food safety vocabulary does not differentiate between intentional and unintentional contamination (Manning and Soon, 2016). PAS 96 (2014) distinguishes between a hazard and a threat in the context of food protection, namely, that a *hazard* is something that can cause loss or harm that arises from a naturally occurring or accidental event or incompetence or ignorance of the people involved – unintentional – while a *threat* is something that can cause loss or harm that arises from the ill intent of people – an intentional act.

If adulteration does not cause a health impact (noting that many adulterants can reduce or negatively impact the nutritional value of food), it may simply go unnoticed by consumers and industry alike. As only the perpetrators themselves know how the food has been adulterated (Manning and Soon, 2014), this increases the overall inherent risk associated with the adulterated product, as the threat may be unconventional and also difficult to detect (Moore et al, 2010; Spink and Moyer, 2011a; Tähkäpää et al, 2015). Further, analytical tests that have been developed to identify the presence of a 'known' adulterant may only be of limited value. Once the perpetrator(s) recognise that there is a test available that will highlight their activity, and that there is an associated testing programme in place, they can either reduce the level of adulteration to be below the limit of detection, or switch their activity to another adulterant for which there is either no analytical test available to determine its presence or where a test is available, but not routinely used in food product verification (Manning et al, 2016). This means that quantifying the prevalence of food adulteration across food groups or the food supply chain proves difficult. Concern over food authenticity and adulteration has been a major driver for establishing food regulations worldwide (Kölbener et al, 2016) and associated surveillance programmes. The *Food Law Code of Practice (England)* April (2012, p 74) states, '"Surveillance" means a careful observation of one or more food businesses, or food business operators or their activities.' Surveillance can be carried out as part of a statutory regulatory programme and/or by organisations seeking to verity the integrity of the foods they sell. Following the recommendations of the Elliott Review (2014), in the UK, the FSA National Food Crime Unit (NFCU) was created to help ensure that prevention measures are put in place to protect consumers from illicit activity associated with food, including adulteration. The associated UK Food Fraud database serves as an important source of intelligence and as a tool to detect emerging patterns of fraudulent and criminal activities (FSA, 2016a, b). In 2011, there were 54 complaints, in 2012, 81 complaints, and in 2013, 134 complaints, of which one was related to adulteration and another to authenticity (Elliot Review, 2014).

Prevalence of types of food adulteration or fraud in the RASFF database

There are two publically available databases that contain information on the incidence of detected food fraud and adulteration: in the European Union (EU), the Rapid Alert System for Food and Feed (RASFF), and in the US, the Economically Motivated Adulteration (EMA) incidents database. Chapter 14 of this book considers the operation of the RASFF database in more detail, and how it facilitates a transnational networked response to food fraud, sharing the burden of regulatory activity and the monitoring of food that has failed to enter the EU at one border point and then is presented for entry elsewhere. The EMA database utilises eight categorisations of food fraud: substitution, dilution, artificial enhancement, counterfeit, transshipment or origin masking, mislabelling, intentional distribution of a contaminated product, and theft and resale (US Food Production and Defense Institute, 2016), all of which could be said to be associated with food processing and the representation of food. There are six food fraud categories in the RASFF database: improper, fraudulent, missing or absent health certificate; illegal or unauthorised import, trade or transit; adulteration, fraud or tampering; improper, expired, fraudulent or missing common entry document (CED), import declaration or analytical report; expiration date; and mislabelling (Bouzembrak and Marvin, 2015).

Analysis of RASFF fraud notifications, from 2002 through and including 2015, identifies fraud linked to products as follows: fish and seafood products (17.4%), nuts (16.4%), meat and meat products (16%), and fruit and vegetables (8%). Marvin et al (2016) studied 1,686 records from the RASFF and EMA systems in their research, and their Bayesian Network model used combined data from the RASFF and EMA databases, suggesting that 'tampering' occurs with the highest probability (35.9%), followed by 'health certificate issues' (27.6%), 'illegal importation' (18.3%), 'origin labelling' (11.6%), 'CED' (4%), 'expiration date' (1.7%) and 'theft and resale' (0.8%). It should be noted that the type of sampling that gives rise to this data may in itself influence data distribution, as the sampling is purposive and not random (Eurostat, 2010), and includes: *routine surveillance sampling*, where samples are taken to check compliance levels in line with regulatory sampling plans; *statutory sampling*, where the frequency of samples is prescribed in law for a selection of materials/products identified within the EU-designated points of entry (for example, ports) for imported food and feed; and *suspect sampling or enforcement related sampling*, where samples are taken as part of ongoing investigations and there is a 'snowball effect'. Thus, as the sampling from which these results are derived is neither random nor of a high frequency, interpretations of RASFF and EMA statistics require caution in terms of how representative the results are in terms of the food supply chain as a whole. Wright et al (2014) determine that:

- for a 0.1% rate of unsatisfactory results, a sample of 4,500 analyses has a 99% likelihood of detecting one or more non-compliant item
- for a 1% rate of unsatisfactory results, a sample of 500 analyses has a 99% likelihood of detecting one or more non-compliant item
- for a 10% rate of unsatisfactory results, a sample of 50 analyses has a 99% likelihood of detecting one or more non-compliant item.

Regulatory sampling programmes are simply not at the sampling frequency where such confidence limits are met, which means that some have suggested that other than as a verification activity this type of purposive sampling is of limited value. Ultimately due to this limitation, the effectiveness of regulatory food sampling for identifying food adulteration is minimal. This means that to be effective, regulatory sampling programmes must be coupled with a formal risk assessment approach that is updated on a regular basis as a result of emerging or changing information, so that sampling is appropriately targeted. While there are advantages to targeted sampling, the data obtained must be interpreted carefully in light of how it relates to actual levels of non-conformity in the wider supply chain. Further, the food industry should develop protocols for the internal reporting and management of potential instances of adulteration, as resolving potential fraudulent practices internally can prevent or reduce loss of profit, reputation and ultimately maintain customer and consumer trust.

The trends in the number of fraud/adulteration incidents recorded are influenced by a range of factors including specific incidents such as the 2013 horsemeat incident and changes in legislation that led to a change in statutory sampling and subsequently a rise in the number of incidents identified after statutory sampling commenced. Legislative requirements can require statutory sampling from a given date (such as with food contact materials). Two notifications of non-compliance were reported in 2011 followed by 17 notifications between 2012–15 after the implementation of the Commission Regulation (EU) No 284/2011 of 22 March 2011, laying down specific conditions and detailed procedures for the import of polyamide and melamine plastic kitchenware originating in or consigned from the People's Republic of China and Hong Kong Special Administrative Region, China.

Prior to 2011 there was no incidence of non-conformity reported, but once statutory requirements were introduced, non-conformity was subsequently identified. This doesn't mean that there was necessarily no previous non-conformity; it may well have occurred and have simply gone undetected, so it is important not to make such assumptions when non-conformity has not been assessed. In the same way, when Commission Implementing Regulation (EU) No 506/2011 of 23 May 2011, amending Regulation (EU) No 297/2011 imposing special conditions governing the import of feed and food originating in or consigned from Japan following the accident at the Fukushima nuclear power station, was introduced, this gave rise to associated incidents of imported product non-conformity that had not been previously recorded. These are two examples of how changes to regulatory sampling requirement can lead to trends appearing in the level of non-conformity. Incidents such as the horsemeat incident in 2013 can give rise to a spike in the number of incidents reported, as 81 cases were due to adulteration of food with horsemeat. Fifty-five of the horsemeat incidents were found in the meat and meat products (including poultry) category, while 26 were reported in prepared dishes and snacks. The other 52 per cent of fraud/adulteration incidents were due to mislabelling, illegal trade and others, such as an absence of declaration of compliance, fraudulent health certificate and absence of a certified analytical report.

In February 2013, notifications with regard to horsemeat were first received into the RASFF database from Ireland. As the notifications increased over time, more reports came in from other member states. Further, the presence of medication was noted in a number of products ($n=4$), showing the potential health risk to consumers of this fraudulent adulteration practice. Thus it can be concluded that the current supply chain process and documentation-based countermeasures such as certification of processes to third party system standards and verification through audit and low-level product testing are wholly inadequate to address illicit practices and levels of food adulteration. Further, risk-based sampling is also of limited use for as yet unknown adulteration risks. This means that new countermeasure approaches such as strengthened whistleblowing channels and other intelligence-gathering measures are crucial to minimising risk and underpinning a risk-based sampling approach.

Countermeasures: mechanisms to control intentional food adulteration

Food criminals are clandestine, stealthy and actively seek to avoid detection (Spink and Moyer, 2011b), and such criminal activity is covert, entrepreneurial and opportunist, making the development of risk mitigation strategies at organisational, supply chain and global levels difficult (Manning, 2016). The use of a pre-requisite programme to minimise and, where possible, eliminate the likelihood of a food safety incident is well established through the hazard analysis critical control point (HACCP) approach. Spink et al (2015) assert that in an existing food control programme the formal systems and procedures are developed to meet the requirements of good manufacturing practice (GMP), good hygienic practice (GHP) and food safety and quality control. Conversely, the protocol for the development of a countermeasures programme to minimise or eliminate the likelihood of a food adulteration incident is not as well formalised. EMA prevention can leverage well-established tools such as Six Sigma and HACCP methodologies (Moyer et al, 2017), and the use of threat analysis critical control point (TACCP) methodologies such as PAS 96.

However, the food industry is playing 'catch-up' in adopting such prevention practices at the processing stage and introducing appropriate countermeasures. Countermeasures developed to minimise food adulteration risk include: the use of unique serial numbers at batch, product or lot level; traceability through measures such as radio frequency identification devices (RFID); and features on the packaging of individual items such as special inks, holograms and so on, in cases of a product or on each pallet (Spink et al, 2010; Manning and Soon, 2016). EMA countermeasures fall into five distinct categories (Spink et al, 2016):

- *Detect*: Identifying the opportunity for EMA by assessing the points along the food chain where vulnerabilities exist using a HACCP or TACCP-style approach.
- *Monitor*: Mapping food chains and using techniques such as hotspot analysis. Hotspots are points in the food supply chain that are vulnerable to EMA. The term 'horizon scanning' describes the systematic way of assessing the degree of protection against potential EMA threats to ensure that there is effective control at organisational and supply chain levels. Appropriate ongoing surveillance needs to be implemented along the supply chains.

- *Deter*: Ensure that penalties for EMA are dissuasive and act as a sufficient deterrent (Spink et al, 2016).
- *Prevent*: Persuade the fraudster to not even try to commit EMA or attack the system.
- *Disrupt*: In some cases, the fraudsters cannot be brought to justice, but the EMA itself must be disrupted (Spink et al, 2016). Moyer et al (2017) reflect that detection and deterrence countermeasures must operate in consort, for example, appropriate process controls must be integrated with product testing.

Hurdles including process and product monitoring and verification activities (including audits and product testing) are formal system components that reduce the opportunity for food adulteration by either assisting detection or proving to be a deterrent (Spink et al, 2015), and form part of an effective countermeasures programme along with awareness training and refresher training when new threats are identified. Therefore, effective countermeasures reduce criminal opportunity (Spink et al, 2015), and will not only lessen the impact of an incident, but, if suitably implemented, will also make intentional adulteration less likely in the first place (Mitenius et al, 2014).

During processing, the risk of adulteration can be minimised by limiting accessibility by process design, which may include covered conveyors, use of sight glasses, zoning (place), use of cameras and fingerprint technology, and codes and passwords to gain access. Creating a buddy system so that workers in high-risk processes such as when using expensive ingredients are not allowed to work alone, stock control measures, password protection of computer terminals and electronic process management systems are all of value. With regard to marketing controls to reduce the risk of adulteration, countermeasures to consider include product substitution profit assessments; suppliers' ranking and ongoing performance monitoring; credit checks on suppliers and determination of their financial position; monitoring of individuals in supplier organisations, noting staff changeover in key roles; assessments to determine the likelihood of adulteration detection, potential severity and impact should it occur; and assessment of the effectiveness of preventive countermeasures and other factors that influence the risk of food fraud such as history of occurrences, seasonality and market prices.

Conclusion

The process sampling activities used within second party audits and third party certification audits, to demonstrate compliance with legal and market requirements, are constrained by the scope of the standards, the time available, planned frequency of verification activities, the volume of data to be assessed and any planned or unplanned sampling bias, meaning that EMA often goes unverified, and there is currently little integration of independent third party certification audits with emerging supply chain intelligence (Manning, 2013; Manning and Soon, 2014). Product sampling is of value as a countermeasure in determining and eliminating EMA, when it forms part of a product positive release control system, and only then if sampling levels provide sufficient confidence in the results. Sampling activities to address the potential for EMA can only be considered as a monitoring activity if the results are received while the product is still under the control of the manufacturer or processor. Otherwise, product sampling can only ever be a verification or surveillance activity. Further validation processes must ensure that the product testing protocols undertaken are reliable, representative and give meaningful results that represent the batch being tested.

The use of countermeasures in the food supply chain as a means for food fraud/adulteration control and ways to minimise risk of occurrence have been discussed, but procedural and policy-driven countermeasures in isolation are of limited value unless they are combined with appropriate product testing protocols. Traceability protocols suggest that given foods and/or component parts can be tracked and traced at least one step forward and one step back, and in some cases from field to fork. Traceability processes can provide consumers with assurance as to the source, safety and authenticity of the food. However, this countermeasure relies on data and people integrity, and is not without its vulnerabilities in terms of EMA control and elimination. Traceability systems are challenged by the inability to link information and/or data across the food chain, the inaccuracy of, and errors in, documentation, which lead to an inability to access essential data (Badia-Melis et al, 2015). Further concepts of provenance include extrinsic value cues such as geographic origin and method of production, and EMA is a risk with provenance-orientated food products where identity preservation is undermined by adulteration.

While third party standards at the stages of farming and manufacturing are being revised to include audit criteria for ensuring that risk assessment processes have been put in place, assessing food adulteration and other instances of food crime risk, the subsequent managing, mitigating and communicating of food crime risk effectively to employees requires additional operational and strategic management mechanisms. Indeed, the nature of a food, or food ingredient, being in some way illicit can be a transient characteristic. While one action undertaken by a perpetrator may be unlawful – such as the adulteration of a food ingredient that is then used within a composite food product – within the wider context of a series of multiple lawful actions that then occur, it may be difficult to identify the exact illicit action that has occurred. Procedural and policy-driven countermeasures and/or traditional process controls alone will not give sufficient protection against food adulteration; instead, additional measures such as risk-based product testing, responsive surveillance and verification mechanisms that are underpinned by real-time supply chain intelligence also need to be in place. This requires food supply chain leaders and managers to first, recognise the risk of food adulteration associated with their organisations and products, and second, to demonstrate competence, not only in risk characterisation, risk assessment and risk mitigation, but also in risk communication, and to understand the pressures and drivers of potential food adulteration in the first place.

References

Badia-Melis, R., Mishra, P. and Ruiz-Garcia, L. (2015) 'Food traceability: New trends and recent advances. A review', *Food Control*, vol 57, pp 393–401.

Bansal, S., Singh, A., Mangal, M., Mangal, A.K. and Kumar, S. (2015) 'Food adulteration: Sources, health risks and detection method', *Critical Reviews in Food Science and Nutrition*, vol 57, no 6, pp 1174–89.

Black, C., Chevallier, O.P. and Elliott, C.T. (2016) 'The current and potential applications of ambient mass spectrometry in detecting food fraud', *TrAC: Trends in Analytical Chemistry*, vol 82, pp 268–78.

Bouzembrak, Y. and Marvin, H.J.P. (2015) 'Prediction of food fraud type using data from Rapid Alert System for Food and Feed (RASFF) and Bayesian network modelling', *Food Control*, vol 61, pp 180–7.

CAC (Codex Alimentarius Commission) (2003) 'Hazard analysis and critical control point (HACCP) system and guidelines for its application', Codex Alimentarius Commission Food Hygiene Basic Texts (Revision 4) (www.codexalimentarius.org).

Charlebois, S., Schwab, A., Henn, R. and Huck, C.W. (2016) 'Food fraud: An exploratory study for measuring consumer perception towards mislabeled food products and influence on self-authentication intentions', *Trends in Food Science & Technology*, vol 50, pp 211–18.

Coleman, J.W. (1987) 'Toward an integrated theory of white-collar crime', *American Journal of Sociology*, vol 93, no 2, pp 406–39.

Commission Regulation (EU) No 284/2011 of 22 March 2011 laying down specific conditions and detailed procedures for the import of polyamide and melamine plastic kitchenware originating in or consigned from the People's Republic of China and Hong Kong Special Administrative Region, China (http://eur-lex.europa.eu/legal-content/EN/ALL/?uri=CELEX:32011R0284).

Commission Implementing Regulation (EU) No 506/2011 of 23 May 2011 amending Regulation (EU) No 297/2011 imposing special conditions governing the import of feed and food originating in or consigned from Japan following the accident at the Fukushima nuclear power station (http://eur-lex.europa.eu/legal-content/EN/TXT/?uri=CELEX%3A32011R0506).

Elliott Review (2014) *Elliott Review into the integrity and assurance of food supply networks – Final report: A national food crime prevention framework*, London: HM Government, July.

Eurostat (2010) *Typology of sampling strategies*, Eurostat European Commission, Working group 'Food Safety Statistics', May (https://circabc.europa.eu/sd/d/2fc47bd9-237a-4c79-93e0-6a4665cf3591/201_Typology_sampling_strategies.pdf).

Food Law Code of Practice (England) April (2012) (www.food.gov.uk/sites/default/files/multimedia/pdfs/codeofpracticeeng.pdf).

FSA (Food Standards Agency) (2016a) 'Whistleblowing' (www.food.gov.uk/enforcement/the-national-food-crime-unit/foodfraud/whistleblowing).FSA (2016b) 'Reporting food fraud' (www.food.gov.uk/enforcement/the-national-food-crime-unit/foodfraud).

Grundy, H.H., Kelly, S.D., Charlton, A.J., Donarski, J.A., Hird, S.J. and Collins, M.J. (2012) 'Food authenticity and food fraud research: Achievements and emerging issues', *Journal of the Association of Public Analysts*, vol 40, pp 65–8.

Hines, T. and Murphy, L. (2016) 'Combatting food fraud with intelligent due diligence', *World Food Regulation Review*, vol 25, no 8, p 20.

Kölbener, P., Bieri, S. and St-Gallen, C. (2016) 'Food fraud and adulteration, a centuries-old practice', *CHIMIA International Journal for Chemistry*, vol 70, no 5, p 318.

Lipp, M. (2011) 'A closer look at chemical contamination', *Food Safety Magazine*, August/September (www.foodsafetymagazine.com/magazine-archive1/augustseptember-2011/a-closer-look-at-chemical-contamination/).

Lutter, R. (2009) 'Addressing challenges of economically motivated adulteration' (www.fda.gov/downloads/newsevents/meetingsconferencesworkshops/ucm163631.ppt).

Manning, L. (2013) 'Development of a food safety verification risk model', *British Food Journal*, vol 115, no 4, pp 575–89.

Manning, L. (2016) 'Food fraud, policy and food chain', Current Opinions in Food Science, vol 10, pp 16–21.

Manning, L. and Soon, J.M. (2014) 'Developing systems to control food adulteration', *Food Policy*, vol 49, no 1, pp 23–32.

Manning, L. and Soon, J.M. (2016) 'Food safety, food fraud, and food defense: A fast evolving literature', *Journal of Food Science*, vol 81, no 4, pp R823–R834.

Manning, L., Smith, R. and Soon, J.M. (2016) 'Developing an organizational typology of criminals in the meat supply chain', *Food Policy*, vol 59, pp 44–54

Marvin, H.J., Bouzembrak, Y., Janssen, E.M., van der Fels-Klerx, H.J., van Asselt, E.D. and Kleter, G.A. (2016) 'A holistic approach to food safety risks: Food fraud as an example', *Food Research International*, vol 89, pp 463–70.

Mitenius, N., Kennedy, S.P. and Busta, F.F. (2014) 'Food defense', in Y. Motarjemi and H. Lelieveld (eds) *Food safety management: A practical guide for the food industry*, Cambridge, MA: Academic Press, pp 937–58.

Moore, J.C., DeVries, J.W., Lipp, M., Griffiths, J.C. and Abernethy, D.R. (2010) 'Total protein methods and their potential to reduce the risk of food protein adulteration', *Comprehensive Reviews in Food Science and Food Safety*, vol 9, pp 330–57

Moyer, D.C., DeVries, J.W. and Spink, J. (2017) 'The economics of a food fraud incident – Case studies and examples including melamine in wheat gluten', *Food Control*, vol 71, pp 358–64.

PAS 96 (2014) *Guide to protecting and defending food and drink from deliberate attack*, BSI, London.

RASFF database (http://ec.europa.eu/food/safety/rasff_en).

Schuchter, A. and Levi, M. (2015) 'Beyond the fraud triangle: Swiss and Austrian elite fraudsters', *Accounting Forum*, vol 39, pp 176–87.

Spink, J. (2011) 'The challenge of intellectual property enforcement for agriculture technology transfers, additives, raw materials, and finished goods against product fraud and counterfeiters', *Journal of Intellectual Property Rights*, vol 16, no 2, pp 183–93.

Spink, J. and Moyer, D.C. (2011a) 'Defining the public health threat of food fraud', *Journal of Food Science*, vol 76, no 9, pp R157–R163.

Spink, J. and Moyer, D. C. (2011b) 'Types of counterfeiters and counterfeiting', Paper presented at the School of Criminal Justice, 75th Anniversary Symposium.

Spink, J., Helferich, O.K. and Griggs, J.E. (2010) 'Combating the impact of product counterfeiting', *Distribution Business Management Journal*, vol 10, no 1, pp 59–63.

Spink, J., Moyer, D.C. and Whelan, P. (2016) 'The role of the public private partnership in food fraud prevention – includes implementing the strategy', *Current Opinion in Food Science*, vol 10, pp 68–75.

Spink, J., Moyer, D.C., Park, H., Wu, Y., Fersht, V., Shao, B. and Edelev, D. (2015) 'Introducing food fraud including translation and interpretation to Russian, Korean, and Chinese languages', *Food Chemistry*, vol 189, pp 102–7.

Tähkäpää, S., Maijala, R., Korkeala, H. and Nevas, M. (2015) 'Patterns of food frauds and adulterations reported in the EU Rapid Alert System for Food and Feed and in Finland', *Food Control*, vol 47, pp 175–84.

US Federal Food, Drug and Cosmetic Act, Section 342 (www.law. cornell.edu/uscode/pdf/uscode21/lii_usc_TI_21_CH_9_SC_IV_ SE_342.pdf).

US Food Protection and Defense Institute (2016) *Economically Motivated Adulteration (EMA) and Intentional Adulteration (IA) Incidents Database* (https://foodprotection.umn.edu/innovations/food-fraudema).

Wallace, C.A., Sperber, W.H. and Mortimore, S.E. (2011) *Managing HACCP and food safety through the global supply chain*, Oxford: Wiley Blackwell.

WHO (World Health Organization) (2008) *Terrorist threats to food. Guidance for establishing and strengthening prevention and response systems*, Food Safety Issues Series, Geneva: WHO.

Wright, M., Ibrahim, F., Manning, L. and McKellar, D. (2014) *Research to explore the current and historic trends in food sampling with particular reference to sampling and surveillance undertaken by local authorities and port health authorities*, FSA project (www.food.gov.uk/sites/default/ files/870-1-1613_GSB_CL2729_Effectiveness_of_sampling_main_ report_R6_V3_ADCR.pdf).

9

Prohibitive property practices: The impact of restrictive covenants on the built food environment

Sugandhi del Canto and Rachel Engler-Stringer

Introduction

Opportunities to obtain food are influenced by physical, socio-cultural, economic and policy factors at both micro and macro levels, the constellation of which is broadly referred to as the food environment. The retail food environment can be characterised by physical attributes such as the density, diversity and distribution of food stores within an area, often at the neighbourhood or census tract level (Glanz et al, 2005). When food environments are assessed in terms of access to nutritious foods, it is these geography-based metrics – density, diversity and distribution – that are examined in terms of where supermarkets (proxies for access to more nutritious foods) and convenience stores (proxies for less nutritious food access) are located, and extrapolated to the overall 'healthfulness' of a neighbourhood food environment. Proximity to a supermarket, and thereby proximity to a wider array of foods, is often considered a positive feature of a neighbourhood, while the absence of a supermarket, or the ubiquity of convenience stores, is perceived as a negative neighbourhood feature (Cameron et al, 2010).

These features of the retail food environment are but one aspect of the broader food environment, focusing on the choice, availability and cost of food within, and among, food outlets. Research strongly suggests that the structure and organisation of the neighbourhood or community food environment might influence food purchasing patterns and, subsequently, diet-related health outcomes (Thompson et al, 2013; Richardson et al, 2014). The rise in adverse nutrition-related health conditions now seen at a population level – such as cardiovascular disease, diabetes and obesity – is now well understood to be a combination of individual and environmental-level influences (Larson et al, 2009). Individual factors include genetics and eating behaviour; environmental factors include, among others, public policy and corporate practices. Increasingly, food environment research focuses on environmental factors to uncover the broad socioeconomic mechanisms that have led to population-level shifts in health outcomes. Although studies exploring behaviour and consumption patterns among individuals were the focus of much research in the past, it is these environmental-level factors and their influence on the social determinants of health that are of increasing interest to food environment researchers (Egger and Swinburn, 1997). Emphasis on environmental factors may be based on considerations that it is more sustainable and cost-effective to change food and activity spaces rather than the behaviour of the broader population (Kurtz, 2013).

A poor diet, one that is nutrient-poor but calorie-rich, is usually characterised by low intakes of fruit and vegetables (Aggarwal et al, 2014). One measure that is used to estimate a community's level of produce intake is residential proximity to a supermarket. Supermarkets and large chain grocery stores are the food store types that carry the widest range of produce, at more affordable prices, when compared to other food store types. The assumption, then, is that neighbourhood or community-level proximity to sources of fruits and vegetables is related to the purchase and consumption of fruits and vegetables (Lotoski et al, 2015). Residential proximity of a supermarket is quite limited as a measure, since it assumes physical access means there are no other significant barriers (such as financial means or cultural appropriateness of food available). However, as the most common source of healthy food in North America, supermarkets are used in this chapter (as it is in much of the literature on this topic) as a proxy for access to nutritious foods (Lamichhane et al, 2013).

In the US, there is extensive evidence of food store disparities in racialised and lower socioeconomic neighbourhoods. Across numerous studies, there is a marked difference in the price, quality and availability of nutritious foods in neighbourhoods of differing socioeconomic status, with lower access and affordability documented in low socioeconomic status communities (Walker et al, 2010). These studies vary in the degree to which differences exist between neighbourhoods, but point to inversely proportional relationships between socioeconomic status and access to healthy foods (Sobal and Bisogni, 2009). A 2007 study found that in wealthier, predominantly white, American neighbourhoods, the ratio of grocery stores to residents was 1:3,816; in US neighbourhoods of lower socioeconomic status, which tend to have higher proportions of black and Latino residents, the ratio was a disturbing 1:23,582 (Morland and Filomena, 2007). A similar study that same year found that poor neighbourhoods have fewer supermarkets – up to 75 per cent fewer than middle-income neighbourhoods (Powell et al, 2007).

The food environments that exist in cities in North America (and in wealthy, and less wealthy, countries around the world) are the result of decades of *action by business interests* seeking ever-increasing profitability within the food system, as well as of *inaction by government* in regulating these interests, even when actions by business are not in the best interests of people (Winson, 2013). This is an issue of food justice, which is aimed at ensuring that both the benefits of and problems with the food system are distributed evenly (Gottlieb and Joshi, 2010). One of the key principles of food justice is equal access to the benefits of healthy food (Alkon and Agyeman, 2011). Food injustice exists currently in retail food access when high-quality, nutritious food (and choice overall) is available in more affluent, urban neighbourhoods while, in contrast, low-income and often racialised neighbourhoods are left with some of the least healthy food sources available, the result of the pursuit of ever-increasing profit (Alkon and Agyeman, 2011).

This chapter provides an overview of how built food environments have changed over time in urban and suburban settings, with a particular focus on the role and impact of restrictive covenants, or land sale prohibitions, as a specific form of food injustice. These restrictions are a corporate real estate practice that places conditions, or land sale caveats, on the future uses of the land being sold – namely, prohibiting the sale of certain products or the development of certain store formats. Such restrictions are a significant barrier to the opening of new supermarkets and become especially problematic in areas already lacking access to nutritious foods. These restrictions disadvantage smaller or independent grocers, reduce competition and, ultimately, concentrate the wealth among a small handful of large corporate supermarket chains. These unethical practices prioritise a corporation's 'right' to reduce retail competition over a person's right to access nutritious food. Examples in this chapter examine the impact of restrictive covenants and how communities have tried to address the resulting inequities. The chapter concludes with a summary of promising approaches to curtail the effects of restrictive covenants and thereby contribute to food justice.

Suburbanisation and the built food environment

The built environment can be understood in terms of physical design, land use patterns (residential, commercial, office, industrial and other activities) and transportation systems (Feng et al, 2010). The built environment consists of the neighbourhoods, roads, buildings, food sources and recreation facilities in which people live, work, are educated, eat and play (Glanz et al, 2007). Mixed land use, connected streets and moderate-to-high population density encourage pedestrian traffic and promote a sense of cohesion and community in neighbourhoods, and such community-promoting features are often lacking from car-dependent food environments (Handy and Clifton, 2001). Grid patterns, pavements and developed public transit are more often found together in older areas of cities, which tend to have a higher density and diversity of building use (Townshend and Lake, 2009). These neighbourhoods were built and developed before the widespread use of personal vehicles, resulting in more pedestrian and cyclist-friendly neighbourhood design. As cities have grown, suburban development has resulted in a design that is significantly more car-dependent, less people-friendly and less encouraging of physical activity overall (Hallett and McDermott, 2011). In line with such changes, supermarkets are increasingly moving to the periphery of cities, where land is cheaper and more abundant. People living in suburban areas, who are more likely to own vehicles due to the car-dependent nature of their neighbourhood's design, are less affected by the out-migration of food stores away from the city centre than those without vehicles (Cummins and Macintyre, 2006).

The last three to four decades have seen considerable fluctuation in food retail environments, with low-income areas experiencing more retail changes (Pothukuchi, 2005; Zenk et al, 2005; Filomena et al, 2013). The food retail trend is moving toward ever bigger stores, particularly in rapidly sprawling cities (Ziff, 2016). Low-income individuals and families are more often affected by their neighbourhood's built environment because they are more likely to be constrained by transportation costs and opportunities for mobility

(Handy and Clifton, 2001; Lytle, 2009). The cost of food increases when transportation costs are factored into travelling to and from grocery stores, such as fuel for a vehicle or money for public transit fares. As supermarkets move further away from city centres and towards the outskirts, where larger tracts of land are more cheaply available, urban dwellers may pay up to 30 per cent more than suburban residents to shop at a supermarket when transportation is taken into account. One must also consider the difference in time between travelling by personal vehicle versus public methods of transport, such as bus or subway. Public transport, in particular, can take significantly longer, depending on distance and time of day (Larsen and Gilliland, 2008).

A *food desert* is a geographic area, or neighbourhood, where affordable and nutritious foods are unavailable, particularly in low socioeconomic status neighbourhoods and communities (Apparicio et al, 2007). Comparably, a *food swamp* is an area of low socioeconomic status with high geographic access to non-nutritious food sources (Spence et al, 2009). In a *food mirage*, there may be a number of grocery stores in the area but, if prices are high, nutritious foods are inaccessible to those with low incomes, which is a common situation in rapidly gentrifying neighbourhoods (Breyer and Voss-Andreae, 2013). These concepts evoke a familiar geographic metaphor that suggests complex socio-spatial processes (Kurtz, 2013), and are useful tools to discuss issues related to food security and food choice. Food deserts and food swamps can co-exist, where neighbourhoods may lack supermarkets but are awash in convenience stores (del Canto et al, 2015). Such areas may be better described as nutrition deserts, since these areas lack access to healthy foods, not necessarily food options altogether (Kurtz, 2013).

In larger US cities, economic segregation became more prominent with more affluent households emigrating from cities to suburban areas between 1970 and 1988, causing the median income in those cities to decrease and contributing to nearly one-half of the supermarkets in the three largest US cities closing (Walker et al, 2010). Other reasons for such closures are the growth in the larger format grocery store during this time, and the consolidation of stores by large grocery chains. Large chain supermarkets on the outskirts of cities, often in more affluent areas, offer consumers better quality, variety and prices for a wider array of food options. These suburban venues tend to have longer business hours and better parking options that are attractive to consumers (Cummins and Macintyre, 2006). The expansion of these supermarkets has often meant that smaller, independent, neighbourhood grocery stores cannot compete and have been forced to close, thereby creating areas where affordable, varied food is accessible only to those with access to a car, or those able to pay public transport costs and carry food home (Larsen and Gilliland, 2008). In poorer neighbourhoods, which often lack large chain grocery stores and, by extension, access to cheaper food resulting from economies of scale, residents find themselves paying a higher price for food in non-chain grocery stores or convenience stores (Chung and Myers, 1999). One might then define a food desert as a geographic area where high competition from large chain food stores has created a void (Kurtz, 2013).

Another important factor that makes the establishment of businesses in inner cities less desirable are zoning laws (Cameron et al, 2010). It is difficult in urban areas for large supermarkets to find land that is appropriate for the size of the store, due to fragmentation of property that results from the ease of selling smaller pieces of land (Pothukuchi, 2005). Arguably, urban nutrition deserts should have a competitive advantage as sites for a supermarket due to their prime locations near city centres, ability to address an unmet demand and access to a large labour force. However, the trade-off of higher real estate prices and delivery costs for prime locations override these favourable characteristics, deterring retailers from establishing in urban areas (Cameron et al, 2010).

Restrictive covenants

Restrictive covenants have received some attention in recent years as cities try to improve access to healthy food in their city centres and particularly in low-income neighbourhoods (Stolte, 2012; Theobald, 2013). Edmonton, a city where much of the Canadian media attention on these covenants has been focused, has at least 14 documented grocery store locations where these covenants exist (Cameron et al, 2010). A restrictive covenant is an aspect of property law that places limitations on what the buyer of that property can do with it (Cameron et al, 2010). In the past, restrictive covenants were most notorious for having been used to restrict people of various ethnic backgrounds from buying property in particular neighbourhoods. More recently, restrictive covenants have been applied by businesses to reduce corporate competition (Competition Commission, 2007).

A restrictive covenant must be negative in its obligations, meaning that it prohibits rather than requires something in the positive, such as doing something specific with a piece of property (Ziff, 2016). There are other, more technical, legal requirements (that it must be intended to 'run with the land', and that the buyer must know that it is part of the property agreement, for instance), but an important element of a restrictive covenant is that the restriction can only continue to exist while land changes hands if it benefits some other identified property. Often that identified property is nearby, but 'nearby' is defined fairly broadly and subject to interpretation. For instance, a large chain may have several stores in an area, and the restrictive covenant on one site could remain in place as long as the other 'nearby' stores of the same chain are open for business.

In a legal text on property law where restrictive covenants exist, Ziff (2016) explains how covenants allow owners to place a 'potentially indelible' mark on large areas of land. A single owner may retain only one small parcel of land transferred away, but can control the fate of many parcels for an indefinite period of time. Noting that restrictive covenants are extraordinarily durable, he suggests that they may last indefinitely, if carefully tended to (Ziff, 2016). He describes this as a 'scorched earth' policy when it comes to grocery chain development in a city over time. He also argues that covenants are considered to be valid by legal scholars except for problems with the way proximity is defined, specifically, that these designations are too vague. Generally, courts would only exercise the power to annul a restrictive covenant if the benefits of removing it far outweigh the potential harm to business interests, due to the risk of a grocery chain seeking compensation for the government's interventions.

While restrictive covenants generally apply to the prohibition of supermarket development, such covenants can also restrict a certain portion of sales related to food, or limit the floor space dedicated to the sale of the prohibited items. Known as *exclusivity arrangements*, a supermarket agrees not to allow another grocery store to operate from the same site, or restricts or limits the sale of groceries by parties other than the supermarket on that site. Unsurprisingly, these arrangements can be confusing to navigate. An example in White City, US, includes a restrictive covenant in which the:

> Landlord further covenants and agrees not to permit or suffer any property located within the shopping center to be used for or occupied by any business dealing in or which shall keep in stock or sell for off-premises consumption any staple or fancy groceries, meats, fish, vegetables, fruits, bakery goods, dairy products or frozen foods. Except the sale of such items is not to exceed the lesser of 500 square feet of sales area or 10% of the square foot area of any storeroom within the shopping center, as [an] incidental

only to the conduct of another business shall not be deemed a violation hereof. (Schoenmeyer et al, 2014, p 14)

Restrictive covenants are a significant barrier to establishing a new store in an older area. The patterns seen in Canada, the UK and US are that once a grocery store moves out, another rarely moves back in. The consequences are interconnected: when food stores act as anchors in a community shopping area, their closure can lead to a loss of neighbourhood-level identity and history. Restrictive covenants make the site more difficult to sell and are a barrier to revitalisation efforts. Ultimately, vacant property contributes to negative perceptions and crime due to vandalism and poor property maintenance. When land sits vacant for long periods of time, it becomes a visual blight that detracts future investors from opening another grocery store, and a community goes longer than necessary before another grocery store *might* open. A case in Chicago, US, highlights this:

> We started to do a little research into the detrimental effect of these restrictions – what we see in Chicago is there are really a limited number of locations where you can site a large grocery store because of available land, and as you start to take those properties out of the market due to restrictions, it's not unreasonable to believe that at some point you're going to run out of opportunities. What also concerned us was seeing what was left. Almost always, these stores sat vacant for a longer period of time than the market might have dictated if another grocery store were allowed to move in. (Springer, 2005, p 6)

Beyond reducing the vibrancy of a neighbourhood, restrictive covenants arguably reduce access to healthy food choices by limiting the amount of food that can be sold in the site of a former grocery store (Cameron et al, 2010; Ziff, 2016). Cameron and colleagues (2010), in discussing the use of restrictive covenants in food retail, explain how supermarket chains have used them to control grocery store access at the neighbourhood level:

> The industry restructuring and subsequent urban locational changes led chains to close their older, smaller neighbourhood stores and to place restrictive covenants on the abandoned sites, so that they could protect the expanded trade areas of their newer and larger stores from

their supermarket competitors. The neighbourhood stores affected by restrictive covenants were located in mature areas of the city with older populations, potentially less mobile and able to respond to these changes. (Cameron et al, 2010, p 912)

Addressing the effects of restrictive covenants

Various jurisdictions have recognised the deleterious effects that restrictive covenants have in some communities, and have tried to implement measures to curb their effects. These include measures to rectify the current situation moving forward, while others look to restructure how policy is developed and implemented. This section describes examples in the UK, Canada and the US, but similar situations can be located globally.

In the UK, where four large supermarket chains dominate the food retail landscape, a report by the Competition and Markets Authority (CMA), a national corporate practices watchdog, made recommendations to attempt to regulate the 'stockpiling' of land by supermarket corporations. The CMA's report ordered supermarkets to remove selected restrictive covenants and enabled local planning authorities to stop a chain opening in a specific location if it already dominates the area (Competition Commission, 2007). Larger corporations argued that assessments of competition added delays and extra costs to an already slow and expensive planning system. The CMA concluded that competition in the groceries market would be improved by requiring supermarkets to release existing restrictive covenants in highly concentrated local markets. In their report, they proposed lifting restrictive covenants in areas of high concentration but, as one advocate asserted, 'The large chains are unlikely to be adversely affected by the renewed grocery use of old sites disposed of when they move to large purpose-built supermarkets, whereas smaller chains become more vulnerable' (McClary, 2008, p 45). The ultimate challenge remains the enforceability of such recommendations (Collinson and Williams, 2011).

In Edmonton, Canada, a large chain supermarket closed several locations in the 1980s and 1990s and placed restrictive covenants on the properties to prevent competing stores from using them. In 2005, the City of Edmonton studied how to remove covenants that they perceived were not in the best interests of neighbourhood residents; in the end, they concluded that the costs of pursuing the removal of covenants was too high (Borkowsky, 2005; Kleiss, 2005). The case of Edmonton is an interesting one. The city faced a situation where an independent grocery store tried to open in the former location of a chain supermarket and, when faced with a prohibition due to a restrictive covenant, the city intervened on the independent store's behalf. The corporate chain was only willing to allow the store to open if they used the corporate chain for the vast majority of their produce. The proposed independent store was unwilling to be bound by such an agreement, choosing instead a different location for their store. Edmonton serves as an example of a city trying to find ways of dealing with food deserts, but not acting out of fear of lawsuits.

Chicago, a large US city, has put an ordinance in place to limit the use of restrictive covenants (Ziff, 2016). Under the ordinance, restrictions may only exist for three years, and only if the grocery store that has closed relocates within a half mile of the former site within two years (although it only applies to new covenants put in place after the ordinance was established). While this ordinance has the potential to improve the food environment over time, it will be slow to improve the situation, and does not affect sites that were closed previously and had covenants placed on them.

In the examples described, several measures have been implemented in an attempt to prevent nutrition deserts and to promote neighbourhood development. However, as these examples demonstrate, rectifying existing nutrition deserts is far more difficult than preventing new ones. While many factors can create a nutrition desert, restrictive covenants mean that when a supermarket chain closes at a particular location, another store cannot open in its place, and thus cannot benefit from the store infrastructure and customer base already in place. There are numerous examples of chain supermarkets moving out of older, more central, urban neighbourhoods to larger formats on larger sites, often to new areas on highways or cheaper tracts of land (Larsen and Gilliland, 2008; Cameron et al, 2010). The deserted neighbourhoods subsequently struggle to attract the development of new supermarkets. Less mobile populations (people with low incomes, older people and people without personal vehicles) are often left to purchase food from convenience and drug stores, where food is often more expensive and less nutritious.

Conclusion

This chapter has detailed the role that the built food environment – which includes the density, diversity and distribution of food stores – can play in equal access to healthy foods across neighbourhoods. Areas that lack stores offering nutritious foods (food deserts) have an abundance of stores offering less nutritious foods (food swamps), and areas with illusory access to nutritious foods due to high prices (food mirages) have a greater impact on individuals and households of lower socioeconomic means. Using the metaphor of nutrition deserts as food injustice to exemplify that it is the absence of *nutritious* foods that is problematic, this chapter focuses on restrictive covenants, a property practice that allows businesses to dictate what can be done with their former properties once they have been sold. The rampant use of restrictive covenants in some cities creates nutrition deserts, and can lead to neighbourhood decline via loss of investment in a community. Prohibitive property practices such as this, aimed at curbing corporate competition, effectively limit or eliminate people's access to nutritious food through mechanisms over which they have no control.

The experiences described in this chapter – and in Edmonton, Canada in particular – serve as a cautionary tale for municipal governments, with their relatively low political clout to act on behalf of food desert neighbourhoods. To contribute towards food justice, given that real estate law is within provincial jurisdiction in Canada (or state or regional governments in other places), regional or national governments should intervene to limit or eliminate restrictive covenants for retail food businesses. Should these more powerful jurisdictions take on corporate actors, they are much more likely to be successful and to be able to protect themselves from legal reprisals.

While regulatory bodies must remain vigilant and act to curb the myriad ways corporations can reduce access through an emphasis on reducing competition, food justice will also require exploring and supporting alternative food channels. For long-term improvements in food environments and health equity, alternative food systems are needed, since supermarkets are profit-driven. The food environment interests of people – namely, access to affordable and nutritious foods – are not the primary concern of corporations. Alternatives that should be supported include urban agriculture, urban greenhouses and cooperative food store models, the latter of which operates to benefit communities over corporate interests and will not impose restrictive covenants as a business practice. Other promising practices include incentivising the development of mobile healthy food vending, as has been done in numerous jurisdictions across the US and Canada (Brinkley et al, 2013; Food Share, 2013), as well as tax abatements or subsidies for healthy food retail in low-income nutrition desert neighbourhoods (Public Health Agency of Canada, 2011). Nonetheless, healthy food retail should be defined carefully, for instance, by the proportion of vegetables and fruit available. What these alternatives all have in common is shifting power within the retail food environment in particular, away from corporate interests, and towards community ones, a significant step towards food justice.

Governments can play a key role by incentivising the development of alternative food channels through various creative means as described here, in conjunction with keeping damaging property practices, such as restrictive covenants, in check. But in order to do so, governments need to recognise the important role they should play in ensuring nutrition equity. Population health depends on improving food environments and contributing to food justice through support for communities that are most vulnerable.

References

Aggarwal, A., Cook, A.J., Jiao, J., Seguin, R., Vernez Moudon, A., Hurvitz, P.M. and Drewnowski, A. (2014) 'Access to supermarkets and fruit and vegetable consumption', *American Journal of Public Health*, vol 104, no 5, pp 917–23.

Alkon, A.H. and Agyeman, A.H. (eds) *Cultivating food justice: Race, class and sustainability*, Cambridge, MA: MIT Press.

Apparicio, P., Cloutier, M.S. and Shearmur, R. (2007) 'The case of Montréal's missing food deserts: Evaluation of accessibility to food supermarkets', *International Journal of Health Geographics BioMed Central*, vol 6, p 4.

Borkowsky, K. (2005) 'Good earth relocating, weary of impasse with Safeway', *Edmonton Journal*, 23 August, B-1.

Breyer, B. and Voss-Andreae, A. (2013) 'Food mirages: Geographic and economic barriers to healthful food access in Portland, Oregon', *Health and Place*, vol 24, pp 131–9.

Brinkley, C., Chrisinger, B. and Hillier, A. (2013) 'Tradition of healthy food access in low-income neighborhoods: Price and variety of curbside produce vending compared to conventional retailers', *Journal of Agriculture, Food Systems, and Community Development*, vol 4, no 1, pp 155–69.

Cameron, N., Amrhein, C.G., Smoyer-Tomic, K.E., Raine, K.D. and Chong, L.Y. (2010) 'Cornering the market: Restriction of retail supermarket locations', *Environment and Planning C: Government and Policy*, vol 28, pp 905–22.

Chung, C. and Myers, S. L. (1999) 'Do the poor pay more for food? An analysis of grocery store availability and food price disparities', *Journal of Consumer Affairs*, vol 33, no 2, pp 276–96.

Collinson, A. and Williams, P. (2011) 'Opening doors', *The Estates Gazette*, p 99.

Competition Commission (2007) *Working Paper on retail competition*, London: UK Government.

Cummins, S. and Macintyre, S. (2006) 'Food environments and obesity – neighbourhood or nation?', *International Journal of Epidemiology*, vol 35, no 1, pp 100–4.

del Canto, S., Engler-Stringer, R. and Muhajarine, N. (2015) 'Characterizing Saskatoon's food environment: A neighbourhood-level analysis of in-store fruit and vegetable access', *Canadian Journal of Urban Research*, vol 24, no 1, pp 1–16.

Egger, G. and Swinburn, B. (1997) 'An "ecological" approach to the obesity pandemic', *British Medical Journal*, vol 315, no 7106, pp 477–80.

Feng, J., Glass, T.A., Curriero, F.C., Stewart, W.F. and Schwartz, B.S. (2010) 'The built environment and obesity: A systematic review of the epidemiologic evidence', *Health & Place*, vol 16, no 2, pp 175–90.

Filomena, S., Scanlin, K. and Morland, K.B. (2013) 'Brooklyn, New York foodscape 2007–2011: A five-year analysis of stability in food retail environments', *International Journal of Behavioral Nutrition and Physical Activity*, vol 10, no 1, p 46.

Food Share (2013) *Stories from the mobile good food market*, Toronto, ON: Food Share.

Glanz, K., Sallis, J.F., Saelens, B.E. and Frank, L.D. (2005) 'Healthy nutrition environments: Concepts and measures', *American Journal of Health Promotion*, vol 19, no 5, pp 330–3.

Glanz, K., Sallis, J.F., Saelens, B.E. and Frank, L.D. (2007) 'Nutrition Environment Measures Survey in Stores (NEMS-S): Development and evaluation', *American Journal of Preventive Medicine*, vol 32, no 4, pp 282–9.

Gottlieb, R. and Joshi, A. (2010) *Food justice*, Cambridge, MA: MIT Press.

Hallett, L.F. and McDermott, D. (2011) 'Quantifying the extent and cost of food deserts in Lawrence, Kansas, USA', *Applied Geography*, vol 31, no 4, pp 1210–15.

Handy, S.L. and Clifton, K.J. (2001) 'Local shopping as a strategy for reducing automobile travel', *Transportation*, vol 28, no 4, pp 317–46.

Kleiss, K. (2005) 'City ponders cost of taking on Safeway over store closures', *Edmonton Journal*, B4.

Kurtz, H. (2013) 'Linking food deserts and racial segregation: Challenges and limitations', in R. Slocum and A. Saldanha (eds) *Geographies of race and food: Fields, bodies, markets*, Abingdon: Routledge, pp 247–64.

Lamichhane, A.P., Warren, J., Puett, R., Porter, D.E., Bottai, M., Mayer-Davis, E.J. and Liese, A.D. (2013) 'Spatial patterning of supermarkets and fast food outlets with respect to neighborhood characteristics', *Health and Place*, vol 23, pp 157–64.

Larsen, K. and Gilliland, J. (2008) 'Mapping the evolution of "food deserts" in a Canadian city: Supermarket accessibility in London, Ontario, 1961–2005', *International Journal of Health Geographics*, vol 7, p 16.

Larson, N.I., Story, M.T. and Nelson, M.C. (2009) 'Neighborhood environments: Disparities in access to healthy foods in the US', *American Journal of Preventive Medicine*, vol 36, no 1, pp 74–81.

Lotoski, L.C., Engler-Stringer, R. and Muhajarine, N. (2015) 'Cross-sectional analysis of a community-based cooperative grocery store intervention in Saskatoon, Canada', *Canadian Journal of Public Health*, vol 106, no 3, pp 147–54.

Lytle, L.A. (2009) 'Measuring the food environment', *American Journal of Preventive Medicine*, vol 36, no 4, pp S134–S144.

McClary, S. (2008) 'Commission rules will jeopardise regeneration', *The Estates Gazette*, p 48.

Morland, K. and Filomena, S. (2007) 'Disparities in the availability of fruits and vegetables between racially segregated urban neighbourhoods', *Public Health Nutrition*, vol 10, no 12, pp 1481–9.

Pothukuchi, K. (2005) 'Attracting supermarkets to inner-city neighborhoods: Economic development outside the box', *Economic Development Quarterly*, vol 19, no 3, pp 232–44.

Powell, L.M., Slater, S., Mirtcheva, D., Bao, Y. and Chaloupka, F.J. (2007) 'Food store availability and neighborhood characteristics in the United States', *Preventive Medicine*, vol 44, no 3, pp 189–95.

Public Health Agency of Canada (2011) *Obesity in Canada: A joint report from the Public Health Association of Canada and the Canadian Institute for Health Information*, Ottawa, Canada: Government of Canada.

Richardson, A.S., Meyer, K.A., Howard, A.G., Boone-Heinonen, J., Popkin, B.M., Evenson, K.R., et al (2014) 'Neighborhood socioeconomic status and food environment: A 20-year longitudinal latent class analysis among CARDIA participants', *Health & Place*, vol 30, pp 145–53.

Schoenmeyer, R.A., Menor, A.J. and Delaney, L.S. (2014) 'Is a burrito a sandwich?', *Probate and Property*, vol 28, no 1, pp 13–15.

Sobal, J. and Bisogni, C.A. (2009) 'Constructing food choice decisions', *Annals of Behavioral Medicine: A Publication of the Society of Behavioral Medicine*, vol 38, Suppl 1, S37–S46.

Spence, J.C., Cutumisu, N., Edwards, J., Raine, K.D. and Smoyer-Tomic, K. (2009) 'Relation between local food environments and obesity among adults', *BMC Public Health*, vol 9, p 192.

Springer, J. (2005) 'Chicago takes aim at retail leases', *Supermarket News*, vol 53, no 34, p 6.

Stolte, E. (2012) 'New report suggests expropriation could eliminate restrictions on former grocery sites', *Edmonton Journal*, 22 January.

Theobald, C. (2013) 'City councillor Don Iveson and Edmonton Federation of Community Leagues take aim at restrictive covenants', *Edmonton Examiner*, 25 September.

Thompson, C., Cummins, S., Brown, T. and Kyle, R. (2013) 'Understanding interactions with the food environment: An exploration of supermarket food shopping routines in deprived neighbourhoods', *Health and Place*, vol 19, pp 116–23.

Townshend, T. and Lake, A. (2009) 'Obesogenic urban form: Theory, policy and practice', *Health & Place*, vol 15, no 4, pp 909–16.

Walker, R.E., Keane, C.R. and Burke, J.G. (2010) 'Disparities and access to healthy food in the United States: A review of food deserts literature', *Health & Place*, vol 16, no 5, pp 876–84.

Winson, A. (2013) *The industrial diet: The degradation of food and the struggle for healthy eating*, Vancouver, BC: Canada: UBC Press.

Zenk, S.N., Schultz, A.J., Israel, B.A., James, S.A., Bao, S. and Wilson, M.L. (2005) 'Neighborhood racial composition, neighborhood poverty, and the spatial accessibility of supermarkets in Metropolitan Detroit', *American Journal of Public Health*, vol 95, no 4, pp 660–7.

Ziff, B. (2016) 'Bumble bees cannot fly and restrictive covenants cannot run', in A. Smit and M. Valiante (eds) *Public interest, private property: Law and planning policy in Canada*, Vancouver, BC: UBC Press, Chapter 2.

Section IV
Corporate food and food safety

10

Regulating food fraud: Public and private law responses in the EU, Italy and the Netherlands

Antonia Corini and Bernd van der Meulen

Introduction

The horsemeat scandal in 2013 brought food fraud to the attention of both the public and authorities in the European Union (EU). 'Food fraud' is used to indicate a wide variety of violations of food law, such as the use of non-authorised ingredients, adulteration of food substances, and irregular labelling or counterfeiting of geographical indications. Such violations may affect consumers' economic interests or health. Depending on the intention of the perpetrator, some distinguish 'food fraud' (economic gain) from 'food defence' (harmful effects) (Spink and Moyer, 2011). The distinguishing factor between these involves their *objective*: economic gain or damage, respectively. In this chapter, food fraud is understood as any *intentional* violation of food laws.

In most EU member states, food fraud may be subjected to either civil or criminal prosecution. In Italy, for example, some violations (for example, incomplete labelling) are punished via administrative fines (see Article 18 of Act 109/1992), while in other cases (Article 440 on adulteration and counterfeiting of food substances) they are subject to criminal sanctions. Similarly, the Netherlands does not specifically define food fraud, but Article 32a of Warenwet (The Commodities

Act) does refer to intentional or reckless infringements that may cause harm to public health or safety.

To contribute to conceptualising food fraud, this chapter analyses public law and policy responses to the horsemeat scandal, both at EU and member state levels (in the Netherlands and Italy), as well as by private standards enforced by food businesses themselves. The chapter is organised as follows. First, it sets out a brief history of approaches to food fraud developed in the EU. Next, the political and legislative responses to the horsemeat scandal are assessed, followed by a presentation of private schemes, including a discussion of their relevance to prevent food fraud. Finally, the added value of private schemes in dealing with food fraud is investigated.

The EU framework, 'mad cow disease' and the horsemeat scandal

In the countries that later formed the EU, falsification of food (now called 'food fraud') was a significant matter of concern, even prior to the formation of the EU. The first half of the 20th century involved periods of food shortages. Unscrupulous businessmen took advantage of this situation by selling counterfeit foods, and governments responded by legislating for the proper composition of food products and enforcing compliance with these standards. At the end of the 1950s, several countries set out to create a supra-national organisation to facilitate a joint market where goods could freely circulate. The mass of differing national food standards created big challenges. Initially, the European legislature tried to overcome this challenge by harmonising product standards at a European level. This was not possible. Food cultures differed too much to bring even the most basic concepts under common denominators. As travellers may experience, even common foods like bread, cheese and beer differ significantly from one country to the next. The vast quantity of products made harmonisation of product standards unattainable.

The European Court of Justice (ECJ) provided a solution. In its landmark judgment Case 120/78 'Cassis de Dijon' [1978], the ECJ articulated the principle of 'mutual recognition' where products adhering to national standards of particular member states cannot be denied access to the EU market if they do not meet compliance standards of other members states. With one stroke of the pen, the ECJ appeared to solve the problem of barriers that food standards presented to trade. As a consequence, national standards could no longer be utilised in attempts to protect consumers from fraudulent practices.

The European legislature took a different approach to protecting consumers by requiring businesses to declare all ingredients on the label of the product (Directive 79/112/EEC), thus enabling consumers to make informed choices. However, in practice, consumers may not read or understand the label, and are therefore not effectively aware of the food that they buy.

Additionally, a series of food safety crises broke out (including bovine spongiform encephalopathy [BSE] or mad cow disease and dioxin) which emphasised risk-based public health concerns, rather than the fraudulent nature of the events. At the beginning of the 21st century the main concern was establishing a legal framework to prevent such crises in the future. As the BSE problem was deemed an unintentional outcome, the reform focused on hazards rather than criminal intent (van der Meulen, 2015). In Article 3(14) of the General Food Law (GFL), the EU legislature defines the concept of 'hazard' to present micro-organisms, toxins and physical agents as the 'enemies' that EU Food Safety Law must overcome, rather than people (van der Meulen, 2015).

The regulations aiming to govern food safety are contradictory. For example, Article 14(1) of the GFL, as the core provision of EU food law (van der Meulen, 2012), states that food shall not be placed on the market if it is unsafe, which, according to Article 14(2), is when it is injurious to health or unfit for human consumption. However, according to the ECJ, a food can be unfit for consumption – that is, unsafe – without being injurious to health (C-636/11). For example, this can occur in case of contamination with non-pathogenic micro-organisms causing an off-flavour or smell, or other failures to meet food safety requirements.

Although there have always been food safety problems, the BSE crisis elevated awareness and put food safety concerns at the top of the political agenda. However, the focus placed on eliminating food safety incidents in EU food law came at the expense of attention to the criminal intent of people. In contrast, the horsemeat scandal redirected awareness to fraud (Poudelet, 2014). Why this particular fraud issue had this impact on food fraud awareness is unclear, but it was certainly significant across the EU as well as within the member states. The remainder of this chapter focuses on the events surrounding the horsemeat scandal and the various responses to them.

The horsemeat scandal and responses

In 2012, horse DNA was found in prepackaged beef lasagne in Ireland. Soon thereafter, throughout much of the EU, horsemeat was found mixed in with or sold as beef in food products. This highlighted the weakness of the system in dealing with problems other than those derived from the presence of measurable hazards. As the most important instruments of EU food law are its enforcement mechanisms, such as withdrawal and recall measures to be taken by food business operators (FBOs) in accordance with Article 19, the question arose as to whether these instruments could be used to deal with this particular situation (van der Meulen, 2014b). Article 19 of the GFL requires FBOs to take the prescribed measures when they consider food products not to be in compliance with food safety requirements. This raises the question: do situations of deceptions come within the ambit of what Article 19 of the GFL has in mind where it refers to 'food safety requirements'?

EU member states took different positions. Ireland and Italy argued that Article 19 requirements had not been met, so they did not recall the involved food products (van der Meulen et al, 2015). A similar position was taken by Germany and France, although they imposed recalls based on national legislation. Greece, the Netherlands and Portugal, on the other hand, considered Article 19 applicable to the horsemeat scandal (van der Meulen et al, 2015). Thus, although EU food law applies uniformly in all member states, its scope and meaning was understood very differently in the face of this new challenge. Essentially, the horsemeat scandal showed weaknesses in the current legal framework, both in its ability to deal with fraud and in terms of law enforcement. The following section looks at the consequential developments and debates in three specific spaces – the EU, Italy and the Netherlands.

The EU

As indicated, no provisions specifically addressing food fraud exist in EU food law. Article 17(1) of the GFL establishes that compliance with food law is the responsibility of FBOs, while Article 17(2) indicates that enforcement of food law is the responsibility of member states. Thus controls are performed by both private and public actors. FBOs must ensure that food satisfies the requirements of food law, and verify that such requirements are met, and member states are responsible for enforcement by organising a system of official controls and designate authorities enabled to verify compliance with food-related rules.

The EU institutions reacted in various ways to the horsemeat scandal. The European Parliament (2013) focused on the causes of the food fraud, and identified elements that may have facilitated it, such as weaknesses within food chains, their complexity and cross-border character, lack of methods to detect fraud and fraudsters, and the fact that there is no unified framework to target food fraud. This led to the 'development of risk profiles and vulnerability assessments for each supply chain and food product' (para 54). The Council of the EU (2014) emphasised the role of public law in combating food crime, such as the use of rules aiming to facilitate an exchange of experience between member state authorities during investigation and prosecution processes, or organising control competent authorities (CAs) which are responsible for the enforcement of food law requirements. Along with these two institutions, the European Commission further discussed the need to provide a harmonised definition of food fraud (Garau, 2014), while the European Parliament considered a uniform definition essential for developing a European approach to combating food fraud, to be based on discussions with member states, stakeholders and experts (European Parliament, 2013).

The European Commission, by recalling the definition provided by the Food Fraud Network – an organisation set up between the Commission and member states – proposed an operational definition for food fraud as 'intentional violation of the rules covered by Regulation 882/2004 (the Official Controls Regulation) which are applicable to the production of food and feed, motivated by the prospect of economic or financial gain' (Garau, 2014, p 3). The Food Fraud group was created in 2013 within the Official Controls Experts group with the purpose of gathering member state representatives in charge of food fraud issues and to promote a dialogue with the European Commission. They proposed adding to the operational definition terms such as 'possible intentional violation' and 'deceit to consumers' in order to better determine the remit of the investigations to carry out and identify the most suitable tools to use. Ultimately, however, no agreement on a definition was reached.

Awareness and concern surrounding food fraud continued to grow. The food industry involved itself by acknowledging food fraud as an increasing concern for society, including the food industry (FoodDrinkEurope, 2016). Additionally, food fraud was understood as the basis of many food scares, regardless of whether it had an impact on human food safety (Eurocommerce, 2015). Developing anti-fraud strategies, including the use of private quality schemes, became of paramount importance (Eurocommerce, 2015).

The European Commission acknowledged system shortcomings in managing food fraud and introduced several tools to combat it. The Food Fraud Network functions to provide connection and administrative support, especially in cases of fraud in the market concerning different member states. The Administrative Assistance and Cooperation (AAC) system was also created, a computer tool to assist in cases of fraud through data and information sharing. The Food and Veterinary Office (FVO), recognising that at present there is no provision for unannounced FVO audits to detect any possible food fraud, argued that several challenges have to be faced to 'give high priority to fraud' (Scannell, 2013). The FVO is now called Directorate F, for Health and Food Audits and Analysis.

Shortly after the horsemeat scandal, a proposal was presented to the European Parliament for a new Official Controls Regulation (OCR). This opportunity led to the inclusion of anti-fraud controls. Tonio Borg, Health and Consumer Commissioner at the time of the proposal, highlighted the economic importance of the agri-food industry for the EU, as well as the high level of EU food safety standards, and argued that 'the recent horsemeat scandal has shown that there is room for improvement, even if no health risk emerged' (European Commission, 2013). The proposal was adopted on 15 March 2017 and published in the *Official Journal* on 7 April 2018 as Regulation (EU) 2017/625. It will be in force 20 days after publication, yet most of its provisions will only be applicable from December 2019.

This new regulation aims to simplify and clarify by creating a single framework for coordinated and rationalised official controls along the agri-food chain. The most important changes regarding fraud are the planning of controls both to verify compliance with food safety requirements and also to detect other possible violations. Several provisions envisage the inclusion of controls to fraudulent or deceptive practices that affect food trade. For example, Recital 32 states that the frequency of official controls shall be established in regards to the need to detect possible violations perpetrated through fraudulent or deceptive practices, while Article 9(2) makes reference to possible intentional violations perpetrated through fraudulent or deceptive practices. Another change is the creation of an Information Management System (IMSOC), a computerised system through which data, information and documents concerning official controls are managed and automatically exchanged.

The Netherlands

In the Netherlands, enforcement of food law is centralised at the national government level. The Minister of Public Health and the Minister of Economic Affairs have powers to impose remedial measures (such as recalls) and administrative fines. On behalf of the ministers, these food chain-wide inspection powers are executed by the Nederlandse Voedsel- en Warenautoriteit (NVWA) (Food and Consumer Product Safety Authority). The NVWA applies a risk-based enforcement policy by taking account of the performance of private controls systems. This approach is known as 'meta supervision' (Verbruggen and Havinga, 2014; van der Meulen and Freriks, 2006). Businesses are colour-coded, as a result of risk measurements based on types of products and the business's history of compliance, ranging from green, amber, orange and red, or low risk to high risk respectively. The higher the risk, the higher the number and intensity of official controls, and the better the performance of the private controls system in place, the lower the priority that is given to official controls. Businesses can improve their colour code through prolonged compliance and certification.

The Netherlands has a special relation to the horsemeat scandal as two of the slaughterhouses that committed the fraud are located there. As the horsemeat fraud events were taken up in the media, the NVWA produced an enforcement policy to prioritise food safety issues. Initially the horsemeat fraud was considered not to cause human food safety concerns, and thus no action was taken. Under media pressure, however, this position became untenable. When the NVWA decided to act, it first considered the fraud a *potential safety issue* as it might have brought residues of illegal veterinary medicines (phenylbutazone in particular) into the food chain, although risk assessment at EU and national levels (EFSA, 2013) showed this risk to be virtually non-existent. The NVWA then took the position that the origin of the horses was unknown, as was their fitness for human consumption in the absence of evidence of ante mortem veterinary controls.

Ultimately, evidence suggests that there was tampering with bookkeeping that disrupted the traceability mechanisms. So the NVWA concluded that due to these fraudulent events, the origin of *all* meat products from the two slaughterhouses was uncertain, not just the horsemeat in question. For this reason, the NVWA considered all products supplied by the two businesses as unsafe, and carried out the largest recall in its history of 50,000 tons of meat products. Simultaneously, the public was informed that there had never been a threat to public health. This led to a discussion in court as to whether the obligation to recall, stated in Article 19 of the GFL, and/or the concept of unsafety described in Article 14, included the situation of disrupted traceability mechanisms as set out in Article 18. Twice, in provisional rulings, the College van Beroep voor het bedrijfsleven (CBB) (Industrial Appeals Board) upheld the authority's interpretation (see *Selten B.V. in liquidation v. Vice Minister of Economic Affairs*, 2013; *Van Hattem Vlees B.V. v. Vice-Minister of Economic Affairs*, 2014). This included both the interpretation that infringement on traceability obligation sparks a recall obligation under Article 19 of the GFL, and the reasoning that disrupted traceability makes a food legally unsafe, and therefore under recall obligation (van der Meulen et al, 2015). While the perpetrators faced criminal prosecution for common fraud, any possible fines under food law would have been very low.

The horsemeat scandal, the lessons learned from it and the actions to be taken were debated in the taskforce Voedselvertrouwen (Food Trust), which consisted of government and food industry representatives. This taskforce was formed to strengthen existing enforcement, fight food fraud and protect food authenticity. Its conclusions focused strongly on the use of private means of enforcement, justified due to the international character of trade and purchase. Public authorities are bound by jurisdiction boundaries, whereas private authorities have no such limitations, especially concerning the EU's internal market. The taskforce recommends that the Global Food Safety Initiative (GFSI) requires participating private schemes (such as FSSC 22000, Food Safety System Certification, the British Retail Consortium [BRC] and International Featured Standards [IFS]) to include 'fraud modules' in their systems. With these modules, businesses require their suppliers to ensure food integrity and traceability based on specific criteria given by the taskforce. Such criteria include the training of auditors, unannounced audits, exchange of information between auditors and public authorities, and private sanction instruments. In this way, businesses may ascertain whether their suppliers are up to standard – or choose different suppliers. The NVWA will accept these schemes in their enforcement policy, granting a lighter inspection regime to certified businesses.

In the Dutch legal framework, the use of private schemes was already quite common even before the horsemeat scandal. Retailers and producers owning high-end brands use them to control the quality and safety of practices performed by their suppliers (van der Meulen, 2011). Additionally, the RiskPlaza, a Dutch assurance scheme established in 2015, requires participating businesses to control the performance of their suppliers by checking the presence of enumerated hazards that may originate from listed products, to ensure the safety of the products.

However, the taskforce also recommended strengthening the role of public authorities and their instruments against fraudsters. Legislative action was consequently undertaken to reinforce the arsenal of punitive measures. Sanctions in food law used to be low, ranging from about €500 to €1,200 per infringement. To be better able to deal with criminal intent in the food chain, the maximum level of administrative fines is being increased to €810,000, and in case of *intentional* infringements, to 1 per cent of the annual turnover of the business.

Italy

In Italy, the control competences are distributed over several levels (state, regional and local), as indicated in Article 2 of the Italian Act 193/2007 and among different CAs (Ministero della salute, 2015a). Specific programmes (such as the *Multiannual national control plan*) exist with the objective to plan controls on the basis of important European principles, including risk analysis, as framed in the GFL.

The horsemeat scandal in Italy was not considered to be a matter of food safety, but a mere commercial fraud (van der Meulen et al, 2015). Nevertheless, the events sparked a shared commitment among the different CAs. Controls were intensified to exclude any risk to health and to verify the possible use of undeclared horsemeat. Only in a few of the samples were there traces of undeclared horsemeat (van der Meulen et al, 2015). No measures of recall or withdrawal of products, based on the GFL, were taken.

The fight against food fraud and counterfeiting has been identified as one of the 'high-level strategic objectives' in the *Multiannual national control plan 2015–2018* (Ministero della salute, 2015b). Furthermore, ministerial guidelines were adopted concerning the procedure to be followed by FBOs regarding the recall of products (Ministero della salute, 2016). The criteria for product recall are derived from the 'guidelines on alert system' (Conferenza permanente per i rapporti tra lo Stato, le Regioni e le Province Autonome di Trento e Bolzano, 2008), and are based on the presence of risk ('serious risk' or a 'serious risk to be ascertained'). There is no reference to situations other than those characterised by the presence of risk that may require the undertaking of recall procedures. Therefore, under such control mechanisms, the horsemeat scandal would not be approached with a recall.

Similar to the Netherlands, in Italy private food law instruments are explored as ways of dealing with food fraud. In the domain of food safety and food quality, standards globally recognised or retail label certifications 'born' in Italy are often used as they serve as an element of distinction from other products (Cristiani and Strambi, 2012). In addition, there are several examples of Italian private schemes providing the infrastructure to respond to food fraud, such as the 'code of self-discipline' and 'manuals of good hygienic practices' adopted by FBO associations, but these instruments have not specifically been connected to the prevention of food fraud.

The horsemeat scandal and the consequential strive for food authenticity is represented by a proposed law to revise food crimes in the Italian legal framework. This proposal (Disegno di Legge S 2231, 2016) argues for the modification of several provisions. For example, the revision of Article 516 of the Italian Criminal Code altered its title from 'Sale of non-genuine food substances as being genuine' to 'Fraud in the commerce of food products'. This proposal establishes harsher punitive-like sanctions and a broader scope of application that may be applied in the context of food fraud.

Overall, the legislative and political responses to the horsemeat scandal in the EU, the Netherlands and Italy are quite different in terms of their conceptualisations, operationalisation and enforcement of food fraud. In varying degrees, private actors are given responsibility for prevention and enforcement of food fraud and other issues of food safety. These private-based control schemes are discussed next.

Private schemes

Since the 1990s food chains have increasingly been regulated by private actors using private law instruments. While chains have grown too long to be effectively covered by contractual arrangements, businesses at one end of the chain depend on performance at the other end of the chain in a multitude of ways. To deal with this situation, private regulatory bodies have provided requirements and standards. Key standards in the field of food safety include the British Retail Consortium (BRC), International Featured Standards (IFS), Safe Quality Food (SQF), FSSC 22000 and GlobalGAP (specifically for primary production). By using standards, FBOs show their additional commitment in conforming to the rules established in the standards, aiming to provide consumers with a certified safety and quality of their products.

Uniform quality assurance food safety standards are important for buyers to assess the conformity of suppliers with requirements, especially involving intentional adulteration (Eurocommerce, 2016). Purchasers are (more) willing to accept that the requirements of standards have been met if this is certified by an independent third party that has audited the business to whom the certification has been issued. Such objective auditing instruments can be used in combating food fraud by acting on behalf of all chain partners to check compliance. After the horsemeat scandal, the food industry pushed for the adoption of food fraud risk management systems and food fraud vulnerability assessments (FoodDrinkEurope, 2016).

The Global Food Safety Initiative (GFSI) is a collaboration between the world's leading retail chains. Participants commit themselves to accepting the standards benchmarked by GFSI and products on their shelves are certified in line with them. In this way GFSI has become the standard of standards. GFSI members convened a food fraud think tank, which then issued several recommendations to combat food fraud; the GFSI board has accepted these and incorporated them into their guidance document, which also includes carrying out a food fraud vulnerability assessment, and to have a control plan in place. The GFSI also wrote a position paper (2014), which distinguishes between food fraud (for economic gain) and food defence (intention to cause harm), with the emphasis on the former.

Unlike most of the other leading standards, FSSC 22000 is not retailer-driven; it is mainly used by high-end brands. FSSC 22000 is an integrative food safety management system, combining food safety, food defence and food fraud. Businesses should address food safety through HACCP (hazard analysis and critical control points), food defence through TACCP (threats analysis and critical control points) and food fraud through VACCP (vulnerability analysis and critical control points). According to the standard, the organisation shall have both a documented and annually reviewed food defence threat assessment procedure and food fraud vulnerability assessment procedure in place, as well as prioritising preventive measures more generally.

These examples of private schemes add to the legal framework not just another set of rules, but also concrete tools that, even if they are not mandatory, may serve to prevent and manage several possible crimes against food.

Discussion

The responses, both during and after the horsemeat scandal, resulted in different actions taken by the various member states. Some responded with food safety measures – recalls in particular – while others thought this not applicable, given the international or national regulations in place. Aiming to adjust the legal framework, governmental and private actions focused on the detection of food fraud. While Italy and the EU aim to prevent food fraud using deterrence and punishment practices, private schemes aim to prevent food fraud through chain integration. The Netherlands uses both methods. As the next subsections exemplify, discussions of food fraud detection, deterrence, and prevention must be accompanied by how these tools are framed.

Framing

While most member states seem unwilling to conceptualise food fraud as a form of food safety problems, the Dutch authorities introduced a new safety concept. In their understanding, a food should not only be considered unsafe if some defect could be measured, but also in the case of an infringement on procedural food safety requirements such as traceability. So, along with the EU and Italy, the Netherlands frames food fraud as a criminal act, which emphasises the role of intent of the perpetrators.

Private schemes also emphasise safety, but from a different angle. They seek to prevent fraud as a potential cause of safety problems, which is understood in a more substantive and conventional way. From this perspective, the core issue is the *effect* of the fraud.

Whether it is wise to include such elements – the effect on safety, intentional deception or the objective of achieving economic gain – in a definition of food fraud largely depends on the purpose of the definition itself. For example, if defining food fraud is meant to achieve a greater understanding of its nature, then including more elements may be helpful, but if defining food fraud is meant to be used to regulate and punish offenders, the more elements included may increase the burden of proof and delay persecution processes.

For this reason, it is probably for the best that the new OCR, as opposed to the European Commission's operational definition, mentions intentional infringements but does not introduce food fraud as a special legal category, nor does it distinguish types of fraud according to motive. In this way, food fraud in the OCR is neither limited nor implied by its potential to create harmful health effects on humans. The new provisions, rules and principles introduced by the new OCR are represented in that intentional violations are clearly mentioned. In addition, as indicated in Article 1(2)(a), official controls include the verification of compliance, further to the area of food and food safety, as well as matters related to the integrity and wholesomeness of the food chain at any stage of production, processing and distribution, and, accordingly, to rules aimed at ensuring fair practices in trade and protecting consumer interests and information.

It may be argued that the intentional element will not always be present. From this perspective, Giddens and Sutton (2014) argue that companies are 'inherently criminogenic'. Consequently, seeing a competitive advantage, they may commit several crimes for economic gain. For example, during production, they may admit dangerous products to the market, or retailers and marketing companies may produce products with misleading labels or utilise anti-competitive or misleading advertising. However, it is not helpful to overly focus on a single characteristic of food fraud, whether it is intentional or pursued when seeking economic gain. Additionally, in our view, defining food fraud as including unintentional behaviour may not serve a practical purpose.

Detection, deterrence prevention and sanctioning

The new OCR, by requiring controls on possible intentional violations, makes an important starting point for the detection of food fraud. Additionally, the information-sharing systems introduced by the European Commission are potential assets in dealing with future food frauds, especially if the quantity of these frauds increase.

The use of self-controls and audit-based private schemes allows private actors to closely regulate their business relations and their products, which assists in identifying possible fraud. By taking responsibility for their business relations and by assessing possible risks in those relations, private actors are able to make a substantive contribution to reducing the occurrence of food fraud. Food companies are rewarded with reductions in official controls if they show themselves as trustworthy by adhering to self-regulatory safety regulations.

Conclusion

The horsemeat scandal raised awareness of intentional infringements of food law. To deal with such infringements, different instruments are needed from those specifically designed to solve regulator food safety issues. Punitive sanctions have been introduced in public law to prevent and identify food fraud, while private schemes offer a different practical-based avenue which may benefit both food companies and consumers interests.

References

College van Beroep voor het bedrijfsleven (www.rechtspraak.nl/ Organisatie-en-contact/Organisatie/College-van-Beroep-voor-het-bedrijfsleven).

Conferenza permanente per i rapporti tra lo Stato, le Regioni e le Province Autonome di Trento e Bolzano (2008) *Linee guida per la gestione operativa del sistema di allerta per alimenti destinati al consumo umano* (www.salute.gov.it/imgs/C_17_pagineAree_1147_listaFile_ itemName_0_file.pdf).

Council of the EU (European Union) (2014) 'Draft Council conclusions on the role of law enforcement cooperation in combating food crime' (http://register.consilium.europa.eu/doc/srv?l=EN&f=ST%20 15623%202014%20INIT).

Cristiani, E. and Strambi, G. (2012) 'Public and privates standards official controls', in L. Costato and F. Albisinni (eds) *Food law*, Padova, Italy: CEDAM.

EFSA (European Food Safety Authority) (2013) 'Joint statement of EFSA and EMA on the presence of residues of phenylbutazone in horse meat' (www.efsa.europa.eu/en/efsajournal/pub/3190).

Eurocommerce (2015) 'Food fraud', Briefing (www.eurocommerce. eu/media/119222/food_fraud__150407.pdf).

Eurocommerce (2016) 'Quality schemes in distribution', 23 June (www.eurocommerce.eu/media/128953/els_bedert_-_quality_ schemes_in_distribution.pdf).

European Commission (2013) 'Smarter rules for safer food: Commission proposes landmark package to modernise, simplify and strengthen the agri-food chain in Europe', Press release (http://europa.eu/rapid/ press-release_IP-13-400_en.htm).

European Parliament (2013) *Report on the food crisis, fraud in the food chain and control thereof,* Committee on the Environment, Public Health and Food Safety (www.europarl.europa.eu/sides/getDoc.do?pubRef=-//EP//TEXT+REPORT+A7-2013-0434+0+DOC+XML+V0//EN).

FoodDrinkEurope (2016) *Position paper on food fraud* (www.fooddrinkeurope.eu/publication/position-paper-on-food-fraud/).

Garau, C. (2014) Conference on food fraud, The EU perspective, An overview of the European Commission's policy initiatives (www.salute.gov.it/portale/ItaliaUE2014/dettaglioEvento.jsp?lingua=italiano&id=205).

GFSI (Global Food Safety Initiative) (2014) 'GFSI position on mitigating the public health risk of food fraud' (www.mygfsi.com/files/Technical_Documents/Food_Fraud_Position_Paper.pdf).

Giddens, A. and Sutton, P.W. (2014) *Fondamenti di sociologia,* Bologna, Italy: Il Mulino, citing Box, S. (1983) *Power, crime, and mystification,* London: Tavistock.

Ministero della salute (2015a) *Piano nazionale integrato 2015–2018, Autorità competenti e organismi di controllo* (www.salute.gov.it/pianoNazionaleIntegrato2015/sezionePianoNazionaleIntegrato2015.jsp?cap=capitolo2&sez=pni-cap2-autoritacompetenti).

Ministero della salute (2015b) *Piano nazionale integrato 2015–2018, Obiettivi strategici* (www.salute.gov.it/pianoNazionaleIntegrato2015/capitoloPianoNazionaleIntegrato2015.jsp?cap=capitolo1).

Ministero della Salute (2016) *Procedure per il richiamo, da parte degli OSA, di prodotti non conformi, ai sensi del Regolamento (CE) 178/2002 e successiva pubblicazione dei dati inerenti i prodotti richiamati per una corretta tutela del consumatore* (www.trovanorme.salute.gov.it/norme/renderNormsanPdf;jsessionid=JXW+9Ex-1qWwIjLH3DQQfg__.sgc3-prd-sal?anno=2016&codLeg=54999&parte=1%20&serie=).

Poudelet, E. (2014) Conference on food fraud, Speech (www.salute.gov.it/portale/ItaliaUE2014/dettaglioEvento.jsp?lingua=italiano&id=205).

Scannell, M. (2013) 'The current veterinary official controls system', Workshop of the European Parliament (www.europarl.europa.eu/document/activities/cont/201306/20130618ATT67996/20130618ATT67996EN.pdf).

Spink, J. and Moyer, D.C. (2011) *Backgrounder: Defining the public health threat of food fraud,* National Center for Food Protection Defense, A Homeland Security Center of Excellence, Michigan State University (http://foodfraud.msu.edu/wp-content/uploads/2014/07/food-fraud-ffg-backgrounder-v11-Final.pdf).

van der Meulen, B.M.J. (ed) (2011) *Private food law*, Wageningen, Netherlands: Wageningen Academic Publishers.

van der Meulen, B.M.J. (2012) 'The core of food law: A critical reflection on the single most important provision in all EU food law', *European Food and Feed Law Review*, vol 3, pp 117–25.

van der Meulen, B.M.J. (ed) (2014a) *EU food law handbook*, Wageningen, Netherlands: Wageningen Academic Publishers.

van der Meulen, B.M.J. (2014b) 'Vitality of the General Food Law. Wear and tear of the substantive approach to food safety', *Journal für Verbraucherschutz und Lebensmittelsicherheit: Journal of Consumer Protection and Food Safety*, doi: 10.1007/s00003-014-0921-9.

van der Meulen, B.M.J. (2015) 'Is current EU food safety law geared up for fighting food fraud?', *Journal für Verbraucherschutz und Lebensmittelsicherheit: Journal of Consumer Protection and Food Safety*, doi: 10.1007/s00003-015-0992-2.

van der Meulen, B.M.J. and Freriks, A.A. (2006) 'Millefeuille. The emergency of a multi-layered controls system in the European food sector', *Utrecht Law Review*, vol 2, no 1, pp 156–76.

van der Meulen, S., Boin, G., Bousoula, I., Conte-Salinas, N., Paganizza, V., Montanari, F., Rodriguez Fuentes, V., and van der Meulen, B.M.J. (2015) 'Horsemeat scandal: Use of recalls in enforcement throughout the EU', *European Food and Feed Law Review* 1: 2-13.

Verbruggen, P. and Havinga, T. (2014) 'Metatoezicht op voedselveiligheid', *Tijdschrift voor Toezicht*, doi: 10.5553/TvT/187987052014005001002.

11

Mass *Salmonella* poisoning by the Peanut Corporation of America: Lessons in state-corporate food crime

Paul Leighton

Introduction

In 2008, the Centers for Disease Control and Prevention (CDC) noticed a multistate outbreak of *Salmonella* that eventually killed nine and officially sickened 714 (CDC, 2009a). It hospitalised at least 166, with total cases estimated between 11,000 (Cavallaro, 2011, pp 601, 607) and 20,700 (Sheth et al, 2011). Public health officials traced the outbreak to the Peanut Corporation of America's (PCA) facility in Blakely, Georgia. PCA was a relatively small business that sold containers of peanut butter and products to snack food makers, schools, the military, nursing homes and disaster relief agencies (Leighton, 2016).

PCA claimed the problem was isolated, but former employee Kenneth Kendrick went on national TV to draw attention to PCA's Plainview, Texas facility. The plant had a flooded basement, rodents, and a hole in the roof that dripped bird faeces on to the production area; it had never undergone a sanitation inspection. The recalls from all PCA facilities included 4,000 products, 'one of the largest food recalls ever in the United States' (FDA, 2009a).

PCA's CEO, Stewart Parnell, appeared in front of the House Subcommittee on Oversight and Investigations, which released information that PCA had on multiple occasions knowingly shipped peanut products that tested positive for *Salmonella*. A representative put recalled peanut products in a jar wrapped with yellow CAUTION tape, and asked Parnell if he would eat any. Parnell pleaded his Fifth Amendment right not to incriminate himself. PCA declared bankruptcy; the victims split US$12 million in insurance (Bottemiller, 2010), and PCA leadership split a US$875,000 insurance policy for their legal bills (Flynn, 2009). The peanut recall was one of several food safety events that led to the Food Safety Modernization Act (FSMA) of 2010. In 2013, the Department of Justice finally returned a 76-count criminal indictment against Parnell and other PCA executives. They were found guilty, and the court sentenced Parnell to 28 years.

Although the appeals process is not completed at publication time (2017), PCA is an important case study of food crime. Because many people do not know where their food comes from, this case study is about a relatively small company that processed peanuts. Nuts came in from China, Mexico and US locations, where they would have the skin removed (blanching) and be roasted. PCA would then chop or grind the nuts into products for resale. They made some peanut butter that was 'rebranded', meaning someone put their own label on PCA's product and sold it – in larger sizes used by institutions such as nursing homes (Layton and Miroff, 2009; DOJ, 2013a). Peanut paste and nuts chopped to different sizes were sold to food producers (like Kelloggs) to be made into peanut butter crackers, cereal, granola bars, snack mix and ice cream, which were among the thousands of products recalled by many manufacturers. PCA is important because it was a small company whose executives were found to have done great harm by being a low-cost supplier to national and multinational food producers.

This case more specifically illustrates the harms done by microbes in the food supply, the process of investigating outbreaks of foodborne illness, and the regulatory oversight of the Food & Drug Administration (FDA). In spite of the seemingly tough criminal sanctions and food safety reform legislation, this chapter presents PCA as a cautionary case study. First, PCA illustrates a larger problem of state-corporate crime, which involves 'the pursuit of profit by corporations along with the failure of a state agency to effectively monitor them [that] resulted in the violent deaths' (Matthews and Kauzlarich, 2006, p 83).

Second, the indictment only named corporate victims, like Kelloggs, who were the immediate purchasers; the dead and sickened were not mentioned at trial. Third while the FSMA is a major reform, Congress has subsequently not increased the FDA budget to fund all the mandates Congress took credit for enacting.

To explore these issues and contribute to an understanding of food crime, this chapter explores the *Salmonella*-based mass victimisation caused by PCA. The first section provides an overview of *Salmonella* in peanuts and bioterrorism, and the investigative process done by public health officials to identify a contamination source. The second section describes the conditions at PCA's facilities, FDA law on adulterated and misbranded food, and the charges against PCA's leadership. The third section discusses state-corporate crime and the failures of regulatory oversight/capable guardians. The conclusion argues against a triumphalist interpretation where justice and reform prevail.

This chapter contains information from the whistleblower Kenneth Kendrick. Mr Kendrick worked as an assistant manager for production for three months in 2006 in the Plainview, Texas PCA plant. He provided helpful background information and details about the plant. Quotes attributed to him that lack a citation are from our email exchanges and telephone discussions from 2012 to 2014.

Salmonella, peanuts and public health investigations

Salmonella bacteria occur naturally in animal and human faeces. For most people, *Salmonella*'s assault on the body results in four to seven days of diarrhoea, fever, abdominal cramps and vomiting (Marler, 2011). While most people recover without treatment, it can lead to hospitalisation, permanent health impairments or even death in the elderly, infants and those with weakened immune systems. Injury can also be financial, especially with the 'precariat' who have a precarious financial existence because of low job security, poor pay, a paycheck-to-paycheck existence and high-deductible healthcare plans.

Given the harm that *Salmonella* and other pathogens can do, they are sometimes used for bioterrorism, which happens substantially less frequently than harms from corporate (in)actions (Dalziel, 2009). In 1984, members of the Rajneesh sect deliberately introduced *Salmonella* into the salad bars of restaurants in the Dalles, Oregon. They were testing a plan to incapacitate voters to sway an upcoming local election and assure approval for building a controversial centre to spread their beliefs. About 750 people contracted food poisoning and 45 were hospitalised (Török et al, 1997). This incident happened before Congress passed biological weapons statutes (18 United States Code [USC] §178), under which *Salmonella* would be considered a 'biological agent,' which means 'any microorganism' that is 'capable of causing (A) death, disease, or other biological malfunction.'

Bioterrorism law does not apply to an agent or toxin 'that is in its naturally occurring environment, if the biological agent or toxin has not been cultivated, collected, or otherwise extracted from its natural source' (18 USC §175). Thus, such statutes have not been used to prosecute food manufacturers, even though PCA's plant conditions were ideal to incubate *Salmonella*, and executives knowingly distributed it. However, the FDA did use the Public Health Security and Bioterrorism Preparedness Response Act 2002 (42 USC §282) to access PCA business records (Harris and Belluck, 2009).

Regulations and best practices seek to minimise microbial contamination. For example, production processes often involve a 'kill step', usually heating the food for a combination of time and temperature to kill pathogens. Raw (potentially contaminated) food should be segregated from a product that has been through a kill step. Nevertheless, contamination can be introduced after a kill step via processing equipment or during storage.

Peanut roasting should kill *Salmonella* (Sheth et al, 2011), but wide variations of peanut types and their moisture content mean that *Salmonella* may survive roasting. Low acid, fatty foods like peanuts are protective of *Salmonella*, which can last up to two years in peanut butter jars (Cavallaro, 2011), and stomach acid may not destroy it (Borrell, 2009). Salmonella in peanut butter is stable, but 'water in a peanut butter processing plant is like putting gasoline on a fire. It will not only spread the *Salmonella*, but the *Salmonella* will grow when water is present' (Borrell, 2009).

When patients with salmonellosis appear, doctors take a stool sample, 'fingerprint' the bacteria's DNA and upload it to CDC's PulseNet (Cavallaro, 2011; CDC, 2013). In 2008, the CDC saw increasing numbers of geographically diverse cases of bacteria with the same DNA fingerprint, which indicated a single source for the contamination. Public health officials interviewed victims about their food consumption, getting details on specific products they ate, and retrieving packaging to identify batch numbers. A TV series like *24* would glorify the intelligence community doing this detective work to track down bioterrorists while the body count continued to mount, but 'Team Diarrhoea' receives no such recognition for its work to find common ingredients the victims ate and trace the contamination back to its source.

With PCA, public health officials matched the DNA fingerprint of the *Salmonella* Typhimurium from patients to the *Salmonella* in food products that left PCA's Blakely, Georgia plant (CDC, 2009b). Officials first identified *Salmonella* in an opened container of King Nut peanut butter, which put their label on PCA's product. Parnell emailed King Nut's Vice President and attached a story 'Salmonella outbreak spreads to 42 states': 'I'm sure it is something we did' (Parnell, 2009). Five days later, Parnell denied responsibility: 'we suspect the *Salmonella* could have been introduced by cross-contamination after the tub was opened. We do not believe the *Salmonella* came from our facility.' He falsely claimed, 'we send hourly PB [peanut butter] samples to an independent lab to test for *Salmonella* during production of peanut butter, and we have never found any *Salmonella* at all' (Lynchburg Office, 2009). However, the identification of King Nut focused attention on PCA.

PCA's facilities, wrongs and crimes

The Blakely plant was 'more circa 1955 than 2009' (Moss, 2009). An FDA inspection in response to *Salmonella* concerns found cockroaches, mould on the ceilings and walls of a cooler that stored the finished product, cracks up to four feet in the roof that dripped water into production and storage rooms, and 'deficiencies in the plant's design and construction that invite contamination' (Layton, 2009b; see also Hartman and Barrett, 2009; Layton and Miroff, 2009; Cavallaro, 2011, p 605). Raw peanuts were stored next to the processed product, allowing for cross-contamination, and 'the roaster was not calibrated to kill deadly germs.' Federal testing 'showed *Salmonella* living on the plant floors. Plant managers had not decontaminated the peanut butter processing line after detecting *Salmonella*' (Moss, 2009).

The Plainview plant had been a hog slaughter and sausage processing operation from 1969 until 1974 (Nestlé, 2006, p 3; Vielmetti, 2009); then it sat vacant until Parnell purchased it three decades later. Inspectors found six leaks in the ceiling, numerous dead mice, faeces (rodent excreta pellets) on counters and in cabinets, and 'what appeared to be a bird's nest' (FDA, 2009b). They also 'found holes in the building's roof' and 'dead rodent remains, rodent feces and feathers in a crawl space above the production area' (Zacher, 2009). The plant's ventilation system sucked debris 'from the infested crawl space into production areas of the plant' (CNN, 2009; Leighton, 2016).

Kendrick called the plant 'disgusting', and the *New York Times* noted that a second former employee 'confirmed Mr. Kendrick's descriptions of the plant and its processes' (Harris, 2009). Kendrick noted the antiquated equipment was used to cook peanuts 'to color, not to kill bacteria'. PCA did not regularly record basic information like the roasting time and temperature of peanut batches. Further, 'the roof leaked so badly that when it rained, workers were instructed to raise tarps to the ceiling to direct the water away from peanuts and plant equipment, the two said. Rain at night went unattended, they said' (Harris, 2009; Harris and Barrett, 2009). In addition, the basement flooded, but the underlying problem was never fixed, so 'the plant always had standing water in its basement' (Harris, 2009). Some products sat in this environment for months until PCA accumulated 1,700 pounds up to tanker truckers to ship. In emails, PCA officials tell employees to 'air hose off the top' of the storage container 'because they are covered in dust and rat crap' (DOJ, 2013a, p 29).

Neither Blakely nor Plainview conducted regular environmental testing – swabbing work surfaces and machinery to check for pathogens. Neither plant regularly tested the finished product, even though PCA claimed 'state-of-the-art Food Safety techniques' (DOJ, 2013a, pp 19, 28). All PCA did was irregularly send samples to lab for testing to generate a Certificate of Analysis (COA) (Hearing on the Salmonella Outbreak [hereafter Hearing], 2009, pp 132–3). Because conditions in PCA's plants maximised the cultivation of *Salmonella*, and Parnell's emails acknowledged regular positive results, getting around positive COAs was an important aspect of PCA's crimes.

When customers did not require a COA, PCA did not test and falsely asserted they did. For one customer that requested testing, 63 per cent of the lots PCA shipped had not been tested (DOJ, 2013a, p 22). PCA sometimes tested up to four samples in order to get a negative result that it would use and then disregard all the positive results (DOJ, 2013a, p 31; Hearing, 2009, p 210). Because of concern that companies can draw repeated samples from a contaminated lot and eventually get a negative, 'you cannot retest away a positive result', said one lab owner at Congressional hearings: 'If you tested 50 samples for a given lot and 49 of those were negative and one was positive, that one positive must trump the 49 negatives' (Hearing, 2009, p 182). But the company 'knowingly shipped out contaminated peanut butter 12 times in the past two years' (Layton, 2009a). Some of the lots that shipped after a positive test were sent to schools (Maugh and Engel, 2009).

PCA also took multiple samples from a relatively clean batch, submitted them for testing under a variety of batch numbers, and then shipped untested batches with those negative test results (DOJ, 2013a, p 21). If a company needed a COA, then a PCA email said they 'would create one.... The girl in TX was very good at white-out' (DOJ, 2013a, p 27). Others were sent COA forms to falsify (DOJ, 2013a, pp 32, 46). In spite of this history, during an interview with an FDA inspector in 2009, Parnell was asked about positive tests for *Salmonella*. He replied: 'This is not something that happens very often and I think I would remember something that came up positive' (DOJ, 2013a, p 49).

In 2011, the victims had a press conference to call for criminal charges, but it received no media attention. Finally, almost four years after Congressional investigators exposed incriminating documents, the DOJ returned a 76-count indictment against four PCA executives (2013b). In addition to Parnell, the indictment named his brother Michael (Vice President of PP Sales and a sales agent for PCA); Samuel Lightsey, Blakely's Operations Manager; and Mary Wilkerson, Blakely's Office and Quality Assurance Manager (DOJ, 2013a). Daniel Kilgore, also a Blakely Operations Manager, was indicted separately and cooperated with the government.

Charges included wire fraud, obstruction of justice and violations of the Food, Drug and Cosmetic Act of 1938 (21 USC Chapter 9), which prohibits the introduction into interstate commerce of any food that is adulterated (contaminated) or misbranded (falsely labelled) (§331a). Section 333a1 creates a misdemeanour strict liability offence, meaning there is no requirement of *mens rea* (intent, awareness) and better protection against wilful blindness and plausible deniability. (This section has very limited application [Klein and Grobley, 2012].) Section 333a2 creates a felony, punishable by imprisonment of up to three years, for repeat offenders or offenders who commit 'a violation with the intent to defraud or mislead.'

The indictment was based on fraud against corporations rather than harm to people. Count 1 is a conspiracy to defraud 'customers', and counts 2 to 67 link to a specified corporate customer (counts 68 to 76 are obstruction of justice). 'Customer #1' – Kelloggs – is identified in 42 of the 67 counts in which the government does not see itself as a victim. The nine dead or many sickened people are not mentioned anywhere. The defence claimed it would be prejudicial for the government to mention them at trial, and the prosecution did not mention public health harms.

Parnell was convicted on 60 felony counts, his brother on 30 counts, and Wilkerson on a count of obstruction of justice (Lightsey and Kilgore were prosecution witnesses under plea agreements). The court sentenced Stewart Parnell to 28 years; Michael Parnell received 20 and Mary Wilkerson five years.

State facilitation: Flaws in guardianship?

While the PCA executives were rightly punished, the government failed in a spectacular way to control a food manufacturer that played 'Russian roulette with children and the elderly' (Hearing, 2009, p 83). Indeed, the appropriate analytic lens is state-corporate crime, which involves 'illegal or socially injurious actions that result from mutually reinforcing interactions' between governments and corporations when they 'pursue goals that intersect' (Aulette and Michalowski, 2006, p 47). State-corporate crime exists on a continuum from acts that are state-initiated to state-facilitated, with the latter including bureaucratic failure and regulatory dysfunction (Kauzlarich et al, 2003, p 247). PCA is a case of state-facilitated crime (Leighton, 2016).

Facilitation happens when the state pursues a business-friendly environment and creates 'regulation deficiency' (Griffin and Miller, 2010, p 223): it minimises criminal liability for corporations and their executives, regulates reluctantly and promotes weak, underfunded, even dysfunctional, regulatory agencies. The problem of state-facilitated crime is most problematic in areas where the government has 'assigned or implied trust/duty' to the public (Kauzlarich et al, 2003, p 247) – and food safety is clearly one of those areas.

The exploration thus involves who was acting as capable guardians (Lanier et al, 2015, p 62) to prevent crime and the ways in which their capabilities were inadequate. With street crime, the police are guardians, but with state-corporate crime, it is legislators and regulatory agencies. Capable guardianship is based on the scope of relevant law, the extent of powers delegated to regulatory agencies, their actual use or implementation of that authority, and the resource level. The main guardian in PCA's case was the FDA, which regulates food (except some meat), drugs (including tobacco, but not herbal supplements), and medical devices, but also cosmetics, pet food and veterinary products. Products regulated by it comprise about 20 per cent of American consumer spending (Hamburg, 2015).

One notable failure by the FDA was in the areas of sanitation and testing. Neither legislation nor the regulatory framework required environmental testing or regular sampling of finished products (Hearing, 2009, p 163). Dr Sundlof, then Director of the FDA's Center for Food Safety and Applied Nutrition, noted in Congressional testimony that it 'is not written anywhere in the law or the regulations but it is common knowledge within the industry that you can't test your way to negative' (Hearing, 2009, p 211).

Further, while testimony from food safety experts was unanimous that a positive test should result in the product being destroyed and equipment disinfected, those steps were in no way required. There was no requirement that positive results on a COA are to be reported to the FDA, which could use them to look for early signs of systematic problems. The FDA had no authority to mandate a recall of any product they determined to be hazardous to health. These deficiencies continued to exist after the 2007 recall of peanut butter that caused 715 cases of salmonellosis (CDC, 2007). Con Agra closed their plant and 'installed new equipment at the manufacturing plant, made repairs to the roof, cleaned and sanitised the plant, ensured separation of raw ingredients from post–peanut-roasting areas that handle processed product, created a new Hazard Analysis and Critical Control Points Plan, and implemented a revised environmental testing program for Salmonella' (Sheth et al, 2011, p 360).

The FDA contracts with states to do inspections, with the FDA maintaining an oversight role. But in 2010, after PCA had been exposed, the Department of Health and Human Service's Office of Inspector General (OIG) 'found that more than half of all food facilities have gone 5 or more years without an FDA inspection and that FDA does not always take swift and effective action to remedy violations found during inspections' (Department of Health and Human Services, 2011, p 6; Layton, 2009d). Resource constraints meant routine inspections involved no environmental or product testing, which is only done in 'for-cause inspections' (Hearing, 2009, p 160).

Both Georgia and Texas conducted inspections under a contract with the FDA, and both had poor records of holding PCA accountable. There is no record of enforcement actions against PCA, even though a buyer for a snack food company that inspected PCA in the mid-1980s said: 'The roofs leaked, the windows would be open, and birds would fly through the building…. It was just a time bomb waiting to go off, and everybody in the peanut industry in Georgia, Virginia and Texas – they all knew' (Layton and Miroff, 2009).

The failure of Texas guardians was extreme. The Texas Department of Agriculture certified PCA's facility as an organic processor, which meant that it separated organic from conventionally grown products and cleaned the machinery used for conventionally grown food before processing organic food. The organic certification depended on the facility being properly licensed and inspected by the Department of

State Health Services for food safety and sanitation, which did not happen during the years PCA operated the plant – and even after they added a small retail outlet that sold directly to the public (Harris, 2009; Layton and Miroff, 2009; Zacher, 2009).

The Georgia Department of Agriculture had conducted nine inspections of PCA's Blakely site between 2006 and 2008, which the *Washington Post* summarised as follows: 'The state inspection reports all seemed to play down deficiencies, saying all that was needed was routine follow-up' (Layton, 2009c). Between 2007 and 2008, the Department tested 35 samples from the five facilities that produce peanut butter in the state; three came from PCA's plant and were negative. Oscar Garrison, Assistant Commissioner responsible for the Department of Agriculture's Consumer Protection Division, stated that because of low laboratory capacity they only tested whatever food product seemed most problematic at the moment (Hearing, 2009, p 118). He explained that the inspection form did not include questions about positive microbial tests. Further, 'when companies are not required to give records, we don't even know if tests have been conducted' (Hearing, 2009, p 120). Indeed, inspectors did not have the authority to examine peanut roasting records to make sure the times and temperatures were even filled in (Hearing, 2009, pp 125–6).

Conclusion

PCA's executives officially killed nine, sickened 700 and caused the largest food recall by product count. Executives lied about having a state-of-the-art food safety process, and their own documents and emails show they knowingly shipped out a product contaminated with *Salmonella* on multiple occasions. But similar to the livelihoods of farm managers in agri-food systems (see Chapter 4, this volume), the deeds of the bad actors and a rogue corporation should not deflect attention from structural problems and larger social, political and economic forces (Leighton, 2016).

First, many larger food producers did not carefully scrutinise PCA because it was a low-cost supplier, which are highly valued by industry. While Nestlé inspected PCA itself and rejected them as a supplier (2006), other major food manufacturers were comfortable relying on a third party inspection system with an inherent conflict of interest. PCA paid the American Institute of Baking (AIB) for an inspection and received a 'superior' rating for its Plainview plant. AIB could not say PCA's facility was unacceptable if they wanted repeat business, and the customer service mentality leads to non-objective ratings.

Further, the embrace of low-cost suppliers extended to government. As a US$30 million a year business, PCA was relatively insignificant, but Parnell was a member of the Department of Agriculture's Peanut Standards Board, which oversees moisture content and peanut size for grading purposes (pathogens are not included in their interpretation of 'quality and handling standards' in the authorising legislation). Parnell was reappointed to a second term, but removed in 2009 (Keefe, 2009). After Congressional hearings, but before the indictments, Parnell was a 'consultant to peanut companies' again (Bottemiller, 2010). Interestingly – and sadly – around Plainview, the community directed more anger at Kendrick for bringing attention to the plant and costing them jobs than at Parnell for killing nine people.

Second, politicians of both parties equate regulation with 'red tape' that hurts the economy, creating anti-regulatory zeal. In contrast to the rhetoric about overbearing regulatory agencies, in the PCA's case inspectors missed and downplayed flaws in the facility they knew about, and were unaware of an unregistered facility that had prominent signage and was registered with other state agencies. Less than two years after the Con Agra hospitalised 715 with *Salmonella* from a plant with leaking roofs, no environmental or product testing and cross-contamination, PCA's Blakely plant – in the same state and 75 miles away – had the exact same problems. No regulations require pathogen testing or require a food manufacturer to destroy the product and clean up after they receive a positive test for pathogens.

One victim of PCA's products commented, 'there was some congresswoman saying we need to enact laws now to not let this happen again. And I was like, "You idiot. What have you all been doing?"' (Moss, 2009). The FSMA became law in 2011, 'the most sweeping reform of our food safety laws in more than 70 years' (FDA, 2013) – but also the only major overhaul of food laws. PCA played a role in generating pressure for its passage, along with high-profile recalls of spinach, 500 million eggs (FDA, 2010) and 143 million pounds of beef (*New York Times*, 2008).

However, FSMA was not a rejection of anti-regulatory zeal. The bill had the support of larger companies that wanted to avoid some of the problems Kellogg had because of PCA. All proposals to create additional food crimes or increase criminal penalties were rejected in committee (Johnson, 2011, p 11). The legislation did not ban third party inspections or even impose standards for those conducting them. The FSMA did not alter the status quo on a number of other problems exposed by PCA. Even worse, Congressional budget appropriations have been about half the level the Congressional Budget Office said was necessary for the FDA to fulfil all of the new mandates (Johnson, 2011, pp 6–7; Goad, 2014; Zuraw, 2015).

Congress seems to have responded to well publicised public health problems by giving the agency broad new mandates, which Congress subsequently did not fully fund. The accretion of unfunded or under-funded mandates over many cycles of 'reform' sets up agencies for continued, visible struggles and failures. Certainly legislators are not responsible for all regulatory dysfunction, but anti-regulatory actions by legislators can have a significant negative impact, including in the area of food safety.

Third, even if Parnell's 28 years was an appropriate sentence for nine negligent (reckless?) deaths and thousands of assaults, the link between punishment and harm to people is not supported by the indictment. The indictment was based on harm to corporate food producers, with no mention of death or illness at the criminal trial.

To be sure, food producers were victims of PCA. Kellogg lost US$65 million – 2 per cent of each year's operating profit – for inventory, recall and disposal, plus an unknown amount in lost sales (Kellogg, 2010, p 53) and millions in civil settlements. This matters because work by Black (1976) and others (Leighton and Reiman, 2014) concludes that the response to a victimisation depends on the relative status of the victim and perpetrator. PCA, a relatively small company, repeatedly lied to federal officials, and the Department of Justice still took four years to return an indictment listing nine national and two multinational companies as customers/victims. If PCA had been bigger and/or sold directly to the public, how would that have changed/reduced the response, even if nine people still died and more than 700 were officially injured?

This analysis recognises that the size, power and interests of corporate victims can affect the intensity, comprehensiveness and nature of the state response to state-corporate crime. Indeed, the reason for describing it is to ask how the balance of corporate interests and public interests played out. Or how the willingness of government to stand up for the regular citizens eating peanut butter would have been different if large food producers were against the legislation and/or not harmed by the wrongdoing?

The mass victimisation perpetrated by PCA makes it a powerful case study of food crime. It demonstrates how a small group of people motivated by profit, not terrorist ideology, can cause death and widespread illness though the industrial food production system. The victims were average citizens, with the inevitable over-representation by age and pre-existing illness. The criminal sentences for PCA executives and food safety legislation were appropriate responses, but the specific conclusion is that justice can (somewhat) prevail where the interests of big food producers and regular citizens align.

References

Aulette, J., and Michalowski, R. (2006) 'The fire in Hamlet', in R. Michalowski and R. Kramer (eds) *State-corporate crime*, New Brunswick, NJ: Rutgers University Press, pp 45–66.

Black, D. (1976) *The behavior of law*, New York: Academic Press.

Borrell, B. (2009) 'How does *Salmonella* get into peanut butter?', *Scientific American*, 13 January (www.scientificamerican.com/article.cfm?id=Salmonella-poisoning-peanut-butter).

Bottemiller, H. (2010) 'PCA exec back to work despite investigation', *Food Safety News*, 9 September (www.foodsafetynews.com/2010/09/peanut-exec-under-criminal-investigation-is-back-to-work/).

Cavallaro, E. (2011) '*Salmonella* Typhimurium infections associated with peanut products', *The New England Journal of Medicine*, vol 356, no 7, pp 601–10.

CDC (Centers for Disease Control and Prevention) (2009a) 'Investigation update: Outbreak of *Salmonella* Typhimurium infections, 2008–2009' (www.cdc.gov/Salmonella/Typhimurium/update.html).

CDC (2009b) 'Multistate outbreak of *Salmonella* infections associated with peanut butter and peanut butter-containing products', *Morbidity and Mortality Weekly Report*, vol 58, no 4, pp 85–90.

CDC (2007) 'Multistate outbreak of *Salmonella* infections associated with peanut butter', *Morbidity and Mortality Weekly Report*, vol 56, no 21, pp 521–4.

CDC (2013) 'Outbreak detection' (www.cdc.gov/pulsenet/outbreak-detection/index.html).

CNN (2009) 'Dead rodents, excrement in peanut processor lead to recall', 12 February (www.cnn.com/2009/US/02/12/peanut.butter.recall/).

Dalziel, G.R. (2009) *Food defense incidents 1950–2008*, Singapore: Centre of Excellence for National Security, Nanyang Technological University.

Department of Health and Human Services (2011) 'Vulnerabilities in FDA's oversight of state food facility inspections', Office of Inspector General (https://oig.hhs.gov/oei/reports/oei-02-09-00430.pdf).

DOJ (Department of Justice) (US) (2013a) *US v Stewart Parnell, et al* (www.justice.gov/iso/opa/resources/61201322111426350488.pdf).

DOJ (2013b) 'Former officials and broker of Peanut Corporation of America indicted related to *Salmonella*-tainted peanut products' (www.justice.gov/opa/pr/2013/February/13-civ-220.html).

FDA (Food & Drug Administration) (2009a) 'FDA's investigation' (https://web.archive.org/web/20091211230556/http://www.fda.gov/Safety/Recalls/MajorProductRecalls/Peanut/FDA%E2%80%99sInvestigation/default.htm).

FDA (2009b) 'Inspection report on PCA facility in Plainview, Texas' (www.fda.gov/downloads/AboutFDA/CentersOffices/OfficeofGlobalRegulatoryOperationsandPolicy/ORA/ORAElectronicReadingRoom/UCM114852.pdf).

FDA (2010) '*Salmonella* enteritidis outbreak in shell eggs' (www.fda.gov/Food/NewsEvents/NewsfromOtherFederalResources/ucm222684.htm).

FDA (2013) Food Safety Modernization Act (FSMA) (www.fda.gov/food/guidanceregulation/fsma/).

Flynn, D. (2009) 'PCA executives to divide $875,000', *Food Safety News*, 11 December (www.foodsafetynews.com/2009/12/pca-executives-get-to-divide-875000-among-themselves/).

Goad, J. (2014) 'Senators, food industry groups call for more FSMA funding', *The Hill*, 3 September (http://thehill.com/regulation/216463-to-do-list-on-food-safety-grows-longer-for-agencies).

Griffin III, O.H. and Miller, B.L. (2010) 'OxyContin and a regulation deficiency of the pharmaceutical industry: Rethinking state-corporate crime', *Critical Criminology*, vol 19, no 3, pp 213–26.

Hamburg, M. (2015) 'Statement of Margaret Hamburg, MD, Commissioner of Food and Drugs', Hearings before the House Subcommittee on Agriculture, Rural Development, Food & Drug Administration and Related Agencies, 4 March (http://docs.house.gov/meetings/AP/AP01/20150304/103059/HHRG-114-AP01-Wstate-HamburgM-20150304.pdf).

Harris, G. (2009) 'After tests, peanut plant in Texas is closed', *New York Times*, 10 February (www.nytimes.com/2009/02/11/health/policy/11peanut.html).

Harris, D. and Barrett, K. (2009) 'Former manager says peanut plant complaints ignored', ABC News, 16 February (http://abcnews.go.com/GMA/story?id=6888169).

Harris, D. and Belluck, P. (2009) 'New look at food safety after peanut tainting', *New York Times*, 29 January (www.nytimes. com/2009/01/30/health/30peanut.html).

Hartman, B. and Barrett, K. (2009) 'Timeline of the *Salmonella* outbreak', ABC News, 10 February (http://abcnews.go.com/Health/ story?id=6837291&page=1).

Hearing on the Salmonella Outbreak (2009) House Subcommittee on Oversight and Investigation, Committee on Energy and Commerce, 11 February (https://web.archive.org/web/20110602100540/http:// democrats.energycommerce.house.gov/index.php?q=hearing/the-salmonella-outbreak-the-continued-failure-to-protect-the-food-supply).

Johnson, R. (2011) 'Food safety issues for the 112th Congress', Congressional Research Service, 10 February (http:// nationalaglawcenter.org/wp-content/uploads/assets/crs/R41629. pdf).

Kauzlarich, D., Mullins, C. and Matthews, R. (2003) 'A complicity continuum of state crime', *Contemporary Justice Review*, vol 6, no 3, pp 241–54.

Keefe, B. (2009) 'Peanut firm's chief an adviser', *Atlanta Journal and Constitution*, 1 February, A15.

Kellogg (2010) Form 10-K, filed with the Securities and Exchange Commission (www.sec.gov/Archives/edgar/ data/55067/000119312510042654/d10k.htm).

Klein, S. and Grobley, I. (2012) 'Debunking claims of over-federalization of criminal law', *Emory Law Journal*, vol 62, no 1, pp 1–120.

Lanier, M., Henry, S. and Anastasia, D. (2015) *Essential criminology*, Boulder, CO: Westview Press.

Layton, L. (2009a) 'Peanut processor ignored *Salmonella* tests, knowingly sold tainted products', *Washington Post*, 28 January (www.washingtonpost.com/wp-dyn/content/article/2009/01/27/ AR2009012702992.html).

Layton, L. (2009b) 'Suspect peanuts sent to schools', *Washington Post*, 6 February (www.washingtonpost.com/wp-dyn/content/ article/2009/02/05/AR2009020500743.html).

Layton, L. (2009c) 'Every peanut product from Ga. Plant recalled', *Washington Post*, 29 January (http://articles.washingtonpost. com/2009-01-29/news/36924188_1_peanut-corporation-Salmonella-contamination-stewart-parnell).

Layton, L. (2009d) 'FDA hasn't intensified inspections at peanut facilities, despite illness', *Washington Post*, 3 April (http://articles. washingtonpost.com/2009-04-03/news/36871609_1_peanut-corporation-Salmonella-illness-peanut-products).

Layton, L. and Miroff, N. (2009) 'The rise and fall of a peanut empire', *Washington Post*, 15 February (www.washingtonpost.com/wp-dyn/content/article/2009/02/14/AR2009021401758.html).

Leighton, P. (2016) 'Mass *Salmonella* poisoning by the peanut corporation of America: State-corporate crime involving food safety', *Critical Criminology*, vol 24, no 1, pp 75–91.

Leighton, P. and Reiman, J. (2014) 'A suitable amount of street crime and a suitable amount of white collar crime: Inconvenient truths about inequality, crime and criminal justice', in B. Arrigo and H. Berscot (eds) *Routledge handbook of international crime and justice studies*, London: Routledge, pp 302–24.

Lynchburg Office (of PCA) (2009) 'Salmonella investigation', 12 January [email] (https://web.archive.org/web/20110602100540/http://democrats.energycommerce.house.gov/index.php?q=hearing/the-salmonella-outbreak-the-continued-failure-to-protect-the-food-supply).

Marler, B. (2011) 'Last peanut corporation of America *Salmonella* death case settled for undisclosed sum', Marler Blog, 9 August (www.marlerblog.com/legal-cases/last-peanut-corporation-of-america-Salmonella-death-case-settled-for-undisclosed-sum/).

Matthews, R. and Kauzlarich, D. (2006) 'The crash of ValueJet flight 592', in R. Michalowski and R. Kramer (eds) *State-corporate crime*, New Brunswick, NJ: Rutgers University Press, pp 82–97.

Maugh, T. and Engel, M. (2009) 'Peanut company lied on *Salmonella* testing, FDA finds', *Los Angeles Times*, 7 February (http://articles.latimes.com/2009/feb/07/science/sci-peanut-fda7).

Moss, M. (2009) 'Peanut case shows holes in safety net', *Washington Post*, 8 February (www.nytimes.com/2009/02/09/us/09peanuts.html?_r=1&hp).

Nestlé (2006) 'NQS Level 1 – Food safety audit report of Peanut Corporation of America', 5 January (https://web.archive.org/web/20140729034750/http://democrats.energycommerce.house.gov/sites/default/files/documents/Audit-Nestle-Peanut-Corporation-2006.pdf).

New York Times (2008) Editorial: 'The biggest beef recall ever', 21 February (www.nytimes.com/2008/02/21/opinion/21thu1.html).

Parnell, S. (2009) 'Salmonella outbreak spreads to 42 states', 7 January [email] (https://web.archive.org/web/20110602100540/http://democrats.energycommerce.house.gov/index.php?q=hearing/the-salmonella-outbreak-the-continued-failure-to-protect-the-food-supply).

Sheth, A.N., Hoekstra, M., Patel, N., Ewald, G., Lord, C., Clarke, C., et al (2011) 'A national outbreak of *Salmonella* serotype Tennessee infections from contaminated peanut butter: A new food vehicle for salmonellosis in the United States', *Clinical Infectious Diseases*, vol 53, no 4, pp 356–62.

Sundlof, S. (2009) Testimony before the House Subcommittee on Oversight and Investigation, Committee on Energy and Commerce, 11 February (https://web.archive.org/web/20110602100540/http://democrats.energycommerce.house.gov/index.php?q=hearing/the-salmonella-outbreak-the-continued-failure-to-protect-the-food-supply).

Török, T.J., Tauxe, R.V., Wise, R.P., Livengood, J.R., Sokolow, R., Mauvais, S., et al (1997) 'A large community outbreak of salmonellosis caused by intentional contamination of restaurant salad bars', *Journal of the American Medical Association*, vol 278, no 5, 6 August, 389–95.

Vielmetti, E. (2009) 'PCA Texas peanut factory – the former Jimmy Dean Meat sausage factory – in Plainview, TX closed' (https://web.archive.org/web/20100505151303/http://vielmetti.typepad.com/vacuum/2009/02/pca-texas-peanut-factory-the-former-jimmy-dean-meat-sausage-factory-in-plainview-tx-closed.html).

Zacher, D. (2009) 'City unaware of outlet store at Plainview peanut plant', *My Plainview*, 20 February (www.myplainview.com/news/article_8652e07b-d45a-5e89-8009-ce8e8fdeb74a.html).

Zuraw, L. (2015) 'Hamburg tells senate budget committee FSMA funding needed to fill "significant" gaps', *Food Safety News*, 13 March (www.foodsafetynews.com/2015/03/hamburg-tells-senate-budget-committee-fsma-funding-needed-to-fill-significant-gaps).

12

Food crime in the context of cheap capitalism

Joseph Yaw Asomah and Hongming Cheng

Introduction

The production and sale of unsafe food, which typifies the concept of cheap capitalism, has become a global concern due to the increasing integration and interdependence of contemporary societies. For instance, the marketing of genetically modified (GM) food worldwide poses potential harm to consumers (Walters, 2006). Additionally, millions of people around the world are exposed to food poisoning, with 350,000 dying annually from it (Sifferlin, 2015). In general, the issue of unsafe food is not a new development. For example, during the Industrial Revolution in the UK, dangerous additives, including lead and mercury, were added to milk production (Philips and French, 2000). Adulteration cases in the US, Canada and Australia led to the passage of anti-adulteration laws in the late 19th and early 20th centuries (Pilcher, 2006).

The recent rise of cases involving unsafe food, however, demonstrate a historic and disturbing pattern of consumers' daily vulnerability to the risk posed by dishonest food corporations sacrificing consumer safety and health for economic gain (Walters, 2006, 2007; Croall, 2009, 2012; Cheng, 2012; Picard, 2012; Young, 2012; Ghazi-Tehrani and Pontell, 2015; Leighton, 2016). In the US, for example, the Peanut Corporation of America (PCA) knowingly distributed *Salmonella*-contaminated peanuts to manufacturers and schools between 2008 and 2009, which led to nine deaths, and about 11,000 illnesses (Leighton, 2016; see also Chapter 11, this volume). Similarly, the Sanlu Group consciously sold its melamine-contaminated infant formula to consumers, which caused the death of at least six babies, and over 300,000 illnesses (Ghazi-Tehrani and Pontell, 2015). These cases of unsafe food, combined with the discursive reframing of human–nature relationships by cheap food (see Chapter 2, this volume), demonstrate the growing problem of cheap capitalism in the food sector globally.

Using secondary data sources, including the media, regulatory bodies, interest groups and scholarly literature, this chapter explores unsafe food within the conceptual framework of cheap capitalism. By examining the nature and scale of unsafe food, it first argues that cheap capitalism is rampant and poses a greater risk to public health locally and internationally. Second, it argues that the state, industry and the processes of globalisation typically constitute the dominant factors driving cheap capitalism in the food sector. Third, it argues that unsafe food in the Canadian context can properly be understood within the global context of cheap capitalism. Finally, it examines steps being taken to address cheap capitalism in the food industry.

Cheap capitalism

In his research on food crime in the Chinese context, Cheng (2012) coined the term 'cheap capitalism' as characterised by degraded business morality, low prices and/or unsafe goods or services, and low-waged labour to maximise profits. Businesses across the supply chain face a strategic and ethical dilemma between seeking new methods of reducing labour and material costs in order to remain competitive, and following legal rules and ethical codes. This has shaped the very nature of today's farmers (see Chapter 4, this volume) and food corporations globally.

'Cheap capitalism', as used in this chapter, integrates and builds on insights from theories of anomie, triple helix and white-collar and corporate crime for analysing food crime. Sutherland (1949) suggests that crimes committed by powerful actors often escape criminal justice systems. Further, the concept of the triple helix – the university–industry–government partnership (Etzkowitz and Leydesdorff, 1996; Etzkowitz and Zhou, 2007) to advance mutual interests – has the tendency to undermine public interests in regard to food safety. In addition, rapid social changes can potentially create anomic conditions (Durkheim, 1951) that lead to social problems such as food crimes and harms. According to Merton (1938), criminogenic conditions take place when material gain trumps collective interests, including consumer safety, alongside the relaxation of the legitimate means for attaining such material interests. In expanding this theory, Robinson and Murphy (2009) suggest that the root cause of contemporary corporate crimes is unrestrained greed.

Incorporating these insights, cheap capitalism is used in this chapter as a framework for explaining and analysing unsafe food. It argues that the state, industry and the processes of neoliberal globalisation typically constitute the dominant factors shaping and driving cheap capitalism in the food sector. In the second sense, it is employed to delineate a general development in which profit-maximisation motives of food corporations are consistently undermining consumer interests through deliberate disrespect for ethical obligations and legal guidelines.

The scale and nature of food crime

Food crime takes on different forms, including food fraud, misleading labelling and packaging, and the sale of outdated and contaminated food (Croall, 2009, 2012), although these dimensions tend to overlap. This section draws on selective cases to analyse the scale and nature of unsafe food from a global perspective with an attempt to emphasise the Canadian context.

Food fraud

Food fraud generally refers to 'the deliberate and intentional substitution, addition, tampering, or misrepresentation of food, food ingredients, or food packaging; or false or misleading statements made about a product for economic gain' (Guajardo, 2016, p 2). Food fraud involves a conscious use of dishonest means to unfairly take advantage of consumers to maximise profit by the seller, distributor or the producer. The recent infamous horsemeat scandals, involving the selling of horsemeat as beef, which hit seven European countries, including Germany, is a typical demonstration of fraud, and, for that matter, cheap capitalism in the food industry (Guajardo, 2016; see also Chapter 10, this volume).

In China, rat meat was passed off and sold as lamb to consumers in 2013 (Martina, 2013). In the UK, following 60 tests carried out on lamb takeaways, *Which?* (2014) reports that 24 of these tests did not contain lamb as described on the label. In addition, beef burgers put on sale in the UK and Ireland were found to contain horsemeat; ABP Food Group and Liffey Meats linked to this scandal supplied the products from their meat factories in the UK and Ireland (BBC News, 2013), which further substantiates cheap capitalism.

Food poisoning

Food poisoning is one of the major sources of death and illness for consumers. In the Philippines, for example, in 2015 the Caraga candy-poisoning incident led to illness among approximately 2,000 people (SunStar, 2015). In Pakistan, the 2016 Punjab sweet poisoning culminated in the death of more than 33 people, including five children; the sweet was tainted with chlorfenapyr, a toxic insecticide (NDTV, 2016).

In Canada, food poisoning affects at least 4 million Canadians every year (Health Canada, 2013a). In 2012, at least 15 people died from consuming food products poisoned with *E. coli* as a result of the unhygienic conditions and the violation of licensing regulations by XL Foods, the Canadian meatpacking company. This poisoning also caused the largest recall of red meat in Canadian history in 2012. The company, however, bounced back to business after one week, and started shipping meat to stores again in just 10 days (Picard, 2012). These cases of food safety concerns demonstrate the increasing threat and potential harm confronting consumers in this era of cheap capitalism.

Food adulteration and contamination

Food products may contain an extensive amount of water and chemical additives beyond legally acceptable limits. In many cases, these additives that are not declared on the food labelling have sparked several food recalls on discovery. In Canada, for example, undeclared food ingredients and chemical additives represented approximately one-third of 350 food recalls in 2010 (CFIA, 2010).

In addition to the issue of adulteration, the sale of contaminated food has been the most serious and dangerous of all forms of cheap capitalism. The case of the major Brazilian meat-processing firms,

Brazil Foods (BRF), and Jose Batista Sobrinho (JBS), which reportedly engaged in the sale and export of meat known to be either rotten or contaminated with *Salmonella*, has been the latest evidence of the global nature and danger of cheap capitalism. These firms allegedly bribed meat regulatory inspectors to sanction the sale of tainted and unwholesome meat products (Freitas et al, 2017). This case confirms the reality of degraded business morality and the state-corporate link in driving cheap capitalism.

In September 2014, Taiwan also witnessed a number of food safety incidents in which cooking oil tainted with recycled waste, animal feed and gutter oil was sold across the country, although this oil product was not fit for human consumption. The Taiwan-based Chang Guann firm involved in this scandal purchased 243 tons of the tainted cheap oil from an unlicensed factory and blended it with other oil to cut down costs and make more profit (*Food Safety News*, 2014). The pattern of these cases demonstrates an evidence of cheap capitalism in which the desire for profit at all costs is privileged over consumer safety and health.

In addition, several food recalls have been issued across the globe due to food safety concerns. In Australia, for example, the Pork Pie Shop recalled pork pies due to possible *Salmonella* contamination (Food Standards, 2017). In the US, Pinnacle Foods voluntarily recalled frozen pancakes, waffles and French toast slices triggered by possible listeria contamination, which can cause high fever, severe headache and abdominal pain, as well as fatal illnesses, particularly among children and elderly people. Similarly, Frito-Lay recalled cooked potato chips believed to contain *Salmonella*, and Lords Organics recalled a ginger powder product from the market due to contamination with *Salmonella* (FDA, 2017).

Canada has also experienced cases of food adulteration and contamination. The August 2008 listeriosis outbreak involving a Maple Leaf Foods plant in Canada was linked to 22 deaths (CBC News, 2009; Weatherill, 2009). This outbreak prompted one of the largest food recalls in Canadian history (Reuters, 2008). In 2013, chloramphenicol, a banned drug in Canada, was detected in food products imported from China (Health Canada, 2013b). Food contamination continues to be a challenge in the Canadian food industry. Between January and early May 2017, approximately 58 food recalls involving food contamination and undeclared food content have taken place. For instance, Montasio DOP cheese was recalled in Ontario in May following listeria contamination (CFIA, 2017). The Canadian and international cases of food adulteration and contamination highlight the continued danger from cheap capitalism.

Food content

Food products indicated as having low proportions of 'natural' ingredients often contradict the labelling information. In Canada, McCain pizza pockets, offered as a healthy food alternative, contain 470 milligrams of sodium per each pizza pocket (CBC News, 2012). In other instances, odd substances, such as pieces of metal and plastic, have been found in food products. For example, chocolate bars were found to contain plastic materials, which prompted a recall in 55 countries, including Germany, France and the Netherlands, in 2016 (Quinn et al, 2016). These cases are rarely prosecuted, as they are typically considered accidental.

Misleading food labelling

Misleading food labels have become a widespread food malpractice. Regulatory food sample tests in the UK confirmed that lamb sold to consumers actually contained beef in most cases, and in other cases, a mixture of beef and lamb (BBC News, 2013). In 2013, Japan was hit with food mislabelling scandals in which labels that indicated high-quality nutrients turned out to be false. Luxurious hotels, restaurants and department stores, including Takashimaya and Daimaru, admitted having sold food with false labels (Japan Today, 2013).

In the Canadian context, following the Canadian Food Inspection Agency's (CFIA) 621 food tests, 58 per cent of the food products tested did not reflect the labelling information on nutrient content. Famous brands, including Unilever, Frito-Lay, Kraft and Heinz, were involved in these cases of misleading food labelling (Chai, 2015). Additionally, Maple Leaf Foods advertises its natural selection line of deli meat as having no preservatives when, in fact, they contain nitrite, which has been linked to cancer (CBC News, 2012). These cases of misleading food labelling demonstrate evidence of cheap capitalism, as they involve a disregard for food labelling standards.

Misleading pictures and packaging

Misleading pictures and packaging deceive consumers into buying food products that may seemingly look larger than they really are. The *Mail Online* (Cliff, 2017), for example, has documented photos of food products packaged and advertised as containing a larger amount that turn out to contain less. It also reports that the labelling information actually contradicts the content, for example, a gluten-free chocolate cookie that was proven to contain gluten. Canadian foods are also not exempt from misleading pictures and packaging, as CBC News (2012) has also catalogued food products with misleading pictures and packaging. Danone's packaging information for the DanActive probiotic drink claims that this product is scientifically proven to prevent colds and flu. This claim was later found to be false; the company was therefore asked to pay a settlement amount of US$21 million in the US. Danone's DanActive food product was also on the Canadian food market with similar claims on its packaging labels without authorisation from the Canadian food regulators (CBC News, 2012).

Vague food descriptions

Food labelling with words such as fresh, natural, pure, traditional, original, authentic, homemade, light, reduced, no added sugar and extra light hardly provide any meaningful information. For example, the phrase 'no added sugar' means that no sugar is added during the processing, but the food contains natural sugar, while 'light fat' means that the product contains less fat, which is not definitive as low fat (Consumer Reports, 2014). Investigations have shown that many products with 'nutritious' or 'low fat' labels turn out to have high amounts of salt, fat or sugar (Deza, 2017). These numerous cases, which highlight various strategies that most food corporations employ to boost sales, cut cost and increase profit by disregarding ethical obligations and food regulations, exemplify cheap capitalism. The FDA (2016) and CFIA (2016) have therefore introduced food labelling guidelines to clarify the legal (or illegal) use of words and phrases, including 'natural' and 'no preservatives', for describing food nutritional content to help consumers make informed choices.

Why cheap capitalism in the food industry?

While the interaction of several factors may be responsible for cheap capitalism in the food sector, this section argues that the state, industry and the processes of globalisation typically constitute the dominant driving forces. Simultaneously these factors help produce a contemporary culture of food fraud and a declining business morality.

Neoliberal globalisation

Neoliberal globalisation has resulted in the greater connectivity and interdependence of contemporary societies at a faster pace. The processes of neoliberal economic and political restructuring have taken the capitalist structure to another level. By its nature, capitalism typically places commercial profit motives over and above collective interests, including the welfare of consumers. It is a system that frees and legitimises greed through rationalisation of profit maximisation. This economic order thrives on human self-interests and greed, as epitomised in the use of illegitimate strategies, including inferior raw materials, to reduce production costs and enhance profit maximisation.

More importantly, the processes of neoliberal globalisation have made it possible for powerful corporations to move their operations to countries where the regulatory framework is weaker. The finished products are then exported back to countries where regulations and enforcement are – comparatively – more stringent. A classic example is the increasing interest of most multinational corporations to relocate to China, where cheap labour and less rigorous health and safety regulations enable corporations to achieve higher productivity at a lesser cost to maximise profit (Cheng, 2012).

Neoliberal globalisation insinuates that risk to food safety in one country can easily be exported to other countries through importing foreign goods. The infamous horsemeat scandal, involving the selling of horsemeat as beef, which affected at least seven European countries, including Germany, demonstrates the contemporary global nature of food safety risk (Guajardo, 2016). Further, the Brazil meat scandal, involving the sale and export of contaminated and rotten meat through a collusion of some meat producers and some members of the food regulatory body (Freitas et al, 2017), demonstrates the constant danger and global nature of food crime. Without robust regulatory enforcement, and sophisticated fraud-detecting technology to counter unlawful capitalist greed, food crime may even get worse.

Within the current global neoliberal climate, however, corporations have increasingly become more powerful actors in local and international spheres due to their economic influences in the creation of jobs. Most politicians not only get resources from corporations to support political campaigns, but also depend on them to reduce the unemployment rate and ensure economic stability. This development has given corporations leverage in shaping the regulatory landscape, often to their advantage but to the detriment of consumer health and safety.

The state

The state's role in food crime is very pronounced given its monopoly over regulatory mechanisms. The way the state impacts crime levels may take different forms, including both actions and inactions. For example, governments can purposely pursue a decriminalisation and deregulation agenda to reduce corporate criminal liabilities under the name of creating a business-friendly climate to attract investors. On the other hand, the state may reduce food safety spending and emphasise heavy reliance on industry regulation, which may pave the way for unscrupulous corporations to exploit this deregulation by engaging in cheap capitalism. Leighton's (2016; see also Chapter 11, this volume) findings, for instance, show evidence of the interaction of lax state regulatory enforcement linked to food safety spending cuts, and the corporation's profit-maximisation agenda as the driving force behind the food scandal involving the PCA. Reduction in food safety funding thus tends to raise food safety concerns among consumers.

In Canada, the planned federal spending cut to CFIA in the wake of the increasing threat to food safety from within and outside Canada will likely impact the Agency's mandate to ensure high food safety standards (Johnson, 2014). Health Canada's 2014–15 report (2016a) on 'plans and priorities' show that the meat and poultry safety programme will see a reduction of $24 million between 2015 and 2017, alongside a drop in full-time employees by 152 within the same period. During this timeframe, reports indicate that funding for the food safety sub-programme will gradually reduce by $35 million, while the number of full-time staff for the programme will also decrease by 192 (Health Canada, 2014). Similarly, funding for the food safety programme will decrease by $115 million between 2017 and 2019 (Health Canada, 2016b). This spending reduction is shifting greater attention to partnership-based regulation (Health Canada, 2014), which emphasises an over-reliance on industry self-regulation. While companies may strive to ensure food safety through self-regulation, a greater reliance on this form of regulation poses a risk of less strict enforcement of food safety standards due to commercial profit motives (see Chapter 1, this volume).

Aside from the food safety spending cut, some countries may have direct stakes in multinational corporations, which may compromise their food safety regulatory enforcement. For example, in the case of the Sanlu Group, the company responsible for the melamine-contaminated formula scandal in 2008, the Chinese government was the majority shareholder, while the New Zealand Company, Fonterra, was the minority stakeholder. Unsurprising, it was the prime minister of New Zealand who pressured the Chinese government to address the scandal. The Chinese government's stake in the company likely contributed to its initial efforts at masking the scandal. Evidence also shows that six other companies had their infant formula certified and exempted from regulatory inspections in China (Ghazi-Tehrani and Pontell, 2015). Such significant trust in industry self-regulation is subject to abuse due to corporations' profit motives, as the case of Sanlu Group exemplifies. Deregulation, food safety spending cuts and states' special interest in corporations typically compromise food regulations that engender food crime.

Industry

Like most businesses, food industries are established with profit maximisation as the ultimate goal. The industries' inordinate desire for uncapped profits often ends up in violations of laws governing food production to reduce costs. The Taiwan food scandal, Japan food scandal and the horsemeat scandal in Europe previously discussed are some cases exemplifying cheap capitalism, and provide compelling evidence of how some corporations endanger food safety for profit gains. Unrestrained corporate profit motives have contributed to a contemporary culture of fraud and declining business morality, which endangers public health.

Contemporary culture of fraud

The classic case of Brazil's 2017 meat scandal shows a consistent pattern of a contemporary culture of fraud within the food business community.

Unrealistic corporate profit targets, with limited opportunities to achieve them, partly sheds light on unscrupulous corporations' increasing use of unethical and illegal strategies to advance corporate profit interests. In today's world, performance and competition pressures are daily features of the prevailing capitalist social order. Corporations are often tempted to overstep legal boundaries to increase and consolidate their market share in order to stay in business, and make more profits, particularly when the chances of detection and sanctions are overly minimal. The apparent unrestrained economic gains is perhaps useful in making sense of why giant meat-supplying firms, including BRF and JBS in Brazil, will knowingly engage in the sale and export of meat known to be either rotten or contaminated with *Salmonella* by bribing meat regulatory inspectors (Freitas et al, 2017).

Declining business morality

Corporate interests unsettle business morality and ethical obligations. Within the current global neoliberal climate, individual and corporate gains seem to have taken primacy over collective human security and safety, due to greater emphasis on unfettered competition and profit maximisation. The several cases cited, including the Taiwan food scandal, Brazil meat scandal, Japan food scandal and the horsemeat scandal in Europe, as evidence of cheap capitalism in the food sector, indicate a consistent pattern of declining business morality. The issue of food crime as driven by profit maximisation without consideration for the health of consumers suggests a demise of moral and ethical consciousness in the marketplace, and in regulatory institutions.

Does regulation work?

The desire for uncapped profits, as an inherent problem in the capitalist economic order, necessitates the need for the institutionalisation of relevant processes, structures and mechanisms to ensure compliance with food safety standards. Food-related regulations, comprising formal and informal measures, seek to achieve this laudable cause to safeguard food safety.

However, state regulatory agencies, for the most part, have failed to deliver in ensuring that corporations fulfil their legal obligations, given that such agencies often tend to advance their interests. Political interferences towards promoting shared corporate and political interests have largely undermined the effectiveness of state regulatory agencies, as noted in previous studies (see Snider, 1993; Coleman, 2006). State regulatory agencies tend to reflect corporate interests more than public interests. In Canada, for example, Health Canada's (2016) emphasis on building partnerships with the corporate sector potentially compromises its regulatory powers in favour of industry self-regulation, which cannot totally be trusted due to profit motives. Canada appears to have a less stringent regulatory framework compared to many other Western countries.

Finally, sanctions linked to corporate offending are typically too lenient to ensure deterrence. For instance, Snider (1993) observes that in cases where fines have been slapped on offending corporations, they represent about 25 per cent of corporations' profits. These sanctions generally do not go far enough to ensure corporate crime deterrence. Aside from these lenient sanctions, the state enforcement of food regulations – which tends to disproportionately affect small to medium-scale businesses – doesn't help deter giant corporations, which commit more serious food-related crimes (Cheng, 2012).

Another factor is the legal requirement of proof of criminal intent, which is often harder to meet to secure convictions in a court of law. In many instances of food safety concerns, prosecutions are rare as a result of the difficulty in demonstrating criminal intent in the commission of such corporate crimes to ensure convictions (see Simpson, 2013). In addition, the over-characterisation of most cases of food crime as a technical fault or accidental situation, rather than as an intentional criminal act to unlawfully maximise profit, provides an escape route for unscrupulous industries. The line between what may be defined as a technical problem and intentional act for illegitimate economic gain is often blurred. While the empirical evidence on the effectiveness of formal regulations is mixed (Simpson, 2013), formal deterrence strategies have been significantly ineffective due to implementation failures, including the state's disproportionate leaning towards advancing capital interests.

Apart from formal state regulations, other forms of regulations, including third party interventions and informal sanctions, exist to check corporate offending. Consumer associations and non-governmental organisations (NGOs) are contributing to addressing cheap capitalism in the food sector. In the Netherlands, for instance, food retailers have established a regulatory body that subjects food producers to meeting set requirements for certification (Havinga, 2006). Food retailers and consumers can therefore use their economic or market power to compel food industry organisations and producers to observe food safety standards. While non-state interventions in food regulation are promising, guaranteeing food safety should not be left to voluntary organisations alone.

Conclusion

This chapter has argued that cheap capitalism is rampant and poses a greater risk to public health locally and internationally. Second, it has argued that the state, industry and the processes of globalisation typically constitute the dominant factors shaping and driving cheap capitalism in the food sector. Third, it has analysed unsafe food in the Canadian context as part of the broader global development of cheap capitalism in the food sector.

This has important implications on food crime in the context of cheap capitalism. First, the pursuit of mutual interests by industry and the state, including its regulatory agencies, partly explains the state's tolerance for corporate offending to ensure profitable capital accumulation. For instance, governmental reliance on powerful corporations to provide jobs and reduce the unemployment rate requires that it takes steps, including decriminalisation and deregulation, to ensure business-friendly environments for corporations to succeed. The success of capital leads to economic stability and growth, and increased state revenue, which ultimately helps politicians stay in power. On the other hand, corporations lobby authorities and sponsor politicians to ensure that regulations contain clauses that cater to their corporate interests. This symbiotic relationship between industry and government undermines state regulatory oversight over corporations.

Second, unrestrained desire for profit creates the tendency for corporations to use illegitimate and unethical techniques to reduce costs and increase returns, often with the support of the state's regulatory agencies, as shown in the Brazilian case. This situation has resulted in the promotion of a contemporary culture of fraud and the demise of business morality that compromises food safety. Third, the processes of neoliberal globalisation have made it possible for powerful corporations to move their businesses to places where the regulatory framework is weaker. This situation has sparked global competition for foreign investments, which may have contributed to laxer health and safety regulations for attracting investors in some countries.

It is promising, however, to note that the recent high-profile food scandals are gradually changing the food regulatory landscape through third party interventions, a reduction in company profits and share values, dwindling state revenue and public pressure on states to address regulatory deficiencies. Food scandals eventually reduce company profits and investment shares, state revenue from taxation and foreign exchange linked to restrictions and bans on the importation of affected products, and consumer responses to food corporations involved in food crimes and harms (see Chapter 23, this volume). Brazil has therefore taken immediate steps, including the swift arrest of accomplices, due to the launching of investigations into the case, to reassure stakeholders' confidence in its resolve to supply high-quality meat products to the rest of the world. On the other hand, shares of JBS and BRF have plunged following the discovery of the wilful sale and export of contaminated meat. States and food corporations ultimately have a high stake in protecting their image of ensuring high food industry standards. In addition, voluntary organisations are beginning to show a greater interest in ensuring food safety, which provides some hope for addressing cheap capitalism.

On a final note, we recommend further research into the food sector, and the sharing of relevant insights and experiences among policy-makers, industry players, regulators and consumer interest groups to help address the increasing risk to food safety in today's globalised world.

References

BBC News (2013) 'Horsemeat found in beef burgers on sale in UK and Ireland', 15 January (www.bbc.com/news/world-europe-21034942).

CBC News (2009) 'Listeriosis outbreak timeline', 11 September (www.cbc.ca/news/listeriosis-outbreak-timeline-1.694467).

CBC News (2012) 'Ten mislabeling food products in Canada', 3 February (www.cbc.ca/news/canada/10-misleading-food-product-labels-in-canada-1.1142301).

CFIA (Canadian Food Inspection Agency) (2010) Food recalls (http://epe.lac-bac.gc.ca/100/206/301/cfia-acia/2011-09-21/www.inspection.gc.ca/english/agen/broch/broche.shtml).

CFIA (2016) Method of production claims: Nature, natural (www.inspection.gc.ca/food/labelling/food-labelling-for-industry/method-of-production-claims/eng/1389379565794/1389380926083?chap=2).

CFIA (2017) Food recall warnings – high risk (http://inspection.gc.ca/about-the-cfia/newsroom/food-recall-warnings/eng/1299076382077/1299076493846).

Chai, C. (2015) 'Food safety: Are food-borne illnesses, recalls on the rise in Canada?', *Global News*, 1 June (http://globalnews.ca/news/2022928/food-safety-are-food-borne-illnesses-recalls-on-the-rise-in-canada/).

Cheng, H. (2012) 'Cheap capitalism: A sociological study of food crime in China', *British Journal of Criminology*, vol 52, no 2, pp 254–73.

Cliff, M. (2017) 'Are these the biggest food lies? Hilarious pictures reveal misleading packages', *Mail Online*, 28 February (www.dailymail.co.uk/femail/food/article-4252170/Are-biggest-food-lies-ever.html).

Coleman, J.W. (2006) *The criminal elite: Understanding white-collar crime*, 6th edn, New York: Worth Publishers Inc.

Consumer Reports (2014) 'Five food claims that can fool you' (www.consumerreports.org/cro/news/2014/09/5-misleading-food-label-claims/index.htm).

Croall, H. (2009) 'White collar crime, consumers and victimization', *Crime, Law and Social Change*, vol 51, no 1, pp 127–46.

Croall, H. (2012) 'Food, crime, harm and regulation', *Criminal Justice Matters*, vol 90, no 1, pp 16–17.

Deza, D. (2017) 'Sixteen most misleading food labels' (www.health.com/health/gallery/0,,20599288,00.html#ad-9).

Durkheim, E. (1951) *Suicide*, New York: Free Press.

Etzkowitz, H. and Leydesdorff, L. (1996) 'A triple helix of academic–industry–government relations: Development models beyond capitalism versus socialism', *Current Science*, vol 70, pp 690–3.

Etzkowitz, H. and Zhou, C. (2007) 'Regional innovation initiator: The entrepreneurial university in various triple helix models', Singapore Triple Helix VI Conference Theme Paper.

FDA (Food & Drug Administration) (US) (2016) 'Changes to the nutritional facts label' (www.fda.gov/Food/GuidanceRegulation/GuidanceDocumentsRegulatoryInformation/LabelingNutrition/ucm385663.htm).

FDA (US) (2017) 'Food recalls' (www.fda.gov/Food/RecallsOutbreaksEmergencies/Recalls/default.htm).

Food Safety News (2014) 'Food company executive detained in Taiwan's ongoing "gutter oil" scandal', 15 September (www.foodsafetynews.com/2014/09/taiwanese-executive-arrested-in-continuing-gutter-oil-scandal/#.WReLFXKrNMt).

Food Standards (2017) *Food recalls* (www.foodstandards.gov.au/industry/foodrecalls/recalls/Pages/default.aspx).

Freitas, G. Jr, Freitas, T. and Batista, F. (2017) 'Brazil's latest scandal: Bribes, acid and tainted meat sales', *Bloomberg News*, 17 March (www.bloomberg.com/news/articles/2017-03-17/brazil-meat-producers-jbs-brf-probed-in-alleged-bribery-scheme).

Ghazi-Tehrani, A.K. and Pontell, H.N. (2015) 'Corporate crime and state legitimacy: The 2008 Chinese melamine milk scandal', *Crime, Law and Social Change*, vol 63, no 5, pp 247–67.

Guajardo, M.F. (2016) 'Global food fraud: Joining forces for a multi-faceted solution' (www.foodqualitynews.com/Industry-news/Food-fraud-history-regulation-and-technology).

Havinga, T. (2006) 'Private regulation of food safety by supermarkets', *Law and Policy*, vol 28, no 4, pp 515–33.

Health Canada (2013a) *Food-related illnesses* (www.canada.ca/en/health-canada/services/food-nutrition/food-safety/food-related-illnesses.html).

Health Canada (2013b) *Chloramphenicol in food products originated from China* (www.hc-sc.gc.ca/dhp-mps/vet/faq/chloramphenicol-eng.php).

Health Canada (2014) *A partner in health for all Canadians* (www.canada.ca/en/health-canada/corporate/about-health-canada/activities-responsibilities/partner-health-canadians.html).

Health Canada (2016a) *2014–15 report on plans and priorities* (www.canada.ca/en/health-canada/corporate/about-health-canada/accountability-performance-financial-reporting/estimates/report-plans-priorities/2014-2015/health-canada-2014-2015-report-plans-priorities.html).

Health Canada (2016b) *2016–17 report on plans and priorities* (www.canada.ca/en/health-canada/corporate/transparency/corporate-management-reporting/report-plans-priorities/2016-2017-report-plans-priorities.html#ii_2.2.1).

Japan Today (2013) 'Food mislabeling scandals spread to department stores', 6 November (https://japantoday.com/category/national/food-mislabeling-scandal-spreads-to-department-stores).

Johnson, G. (2014) 'Cuts to Canadian Food Inspection Agency risk food safety' (www.straight.com/life/705321/cuts-canadian-food-inspection-agency-risk-food-safety).

Leighton, P. (2016) 'Mass *Salmonella* poisoning by the Peanut Corporation of America: State-corporate crime involving food safety', *Critical Criminology*, vol 24, no 1, pp 75–91.

Martina, M. (2013) 'China: Rat meat sold as lamb in latest food scandal', *The Scotsman*, 3 May (www.scotsman.com/news/world/china-rat-meat-sold-as-lamb-in-latest-food-scandal-1-2919340).

Merton, R.K. (1938) 'Social structure and anomie', *American Sociological Review*, vol 3, pp 672–82.

NDTV (2016) 'Mass food poisoning kills 33 in Pakistan', 1 May (www. ndtv.com/world-news/mass-food-poisoning-kills-33-including-5-children-in-pakistans-multan-1401483).

Picard, A. (2012) 'Despite *E. coli* scandal, it's business as usual for XL Foods', *Globe and Mail*, 16 October (www.theglobeandmail.com/ news/national/despite-e-coli-scandal-its-business-as-usual-for-xl-foods/article4617285/).

Pilcher, J. (2006) *Food in world history*, New York: Routledge.

Philips, J. and French, M. (2000) *Cheated not poisoned? Food regulation in the United Kingdom*, Manchester: Manchester University Press.

Quinn, B., Butler, S. and Smithers, R. (2016) 'Mars recalls chocolate bars in 55 countries', *The Guardian*, 23 February (www.theguardian. com/lifeandstyle/2016/feb/23/mars-chocolate-product-recalls-snickers-milky-way-celebrations-germany-netherlands).

Reuters (2008) 'Canada says 12 dead in food poisoning outbreak', 26 August (www.reuters.com/article/us-meat-idUSN2526525120080826).

Robinson, M. and Murphy, D. (2009) *Greed is good: Maximization and elite deviance in America*, Lanham, MD: Rowman & Littlefield Publishers.

Sifferlin, A. (2015) '351,000 people die of food poisoning globally every year', *Time*, 12 April (http://time.com/3768003/351000-people-die-of-food-poisoning-globally-every-year/).

Simpson, S.S. (2013) 'White-collar crime: A review of recent developments and promising directions for future research', *Annual Review of Sociology*, vol 39, no 1, pp 309–31.

Snider, L. (1993) *Bad business – Corporate crime in Canada*, Scarborough, ON: Nelson Canada.

SunStar (2015) 'Five charged in Caraga food poisoning', 4 July (http://m. sunstar.com.ph/cagayan-de-oro/local-news/2015/07/14/5-charged-candy-poisoning-caraga-418793).

Sutherland, E.H. (1949) *White-collar crime*, New York: Dryden.

Walters, R. (2006) 'Crime, bio-agriculture and the exploitation of hunger', *British Journal of Criminology*, vol 46, no 1, pp 26–45.

Walters, R. (2007) 'Food crime, regulation and the Biotech harvest', *European Journal of Criminology*, vol 4, no 2, pp 217–35.

Weatherill, S. (2009) *Report of the independent investigator into the 2008 listeriosis outbreak*, Government of Canada (http://publications.gc.ca/ collections/collection_2009/agr/A22-508-2009E.pdf).

Which (2014) 'Food fraud: What's in your takeaway?', 16 April (www.which.co.uk/news/2014/04/food-fraud-whats-in-your-takeaway-362886/).

Young, T. (2012) *Facts on prescription drug deaths and the drug industry*, Common Ground (http://dcawatch.com/facts-on-prescription-drug-deaths-and-the-drug-industry/).

Section V
Food trade and movement

13

Crime versus harm in the transportation of animals: A closer look at Ontario's 'pig trial'

Amy Fitzgerald and Wesley Tourangeau

Introduction

On a hot June day in 2015, Anita Krajnc, an animal advocate with Toronto Pig Save in Ontario, Canada, approached a truck transporting nearly 200 pigs. They were making the approximately 100 kilometre (60 mile) trip to slaughter. She observed the apparently thirsty pigs, and through the slats in the side of the stopped truck, gave the overheated animals some water from a bottle. The truck driver reportedly emerged and used his phone to video record what was transpiring. The exchange between the two of them as recorded went as follows:

Truck driver: "Don't give them anything! Do not put anything in there!"
Krajnc: "Jesus said 'If they are thirsty, give them water.'"
Truck driver: "No, you know what? These are not humans you dumb frickin' broad! Hello!" (quoted in Wang, 2016)

This was not the first time that activists had given water to pigs being transported to this slaughterhouse (Carter, 2016a). Nonetheless, this time the driver called the police prior to taking the pigs to the slaughterhouse. Krajnc was charged with criminal mischief, which carries with it the potential of imprisonment (originally with a potential maximum of 10 years, but later reduced to a summary conviction offence with a maximum of six months) and a fine of up to $5,000. The trial began in August 2016; Krajnc pleaded not guilty. In the first week of May 2017 – eight months after the first court appearance (well above the average for such cases[1]) – Ontario Court judge David Harris dismissed the charge of criminal mischief.

Although interesting in its own right, this case provides a useful context for exploring the legal and social constructions of 'food crime'. If one were to simply employ a legalistic definition, this case would be considered a food crime because of the potential of food adulteration caused by Krajnc's 'criminal mischief'. However, this chapter presents the argument that while this case is in fact a food crime, it is not because of Krajnc's actions. It begins by exploring two aspects of Canadian law that provide the backdrop for this case: the legal status of animals as property, and transportation regulations that mandate the minimum amount of care required when transporting animals to slaughter. After laying that groundwork, this chapter examines the arguments made on both sides of the case. Insights from green criminology and Joel Feinberg's legal and moral philosophical works are applied to support the assertion that this is a food crime in accordance with the actions of the state and industry, not because of those of the defendant.

Background on animal cruelty and welfare laws in Canada

In Canada, all animals[2] are theoretically protected under the Criminal Code (RSC, 1985, c. C-46) from treatment that is unnecessarily cruel and injurious. Importantly, the segments of the Code pertaining to animal cruelty legislation are located in a section titled 'Wilful and Forbidden Acts in Respect of Certain Property'. Although the 'unnecessary suffering' of animals is prohibited, these protections are situated within a context where animals are legally defined as property, and protected vis-à-vis their ownership. This categorisation of animals works to limit the moral considerations of animals to the context of personal property – a legal status that has already been modified in other countries. For instance, in 2015, New Zealand's Animal Welfare Amendment Act (No 2) recognised under law that 'animals are sentient', helping re-define how animals are viewed in legal contexts.

Meanwhile, in Canada, in February 2016, Liberal Member of Parliament (MP) Nathaniel Erskine-Smith introduced Bill C-246, the Modernizing Animal Protections Act. This private members' Bill[3] sought several changes to legislation designed to protect animals. Among other things, it proposed moving the animal cruelty provisions from property offences to a new section entitled 'Offences against Animals.' According to MP Erskine-Smith,

> This is a symbolic change. Animals will remain property at law, but it recognizes that animals are different from tables and other kinds of property. It recognizes that an offence against animals is wrong because it is wrong to harm animals, not because it is wrong to damage another person's property, which just happens to be an animal. (House of Commons Debates, 2016)

This Bill came in the wake of a widely publicised case of animal abuse in Windsor, Ontario, where a dog was bound in electrical tape and abandoned in December 2015. As Stanley Coren (2016) writes in an op-ed in *The Globe and Mail*, this case resulted in a two-year prison sentence and a 25-year ban on pet ownership, which may point to 'significant change in the way that our society is treating dogs and their legal status. The judge, the protesters and the general public all seem to be finally recognising that dogs are sentient beings with real feelings and emotions' (para 3). Although justice may be said to have been served in this case (in fact, the dog was renamed Justice by the Humane Society that cared for him), the Bill inspired by the case was defeated in October 2016. Canadians may be fond of their companion animals, but attempts to strengthen animal cruelty laws, even symbolically by moving the placement of the anti-cruelty sections of the Canadian Criminal Code, have been consistently opposed by the animal-use industries, notably animal agriculture.

Animal transport laws in Canada and elsewhere

Under the authority of the Health of Animals Act (SC, 1990, c. 21), the Health of Animals Regulations (CRC, c. 296) lay out the requirements for the transportation of animals in Canada (including entering or leaving the country). Among the requirements, every animal transported is subject to inspection at any time, no animals can be loaded or transported if ill, injured or likely to give birth during transport, no animals can be crowded to an extent likely to cause injury or undue suffering, and each animal must be able to stand in his/her natural position (Health of Animals Regulations, 2015, pp 75–8). More pertinent to the Krajnc case, these regulations limit the length of confinement to a transport container to 36 hours for pigs and horses (or other monogastric animals), 48 hours for cattle, sheep, goats or other ruminants, and 72 hours for chicks of any species. Further, these regulations stipulate that when unloaded for rest, animals are to be 'provided with an ample quantity of suitable food and potable ice-free water', and rested for at least five hours (Health of Animals Regulations, Section 148(4), p 81). From the perspective of the Canadian Food Inspection Agency (CFIA), with these regulations in place, Canada is able to govern the humane transport of animals and protect their welfare (see CFIA, 2016). Yet these regulations are relatively weak compared to other jurisdictions.

Laws and regulations in the European Union (EU) offer a suitable comparison. The EU regulates the protection of animals during transport under Council Regulation (EC) No 1/2005. These regulations consider transportation times exceeding eight hours to be 'long journeys', which are given additional considerations. Regarding pigs specifically, the total transportation period must not exceed 24 hours and there must be continuous access to water, as well as a rest period of 24 hours following a journey (Council Regulation (EC) No 1/2005, p 25). The EU's regulations are decidedly more stringent than Canada's, including provisions that account for the many stressors of transportation and the basic needs of these animals. Nevertheless, these regulations are still considered to have room for improvement (Axberg, 2014), and are currently under review.

On 3 December 2016 the *Canada Gazette* published a notice for CFIA's proposed amendments to the Health of Animals Regulations (Government of Canada, 2016). These changes are meant to address growing concerns over the out-of-date regulations regarding animal handling processes while accounting for food safety and economic impacts (Government of Canada, 2016). The regulatory proposal reduces the maximum time intervals that animals can be transported without food or water (which varies by species). Regarding the transportation of pigs specifically, the proposed maximum journey time is 28 hours (without food and water), reduced from 36 hours, and when the maximum is reached, the minimum mandatory rest period of 5 hours is proposed to increase to 8 hours (Government of Canada, 2016). What is particularly interesting is that this proposal is based on CFIA's own comparative assessment of transportation laws in the EU, New Zealand, Australia and the US. Notably, CFIA's proposed changes are in line with current regulations in the US, which are the least restrictive (see Table 13.1).

Table 13.1: Comparison of maximum journey lengths

EU	New Zealand	Australia	United States	Canada
Pigs can be transported for up to 8 hours without water, or for up to 24 hours with continuous access to water	Pigs can be transported for up to 8 hours without water and for up to 24 hours without food	Pigs can be transported for up to 24 hours without food or water (piglets are limited to 12 hours)	Pigs can be transported for up to 28 hours and then must be unloaded for food, water and rest	Pigs can be transported without food and water Current: up to 36 hours Proposed: up to 28 hours

Source: Adapted from Government of Canada (2016)

Animal advocates in Canada are not pleased with the proposed amendments. A lawyer with Animal Justice, an animal advocacy organisation, recently wrote in an op-ed in *The Globe and Mail* that 'the proposed regulations are disappointing, barely improving some key areas and entirely failing to address others. A CFIA statement says 98 per cent of shipments are already compliant with the new regulations – in other words, not much is changing' (Pippus, 2016). For instance, even with the proposed changes in place, animals could still be transported in trucks that are not climate-controlled in extreme heat and cold, they could still go anywhere from 24–36 hours without water (depending on the species), overcrowding would still be permissible, and bolt cutters and electric prods could still be used to make animals compliant (Pippus, 2016). Opponents of significant regulatory changes argue that they would increase costs. Research indicates that the 2004 regulatory changes in the EU resulted in improved animal welfare, as well as increased costs for transport companies due to necessary truck modifications. However, these costs have not been passed on to consumers or negatively impacted trade flow (Baltussen et al, 2011).

It is worth noting that the enforcement of the new regulations across EU member countries has varied significantly, which can compromise animal welfare and reduce the likelihood of a level playing field for operators that was intended as part of the regulatory changes (Baltussen et al, 2011). This is due, in part, to inconsistencies in the type and frequency of inspections, inadequate reporting and a lack of data on penalties (Baltussen et al, 2011). CFIA's proposed changes to Canada's regulations do include provisions for improving the clarity of prohibitions and standards of conduct in order to improve compliance as well as enforcement (Government of Canada, 2016). However, effective enforcement of regulations is not only linked to the clarity of regulations, adequate resourcing of enforcement across jurisdictions is also critical.

Animal transport as contested practice

The Krajnc case invokes two very different constructions of harm and crime. Activists, such as Krajnc, have argued for years that the regulation of animal welfare is grossly inadequate, and that those animals destined to be food are especially overlooked. Animal transport laws, particularly in Canada, have been targeted as being woefully inadequate, and described as the weakest among Western countries (see Sorenson, 2010; Fitzgerald, 2015). Put simply, activists argue that animals are being harmed in the interests of profit, and that the state has been facilitating these injustices, although animal advocates would no doubt object to the construction, legal or otherwise, of these animals as food.

In court and in the media, Krajnc and her legal team focused on three main points to make their case: the welfare of the pigs at the time of the incident, inconsistencies between the treatment of 'livestock' animals and 'companion' animals, and how her motivations for the actions she took were at least partially grounded in her religious beliefs. In short, the argument is that she was acting in the public good.

Regarding the welfare of the pigs, Krajnc wrote in an op-ed in *The Guardian*, 'the pigs I was trying to help on that fateful day were undoubtedly suffering. Crammed into a transport truck on a sweltering day, these helpless animals – covered with their own excrement, being crushed together and slowly suffocating from heat – stared at me through the trailer's metal slats with their pleading eyes' (2016). According to the animal rights community, this was not an isolated incident, as the current regulations allow for transport conditions that can be quite gruelling for animals:

> Under the current laws, farmed animals can be transported for days without food or water. Transport trucks are not required to protect animals from severely inclement weather, resulting in the deaths of millions of animals from exposure to extreme temperatures. Additionally, lack of training and

supervision results in the cruel beating and torturing of animals by workers during loading and unloading. (Mercy for Animals, 2016)

During the trial, Krajnc's defence called an expert witness on animal welfare who testified that the pigs in the video-recorded evidence appeared to be in distress (Carter, 2016a). According to Mercy for Animals (2016), this is not an anomaly: every year approximately 8 million animals arrive at slaughterhouses in conditions (that is, dead, dying, ill or severely injured) that preclude them from being slaughtered for human consumption. Presumably the condition of some of these animals is due to what transpires during transport.

Krajnc's legal team also urged the court to think about what would have been expected of Krajnc if the pigs had been dogs. Dogs are also legally defined as property, yet exceptions are made for acting in their best interests. Krajnc writes, 'there's little doubt in my mind that if those were dogs in distress in that truck instead of pigs, my actions would be applauded and it would be the driver facing charges instead' (2016). Her accurate assessment points to the differing ways that these two species of animals are socially constructed. Psychologists have been trying to make sense of humans' paradoxical attitudes towards different species of animals for years (see Herzog, 2011; Joy, 2011). One contributing factor is that most people live in closer proximity to dogs and other companion animals than those raised for consumption, who are generally intentionally kept out of view of the public. To bring those animals into view, Krajnc's lawyers offered evidence during the trial of videos of pigs being transported to slaughter as well as slaughterhouse footage. Media accounts described people in the court reacting with discomfort to the footage (Carter, 2016a).

Finally, religion was also been invoked in the case. Krajnc testified that giving the pigs water was a natural extension of her Christian beliefs about compassion. This argument has drawn sympathisers, such as Matthew Scully, author and former speechwriter for George W. Bush, who wrote an op-ed about the case in the *National Review* (2016). Krajnc and Scully raise the question of what one who has a deep-rooted commitment to compassion ought to do in this situation. Is failure to act a violation of their beliefs? In fact, in late 2015, the Ontario Human Rights Commission (OHRC) added ethical veganism as a potential creed designation that could be protected, depending on the specific context (such as if it is integral to the person's identity, if the associated beliefs guided the individual's actions, and so forth) (OHRC, 2015).

The second conceptualisation of food crime in this case views the actions of activists giving water to animals destined for slaughter as harmful and tantamount to food adulteration, and potentially even posing broader terroristic threats to security. The industry argues that the food supply is a potentially attractive target for those aiming to do significant harm, and there is no way to definitively know the motivation of someone approaching a truckload of animals soon to be rendered into food. Comment on the case from the animal production, processing and transport industries has been hard to come by, but the discourse they have conveyed is of this case as being a property crime against food, specifically, product tampering (Hanson, 2016).

Through this tampering, the actions of the activists notably also threaten profits. Profits may also be threatened more indirectly through the activity of 'bearing witness' that these activists engage in by holding vigil as animals arrive at the slaughterhouse; this threatens to draw attention to the intentionally veiled process of rendering animals into food (on this process, see Pachirat, 2011; Fitzgerald, 2015). It is unclear which of these ways that profits could be compromised that the truck driver was referring to in court when he stated he had called police because the activists 'had to be stopped because they were "messing with our livelihood"' (Wang, 2016).

It is also unclear why exactly the truck driver chose to call the police that day, and why the owner advocated for charges to be laid against Krajnc. Apparently the activists had been standing vigil at the slaughterhouse for three years and had previously given water to the pigs, all under the periodic supervision of the police without such significant intervention (Carter, 2016a). This case does not technically meet the definition of a Strategic Lawsuit Against Public Participation (SLAPP), a term that refers to civil lawsuits intended to have a chilling effect on activists. In this case, criminal charges were pursued by the state. Nonetheless, the decision of the truck driver and company to involve the police at this point in time, after years of similar behaviour, and against the backdrop of growing momentum among the activist group, is intriguing.

As happens with some SLAPPs, involving the criminal law apparatus here may result in unintended consequences. This case has focused a spotlight on Canada's animal transport regulations. Prior to this case, it is likely that few citizens were aware of what the transport regulations were, or had considered in any sustained way the wellbeing of animals being transported as part of the food commodity cycle. In contrast, a recent survey of a sample of 1,000 people from across Canada conducted by NRG Research Group found that 97 per cent believe that the animal transport regulations need to be updated to better protect animals. What is perhaps even more foreboding for the meat production and processing industries is that 71 per cent of these respondents would like the regulations to be as strong as those in the EU, and 87 per cent support stronger penalties for companies that violate transport regulations (Mercy for Animals, 2016).

The 'pig trial' as food crime: insights from green criminology and the work of Joel Feinberg

As with other strands of critical criminology, green criminology has challenged relying on state definitions of criminally harmful behaviour to delimit the boundaries of the discipline of criminology (see Beirne and South, 2007). Instead, many green criminologists advocate for using a social harm-based approach (see Hillyard et al, 2004) that makes it possible to attend to environmental harms and those endured by non-human animals that are often outside of the purview of criminal law, and sometimes even facilitated by law, including administrative and civil law (see Chapter 1, this volume). The impacts of these harms on humans alone are often well beyond the magnitude of impacts of violations of criminal laws, as illustrated by Lynch and Barrett (2015) in their examination of the death toll of homicides in the US versus deaths caused by environmental pollution via particle matter from coal-fired plants. Green criminologists also challenge speciesist assumptions that have infused the discipline of criminology as well as regulations, legislation and enforcement (see Beirne, 2007; Fitzgerald et al, 2009; Fitzgerald, 2011).

From this perspective, it is argued here that animal transport regulations that make it legal to transport 'livestock' animals for 36 hours (28 hours, if the proposed changes are accepted) without food and water are problematic in that they produce harm, even though that harm is not criminalised. In the very least, distress would result from going without food or water for that amount of time, particularly during periods of extreme heat or cold, as evidenced by the fact that it is not uncommon for animals to arrive at slaughterhouses already dead. Furthermore, these transport conditions would not be tolerated if different species of animals (specifically those kept as 'pets') were involved, as argued in the Krajnc case. It is not that this type of transport never takes place with companion animal species, but mass transport of companion animals, visible by the public, would likely result in a public outcry, or in the least, the provision of water by a bystander would be applauded.

From a green criminological perspective, then, current animal transport regulations in Canada can be understood as falling under the umbrella of food crime, as a form of harm perpetrated against those animals being transported to be rendered into food (although this ought not imply an acceptance of the practice of consuming animals per se). It is doubtful that this conceptual understanding will elicit much debate. However, a potentially more contentious argument can also be made: the Krajnc case would fall under the definitional umbrella of 'food crime', even if a more narrow definition of food crime that precludes harms is employed. To set the stage for this argument, it is useful to turn to a necessarily brief discussion of the work of political and legal philosopher, Joel Feinberg.

Feinberg's (1984) approach to understanding the appropriate uses of criminal law is helpful in further illuminating the problem at hand here. In *Harm to others: The moral limits of the criminal law*, Feinberg (1984) outlines an argument for how much the state can justifiably impose prohibitions on behaviours, and which activities should fall outside the legal realm. Put simply, Feinberg's exercise in applied moral philosophy results in principles for determining when legal sanctions are needed to place limits on individual liberty. Four 'liberty-limiting principles' (Feinberg, 1984) are outlined to guide this discussion:

- the *harm principle* defends penal sanctions for actions causing harm to others – this provides a suitable baseline for legal sanctions against crimes like homicide and assault, the prohibition of which are generally non-controversial;
- the *offence principle* holds that it is reasonably necessary to prevent offence to others (for example, indecent exposure);
- *legal paternalism* uses the law to protect individuals from harming themselves (for example, assisted suicide); and
- *legal moralism* defends sanctions against inherently immoral conduct, whether or not it is harmful or offensive to anyone (for example, bigamy).

Feinberg (1984) argues that the concept of liberalism can be usefully applied to develop laws with a commitment to liberty, ensuring that the state places as few limits on individual liberty as possible. To this end, liberalism is defined as a combination of the harm and offence principles, which between them exhaust all the relevant reasons for criminal prohibition: legal paternalism and legal moralism, in this view, do not warrant penal legislation (Feinberg, 1984).

Less well known than his work on the philosophy of law are Feinberg's writings on the rights of animals (Feinberg, 1974), which are also applicable to this debate. He admits that animals do not possess the corollary of rights – duties and obligations – but argues that this is not a necessary requirement to be a rights-holder. He also argues that it is not necessary for animals to be able to claim rights for themselves, as people can stand in as proxies and make these claims on their behalf, as is done in the legal system with children and those *in absentia*. Therefore, animals would require representation to make their rights claims.

In anticipating the critique that his argument could be applied to argue for the rights of inanimate objects, Feinberg argues that interests are essential to rights (although not all agree; see Regan, 1976). He writes, 'a mere thing, however valuable to others, has no good of its own', things or inanimate objects have no interests in that they have no conscious or unconscious desires, ambitions or impulses to act on (Feinberg, 1974, p 49). He goes on to assert that claims for animals to be humanely treated serve as evidence that they have rights:

> ... if we hold not only that we ought to treat animals humanely but also that we should do so for the animals' own sake, that such treatment is something we owe animals as their due, something that can be claimed for them, something the withholding of which would be an injustice and a wrong, and not merely a harm, then it follows that we do ascribe rights to animals. (Feinberg, 1974, p 50)

According to Feinberg's conceptualisation, protecting animals who are legally categorised as property through the force of criminal law would be challenging. It is not clear how to apply the harm and offence principles to property that experiences suffering; therefore, as per Feinberg's liberalism, protecting these animals in transport would be considered legal moralism, and these harms would not fall under the scope of criminal law. Alternatively, combining Feinberg's writings on animal rights and legal philosophy, one might argue that animals have interests, and as such, they have rights. This applies an entirely different calculus, where the presence of animal welfare guidelines (the animal transport regulations in this case) provide evidence that the interests and 'rights' of animals are at least implicitly acknowledged. Further, the inhumane transportation of these sentient beings could then be conceptualised as causing significant offence and harm to others, and would thus be situated within Feinberg's metric for criminal prohibitions. As Feinberg (1974, p 50) states, disregarding these rights is not simply a matter of harm, it 'would be an injustice and a wrong.' In this way, transport that violates the interests of the animals involved could fall within an even stricter definition of food crime than one that is extended to include harms.

Conclusion

At the beginning of this chapter it was proposed that the 'pig trial' is a food crime case, but because of the actions of the state and industry, not because of the actions of the defendant. Subsequently, the argument was made for why the actions of state and industry actors regarding animal transport represent an illustrative case of food crime. This chapter concludes that there are (at least) three reasons for not accepting definitions of this as a food crime case because of the actions of the defendant. First, although industry representatives suggested in the media that this was a food adulteration case, criminal mischief charges were laid, not food-specific charges. Thus, although the industry might like to frame Krajnc's actions as a threat to food, she was not charged as such.

Second, defining this case as a food crime due to Krajnc's actions would mean accepting the speciesist assumption that animals destined to be food are deserving of different (and lesser) treatment than animals used for other purposes (namely, as companions), and that bystanders should be treated differently based on the species of animal they intercede on behalf of. This assumption has found its way into law. For instance, several jurisdictions in Canada and the US have introduced legislation to protect bystanders who break into vehicles to protect companion animals who appear to be suffering from high temperatures (Gajanan, 2015). Instances where emergency responders have rescued animals from hot cars, and owners are subsequently charged under laws such as the Ontario Society for the Prevention of Cruelty to Animals Act, further illustrate this contrast (see Donkin, 2012). Animals who are to become food, and the bystanders who intervene on their behalf, are not afforded these protections.

Finally, this case can be problematised as a type of SLAPP. As discussed earlier, this case does not fit within the traditional definition of a SLAPP suit because it is a criminal instead of a civil case; however, it is evident that this was not the first time that pigs being sent to slaughter were given water by protesters, allegedly in the presence of police officers on occasion. One might speculate that the timing of involving the criminal law apparatus may be related to the growing momentum of Toronto Pig Save and similar organisations. To compare, in the US state of Virginia, a woman was charged with a traffic offence for giving water to pigs headed for slaughter. The judge in that case dropped the charges at the first court appearance (Craggs, 2016). Meanwhile, more recently in Ontario, Canada, Anita Krajnc faced new charges for obstructing the police and breaching bail conditions when she attempted to assist pigs who had been injured after the truck they were being transported in crashed on the way to the slaughterhouse (see Carter, 2016b).

The May 2017 decision to dismiss Krajnc's charge of criminal mischief represents an important win for animal rights activists, although Judge Harris made it clear that animals are property under the law, and that the basis of the decision was that Krajnc did not interfere with the lawful enjoyment (in this instance, slaughter and sale) of the property (Craggs, 2017). Nonetheless, Krajnc and the organisation she helped found – Toronto Pig Save – have been an inspiration to people in other countries, where similar organisations have begun to pop up. In Canada, the media-attentive public has received an education in animal transport laws, and the transport regulations will be – however conservatively – updated. The decision of the company transporting the pigs to involve the police and pursue charges has certainly had an impact on this specific 'food crime,' although perhaps not in the ways they had envisioned.

Notes

[1] According to the statistics compiled by the Ontario Court of Justice (nd), the average number of days between the first and last court appearance for mischief cases was 123 days in 2015; the Krajnc case took approximately twice as long. Also, the rate at which mischief cases went to trial in 2015 was only 1.3 per cent.

[2] The term 'animals' is used in this chapter to refer to all non-human animals, and when specification is needed, terms such as pigs, ruminants and companion animals ('pets') are used.

[3] Private members' bills introduced in the House of Commons are put forward by MPs who are not Cabinet Ministers. These bills do not often become law.

References

Axberg, J. (2014) *Impact of EU-regulation on pigs' welfare during transport*, Swedish University of Agricultural Sciences, Faculty of Veterinary Medicine and Animal Science.

Baltussen, W., Gebrensbet, G. and de Roest, K. (2011) *Study on the impact of Regulation (EC) No 1/2005 on the protection of animals during transport*, European Commission: Directorate-General for Health and Consumers (https://ec.europa.eu/food/sites/food/files/animals/docs/aw_practice_trans_study_report_en.pdf).

Beirne, P. (2007) 'Animal rights, animal abuse, and green criminology', in P. Beirne and N. South (eds) *Issues in green criminology: Confronting harms against environments, humanity, and other animals*, Portland, OR: Willan Publishing, pp 55–83.

Beirne, P. and South, N. (eds) (2007) *Issues in green criminology: Confronting harms against environments, humanity, and other animals*, Portland, OR: Willan Publishing.

Carter, A. (2016a) 'Vegan who gave water to pigs headed for slaughter finds it "unfathomable" she was charged', CBC, 3 October.

Carter, A. (2016b) 'Woman already on trial for giving water to pigs arrested after pig truck rollover', CBC, 5 October.

CFIA (Canadian Food Inspection Agency) (2016) 'Humane transport/animal welfare' (www.inspection.gc.ca/animals/terrestrial-animals/humane-transport/eng/1300460032193/1300460096845).

Coren, S. (2016) 'Humanity's best friend deserves legal recognition', *The Globe and Mail*, 5 February.

Craggs, S. (2016) 'Virginia judge throws out water for pigs charge inspired by Anita Krajnc case', CBC, 3 December.

Craggs, S. (2017) 'Pig trial: Anita Krajnc found not guilty of mischief charge for giving water to pigs', CBC, 4 May.

Donkin, K. (2012) 'Man charged after leaving dog unattended in hot car', *Toronto Star*, 1 August.

Feinberg, J. (1974) 'The rights of animals and unborn generations', in W. Blackstone (ed) *Philosophy and environmental crisis*, Athens, GA: The University of Georgia Press, pp 229–42.

Feinberg, J. (1984) *Harm to others: The moral limits of the criminal law*, vol 1, New York: Oxford University Press.

Fitzgerald, A. (2011) 'Doing time in slaughterhouses: A green criminological commentary on slaughterhouse work programmes for prison inmates', *Journal of Critical Animal Studies*, vol 10, pp 12–46.

Fitzgerald, A. (2015) *Animals as food: (Re)connecting production, processing, consumption and impacts*, East Lansing, MI: Michigan State University Press.

Fitzgerald, A., Kalof, L. and Dietz, T. (2009) 'Slaughterhouses and increased crime rates: An empirical analysis of the spillover from "The Jungle" into the surrounding community', *Organization and Environment*, vol 22, no 2, pp 158–84.

Gajanan, M. (2015) 'New Tennessee law allows people to break into cars to save animals', *The Guardian*, 9 July.

Government of Canada (2016) 'Regulations amending the Health of Animals Regulations', *Canada Gazette*, vol 150, no 49 (www.gazette. gc.ca/rp-pr/p1/2016/2016-12-03/html/reg2-eng.php).

Hanson, H. (2016) 'A woman is on trial in Canada for giving water to pigs headed for slaughter', *Huffington Post*, 3 November.

Health of Animals Regulations, CRC, c. 296 (http://justice.gc.ca/ eng/regulations/C.R.C.,_c._296/).

Herzog, H. (2011) *Some we love, some we hate, some we eat: Why it's so hard to think straight about animals*, New York: Harper Perennial.

Hillyard, P., Pantazis, C., Tombs, S. and Gordon, D. (eds) (2004) *Beyond criminology: Taking harm seriously*, Black Point, NS: Fernwood Publishing.

House of Commons Debates (2016) *Modernizing Animal Protections Act, Official report* (Hansard), 9 May.

Joy, M. (2011) *Why we love dogs, eat pigs, and wear cows: An introduction to carnism*, San Francisco, CA: Conari Press.

Krajnc, A. (2016) 'I'm on trial for giving water to thirsty pigs. If they were dogs, I would be a hero', *The Guardian*, 17 October.

Lynch, M. and Barrett, K. (2015) 'Death matters: Victimization by particle matter from coal fired power plants in the US, a green criminological view', *Critical Criminology*, vol 23, pp 219–34.

Mercy for Animals (2016) 'Canada's animal transport regulations worst in the Western world, causing millions of deaths each year; Mercy for Animals calls on new Agriculture Minister MacAuley to strengthen regulations', News release, 17 March (www.newswire.ca/news-releases/new-poll-finds-97-percent-of-canadians-support-stronger-federal-transport-protections-for-farmed-animals-572368961.html).

OHRC (Ontario Human Rights Commission) (2015) *Policy on preventing discrimination based on creed* (www.ohrc.on.ca/en/policy-preventing-discrimination-based-creed).

Ontario Court of Justice (no date) 'Criminal court statistics' (www. ontariocourts.ca/ocj/stats-crim/).

Pachirat, T. (2011) *Every twelve seconds: Industrialized slaughter and the politics of sight*, New Haven, CT: Yale University Press.

Pippus, A. (2016) 'Canada: We must do better for our animals (even those we want to eat)', *The Globe and Mail* (Op-ed), 7 December.

Regan, T. (1976) 'Feinberg on what sort of beings can have rights', *The Southern Journal of Philosophy*, vol 14, no 4, pp 485–98.

Scully, M. (2016) 'Showing mercy to suffering animal is not "criminal mischief"', *National Review*, 7 November.

Sorenson, J. (2010) *About Canada: Animal rights*, Halifax, NS: Fernwood Publishing.

Wang, A. (2016) 'An animal activist gave water to slaughterhouse-bound pigs. Now, she's on trial for mischief', *The Washington Post*, 25 August.

14

Coming together to combat food crime: Regulatory networks in the EU

Richard Hyde and Ashley Savage

Introduction

As food fraud is international in scope, steps must be taken to ensure international cooperation in responding to food fraud. Food fraud is increasingly a policy priority for the European Union (EU) and its member states (European Parliament, 2016), leading to increased networking. This was stimulated largely by the horsemeat scandal of 2013 (FSAI, 2013), which provided a wake-up call to European policy-makers to ensure inter-EU and international regulatory networks were fit to respond to food fraud. This chapter examines how regulatory networks are used to prevent and respond to food fraud incidents, and argues that networked governance is essential in dealing with modern food crimes and harms. Networked governance is essential in the response to food crime.

Food crime is not a new phenomenon (Paulus, 1974). It has the potential to damage both consumers' safety and their economic interests. Consumers may be injured by food that has unsafe elements or that has been processed in an unhygienic environment (Spink and Moyer, 2011). For example, chemicals may be introduced into food products to provide desirable characteristics or meat that has been illegally slaughtered may be fraudulently placed on the market. Consumers' economic interests will be damaged as they will be induced to pay for fraudulent food, which professes particular characteristics that it does not possess. For example, a consumer will pay more for Manuka honey than for other honeys, more for olive oil than other oils, or more for cod than other forms of white fish. When food is deceptively sold with valuable characteristics that it does not possess, enforcement bodies should intervene. However, regulators acting alone may not have either the information or the power to take action against the perpetrators of food crime, and may not have the geographical reach to remove deceptive food from our shelves and our homes.

Article 8 of the EU's General Food Law (GFL) evinces an aim to prevent 'fraudulent or deceptive practices.' While there is no formal definition of such practices, they can be understood as 'violations of food law motivated by the intention to obtain an undue benefit' (European Commission, 2017). Spink and Moyer (2011, R157) define food fraud as 'an intentional act for economic gain.' Food fraud also amounts to a violation of Regulation 1169/2011 on food information, as information that accompanies fraudulent food will inevitably be misleading to consumers. Therefore, regulators in every EU country will be taking future action in response to food fraud, and have been doing so at some level for a significant period of time.

In order to combat food fraud in the EU it is necessary that diverse actors work together to take steps to identify fraudulent food and remove it from the market with the least possible amount of harm done. While this chapter focuses on the EU, regulatory networks must extend much further, from the countries from which food is sourced, to the countries (sometimes the same) that process food, to countries that import these food products. Regulatory cooperation is increasingly important in the governance of food risks (Black, 2007; Havinga, 2015; Savage and Hyde, 2015). Actors include national regulators, EU institutions, other international bodies, law enforcement agencies, customs bodies, food businesses and consumers themselves. These actors form complex regulatory networks that obtain, analyse, utilise and transmit information about fraudulent food, and take action on the basis of that information. In particular, regulators in different member states communicate with each other to share information concerning the risks of food fraud, enabling regulatory action to take place, and fraudulent food to be eliminated from the market. This chapter considers how regulatory networks function to share information about food fraud, focusing on the role of the EU in creating an appropriate legal environment for the necessary sharing. It begins by considering the importance of regulatory networks, before turning to consider three networks and their methods of information sharing: the Rapid Alert System for Food and Feed (RASFF), the Food Fraud Network (FFN), coordinated control plans (CCPs), and coordinated law enforcement activity. The challenges posed by information sharing are discussed, and it is concluded that the positive enhancement of regulatory abilities due to shared information outweighs the difficulties.

Cross-border regulatory networks and information sharing

Regulatory networks play a central role in modern regulatory governance (Black, 2007). The complexity of modern society means that simple conceptions of actors as objects and subjects of regulation are obsolete. Multi-level, multi-actor governance is the norm, and simple command and control regulation, where the regulator tells and the regulated do, is insufficient. Multiple actors within a system have the ability to influence actions, leading to compliance with regulatory requirements. These regulatory actors, who have different regulatory capacities, must work together in order to ensure that the maximum regulatory capability is brought to bear on a problem.

The food system involves a multitude of actors, all with different powers, sometimes overlapping and sometimes complementary. In order to govern the complexity of the food system, actors need to be enrolled into the regulatory network and work together and use these powers. The cooperative convergence of regulatory capacity is manifest in food governance at a national level, and it is an important enabler of the response to food crime nationally (Hyde, 2015).

As food is an increasingly globalised commodity, such networks must be supported internationally. Supply chains stretching from farm to fork frequently cross jurisdictional boundaries. To illustrate, one needs only to look at the country of origin information on foods in the local supermarket. Such long supply chains distance the consumer from the production of their food (see Chapter 1, this volume, for a discussion of the consequences of this distancing for a food crime perspective), providing the opportunity for fraudulent food to enter the food system in circumstances where consumers become unable to assess the provenance and safety of the food they are buying (NSF International, 2014). This necessitates coordination to reduce the risk to consumer safety and of consumer detriment. While nation-states hold some power over food standards of imports, in general national-level regulation cannot effectively or significantly regulate global supply chains or distribution chains that extend beyond their political and legal jurisdiction (Havinga, 2015). Given the global structure of contemporary food systems, international regulatory networks are necessary to ensure that the governance of food in the interest of consumers is possible.

A number of different mechanisms may be adopted to enrol actors into such networks. Formal or informal mechanisms may be adopted to allow information sharing, including channels created to encourage actors to share information on an ad hoc basis. Actors have limited power to regulate food, and minimal involvement in the enforcement of food law beyond separate spheres of control, but can provide vital information about non-compliance. Supra-national bodies (such as the EU, Interpol or the Food and Agriculture Organisation) may coordinate actions by member states. Formal combined operations can draw together those bodies with the necessary regulatory capacities to formally achieve objectives that reduce food crime. Informal sharing mechanisms include ad hoc information sharing between colleagues in different regulatory agencies, by using telephone or email, or reports made to regulatory agencies by individuals or businesses outside of a formal network. Informal networks are flexible, but do not ensure that all information is shared, and depend on the pre-existing personal relationships or the ease of contact between the network members.

In the case of food fraud, standards are set by governmental and supra-national bodies. Enforcement is also generally the domain of the government. However, private bodies play an important role, by providing information and providing the mechanism through which risky food can be removed from the shelves if necessary. The next three sections examine three different mechanisms that enrol actors in regulatory networks to respond to food crime.

Rapid Alert System for Food and Feed (RASFF)

The EU has adopted a unified system to share information concerning serious direct or indirect risks to health is shared through the Rapid Alert System for Food and Feed system (Regulation 178/2002, Article 50; European Commission, 2015). The RASFF is a database on to which designated national bodies upload details about food that poses health risks to consumers and the steps that have been taken to control any risk. The national bodies obtain the information from a variety of sources (Hyde, 2015). Reports may be made by consumers who either discover unexpected items in food or become ill following the consumption of food, businesses that notice their food does not comply either through their own compliance processes or following reports form consumers, doctors who report instances of foodborne illness, or routine sampling exercises conducted by the regulators exposing food that is dangerous or does not comply with regulatory requirements.

The RASFF system is open to non-member states (including Norway, Liechtenstein, Iceland and Switzerland) for information about unsafe food likely to circulate within the EU. In the event that the risk is detected at a border point, the information will be transmitted to the country from which the product originated in order to allow authorities in that state to investigate and respond. Consumers have access to their own tool – the RASFF consumers' portal – that provides information on food recalls in all the participating states.

While the RASFF is not in itself a transnational network, it is facilitative of a transnational networked response to food fraud. It allows regulatory actors to identify food that has failed to enter the EU at one border point and seeks re-entry elsewhere. Consumers can participate in the network, by assessing whether they have any risky food in their fridges or cupboards, taking action to remove the food from the food chain if they do. Thus the RASFF enrols further actors into the regulatory enterprise, bringing on board enforcement bodies of the home state of an importer, or the consumer who purchased the food. It allows these network participants to take action to control the risk in their sphere, creating a regulatory structure that has the potential for global chain-long action.

By sharing information through the RASFF, the burden of regulatory activity is shared, with investigation and enforcement functions not necessarily carried out by the same network actors. While this is unlikely to be sufficient alone to control the risk, such enrolment increases the reach of the information shared, and ensures that the network works to remove risky food through numerous mechanisms. Additionally, the RASFF does not direct the actions of the member states. While it shares information about actions of national regulators, actors within other jurisdictions are not required to act on such information.

As well as informing regulatory network members about current breaches of food law, the RASFF can play an important role in informing regulatory actors about future threats. For example, Article 35 of Regulation 178/2002 states that data shared through the RASFF can be used to predict future dangerous food (Bouzembrak and Marvin, 2011; Petrozci et al, 2011), allowing the targeting of regulatory resources at the most risky products. While such targeting will not identify all fraudulent food, it may be used to allow *more* proactive action by participants in the regulatory network.

The RASFF is not a solution to cases of food fraud. Where fraudulent food does not pose a risk to consumers' health, data will not be entered into the RASFF database. So, for example, if a product sold as '100% olive oil' is recalled because it is found to be a mixture of olive oil and sunflower oil, but does not pose a direct or indirect risk to human health, it will not be entered into the RASFF database. The RASFF is, at best, a partial tool in facilitating enrolment into a transnational regulatory network. Therefore, it is necessary for further steps to be taken to ensure that the network can respond to all forms of food crime, coordinating information sharing and regulatory action.

Food Fraud Network (FFN)

The RASFF is reactive and ad hoc, constructing new networks in response to each detected and uploaded incident. A more permanent network is desirable, which has led to the creation of the Food Fraud Network (FFN). Regulation 882/2004 on official controls performed to ensure the verification of compliance with feed and food law provides the architecture for cooperation between member states in the enforcement of all food law. Regulatory bodies may turn to their counterparts in other EU member states and request assistance, including with obtaining information and documents that are necessary to verify compliance with food law (Article 36), or when information is uncovered in one suggesting that there is non-compliance with food law in another, that information may be passed on without a request for such information (Article 37). This ensures that state national bodies are enrolled into the regulatory network where further investigation is needed in those states, or where non-compliance in some states is noted.

In order to enhance the capacity of the network, and to ensure that assistance can be easily obtained, the European Commission has established both a network of Food Fraud Contact Points and a technological tool to facilitate the exchange of information relating to requests for assistance regarding food fraud. The FFN allows the sharing of information regarding food fraud, filling the gap in the RASFF referred to previously. Network members can inform others of the presence of fraudulent food on the market in order to allow them to take action to remove such food from the market within their jurisdiction. Information about over 200 cases has been shared to date between members of the FFN (FFN, 2015). In order to expedite the exchange of information, as situations involving food fraud are often time-critical, the Administrative Assistance and Cooperation (AAC) system allows members of the FFN to electronically exchange information about food fraud and in support of cross-border regulatory cooperation. The FFN and AAC function to expand the capacity of national regulators by providing them with the ability to take advantage of investigative steps undertaken in other member states, providing them with the capacity to take steps in other member states where their investigation reveals cross-border food fraud.

Coordinated control plans (CCPs)

Similar to the RASFF, the FFN functions to enhance the ability of regulatory actors reactively. Where it is perceived that there are violations of food law that have implications across the EU, the Commission has the power to coordinate activities throughout the Union (Regulation 882/2004, Article 40), by enabling the recommendations of ad hoc plans aiming to establish the prevalence of hazards in food (Article 53). This power has been witnessed and utilised increasingly during and following the horsemeat scandal, which demonstrated that coordination and communication was lacking in the cross-border regulatory network, despite the representation of power in Regulation 882/2004.

The inadequacy of the response to the horsemeat scandal was partially due to a focus on cooperation surrounding safety issues, at the expense of successful regulatory responses to food fraud (European Parliament, 2016, paras 30 and 57). Therefore, the European Commission has sought to proactively coordinate the response of national bodies to particularly prevalent instances of food fraud. Coordinated control plans (CCPs) have been issued in respect to horsemeat (Commission Recommendation 2013/99/EU) and honey and fish substitution. CCPs apply across the EU and to certain European Free Trade Association countries. In this chapter, the examination of CCPs is limited to those covering fish substitution and honey, as these perform the function of a day-to-day governance response to perceived food fraud, whereas the CCP for horsemeat was a response to a particular governance crisis (see Chapter 10, this volume, for a discussion of a networked response to the horsemeat scandal).

The CCP for fish substitution, set out in Annex II to Commission Recommendation C(2015) 1558 with a view to establishing the prevalence of fraudulent practices in the marketing of certain foods, was made because information suggested prevalent mislabelling of the species of origin of white fish (FSA, 2016, para 6.4.3). The plan provided a methodology for all EU member state regulators to take steps to establish whether the fish in food products (or pure fish) conforms to the species declared on the label, and if it does not, to establish the species contained within the product. The CCP provided a sampling programme across the supply chain, predominantly targeting major white fish species consumed in the territory of member states as well as those products that are more susceptible to species substitution.

Samples were analysed by isoelectric focusing, polymerase chain reaction coupled with restriction fragment length polymorphism, DNA barcoding or real-time polymerase chain reaction methods to establish whether the fish species in the product matched the fish declared on the label. In June and July of 2015, 3,906 samples were taken and tested with 6 per cent not in conformity with the declared species, the most common mislabelled species being grouper and common sole (DG SANCO, 2015a). While 6 per cent of unprocessed fish products were mislabelled, only 5 per cent of the products containing processed fish sampled were mislabelled.

The CCP for honey authenticity, set out in Annex I to Commission Recommendation C(2015) 1558, was made in order to establish the presence of mislabelled honey regarding botanical or geographical origin or sold as honey despite the presence of non-honey sugars in the product. Concerns about honey authenticity have been present for a number of years (Rouff and Bogdanov, 2004). The high economic value of specialist honeys, such as Manuka, provides a clear incentive for fraudulent mislabelling, in order to increase the value that can be realised for the product (FSA, 2016, para 6.13.17). The plan requires each member state to sample and test honey to determine whether it complies with the information declared. Honey products labelled with a range of origins or from a range of places in the supply chain are included in the sampling plan. Unblended honeys would be submitted to different tests that intended to determine the botanical and geographic origin of the honey, as well as that they had compliant sugar profiles. For blended honeys, only analysis aimed at the detection of unexpected sugars was performed.

Analysis revealed that 7 per cent of samples were non-compliant with regard to their declaration of botanical source, 6 per cent contained exogenous sugar and 2 per cent were non-compliant with regard to their declaration of geographical origin. In addition, 13 per cent of samples were characterised as suspicious because, although the results of analysis were within expected limits, the results were unusual or questionable. The most common sampling location in the food system for non-compliant samples was the importer or wholesaler, where 19 per cent of the samples taken were found to be non-compliant (DG SANCO, 2015b).

The CCPs are an important governance mechanism for identifying the prevalence of misidentified food in the food system. They enrol regulatory actors across numerous member states in a dedicated programme that examines the non-compliance with labelling requirements. Each of the actors has a similar regulatory capability, but covers a different geographical area. Therefore, the geographical scope of the regulatory network is broadened, and the information-gathering capacity of the network advanced, providing a fuller picture of the food system than would be possible for any one regulatory actor alone.

However, the CCP is a sampling-based methodology that cannot identify the reasons for the misidentification, which may include intentional fraud, poor management practices or other non-deliberate reasons. The CCP is therefore primarily an information-gathering exercise and the initiation of member states' response to food crime, not the end. It is successful in coordinating regulatory capacities to collect and analyse samples in response to single identified problems, but does not function to coordinate regulatory capacities beyond that. The regulatory network created is therefore limited, with further steps needed to build the network through the entire regulatory process.

For example, following a sample result demonstrating food fraud, a decision must be made about the steps to remove that food from the supply chain. Formal enforcement may be taken against those who are suspected of engaging in fraudulent practices, which will require evidence gathering beyond simple sampling, such as engaging with other actors in the regulatory network, including food scientists, food businesses, employees and consumers. Further, the presence of adulterated food in the food chain may require engagement with commercial stakeholders not involved in the sampling programme, in order to alert them to the possibility of fraudulent food in the food chain. This can enrol them in the regulatory network, utilising their ability to govern the contents of their food supplies through contractual standards and sampling in order to ensure conformity.

Beyond the CCP itself, the results have the potential to enrol private actors in other mechanisms for the governance of food supplies, such as certification schemes, with the evidence gained through the

CCP as a motivator for enrolment. Similarly, a media campaign based on the results of a CCP has the potential to engage consumers in the possibility of fraudulent food in the system, by alerting them to the areas of risk, and incentivising them to play a fuller role in scrutinising food products for potential problems.

CCPs therefore play an important role in the response to food crime in Europe. They allow the coordination of investigations across the whole European market. However, they do not target intentional non-compliance, and do not coordinate the response of member states when non-compliance is discovered. Further, they do not generally extend beyond the European market. Therefore, the need for mechanisms for networking beyond the FFN and CCPs exists, one that is aimed at ensuring the capacity to enforce against food fraud is enhanced.

Europol and the Opson operations

A proactive network aimed at enforcement necessarily involves more actors, with more diverse regulatory capacities than the CCPs and FFN. Law enforcement requires long-standing international cooperation mechanisms that extend in scope beyond Europe, and include international organisations, such as Interpol, and national law mechanisms, such as extradition and mutual legal assistance. The move from a 'food law' to a 'crime' perspective on food fraud is a recommendation of the European Parliament's resolution on fraud in the food chain (European Parliament, 2016, para 53). The food law perspective focuses on consumers, and seeks to ensure that they are not misled by removing, for example, mislabelled food from the market. The food crime perspective seeks to allocate responsibility to the individuals or corporations that caused the mislabelling. Both perspectives can coexist, but some networking techniques, such as RASFF, exist in a food law paradigm, whereas law enforcement cooperation is necessarily focused on criminal responsibility for breach.

Europol is the EU institution responsible for assisting member states in combating serious organised crime. Food fraud is a priority area for Europol, and also interacts with other priority areas such as organised crime and counterfeiting. As part of this role, Europol (2016) has coordinated yearly operations aimed at 'fighting against organised crime groups involved in the trade of fake and substandard food'. The fifth operation, Opson V, constructed a regulatory network consisting of Europol and Interpol, law enforcement and food regulators from 57 countries and 21 food businesses and trade associations. This operation led to over 350 administrative and criminal cases and the seizure of over 5.5 million food items (Europol, 2016).

Opson V created a regulatory network with a broad regulatory capacity. Europol and Interpol were able to provide intelligence about food fraud, and share information emanating from states or businesses involved in the operation with those that had the capacity to take action. Interpol hosted an operational headquarters, which was available to provide support to those taking part in the operation. States were able to share intelligence and to take action against food fraud taking place within their jurisdiction. While states were not directed regarding the regulatory or criminal action to take during the operation, they were expected to act on the information received. This illustrates the facilitative, rather than directive, nature of the network. The Opson network is not about determining the consequences of non-compliance with law, but about detecting such non-compliance. While transnational measures can be put in place, they do not function to ensure enforcement of law, which remains within the power of states.

The Opson operations bring together a large amount of regulatory capacity to target the resolution of particular problems. By combining the capacity of multiple actors within the regulatory network, actions are better targeted, and enforcement is more likely to be successful: fraudulent food is more likely to be removed from the food system, and criminal actors identified and eliminated. The geographic scope of the Opson operation is particularly important. While RASFF provides the facility to inform states beyond the boundaries of Europe about fraudulent food, Opson commits these states to active involvement in the proactive response to food fraud. This expansion of regulatory capacity beyond the borders of Europe is a useful tool in the networked response to food crime.

The problems of networking

While networked solutions have the potential to enhance regulatory capacity, they also have potential drawbacks. As a number of actors are involved in the response, the sense of responsibility for responding to food crime may become dispersed. This may particularly be the case in systems where networking is reactive, such as RASFF. Unless the information is responded to with diligence, the benefits of networking will not accrue. A network where particular responsibilities are allocated to each actor, like the CCPs, is less likely to have this problem, albeit this does not negate its potential.

As networked solutions rely on information, data security is crucial. Without sufficient data safeguards there is a potential for information to either be lost or to be obtained by unintended actors. The information may have value, for example, if it identifies shipments scheduled to be sampled, and therefore criminal actors may seek to obtain it in order to utilise or sell it to corporations or industries seeking to avoid being caught. Beyond information loss, networking can lead to a loss of control for each of the individual network participants. It is necessary to rely on others to perform actions, rather than all actions being performed by a single actor. This loss of control reduces the ability to protect information, and to take steps to ensure that it, and its source, is protected. This is particularly problematic if the information is derived from anonymous sources that require protection. For example, information derived from whistle blowers, if not properly protected, can be detrimental for the person who makes the disclosure (Hyde and Savage, 2013).

Networking may also have potential to lead to biases and regulatory capture. In networks such as the one constructed by the Opson operations, the involvement of corporate actors means that the focus tends not to be on potential food crime committed by those specific participants. The food businesses involved are constructed as victims, rather than as potential non-compliant entities. They are, of course, both, and it is necessary for this to be acknowledged by participating enforcement agencies. Involvement in regulatory networks does not render a business virtuous, but simply economically savvy, as enforcement against food crime will remove imitation products from the marketplace, making consumers more likely to purchase the 'real' thing.

Conclusion

Despite these challenges, regulatory networks play a vital role in the response to regulatory non-compliance, food fraud and food crime more generally. Networks function to identify food that does not meet regulatory standards, as well as those responsible for such non-compliance. The wrong may be presenting one food as another, but it may be broader than that, including contamination, poor hygiene or use of unapproved novel foods. All of these matters are food crimes. Therefore, rather than focusing on regulatory non-compliance as an issue separate from food crime, the crime-fighting techniques represented by the information-sharing networks considered above should be adopted across the food sector. From information sharing to more formal enforcement cooperation, regulatory capacity to respond to food crime, and regulatory non-compliance more generally, is enhanced by networks. The benefits of networking are particularly acute in the context of transnational food supply chains.

The networking mechanisms explored in this chapter each contribute to the prevention of, or response to, food crime in different ways. RASFF is reactive, allowing regulators, business and consumers to assess whether particular food is within their control, and the steps that can be taken to respond. The FFN and AAC fill gaps within the RASFF, allowing active cooperation rather than passive receipt of information, and allowing information to flow, facilitating action and enhancing the capacity of nationally bound regulators by enabling cooperation in investigation. CCPs allow a proactive coordinated response to a particular problem, but do not dictate the enforcement consequences of the coordinated investigation. The results of a CCP may trigger further actions, and may be used to enrol further members into a regulatory network, reducing the prevalence of fraud in the food system. Law enforcement-led networking, such as the Opson operations, produces a response, but is dependent on information sharing. A broad range of actors, with differing regulatory capacities, must work together to respond to food crime.

References

Black, J. (2007) 'The decentred regulatory state?', in P. Vass (ed), *CRI regulatory review 2006/2007*, Bath: Centre for the Study of Regulated Industries, University of Bath.

Bouzembrak, Y. and Marvin, H. (2016) 'Prediction of food fraud type using data from Rapid Alert System for Food and Feed (RASFF) and Bayesian network modelling', *Food Control*, vol 61, p 180.

DG SANCO of the European Commission (2015a) 'Fish substitution test results' (https://ec.europa.eu/food/safety/official_controls/food_fraud/fish_substitution/tests_en).

DG SANCO of the European Commission (2015b) 'Coordinated control plan to establish the prevalence of fraudulent practices in the marketing of honey: Preliminary results' (https://ec.europa.eu/food/sites/food/files/safety/docs/official-controls_food-fraud_honey_control-plan-results.pdf).

European Commission (2015) *The Rapid Alert System for Food and Feed: 2015 annual report* (https://ec.europa.eu/food/sites/food/files/safety/docs/rasff_annual_report_2015.pdf).

European Commission (2017) 'Food fraud' (https://ec.europa.eu/food/safety/official_controls/food_fraud_en).

European Parliament (2016) Resolution of 14 January 2014 on the food crisis, fraud in the food chain and the control thereof, [2016] OJ C482/4.

Europol (2016) *Report: Operation Opson V* (www.europol.europa.eu/sites/default/files/documents/report_opson_v.pdf).

FFN (Food Fraud Network) (2015) *Food Fraud Network activity report 2015* (https://ec.europa.eu/food/sites/food/files/safety/docs/official-controls_food-fraud_network-activity-report_2015.pdf).

FSA (Food Standards Agency) (2016) *Food Crime: Annual strategic assessment – A 2016 baseline*, London: FSA.

FSAI (Food Safety Authority of Ireland) (2013) 'FSAI survey finds horse DNA in some beef burger products' (www.fsai.ie/details.aspx?id=11878).

Havinga, T. (2015) 'Conceptualizing regulatory arrangements. Complex networks and regulatory roles'. in T. Havinga, F. van Waarden and D. Casey (eds) *The changing landscape of food governance. Public and private encounters*, Cheltenham: Edward Elgar Publishing, pp 19–36.

Hyde, R. (2015) *Regulating food-borne illness: Investigation, control and enforcement*, Oxford: Hart.

Hyde, R. and Savage, A. (2013) 'Cross-border concerns: Perils and possibilities', *E-Journal of International and Comparative Labour Studies*, vol 2, no 3, p 116.

NSF International (2014) 'The "new" phenomenon of criminal fraud in the food supply chain: The rapid rise of food fraud and the collective responses to the global threat' (www.nsf-food-conf.eu/assets/nsf-food-fraud-whitepaper-final-sept2014.pdf).

Paulus, I. (1974) *The search for pure food: A sociology of legislation in Britain*, London: Martin Robertson.

Petrozci, A., Nepusz, T., Taylor, G. and Naughton, D. (2011) 'Network analysis of the RASFF database: A mycotoxin perspective', *World Mycotoxin Journal*, vol 4, no 3, p 329.

Rouff, K., and Bogdanov, S. (2004) 'Authenticity of honey and other bee products', *Apiacta*, vol 38, p 317.

Savage, A. and Hyde, R. (2015) 'The response to whistleblowing by regulators: A practical perspective', *Legal Studies*, vol 35, no 3, pp 408–29.

Spink, J. and Moyer, D. (2011) 'Defining the public health threat of food fraud', *Journal of Food Science*, vol 76, no 9, R157–R163.

15

Fair trade laws, labels and ethics

Will Low and Eileen Davenport

> If the misery of the poor be caused not by the laws of nature,
> but by our institutions, great is our sin. (Charles Darwin)

> Nothing is illegal if one hundred businessmen decide to do
> it. (Andrew Young, former United Nations ambassador)

Introduction

The fair trade movement is arguably one of the most successful social
movements of the late 20th and early 21st centuries. In contrast to its
humble origins in charity shops run by Oxfam in the UK, and the
Mennonite Central Committee and Church of the Brethren in the
US, the largest of the three major networks of fair trade[1] organisations,
Fairtrade International, generated global sales of €7.3 billion in 2015
from 1,200 producer organisations which served more than 1.65
million farmers and farm workers in over 70 countries (Fairtrade
International, 2016).

Having emerged to assist Second World War refugees, a global
social movement evolved as a response to the perceived economic and
social inequities of the international food production and distribution
system, first under a banner of 'alternative trade' and later as 'fair trade'.
The movement's members and supporters reflect diverse approaches
to 'alternative' social relations of production and consumption,

including mutualism (producer and consumer cooperatives), Utopian industrialism, religiously inspired views linking business and social justice (including liberation theology), 'alternative lifestyles' based on communalism and anti-capitalist 'counter-culture', and anti-colonialism. For example, 'Third World solidarity groups' in the Netherlands started selling cane sugar in the 1950s as a vehicle for educating consumers about international development issues (Kocken, 2006).

A key goal of the movement is to offer both a theoretical and practical alternative to the existing power relations in global trade that are argued to structurally disadvantage producers in the Global South (Barratt Brown, 1993). Hence the fair trade movement has built its practice around two key principles: payment of a 'fair price' (Zadek and Tiffen, 1998) and a primary focus on producer wellbeing. Littrell and Dickson (1999, p 5) neatly summarise these two principles as 'an ideological focus on paying producers "as much as possible" rather than "as little as possible"'.

Fridell (2007, p 24) says, '[f]rom a theoretical perspective, the origins of the [fair trade] network's development vision lie in the structuralist, dependency and world systems theories...', which argue that the existing gap between core (rich) and periphery (poor) countries is maintained, in part, through international trade policies. Export of food commodities from the Global South bears the legacy of imperialism and colonialism, as tropical crops such as tea, coffee and sugar were introduced to third world colonies to supply first world markets. World systems theory (Wallerstein, 1974) and dependency theory (Prebisch, 1950) both identified the need for the Global South to gain more benefit from its agricultural sectors. The Non-Aligned Movement, a group of 77 countries so called because they considered themselves independent of the West and the Soviet Bloc, argued that commodity agreements could regulate the price of raw agricultural and mineral products to ensure 'just and equitable terms of trade' (Prashad, 2007). Producer countries established a wide range of commodity agreements during the 1960s, covering, for example, tin, sugar, coffee and oil. Only the agreement on oil production remains today, in the form of the Organisation of Petroleum Exporting Countries (OPEC).

It was the collapse of these supply mechanisms, in particular the International Coffee Agreement in 1989, which proved pivotal in broadening the base of support for fair trade. Dire need ensued as the price of exported green coffee beans fell from US$1.34 per pound to US$0.77 per pound for the first five years thereafter (Daviron and Ponte, 2005). Coincidentally Catholic 'liberation theology'-inspired activists began working with a cooperative of indigenous coffee farmers from Oaxaca, Mexico, to establish the Max Havelaar label to signal to Dutch consumers that the cooperative's coffee had been produced and sold according to 'fair trade' principles (Nicholls and Opal, 2005). The label's name was taken from a novel, published in 1860 and set in the Dutch East Indies, whose eponymous protagonist comes to realise and work against the inhumanity and inequality of the colonial plantation system. The novel raised public awareness in the Netherlands and elsewhere, of the way in which colonialism forced peasant farmers to grow cash crops (such as coffee) rather than staple crops, which imposed and perpetuated rural poverty.

This chapter argues that the emergence and evolution of the fair trade movement can be understood through a food crime perspective developed by Croall (2007) and expanded by Gray and Hinch (2015; see also Chapter 1, this volume). According to Croall (2007, p 206), food crimes refer to the 'many crimes that are involved in the production, distribution and selling of basic foodstuffs.' Fair trade can be seen as a response to 'macro-level' food crimes – systemic harms and injustices caused by the global food production and distribution system against people involved in the food industry – rather than 'micro-level' instances of food adulteration and the misrepresentation of food quality highlighted elsewhere in food crime literature (Gray and Hinch, 2015). The chapter starts by describing the fair trade movement in more detail, in order for the reader to understand its organisation and its operating principles. The next section highlights where the literature on fair trade has identified perceived systemic shortcomings of the movement in meeting its goals and objectives. Then, in the longest section of the chapter, the focus is on issues of labour rights within fair trade, an issue into which we have done direct fieldwork.

The chapter concludes with an assessment of the role fair trade has played in creating and maintaining positive social change in response to systemic inequality and injustice in the global food distribution system. Nonetheless, fair trade is not on its own presented as the solution to the economic and physical harms facing farmers, workers and farming communities in the Global South who are working in export markets. The fair trade movement is one of many attempts by non-state private actors (Reed et al, 2012) to regulate the capitalist system of production and trade, especially across international boundaries, by offering alternatives that meet 'higher' social and environmental standards, which pressure for-profit corporate entities to observe basic human and labour rights and to practice environmental sustainability. However, while championing the agenda of global trade reform alongside anti-globalisation, ethical consumption and anti-sweatshop activists, fair trade has offered a practical alternative for a small but growing number of structurally disadvantaged producers to sell coffee, tea, bananas, coffee, sugar, rice and many other foods to take direct action against the hegemonic forces of 'free trade'.

'Let a hundred flowers bloom; let a hundred schools of thought contend'

In a series of papers, we have traced the evolution of the fair trade movement (Low and Davenport, 2005a, b, 2006, 2007; see also Raynolds, 2002; Renard, 2003). Alternative trade organisations developed a 'charity trade' strategy to sell handcrafts made by refugees, displaced people or marginalised groups in order to fund relief efforts. Increasingly, secular organisations took up this strategy and augmented it with two concurrent strategies, referred to as 'development trade' and 'solidarity trade', where food and handcraft products from the third world were sold to support calls for decolonisation and trade justice across Africa, Asia and Latin America. A broad-based social movement evolved in the 1970s around a common strategy of 'alternative trade', as groups affiliated with organised labour, leftist political parties and church networks facilitated access to northern markets for marginalised southern producers. The southern partners included associations of landless urban poor, divorced and widowed women or small family farmers, who used the system to access northern markets without having to deal through commercial 'middle-men'.

Non-mainstream distribution channels were used to reach consumers, including third world shops, health food shops, church organisations, women's organisations, student and political groups, local fairs and mail order. The alternative trade approach therefore embodied systemic limitations in terms of accessing a broad consumer base, but also suffered from poor product selection and quality (Nicholls, 2002). But just as sales across the alternative trade system seemed to be bumping up against these constraints in the late 1980s, the Max Havelaar label opened up the opportunity for expansion through 'mainstreaming' food products into supermarkets.

It was important to have undifferentiated food commodities such as coffee, tea, cocoa and sugar products labelled, as this acts as a guarantee behind the simple messaging of paying a fair price to producers. This contributed to the success of fair trade-labelled products on supermarket shelves and in high street cafes, not just among 'ethical consumers', but also to the wider public that the alternative trade model did not reach. Mainstreaming these products has made practising 'fairness' an almost daily activity for many consumers in the Global North, thus greatly expanding the movement's reach and helping more producers. While only a small portion of their global markets, the influence of fair trade food products extends beyond impressive growth of sales with its contribution to debates about international trade justice during the late 20th century.

Institutionalisation of fair trade

Kocken (2006) argues that having met informally in conferences every couple of years during the mid-1970s, starting in the mid-1980s fair trade organisations (FTOs) came together more formally in a variety of associations such as the International Federation for Alternative Trade (IFAT). The tenets of fair trade evolved to encompass five key elements agreed by the key actors within the fair trade movement:

- facilitating access to northern markets for marginalised producers who are organised under cooperative governance without resort to commercial middlemen;
- fostering long-term relationships between southern suppliers and northern distributors that allow producers to plan their investment and spending over several years;
- paying a 'fair price' that covers the costs of sustaining production;
- extending credit or advanced payment to producers to cover costs between order and delivery;
- paying a social premium above the fair price that creates a fund for wider community social development (see Nicholls and Huybrechts, 2015, p 1).

Having said that, the movement itself is not unified in terms of its approach to fair trade; the main split is between fair trade as 'cooperative-based, endogenous development' versus 'socially regulated, corporate-led growth' (Reed, 2015, p 218). The former approach adheres more closely to the original model of alternative trade by working with smaller, more marginal producers. The latter approach dominates labelled 'fairtrade' products based on larger, better-organised producers supplying multiple outlet retailers.

There are currently three main networks that govern what is broadly referred to as fair trade. Two are labelling organisations –

Fairtrade International (FI) and the Institute for Marketecology (IMO). The other one is a membership organisation, the World Fair Trade Organization (WFTO).

Fairtrade International (FI) (previously Fairtrade Labelling Organizations International)

Following the development of the Max Havelaar label in the Netherlands, use of a label to identify fair trade goods was subsequently reproduced during the 1990s in other European markets, as well as in North America, Oceania and Japan. These national labelling initiatives became centralised under the Fairtrade Labelling Organizations International (FLO) in 1998. In 2002, a universal registered trademark – the Fairtrade mark – was established, along with various national labels. Since 2011, the organisation has been known as Fairtrade International (FI). In addition to the five fair trade principles identified previously, FI's standards also set criteria to ensure that the conditions of production and trade are environmentally responsible. According to Smith (2014), the typical cost of certification in 2013 was €2,520 for a producer group or €1.44 per farmer/worker.

Institute for Marketecology (IMO)

A certification programme called Fair for Life (FfL) was created in 2006 through a partnership between the IMO and the Bio-Foundation. FfL offers 'brand-neutral' third party inspection and certification for both food and non-food commodities (such as cosmetics, textiles or tourist services). Use of the label is free of charge and at all verified stages of the chain of custody to the final product. FfL covers over 4,600 operations with more than 140,000 small-scale producers in 40 countries (Blanco, 2013).

World Fair Trade Organization (WTFO) (previously International Federation for Alternative Trade)

IFAT was established as a membership organisation in 1989 to coordinate the efforts of individual northern and southern FTOs, and to give its members a common voice and forum. Its initial membership of around 30 organisations was dominated by the northern wholesalers and retailers. Named the World Fair Trade Organization (WFTO) as of 2009, it estimates that it represents the interests of '110 million artisans, farmers, growers, producers, and supporters' in the South and the North through 400 members operating in 73 countries across five regions (WFTO, 2011).

Food crimes in fair trade

We draw on an extensive and growing literature to analyse the structure of the movement and attempt to assess the impact of that system. The majority of studies of fair trade focus on the FI certification system, as the largest component of sales and the main proponent of mainstreaming. Coffee is the main food commodity studied, followed by cocoa, tea and bananas, which round up the top four sellers, with cut flowers also attracting much attention. There are some discussions of the governance of WFTO but limited studies of its handcraft or food product producers. Given its more recent emergence it is not surprising that FfL has not yet been subject to detailed study. These studies show that in terms of 'micro-level' food crimes, fairtrade has not been subject to major scandals or criminal prosecutions. Baughen (2003) suggested that fraudulent selling of conventionally grown bananas as certified fairtrade bananas to meet excess demand is an example of threats to the legitimacy of the system, but no subsequent scandal has developed. In part this is because, since the mid-2000s, fairtrade supply has exceeded demand for certified products, and policing of the licensing agreements for use of the label appears to have been effective.

However, a number of concerns about economic and physical harms to humans in the value chain emanating from macro-level systemic sources remain. The remainder of this section deals with a variety of concerns that relate to fundamental principles of the fair trade system identified previously, and then extensively analyses a key area of concern in global trade: labour rights.

Systemic biases

As suggested earlier, an originating principle of fair trade was to serve producer need and to start from what producers had to sell – a 'producer-driven' value chain (Barrientos and Smith, 2007). Smith (2013) highlights a number of empirical investigations showing that access to fair trade markets is often dictated by market and retailer demands rather than producer need (a 'buyer-driven' value chain). This is especially the case where supermarkets have a very specific way in which they wish to align their products with their brand. For example, Moberg (2005) examined how UK supermarket Tesco's branding decisions led it to ignore the Windward Islands fairtrade banana producers' desire to allocate export quotas equally across the islands, and instead bought the majority of its fruit from just one island to simplify its marketing message.

One of the main criticisms of mainstreaming was that in order to serve the needs of large multiple outlet retailers such as supermarkets, sourcing would favour larger, export-ready cooperatives rather than the marginal and 'poorest of the poor' on which the fair trade movement was established. For example, certification was not available in countries deemed as 'low income' under United Nations (UN) classifications such as Ethiopia, in favour of 'middle-income' countries such as Mexico (Sidwell, 2008).

The FI certification system has also been accused of being an opaque process that leads to seemingly random decisions differentiated by both geography and product characteristics. For example, Smith (2013) highlights how conventional raisins can be certified in Southern Asia, Central Asia and South America, whereas only organic raisins are certified from South Africa.

Fair price

The raison d'être of fair trade has always been paying a 'fair price' to southern producers. Nicholls and Opal (2005, p 10) suggest that even though fair trade cocoa producers capture as little as 4 per cent of the northern selling price of a chocolate bar, this is a higher share than through conventional trade. The ideological roots of paying a fair price reflect perspectives that evolved through the mid-1990s related to 'development and underdevelopment', anti-colonialism, anti-capitalism, mutualism and social justice. Zadek and Tiffen (1998) suggest that a 'fair price' can represent several meanings: more than the local price; more than the price available from other international traders; enough for producers to attain a reasonable living standard; or a trading regime that allows southern producers to earn the same as their northern trading partners.

The fair trade labelling movement institutionalised a fair price by imposing a guaranteed floor price per pound of coffee in the late 1980s when the market price of green beans fell below the estimated cost of production (Low and Davenport, 2005a). Despite ease of translating the message of a fair price into a marketing message that could underpin mainstreaming and the growth of fairtrade coffee sales, the minimum price guarantee has not been extended to other FI certified products. The requirement for FfL certification is that price should be 'slightly above local market rates for non-FairTrade products of similar quality' (quoted in Smith, 2013, p 64). For all three organisations, the key is that the fair price is decided between buyer and seller 'to ensure that producers can cover their average cost of sustainable production' (Berlan and Dolan, 2016).

The impact of this fair price (and fair wage in the case of WFTO) is highly contentious. Nelson and Pound's (2010) review of fair trade studies conclude that the greatest impact is generating higher *revenue* for the fair trade producer organisations than would be the case for organisations outside the fair trade system. This is a natural outcome of the price floor that guarantees a minimum price for fairtrade production. However, it is difficult to determine whether or not individual farmer *incomes* rise significantly as a result of the greater total revenue. Costs of running the cooperative structure are deducted from the revenue received, and therefore the net income received by farmers is naturally less than the revenue generated by the system. No impact studies demonstrate that the net income of fair trade farmers translates into a 'living wage'.

In the most extensive and widely discussed study of the impacts of FI certified fairtrade, funded by the UK Department for Foreign and International Development, Cramer and colleagues (2014, pp 15–16) argue:

> This research was unable to find any evidence that Fairtrade has made a positive difference to the wages and working conditions of those employed in the production of the commodities produced for Fairtrade certified export in the areas where the research has been conducted.... In some cases, indeed, the data suggest that those employed in areas where there are Fairtrade producer organisations are significantly worse paid, and treated, than those employed for wages in the production of the same commodities in areas without any Fairtrade certified institutions (including in areas characterised by smallholder production).

Social premiums

Fairtrade championed the notion of a 'social premium', a payment above the fair price intended for broad social development projects. Both FI and FfL mandate that the use of the social premium should be 'democratically' determined to support sustainable social or environmental community projects or social projects for the workers and their families. WFTO has not instituted an additional premium, although its principle of fair price and fair wage refers to an agreement between producer and consumer organisations on a level that reflects costs of production and some additional costs. The literature often cites confusion among members over the purpose and use of the social premium, which should not be considered a direct contribution to farmers' incomes. Some farmers, according to Nelson and Pound (2010), have complained that they would prefer to see direct benefits of the fairtrade premium on their household incomes, especially in times of hardship. The situation can be even more complex on plantations because the social premium is intended to provide 'community' benefits. The concept of the worker's community is a contested one in a plantation context, as workers usually come from other districts to live and work on the plantation, and still see 'home' as elsewhere.

Labour rights in fair trade

We now turn to a major concern of many pressure groups working to reform global trade – the rights of workers – which has manifested most notably in clothing and textiles, minerals and renewable resources extraction, electronics manufacturing and agricultural sectors. An example would be child labour, a crime defined in international agreements such as the UN Convention on the Rights of the Child, and by national/local law on the employment of children. Fair trade organisations agree with the principle that young workers should never perform any work that is hazardous or that could jeopardise their emotional, social or physical development. Nonetheless, children working on a family farm are likely to be a reality, especially in the Global South. Thus the principled stand against child labour is fraught with complexity, as pointed out by Berlan (2009, p 144): '... the ILO campaign to end child labour in part bears the marks of a Western conceptualisation of childhood which assumes labour to be detrimental and is at odds with the views the children in Ghana expressed.' While abuse of child workers has not been recorded within the fair trade system, the broader issue of worker rights has been critically examined within the fair trade literature. There are 170,000 workers on FI certified plantations around the world and nearly the same number of workers on FI certified smallholder farms (Fairtrade International, 2016). Neither WFTO nor FfL produce such exacting figures of farm workers within their systems of fair trade.

Workers employed by small-scale producers

Luetchford (2008, p 165) suggests that '[m]uch of the fair trade literature to date focuses "up" from "producers" (which usually, somewhat bafflingly, refers to cooperatives and administrators) and their relations with NGOs and consumers. But we also need to focus "down" on relationships between growers and their cooperatives ... and ... between farmers and workers.' Davenport and Low (2012, p 330) also argue that 'the imagery of the peasant farmer hides ... the presence of hired labourers and their material conditions in the fair trade value chain.'

This is true across the range of fair trade food products. Utting (2009, p 142), in her study of Nicaraguan fairtrade coffee cooperatives, says small producers can (and do) hire landless peasants to work for them. The Fair Trade Foundation (FTF, 2010, p 7) states that 'only the smallest (tea) producers farm their land entirely with family labour, and many smallholders employ workers, often on a casual basis.' The same is true for fairtrade smallholder banana farmers who 'generally employ one or two permanent workers and bring in casual labour for the fortnightly harvest' (FTF, 2008, p 8).

These studies highlight how, hidden behind the fair trade marketing message of paying the peasant farmer a 'fair price' is the employment relationship between the small farmer and labour. The trickle-down of fair trade benefits to these workers is uneven at best, and falls far short of the expectation of the empowerment of all 'producers' that fair trade promises. Davenport and Low (2012) highlight how landless labourers working for wages in Kenyan tea production, who live permanently within the farming community, cannot have a voice in fair trade processes, a role reserved for landowning 'farmers'. Other casual or seasonal migrant labourers are excluded altogether from fair trade benefits unless the fair price paid to the farmer organisation translates into higher wages than would otherwise be paid. However, payment of a:

... "fair wage" (to parallel the "fair price") is not required by the FI standard for small producers and is at the discretion of the individual farmer employing waged labour. At best, an FI member organisation *is expected to encourage* its members to share the benefits of Fairtrade with their workers and to improve the working conditions in line with these Standards ... including casual, seasonal and permanent workers. (Davenport and Low, 2012, pp 332–3; emphasis added)

Lyon (2015) cites two examples in Central America where fairtrade coffee certification has not significantly improved the lot of workers. In Guatemala, many FI certified farmers she spoke with admitted they hired labourers on an as-needed, day-to-day basis in order to avoid complying with national labour laws that require permanent workers to be paid monthly. She also highlights a study by Valkila and Nygren (2010), which found that the labour rights of hired workers on Nicaraguan coffee farms and in coffee-processing facilities had not been significantly enhanced above existing Nicaraguan norms and legislation through fair trade participation. Therefore, a 'hidden' hierarchy of labour relationships remains in the fair trade discourse, despite its often stated goal of 'lifting the veil' obscuring the social relationships in food and craft production (Hudson and Hudson, 2003).

Workers employed in plantation production

FI certification standards have been developed for six product categories – bananas, fresh fruit, cut flowers, juices, tea and wine – grown on plantations or large farms. There have been numerous reports and documentaries since the mid-1990s onwards (such as SOMO et al, 2006; KHRC, 2008) that have focused on the woeful conditions of plantation workers, although not specifically targeting the fairtrade movement. These studies highlight the prevalence of bad housing, low wages, few or no opportunities for schooling and advancement, harassment of women workers, discrimination against minority ethnic groups and child labour in plantation agriculture.

Our own field research in 2009 did not support other studies, such as the Kenyan Human Rights Commission report (2008), which suggests that sexual harassment is rife in tea and flower production in Kenya. In the FI registered tea plantation we visited, certification coincided with the takeover of the plantation by a large multinational corporation that had its own strong policies and procedures to prevent sexual harassment, but fairtrade was also argued to have played a role. In part this was attributable to worker empowerment: workers felt confident that they could speak out because there was a potential sanction against the company from fairtrade organisations and consumers if complaints were ignored.

Engaging with plantation production is both critical and contentious as it opens the fair trade door to more workers in key food commodity categories while diluting the movement's original focus on smallholder farmers. Challenges remain in ensuring that workers on smallholder farms and on plantations see direct benefits to incomes and social development from the fair trade system.

Conclusion

Despite not being guilty of high crimes, such as an act of fraud that might lead to legal actions, Williams (2008, p 7) argues that:

> ... the expectation of consumers is unequivocally that Fairtrade should guarantee better wages, rights and conditions of work as well as delivering Premium to workers' communities. Working conditions in the Fairtrade certified plantations visited are generally below public expectations (and in some cases below those of non-Fairtrade competitors). The lack of a differential between Fairtrade-certified plantations and conventional plantations ... represents a major reputational risk to Fairtrade.

It is important to understand how fair trade interacts with social, business and political institutions and laws to create the conditions under which workers find themselves. A focus solely on the fair trade movement risks marginalising the role played by other agents of social change, in particular, trade unions and their place in promoting worker rights in democratic societies. As Besky (2008, p 5) says in relation to Indian tea plantations: 'the [Indian] Labour Act attempts to concretize socially just wages as opposed to [fair trade's] abstract claims of fair wages....' Regular interactions between trade unions and fair trade bodies might be one way to ensure that existing labour standards are met, and ongoing improvements in the lives of all workers can occur. The fair trade system may serve to reinforce the power and legitimacy of trade unions, and by bolstering monitoring of workers' rights through the threat of consumer boycott actions. Fair trade is not, and never could be on its own, a panacea for the many social and economic challenges facing farmers, workers and farming communities. However, fair trade, especially in the context of a favourable environment for unions and bolstered by ongoing implementation of corporate social responsibility policies by the companies, has a role to play in creating and maintaining positive, systemic social change to prevent the injustices that are central to the analysis of food trade using a food crime perspective.

Note

[1] We follow a convention of using fair trade as two words when referring to the movement in general, whereas fairtrade as one word is used when referring to the labelling initiatives and their certified products.

References

Barratt Brown, M. (1993) *Fair trade: Reform and realities in the international trading system*, London: Zed Books.

Barrientos, S. and Smith, S. (2007) 'Do workers benefit from ethical trade? Assessing codes of labour practice in global production systems', *Third World Quarterly*, vol 28, no 4, pp 713–29.

Baughen, C. (2003) 'What are the limits of fair trade?' (www.alternatives.ca/article1016.html).

Berlan, A. (2009) 'Child labour and cocoa: Whose voices prevail?', *International Journal of Sociology and Social Policy*, vol 29, nos 3/4, pp 141–51.

Berlan, A. and Dolan, C. (2016) 'Of red herrings and immutabilities: Rethinking fairtrade's ethic of relationality among cocao producers', in M. Goodman and C. Sage (eds) *Food transgressions: Making sense of contemporary food politics*, Abingdon: Routledge, pp 39–60.

Besky, S. (2008) 'Can a plantation be fair? Paradoxes and possibilities in fair trade Darjeeling tea certification', *Anthropology of Work Review*, vol 29, no 1, pp 1–9.

Blanco, T. (2013) 'Introduction to Fair for Life certification', Presentation (http://wfto.com/sites/default/files/IMO%20Fair-for-Life---WFTO-AGM-final.pdf).

Cramer, C., Johnston, D., Oya, C. and Sender, J. (2014) *Fairtrade, employment and poverty reduction in Ethiopia and Uganda*, London: SOAS, University of London, for the Department for International Development.

Croall, H. (2007) 'Food crime', in P. Beirne and N. South (eds) *Issues in green criminology: Confronting harms against environments, human and other animals*, Portland, OR: Willan Publishing, pp 206–29.

Davenport, E. and Low, W. (2012) 'The labour behind the (fair trade) label', *Critical Perspectives on International Business*, vol 8, no 4, pp 329–48.

Daviron, B. and Ponte, S. (2005) *The coffee paradox: Global markets, commodity trade and the elusive promise of development*, London: Zed Books.

Fairtrade International (2016) *Driving sales, deepening impact: Annual report 2015–2016* (https://annualreport15-16.fairtrade.net/en/).

Fridell, G. (2007) 'Fair trade coffee and commodity fetishism: The limits of market-driven social justice', *Historical Materialism*, vol 15, no 4, pp 79–104.

FTF (Fair Trade Foundation) (2008) *Unpeeling the banana trade*, London: FTF.

FTF (2010) *Stirring up the tea trade: Can we build a better future for tea producers?*, London: FTF.

Gray, A. and Hinch, R. (2015) 'Agribusiness, governments and food crime: A critical perspective', in R.A. Sollund (ed) *Green harms and crimes: Critical criminology in a changing world*, London: Palgrave Macmillan, pp 93–115.

Hudson, I. and Hudson, M. (2003) 'Removing the veil? Commodity fetishism, fair trade, and the environment', *Organization and Environment*, vol 16, no 4, pp 413–30.

KHRC (Kenyan Human Rights Commission) (2008) *A comparative study of the tea sector in Kenyan: A case study of large-scale tea estates*, Nairobi: KHRC.

Kocken, M. (2006) 'Sixty years of fair trade: A brief history of the fair trade movement', November (www.european-fair-trade-association.org/efta/Doc/History.pdf).

Littrell, M.A. and Dickson, M.A. (1999) *Social responsibility in the global market: Fair trade of cultural products*, Thousand Oaks, CA: Sage.

Low, W. and Davenport, E. (2005a) 'Postcards from the edge: Maintaining the "alternative" character of fair trade', *Sustainable Development*, vol 13, no 3, pp 143–53.

Low, W. and Davenport, E. (2005b) 'Has the medium (roast) become the message? The ethics of marketing fair trade in the mainstream', *International Marketing Review*, vol 22, no 5, pp 494–511.

Low, W. and Davenport, E. (2006) 'Mainstreaming fair trade: Adoption, assimilation, appropriation', *Journal of Strategic Marketing*, vol 14, no 4, pp 315–28.

Low, W. and Davenport, E. (2007) 'To boldly go... Exploring ethical spaces to re-politicise fair trade and ethical consumption', *Journal of Consumer Behaviour*, vol 6, no 5, pp 1–13.

Lyon, S. (2015) 'The hidden labor of fair trade', *Labor: Working class history of the Americas*, vol 12, nos 1–2, pp 159–76.

Luetchford, P. (2008) 'The hands that pick fair trade coffee: Beyond the charms of the family farm', in G. de Neve, P. Luetchford, J. Pratt and D.C. Wood (eds) *Hidden hands in the market: Ethnographies of fair trade, ethical consumption, and corporate social responsibility*, Research in Economic Anthropology, vol 28, Bingley: Emerald Group Publishing Ltd, pp 143–69.

Moberg, M. (2005) 'Fairtrade and Eastern Caribbean banana farmers: Rhetoric and reality in the anti-globalization movement', *Human Organization*, vol 64, no 1, pp 4–15.

Nelson, V. and Pound, B. (2009) *The last ten years: A comprehensive review of the literature on the impact of fair trade*, London: Natural Resources Institute, University of Greenwich.

Nicholls, A.J. (2002) 'Strategic options for fair trade retailing', *International Journal of Retail and Distribution Management*, vol 30, no 1, pp 6–17.

Nicholls, A.J. and Huybrechts, B. (2015) 'Fair trade and co-operatives', in J. Michie, J. Blassi and C. Borzaga (eds) *The handbook of co-operative and mutual businesses*, Oxford: Oxford University Press, pp 470–9 (http://orbi.ulg.be/handle/2268/179498).

Nicholls, A.J. and Opal, C. (2005) *Fair trade market-driven ethical consumption*, Thousand Oaks, CA: Sage Publications.

Prashad, V. (2007) *The darker nations: A people's history of the third world*, New York: The New Press.

Prebisch, R. (1950) *The economic development of Latin America and its principle problems*, New York: United Nations.Raynolds, L. (2002) 'Consumer/producer links in fair trade coffee networks', *Sociologia Ruralis*, vol 42, no 4, pp404–24.

Reed, D. (2015) 'Co-operatives, corporations and fair trade', in L. Raynolds, and E. Bennett (eds) *Handbook of research on fair trade*, Cheltenham: Edward Elgar, pp 211–29.

Reed, D., Mukherjee, A. and Utting, P. (2012) *Business, non-state regulation and development*, New York: Routledge.

Renard, M.C. (2003) 'Fair trade: Quality, market and conventions', *Journal of Rural Studies*, vol 19, no 1, pp 87–96.

Sidwell, M. (2008) *Unfair trade*, London: Adam Smith Institute.

Smith, A.M. (2013) 'What does it mean to do fair trade? Ontology, praxis, and the "Fair for Life" certification system', *Social Enterprise Journal*, vol 9, no 1, pp 53–72.

Smith, A.M. (2014) 'Access to the Fairtrade system: The geography of certification for social justice', *Food Chain*, vol 4, no 1, pp 49–65.

SOMO (Centre for Research on Multinational Corporations), ProFound and India Committee of the Netherlands (2006) *Sustainabilitea: The Dutch tea market and corporate social responsibility*, Utrecht: SOMO.

Utting, K. (2009) 'Assessing the impact of fair trade coffee: Towards an integrative framework', *Journal of Business Ethics*, vol 86, pp 127–49.

Valkila, J. and Nygren, A. (2010) 'Impacts of fair trade certification on coffee farmers, cooperatives, and laborers in Nicaragua', *Agriculture and Human Values*, vol 27, no 3, pp 321–33.

Wallerstein, I. (1974) *The modern world-system, vol I: Capitalist agriculture and the origins of the European world-economy in the Sixteenth Century*, New York and London: Academic Press.

WFTO (World Fair Trade Organization) (2011) 'About WFTO', 'Who we are' (www.wfto.com/index.php?option=com_content&task=view&id=890&Itemid=292).

Williams, P. (2008) *Fairtrade hired labour standards*, London: Fairtrade Foundation.

Zadek, S. and Tiffen, P. (1996) '"Fair trade": Business or campaign?', *Development*, vol 3, pp 48–53.

Section VI
Technologies and food

16

Food, genetics and knowledge politics

Reece Walters

Introduction

The *Routledge international handbook of food studies* is arguably the most comprehensive cross-disciplinary exposé of food in contemporary social life. Interestingly, its 34 chapters from internationally recognised scholars do not mention or address issues relating to crime or genetic technologies (Albala, 2013). This is perhaps unsurprising given the relatively recent advent of 'food crime' and the rapid advances in agro-technologies. Indeed, criminology's interest in global debates of food insecurity is relatively new, and even less interest, from a criminological standpoint, has been devoted to food and technology (Johnson and Walters, 2014). This is surprising given the links between corporate greed, governmental negligence and human starvation (Raghib, 2013). This edited volume seeks to redress this oversight with a dedicated collection devoted to food crime and associated harms.

The United Nations (UN) World Food Programme (WFP) reports that there are 795 million people worldwide who are undernourished (2017). The fact that 10 per cent of the world's population lives in a daily state of starvation and food insecurity is an international crisis that criminology can no longer ignore. As a discipline devoted to, *inter alia*, exposing and examining behaviours and actions that cause social harm, human suffering, dislocation and disadvantage, it is imperative that issues of world hunger are critiqued through a pervasive lens of state and corporate power (Coleman et al, 2010; Tombs and Whyte, 2015). In doing so, this chapter draws on innovative discourses in green criminology to explore the issues of genetic technologies and the politics and power of food production and distribution. It argues that food crime must also be understood within the discourses, debates and contestations surrounding 'knowledge' and its application to food security, distribution and consumption. Those in positions of state and corporate power that have the means to shape the contours of global food trade, notably, what is safe to eat and what is not, requires an academic examination of the ways in which 'knowledge politics' plays a crucial role in shaping public discourse and influences political debate. In doing so, this chapter extends definitions of 'food crime' to include a political economy analysis of food production, distribution and consumption and the ways in which 'knowledge' becomes imperative in a global politics of power and profit.

Green criminology and genetically modified (GM) food

Green criminology has blossomed into a range of critical discourses examining environmental concerns within notions of power, harm and justice (Walters et al, 2013). Since its emergence in the late 1980s, discourses in the greening of the criminological enterprise have adopted various terms and nomenclature in an attempt to harness and capture evolving debates. As a result, the use of 'green criminology' (Lynch, 1990), 'eco-critical criminology' (Seis, 1993), 'conservation criminology' (Herbig and Joubert, 2006) and 'eco global criminology' (White, 2011) have all been used in various intertwined ways to explore state and corporate exploitation of the environment for power and profit. In 2013, Nigel South and Avi Brisman compiled the first *International handbook of green criminology*, and in their introduction they describe the subject as a 'capacious and evolving perspective', where 'diversity is one of its great strengths'. They further add that it includes a '… set of intellectual, empirical and political orientations towards problems (harms, offences and crimes related to the environment, different species and the planet). Importantly, it is also an "open" perspective and framework, arising from within the tradition(s) of critical criminology; at the same time, it actively seeks inter- and multi–disciplinary engagement' (South and Brisman, 2013, p 18).

It is also important to note that South (2010, p 242), one of the pioneers of green criminology, rightly identifies that emerging environmental harms and injustices requires 'a new academic way of looking at the world but also a new global politics.' This includes an intellectual discourse that moves 'beyond the narrow boundaries of traditional criminology and draws together political and practical action to shape public policy.' Green criminology continues to evolve as a dynamic knowledge of resistance and innovation, one that challenges mainstream crime discourses, and critically examines the policies and practices of contemporary governments and corporations. It is a collection of new and thought-provoking voices within the criminological lexicon, and its engagement with diverse narratives seeks to identify, theorise and respond to environmental issues of both global and local concern. The expansion of green criminological perspectives serves to harness and mobilise academic, activist and governmental interests to preserve, protect and develop environmental issues. Such an approach utilises discourses on power, harm and justice to explore the ways in which the natural environment is compromised, manipulated and abused (Walters et al, 2013). The global debates about food insecurity and injustice necessitates adopting a pluralistic analytical lens capable of transcending disciplinary boundaries to understand the complexities of food production, trade and consumption – a *food crime perspective* (see Chapter 1, this volume).

The Global Sustainability Institute has predicted that catastrophic food shortages by 2040 will cause worldwide riots and death, and society as it is known 'will collapse' (Doré, 2015). Such forecasts are indeed alarming; however, the rhetoric of 'warning' and 'emergency' about food production and distribution are not new. In 2009, the UN Secretary-General Ban Ki-Moon stated that food security was a 'forgotten crisis' (Ki-Moon, 2009), and the future shortages of world food supplies is an accumulating and dangerously quiet but deadly 'tsunami' (Johnson and Walters, 2017). The challenges to long-term global food security are compounded by resource scarcity, environmental degradation, biodiversity loss, climate change, reductions of farm labour and a growing world population. These issues are arguably caused and aggravated by the spread of corporatised and monopolised food systems, dietary change and urbanisation. These factors have rapidly brought food under the umbrella of emerging global security threats, where social, political, economic and military security is linked to the long-term sustainable development of food supplies (van Heukelom, 2011). For some, however, the insecurities brought about by food shortages have substantial fiscal opportunities.

For some, humanitarian crises associated with food insecurity are a pending peril, notably for the world's poorest and most vulnerable people. For others, it is an emerging market with unprecedented profits, where 'national and international institutions and governments make use of human hunger for their own survival' (Raghib, 2013, p 1). The global food crisis has also reinvigorated debates about agricultural development and genetically modified (GM) food, as well as posing deeply divided debates about poverty, debt and security.

Elsewhere I have explored the intersections between GM crops and criminology (2011, 2006, and 2004). These accounts have detailed the monopolisation of food and included debates about eco sovereignty and GM organisms. For almost two decades, proponents of GM food have exploited moments of severe drought and food shortages to promote the advantages of biotechnology and food production. Such moments have been continually met with opposition from the world's hungry. It has been proven that GM plants can irreversibly contaminate other plants and biodiversity (Walters, 2011). With the production of GM products controlled by a diminishing number of biotech giants, there is a growing form of 'monopoly capitalism' (Walters, 2006, p 35). The aggressive corporate policies of control have been openly acknowledged by the directors of the biotech industries. Mr Rob Fraley, from DuPont, has stated that 'what we are seeing is not just a consolidation of seed companies, it's really a consolidation of the entire food chain' (quoted in Walters, 2011, p 29). Such monopoly capitalism infringes human rights and international trade law, and is in direct opposition to the competitive and free trade policies of the World Trade Organization (WTO). The overwhelmingly majority of GM food and its accompanying fertilisers, seeds and herbicides are produced from four chemical corporations, namely, Monsanto, Syngenta, DuPont and Bayer (Shemkus, 2014). Yet free-trade ideologies espoused by the WTO to enhance notions of competitive capitalism are compromised by a status quo of monopoly capitalism. As Winston (2002, p 174) argues, 'genetically modified organisms would be only an interesting academic sideline if there was no money to be made. The heavy investments in research that have driven corporate biotechnology would not have been forthcoming without the product protection provided by patents.' The biotech corporate lobbying of government officials, the bribing and threatening of scientists, the theft, manipulation and subversion of scientific data, the strategic placement of GM corporate employees on regulatory, funding and government decision bodies have all been documented and continue to raise serious concerns about the actions and motives of the GM giants (Walters, 2011).

In 2015, thousands of people united in protest across the world to oppose the expansion and adoption of GM food technologies (BBC News, 2015). After decades of scepticism, China finally approved the growing of GM crops under tight regulations (Baxter, 2016). However, within months, and due to public opposition, Chinese provinces placed a five-year moratorium on all GMO activities (*Financial Times*, 2016). Indeed, scientists remain at odds over the future of GM foods, and as a result, the public continue to be confused and polarised (Edwards, 2015). This has resulted in GM biotech giant, Monsanto, stepping up its public relations activities and directly targeting consumers with a new branding that includes positive messaging. This targeting to end users is reportedly the result of Monsanto's bottom line being effected by continued global consumer protest and opposition (Alseci, 2016).

The following section of this chapter examines the ways in which 'knowledge' about genetic food technologies has become a means to control political, public and commercial discourses – notably, the way knowledge production is increasingly privatised, controlled and selectively utilised by corporate interests and how this is transformed into economic and political power, in what Stehr (2005) refers to as 'knowledge politics'.

Knowledge politics and GM food technologies

The development of GM crops is a prime example of an environmental regulatory issue featuring a proliferation of contested knowledge – from detailed agronomic and ecological research data, to scientific reviews, technology assessments, public inquiries, economic and risk analyses, media reportage and policy documents. Notwithstanding, little clarity or social agreement exists on the productive capacity, ecological or social consequences of GM crop regimes, or confidence in GM commercialisation. Such knowledge contestations reflect conflicts between expert scientific knowledge and local knowledge and understanding (Liberatore and Funtowicz, 2003).

The GM crops debate intersects a number of highly controversial 'science, technology, environment and society' debates including anthropogenic global warming, deterioration of the ozone layer and nuclear energy. All are characterised by considerable complexity and uncertainty, high risk, susceptibility to politicisation by interested parties, and a divisive polarisation of viewpoints. In these issues, 'authoritative' knowledge is a valuable commodity and those in the position to control knowledge production and communication can exert significant political and economic power. With highly contested issues such as GM technologies, much is at stake. Considerable capital investment has occurred, and large profits are potentially available to transnational corporations. The state is eager to attract capital and to harvest tax revenue in a political environment where 'balanced' budgets are seen as a measure of government competency. In agriculture, successive governments in Australia, Canada and the US have been withdrawing state support, hoping to create an economic environment that encourages private interests in farming and farming support services. The introduction of GM technologies reduces reliance on local knowledge through restrictions on farmer experimentation and evaluation, and with the decline in independent sources of knowledge, farmers are more reliant on private knowledge sources from those who are also beneficiaries of the technology. These 'structural' changes to the knowledge networks of farmers, intensified by patent-protected GM resources and knowledge exclusivity, influence what and how decisions are made about GM crop adoption.

The battlegrounds of GM crop technologies

Biotechnology, through the development of new transgenic organisms, denotes a new phase in the industrialisation of agriculture. Novel traits, such as herbicide or pesticide resistance, can be engineered into crops. GM proponents argue that current technology promises increased agricultural productivity, lower costs and improved environmental outcomes, or that GM is a breakthrough technology that promises to feed the world's hungry (Hindmarsh, 2008) and contribute to global food security (Tait and Barker, 2011). Further, the burden of contractual arrangements, increased liability and market risk, significant payouts to seed companies (either owned or licensed by biotech companies) and greater transport and segregation are additional costs farmers have to bear. Critics of the new agrigenetics technology raise a number of issues, including:

- *risk and uncertainty* regarding the development of GM crops, particularly when regulated by a narrow scientific cohort (Hindmarsh, 2008);
- *economic harm* created through GM contamination via gene flow (of non-GM conventional to organic produce) or inadequate storage and transportation loss;

- *environmental harm* including the breeding of wild weed species (Knispel et al, 2008), and the demise of beneficial insects (Zhao et al, 2011);
- *Bt toxin persistence and unintended effects* on soil biota (Vadakattu and Watson, 2004);
- *safety of long-term ingestion of GM foods* (Carman, 2004), consumer choice and the 'right to know';
- *concentration of capital and privatisation* of genetic information and its influence on the control of agricultural production (Pechlaner and Otero, 2010);
- *deviant and illegal activities of corporate actors* in controlling and monopolising the production, distribution and regulation of GM technologies, seeds and plants (Walters, 2011).

As in Canada and the US, the minimalist regulatory regime for GM crops in Australia also side-steps concerns regarding broader and interrelated socioeconomic risks of the technology (Dibden et al, 2013). These include market risk, transportation and storage separations and cost, increased corporate control over farming and the actual production and economic value to farmers in using this technology. These issues are then expected to be mediated by farmers and their representatives, and partners in crop production, transportation and storage. Clearly, a key aim for bio-development is to reduce the financial and regulatory hurdles for GM crops, and that risks should be handled by industry self-regulation. The primary assertion is that technology users should have the freedom to choose between growing GM or non-GM crops. However, 'freedom to choose' relies heavily on independent knowledge of the agronomic, economic and environmental consequences of the technology. Others also argue persuasively that once GM crops are established it would be difficult to turn back because of contamination issues and the increased control of seed production and licensing by the biotechnology sector (Dibden et al, 2013, pp 67–8).

The 'freedom to choose' discourse – frequently wheeled out to support low levels of technology regulation – is useful for conceptualising the way power is deployed through the control of knowledge production and deployment. Freedom to choose and related neoliberal discourse assumes an 'ideal type' of an individual actor acting rationally with perfect information and negligible transaction costs. The way the GM crop knowledge economy is structured leaves the farmer, consumer and social actor with a 'freedom of choice' based on biased knowledge, and limited discursive resources for politicisation.

Power and knowledge

The successful establishment of GM-'friendly' national regulatory institutions has been critically examined in previous work in Australia (Hindmarsh and Parkinson, 2012) and the UK (Walters, 2011). Such works concluded that the direct application of economic power, astute policy alliances and ownership and privileging of certain knowledge has contributed to the dominance of the GM lobby. More broadly, biotech companies have sought political influence through substantial public relation campaigns, focused lobby groups and through sponsorship and advertising in influential scientific journals (Walters, 2011, pp 23–6), as well as through public exhibitions (Hindmarsh, 2008) and public inquiries as forms of knowledge/power (Hindmarsh and Parkinson, 2012). Widespread evidence exists in the US of orchestrated attacks on scientific research exposing the environmental risks of GM crops (Waltz, 2009). Public sector scientists in the US have complained that it has been difficult to obtain GM seeds for comparative agronomic research, and that in some cases, adverse agronomic studies have been prevented from being published (Waltz, 2009).

Studies on the role of truth and knowledge claims in the resolution of complex social problems are not new. The sociology of knowledge is a well-established field, and scholars have long debated the relationship between knowledge and interests in social theory (Habermas, 1971), and explored the interrelationships between the regimes of truth/knowledge and power relations (Foucault, 1981). Critiques of 'expert knowledge' abound in the sociology of knowledge literature, and have contributed to understandings of the importance of 'local/contextual/tacit' knowledge (Kaup, 2008). The efficacy of expert knowledge in contributing to enhanced development or agricultural productivity has often been questioned, particularly in in development contexts, where local cultural traditions provide significant barriers to implementation. Similarly, in the agricultural extension literature, critiques of the linear model of extension of agricultural science to farmers highlighted low adoption and/or inappropriate outcomes. Further, these critiques had a normative element that characterised expert–layperson relations as a form of domination.

These critiques at both policy and local contexts support a democratisation of knowledge, but rarely attempt to interrogate links between knowledge ownership and production – how certain knowledge gains 'authority' and the power effects of particular knowledge appropriation and insertion into influential discourses. There is a sense that the critiques of scientific knowledge and the focus on its limitations has displaced a concern for the materialist aspects of (scientific) knowledge – the way this knowledge production is increasingly privatised, controlled and selectively deployed by corporate and state interests and how this is transformed into economic and political power.

Controlling GM food knowledge production

Probably the most widely known and instructive examples of corporate control of the means of knowledge production in GM crops relate directly to patenting of GM products. The specificity of engineered biological material allows simple identification, and the state has instituted laws that provide total control to patent holders over the GM product. Pechlaner and Otero (2010, p 254) argue that the legal framework developed by the state to support patents and contractual arrangements between growers and seed suppliers is significantly distinct from other forms of agricultural industrialisation to require a new concept, which she names 'expropriationism'. Central to this concept is the partisan nature of the legal framework that gives strong protection to the patent owner over use of their genetic material, but no responsibility over its risk and economic damage. Further, the contractual framework for use of the GM germplasm, often called a 'technology package', places restrictions on farming practices. The contract requires certain farming practices to occur – such as the inspection and destruction of 'volunteers' – and obligates the farmer to allow 'inspections' of their property, testing of soils and grain bins and inspections of farm records by the technology owner for a further three years after purchasing seed (all at the cost of the farmer). Any legal or investigatory action by the technology owner must be paid for by the farmer, and within this contract, the technology owners' liability is limited to the cost of the seed and the warranty specifically excludes economic loss due to crop failure. Any external punitive action that is taken to recover economic loss due to GM canola spread leaving and liability on the contacted farmer. The sale of land that has grown GM canola within the last six years must include an agreement from the purchaser to abide by the technology agreement originally entered in to by the vendor. Further, the contract specifies technology charges based on yield at delivery in addition to seed costs. However, one of the most powerful aspects of the patent is the exclusive control over the use of GM seed for research by independent science. These characters socially restrict the reincorporation of seed production into farm processes through state regulations that protect the patented gene. At the same time, public sector research and development into new seed varieties has diminished, leaving farmers more dependent on a few large corporations for their supply of seed.

The agricultural knowledge economy

The introduction of new technology and innovations in agriculture has always been accompanied by discourses on the benefits of the particular technology. However, historically, innovations have come from a diversity of sources including farm-level experimentation and experience, public sector research from the state and universities and private sector research. The extension or communication of these innovations has also occurred through multiple pathways or what might be called 'knowledge networks'. They may include local farmer communication, rural media, field days and on-farm demonstrations, collaborative on-farm research (Crawford et al, 2007), state and private sector extension agents and farmer groups and commodity organisations. Significantly, there has been direct involvement of farmers in knowledge production and innovation through invention, experimentation and plant selection. The challenge of agricultural development is significantly different from other industry sectors. Rural wellbeing, which in the past has been seen to be intimately connected to the fortunes of agriculture, has been a political priority for successive governments. These complex developments have created an agricultural knowledge economy that is vulnerable to colonisation by large capital and private interests. These changes were not simply driven by neoliberal approaches to agriculture, but were also enabled by strident criticism of the state extension model by rural development scholars and some extension practitioners. These discourses provided space for new conceptions of knowledge production and communication based on the more forthright entry of private interests. To further complicate this, there was an increasing realisation of the degradation of rural environments through farming, which could not be simply internalised by private interests. Rural industry was also considered less important to the economy and economic activity in rural areas was diversifying beyond agriculture, for example, in mining and tourism, and more plural interests have emerged such as energy supply and environmental values (Daugbjerg and Swinbank, 2012). These vulnerabilities in the knowledge economy of agriculture provide opportunities for private knowledge colonisation by GM technology companies.

Because of the risk inherent in agricultural production and the difficulty in controlling the biophysical environment of farming, the industrialisation of agriculture has mainly developed in a piecemeal fashion (Goodman et al, 1987). While large capital has made some incursions into farmland ownership, the difficulties of intensification and control of natural processes, the relative lack of control of labour and the limited economies of scale are often a disincentive to corporate ownership (McCabe and McCabe, 2008). As a result, capital has endeavoured to appropriate endogenous farming processes (such as seed saving and nutrient recycling) with industrialised inputs (such as seeds and fertilisers) (see also Goodman et al, 1987). The commodification of inputs increases reliance on large capital and shapes the type of farming processes. 'Substitution' by industrial capital seeks to mediate between farm production and consumption by utilising farm produce as industrial inputs, and therefore exerts control over the production process through demanding particular farm produce characteristics and determining the price paid for products.

Significantly, capital accumulation through substitution and appropriation are historically and spatially contingent processes. The relative abundance of land and the predominant farm production systems determine what aspects might be best appropriated (e-mechanisation vs input fertilisers) and what products might be best substituted. Science and technology development have a major effect on the type and intensity of capital accumulation strategies because they provide new opportunities for controlling aspects of the farm production process. Similarly, state policy also has a major influence through regulating markets, facilitating and/or funding technological development and regulating aspects of industrial and farm production.

The specificity of engineered biological material allows simple identification and a potentially patentable product. These characteristics socially restrict the reincorporation of seed production into farm processes through state regulations that protect the patented gene. At the same time, public sector research and development into new seed varieties has diminished, leaving farmers more dependent on a few large corporations for their supply of seed. The reduction in choice for farmers through a monopolisation of seed sources, and prohibition of seed saving, opens up possibilities for a more subservient role of farm production to industrialised capital. Large capital control of genetic resources for farming increases the possibilities for appropriation by linking specific inputs to the genetic needs of the production process. For example, the GM 'Roundup Ready' canola requires the application of a specific herbicide, glyphosphate, which is an important product of the developers of RR Canola (Monsanto). For the future, the potential linkages could include genetic traits requiring specific nutrient regimes, growth promoters or inhibitors and chemical harvesting – the list is only limited by imagination. The commodification and exchangeability of these inputs threatens natural crop sources from developing countries.

It is clear that the 'new' GM technology, facilitated through patent and contract law, serves to extract property rights from farmers and allow large capital closer control of farm processes. In so doing, the contracted farmers are not only exposed to production risks but also legal liability from other farmers (for economic loss through adventitious presence) and from the technology owner.

Conclusion

There is no doubt that science and technology per se have significantly and positively impacted on global food production, distribution and consumption. The advent of food genetics and biotechnology, however, has provided deeply divided and politicised dimensions to discourses, policies and practices about food security. Within such global debates, scientific knowledge resources have been selectively produced and deployed to counter the politicisation of GM crops and to encourage the rapid adoption of this technology. In highly contested social and environmental issues, what is researched – and what is not – and how that knowledge is authorised and deployed has significant power effects that may pose serious social, economic and environmental consequences.

The chapter concludes that scientific knowledge is very important in decisions to adopt and establish new technologies – not through some rational calculus of cost-benefit, but through the provision of discursive resources for democratic debate and politicisation, and for the knowledge needed for farmers and consumers to enable *true* 'freedom to choose'. One of the most crucial resources is knowledge. Who develops and 'owns' knowledge, what knowledge is seen to be authoritative in these contexts, and how it is extended to decision-makers are important questions. At present, there remains a corporate colonisation of food biotechnology and its associated knowledge politics with trade and fiscal imperatives underpinning motivations and developments. It is within these corridors of knowledge that we must inculcate discourses of food crime and examine the ways in which power is undemocratically used and abused. It is clear that the production and dissemination of GM food knowledge remains deeply politicised and polarised. Given the money to be made from world hunger, and the monopolisation of the biotech industry, it is not surprising that the Monsantos of the world are entering the next phase of the GM food technology era firmly focused on public relations in re-branding and messaging their genetic products. The shift has now moved from farmers, politicians, supermarkets and scientists to the global consuming public in an attempt to capture the hearts, minds, stomachs and pockets of future generations.

References

Albala, K. (ed) (2013) *Routledge international handbook of food studies*, London: Routledge.

Alseci, A. (2016) 'Monsanto CEO frustrated over polarised GMO debate', *CNN Money*, 18 April (http://money.cnn.com/2016/04/18/news/companies/monsanto-ceo-gmo/).

Baxter, A. (2016) 'After decades of weariness, China to go GMOs', *Marketplace*, 11 August (www.marketplace.org/2016/08/11/world/china-gmo).

BBC News (2015) 'Is opposition to genetically modified food irrational', 3 June (www.bbc.com/news/science-environment-32901834).

Brisman, N., and South, N. (2013) 'Introduction. Horizons, issues and relationships in green criminology', in N. South and A. Brisman (eds) *Routledge international handbook of green criminology*, London: Routledge, pp 1–23.

Carman, J. (2004) 'Is GM food safe to eat?', in R. Hindmarsh and R. Lawrence (eds) *Recoding nature: Critical perspectives on genetic engineering*, Sydney, NSW: UNSW Press, pp 82–93.

Crawford, A., Nettle, R., Paine, M. and Kabore, C. (2007) 'Farms and learning partnerships in farming systems projects: A response to the challenges of complexity in agricultural innovation', *The Journal of Agricultural Education and Extension*, vol 13, no 3, pp 191–207.

Coleman, R., Sim, J., Tombs, S. and Whyte, S. (eds) (2010) *State, power, crime*, London: Sage.

Daugbjerg, C. and Swinbank, A. (2012) 'An introduction to the "new" politics of agriculture and food', *Policy and Society*, vol 31, pp 259–70.

Dibden, J., Gibbs, D. and Cocklin, C. (2013) 'Framing GM crops as a food security solution', *Journal of Rural Studies*, vol 29, pp 59–70.

Doré, L. (2015) 'Society will collapse by 2014 dues to catastrophic food shortages, study says', *Independent*, 22 June (www.independent.co.uk/environment/climate-change/society-will-collapse-by-2040-due-to-catastrophic-food-shortages-says-study-10336406.html).

Edwards, J. (2015) 'Scientists against GMOs hear those who have done the research', *Organic Lifestyle*, 5 August (www.organiclifestylemagazine.com/scientists-against-gmos-hear-from-those-who-have-done-the-research).

Financial Times (2016) 'China province bans GMO crops for five years' (www.ft.com/content/a221fb5e-c750-11e6-8f29-9445cac8966f).

Foucault, M. (1981) *The history of sexuality* (vol 1), Harmondsworth: Penguin.

Goodman, D., Sorj, B. and Wilkinson, J. (1987) *From farming to biotechnology*, Oxford: Basil Blackwell.

Habermas, J. (1971) *Toward a rational society*, London: Heinemann.

Herbig, F. and Joubert, S. (2006) 'Criminological semantics: Conservation criminology – vision or vagary', *Acta Criminologica*, vol 19, no 3, pp 88–103.

Hindmarsh, R. (2008) 'Food and environmental security in the Indian Ocean region: Questioning the GM doubly green revolution', in T. Doyle and M. Risely (eds) *Crucible for survival: Environmental security in the Indian Ocean region*, New Brunswick, NJ: Rutgers University Press, pp 182–214.

Hindmarsh, R. and Parkinson, A. (2012) 'The public inquiry as a contested political technology: GM crop moratoria review in Australia', *Environmental Politics*, vol 23, no 2, pp 293–311.

Johnson, H. and Walters, W. (2014) 'Food security', in M. Gill (ed) *The handbook of security* (2nd edn), London: Palgrave, pp 404–26.

Kaup, B. (2008) 'The reflexive producer: The influence of farmer knowledge upon the use of Bt corn', *Rural Sociology*, vol 73, no 1, pp 62–81.

Ki-Moon, B. (2009) 'Food security: Our forgotten crisis', United Nations Secretary-General (www.un.org/sg/articles/articleFull.asp?TID=90&Type=Op-Ed&h=0).

Knispel, A., McLachlan, S., van Acker, R. and Friesen, L. (2008) 'Gene flow and multiple herbicide resistance in escaped canola populations', *Weed Science*, vol 56, no 1, pp 72–80.

Liberatore, A. and Funtowicz, S. (2003) '"Democratising" expertise, "expertising" democracy. What does it mean and why bother?', *Science and Public Policy*, vol 30, no 3, pp 146–50.

Lynch, M. (1990) 'The greening of criminology: A perspective on the 1990s', *The Critical Criminologist*, vol 2, no 3, pp 1–12.

McCabe, L. and McCabe, E. (2008) *DNA: Promise and perils*, Berkeley, CA: University of California Press.

Pechlaner, G. and Otero, G. (2010) 'Neoliberalism and food vulnerability: The stakes for the South', in G. Lawrence, K. Lyons and T. Wallington (eds) *Food security, nutrition and sustainability*, London: Earthscan, pp 79–86.

Raghib, Q. (2013) 'Pitfalls and perils of politicised food insecurity', *News Daily* (www.dailytimes.com.pk/default.asp?page=2013%5C06 %5C28%5Cstory_28-6-2013_pg3_4).

Seis, M. (1993) 'Ecological blunders in US clean air legislation', *Journal of Human Justice*, vol 10, no 2, pp 22–42.

Shemkus, S. (2014) 'Fighting the seed monopoly – "We want to make free seed a sort of meme"', *The Guardian*, 2 May (www. theguardian.com/sustainable-business/seed-monopoly-free-seeds-farm-monsanto-dupont).

South, N. (2010) 'The ecocidal tendencies of late modernity: Transnational crime, social exclusion, victims and rights', in R. White (ed) *Global environmental harm. Criminological perspectives*, Cullompton: Willan, pp 228–47.

South, N. and Brisman, N. (2013) 'Introduction. Horizons, issues and relationships in green criminology', in N. South and A. Brisman (eds) *Routledge international handbook of green criminology*, London: Routledge, pp 1–32.

Stehr, N. (2005) *Knowledge politics: Governing the consequences of science and technology*, Boulder, CO: Paradigm Publishers.

Tait, J. and Barker, G. (2011) 'Global food security and the governance of modern biotechnologies', *Science and Society*, vol 12, no 8, pp 763–88.

Tombs, S. and Whyte, D. (2015) *The corporate criminal. Why corporations must be abolished*, London: Routledge.

UN WFP (United Nations World Food Programme) (2017) 'Hunger' (www.wfp.org/hunger).

Vadakattu, G. and Watson, S. (2004) *Ecological impacts of GM cotton on soil biodiversity*, CSIRO (www.environment.gov.au/system/files/pages/ca807cf6-8ad9-478f-9d7d-f3894704642d/files/bt-cotton.pdf).

van Heukelom, T. (2011) 'A human approach to food security: Land grabs and the limelight', *Journal of Human Security*, vol 7, no 1, pp 6–20.

Walters, R. (2006) 'Crime, bio-agriculture and the exploitation of hunger', *The British Journal of Criminology*, vol 46, no 1, pp 26–45.

Walters, R. (2011) *Eco crime and genetically modified food*, London: Routledge.

Walters, R., Westerhuis, D. and Wyatt, T. (eds) (2013) *Emerging issues in green criminology: Exploring power, justice and harm*, London: Palgrave.

Waltz, E. (2009) 'Battlefield', *Nature*, vol 461, 3 September (www.nature.com/news/2009/090902/pdf/461027a.pdf).

White, R. (2011) *Transnational environmental crime: Toward an eco-global criminology*, London: Routledge.

Winston, M. (2002) *Travels in the genetically modified zone*, Cambridge, MA: Harvard University Press.

Zhao, Y.Y., Liu, F., Yang, G. and You, M.S. (2011) 'PsOr1, a potential target for RNA interference-based pest management', *Insect Molecular Biology*, vol 20, no 1, pp 97–104.

17

Technology, novel food and crime

Juanjuan Sun and Xiaocen Liu

Introduction

Food is a gift from nature. While technological innovation and science development have helped human beings produce food in larger quantities and in a variety of different ways, what food has become is fundamentally different now from what it was in previous generations. In this respect, how food is produced has also considerably changed through the addition of new substances such as colouring agents, flavours, or with the use of science such as biotechnology or nanotechnology. Consequently, there are critical questions that need to be considered about whether food produced as a result of developments in science and technology is generally recognised as 'safe'. In response, regulations at the national and regional levels have taken different countermeasures, and with continual scientific and technological innovation comes new opportunities for food crimes and harms. This chapter addresses first, the regulation of food along with science and technology development, and the regulation of 'novel food' in particular. Second, it introduces the role of technology in the food domain, in both criminal opportunities and crime control. Last, China is discussed as a case study, looking at novel food regulation.

Food regulation in a context of advancements in science and technology

For certain decades, technology, and in particular, science-driven technology, has transformed human life (Committee on Science, Engineering and Public Policy 1993), producing products that have become essential elements of everyday life. While science and technology are quite different concepts, they are used together in this chapter in order to direct a broader discussion of their impact on foodstuffs and food systems. The way food is produced as well as how food is treated has changed dramatically, creating benefits such as diversity, convenience and affordability. But there are also risks to human health due to technological changes in physical, chemical or biological processes involving food production and manufacturing. This corresponds with elevated concern about, and demand for, reinforcing food safety regulation in the interests of the public.

Food fraud (Bee, 2008) is a long-standing issue, giving rise to both safety and quality concerns. As a result, food law originated to fight against food adulteration, and thus to ensure the authenticity and purity of food. Taking the US Pure Food and Drug Act of 1906 as an example, both adulterated and misbranded food were targeted. Adulteration is addressed from the point of substance, including contamination and deleterious substances, while misbranding is defined by information, such as incorrect labelling. This chapter focuses on the adulteration of food. To ensure its purity, a standard of identity was added to ensure that the food was produced according to its legally required composition. Official controls were carried out in the market to prevent both hazardous adulterants such as foreign substances, and non-valuable substances aiming to substitute for expensive and high-value substances.

When food additives can help produce food in a diverse way, and preserve food for longer, the original standard of identity regulations become obstacles, so a more general and flexible safety standard is provided in the form of pre-marketing approval. This means that substances can be used in food as long as their safety has been proved scientifically, which may be accompanied by requirements such as maximum use level and scope of use. This illustrates how scientific and technological developments have changed food supply as well as the corresponding safety regulation. Although the broad application of science and technology in the food supply chain is both beneficial and risky, the regulation of science and technology for preventing technological risks also relies on such science and technology, including the rigorous assessment of a given substance before its use in food, or the detection of adulterants through testing final food products.

Indeed, science and technology have contributed in improving the food supply and promoting human health, as in the case of nutritional food and functions food, where new ingredients or more of existing ingredients can be added. In order to make better use of technological change to bring about a higher quality of life, a supportive policy and law regarding the role of science and technology within food systems may be wise. Yet, in light of the technological risks, environmental degradation and food safety crises, it is also necessary to be cautious. As a result, regulating the technological risks in the food domain is both controversial and non-universal, as there are differences across (inter-)national and regional regulation regarding these so-called 'novel food', a type of food that doesn't have a significant history of consumption or is produced by a method that has not previously been used for food. 'Novel food' is nothing new (Chris, 2013), but was formally conceptualised in response to the advent of biotechnology in food systems. However, the regulation of this kind of newly invented food, either through pre-marketing approval with a safety assessment or deregulation without such a prerequisite, has become a subject of dispute. As far as the European Union (EU) is concerned, novel food refers to food that is newly developed, innovative or produced through the use of new technologies and production processes. Notably, it also refers to food traditionally eaten outside of the EU, but this aspect is beyond the scope of this chapter. Although different from concerns involving the regulation of novel food, the principle of substantial equivalence has been applied to non-regulation of food from new technology. If a new food or a food component is found to be substantially equivalent to an existing food or food component, it can be treated in the same manner with respect to safety (OECD, 1993).

The geographical and political differences in the regulation of science and technology regarding food is due to difficulties balancing the different interests of technological innovation, free trade and economic growth, alongside safety concerns such as human health and environment protection from the point of biodiversity and biosafety. Taking advantage of new science and technology is a common policy for government since advances can bring about higher economic productivity. For example, the application of biotechnology in the agriculture and food domains was regarded as a triumph of modern science in Europe. To this purpose, the harmonised regulation of new tech food by the EU may facilitate the establishment of a common market both inside and outside the EU. With the ongoing debates around the uncertainty of new science and technology, consumers' negative perceptions have become a significant pressure for governments to tighten the regulation of novel food (see Chapter 23, this volume), including requirements such as licensing, labelling and monitoring (Joachim, 2005).

The prioritisation of food safety in food policy, law and forms of regulation was primarily a reaction to recent food crises (Sun, 2012). Scientific risk assessments have helped harmonise food safety regulation at an international level through the World Trade Organization's Agreement on the Application of Sanitary and Phytosanitary Measures, in particular, and the application of risk assessment and food standards provided by international organisations such as the Codex Alimentarius Commission, which is the central part of the Joint FAO/WHO Food Standards Programme and was established by FAO and WHO to protect consumer health and promote fair practices in food trade. In this aspect, it is important to mention the role of science in decision-making regarding food risk management, and the participation of experts through risk assessment, in order to identify risks and hazards, and so to ensure the scientific basis for food safety regulation. Scientific experts originally only played an advisory role, but with scientific food and nutrition discourses increasingly understanding food through their chemical composition, there has been greater reference to scientific opinion. Contemporary food scientists now also play the role of de facto policy-makers.

There is also a risk that non-scientific factors, especially consumers' opinions, may be underestimated or ignored. This is important, as it is the public who are directly exposed to these risks, although laypeople often have different opinions to experts regarding technological risk. For example, the public base the ranking of risk not on statistics, but on qualitative dimensions, such as whether risk-taking is voluntary or involuntary, if the outcome may be chronic or catastrophic, known or unknown to science, controllable or uncontrollable (Arcuri, 2011). The public also tend to overestimate the probability of unfamiliar, catastrophic and well-publicised events (Ruckelshaus, 1984). The public perception of risk eventually matures into public concerns and, in turn, informs decision-making and shapes regulations (Alemanno, 2012).

In this way, one of the challenges in novel food regulation is to deal with the risks resulting from the application of new science and technology. Although risk assessment involves elements of science and technology for prevention and control, the involvement of the public also contributes to increasing the social acceptance of a given risk. For example, when the EU tried to reform the regulation of novel food with the purpose of improving conditions so that businesses could more easily bring new and innovative food to the EU market, the debates concerning the regulation of nanomaterial and the cloning of animals for food production blocked the legislative process, as there was no scientific consensus of such practices' safety for human health (Sarantis, 2015). Similarly, crises such as the BSE scandal exemplify that scientific uncertainty can present a form of scientific controversy, thus precaution should be taken to put public health first; otherwise it could lead to the loss of consumer confidence in both the food business and public administration. As previously discussed, legal frameworks in the EU embrace the precautionary principle to guide decision-making in cases of scientific or technological uncertainty.

Technological innovation and food crime

The case in China involving the addition of melamine in infant formula is a key example of the complexities accompanying scientific and technological innovations within food systems. Melamine was added to infant formula to increase its protein content. However, this melamine-tainted milk was linked to a rise in kidney stones in babies who were given it. As an issue in food safety, food fraud and corporate economic crime, this case became a catalyst driving the reform of food safety regulation in China, leading to the criminalisation of the use of melamine in infant formula.

Another key example is the horsemeat scandal in the EU, where beef was found to be contaminated with (cheaper) horsemeat. In this case there were no detected food safety issues (Fergus, 2013), so it was defined as a case of economically motivated adulteration (Renee, 2014).

Indeed, food crime is plural in nature (see Chapter 1, this volume), which makes it difficult to understand its intersections across concerns of food safety, food quality and food fraud (Manning and Soon, 2016). On the one hand, organised crime has a growing appetite for food crime, in particular, food fraud with economic gain, since the sanction is relatively low if there is no safety concern and there is generally less investigation due to limited public resources (*The Economist*, 2014). On the other hand, technology can make the detection of food fraud more difficult, as in the case of fake honey (Andrew, 2011). Consequently, there is a rising global trend to strengthen the fight against food crime. This has led to the National Food Crime Unit in the UK, functioning to protect consumers from serious criminal activities involving the safety or authenticity of the foods and drugs they consume.

Generally speaking, technological innovation has facilitated both safety regulation as well as offending behaviour and crime opportunities that threaten safety. This is why it is continually questioned whether science and technology are good or bad for food systems. Although the discussion regarding this aspect is beyond the scope of this chapter, it is important to emphasise that technical norms alone are not adequate for benefiting human beings from technological innovation. In other words, government intervention may be essential to protect public interests such as health in the face of technical risk tending to undermine them. What can be defined as technological misuse or crime, and how to carry out technological regulation, differs from country to country due to divergences in legal systems and criminal laws. To work around these inconsistencies, food crime can be addressed in a more comprehensive context, especially in regard to chemical, biological and nuclear technologies (CBNTs) (McGuire, 2012). In fact, food crime has already been an emerging area of criminological scholarship, as in the case of the illegal use of chemicals, or the food crime debate on the use of genetics in food production (Reece, 2007). CBNTs have played a central role in shaping the most crucial ingredients that composite foods and production practice, including methods of biotechnology and radiation.

To promote the benefit brought about by CBNTs, and to fight against the damages caused by misusing them, a traditional criminal sanction can be imposed on the offender and civil compensation given to the victims. As far as the risk and its potential damage are concerned, Beck (1992) claims that in a 'risk society' the risks are by-products of science and technology. In legal terms, risk is the uncertainty of a result, usually, a negative result, having the chance of injury, damage or loss (Gamer, 2004). Since these technological risks deal with potential harms, they should be managed in an anticipatory way. In other words, novel food and other food crime risks – and their regulation – depend on scientific and technological expertise and assessment. This is why risk analysis has become a general principle in managing food risks.

Therefore one of the distinguishing characteristics of the regulation of novel food is to shift from a reactive to a preventive approach. Accordingly, novel food regulation is a specific case to extend the umbrella of technological application and regulation in the food domain. It can also involve a political reason to govern through fear of crime, which is a reaction to people's feelings of insecurity and the resulting demands for stricter laws against (potential) food crimes. As a result, food has become a subject to illustrate how crime control is no longer dominated by the traditional questions of culpability and punishment, but rather by the issues of risk and dangerousness, and by the future-oriented themes of prevention and security (Ulrich, 2016).

In addition to criminal sanctions in fighting food crime, concern about technological risks and potential irreversible damages also influences legal liability. The trend to make criminal sanctions tougher in China is closely linked to the fact that more food safety issues are intentionally introduced by food producers and sellers while ignoring human life and health. While the revision of criminal and food safety law has contributed considerably in this aspect, there is still a call for increased criminal sanctions in food crime by shifting it from its current economic crime category into a public order crime category, since public health is deliberately endangered, and sanctions in the latter are tougher than in the former.

The case of China

In China, the Food Safety Law from 1 June 2009 and its revision in 2015 have provided the legal foundation for regulating novel food and materials. This has made food producers using novel food material submit safety assessment documents, which are only approved if the food safety requirements are legally satisfied. Elsewhere, Sun (2015) has analysed the historical evolution of these rules, and the contemporary food safety requirements. In view of this, how official control is carried out in the case of novel food in China can be further addressed in both ex ante regulation and ex post liability in the following discussion.

The evolution of novel food regulation in China

Although Measures on the Hygiene of Novel Resources for Food in 1987 was established as one of the implementing acts for the Food Hygiene Law of 1983, the definition of 'novelty' had not been clarified until the arrival of Measures on the Hygiene of Food from Novel Resources in 1990. Transitioning from a novel food orientation towards a novel food material orientation (News, 2007), Measures on Food from New Resources in 2007 has further clarified the definition and scope of what novelty means from a legal perspective. It re-grouped novel foods into four categories, and took a process-based criterion for safety assessment (David, 2006). Later, with the establishment of

Food Safety Law in the place of Food Hygiene Law in 2009, the term 'novel food material' was used instead of 'food from novel resources'. The updated Measures on the Safety Review of Novel Food Material in 2013 has further broadened the definition of novel food material to include untraditional items in China's eating habits, such as animals or ingredients extracted from animals. Although the Food Safety Law was revised in 2015 and put into effect on 1 October in the same year, regulation regarding novel food remains based on the 2013 measures at the time of writing.

With the updates, the current definition and scope regarding novelty involves a few key concerns or changes. First, the non-inclusion of traditional foods in China means certain types of food have been produced or traded as standard-packaged or non-standard-packaged food for over 30 years, and have not been listed in the *Pharmacopoeia of the People's Republic of China*. Second, categories of animals, plants and microorganisms, ingredients extracted from animals, plants and microorganisms, food ingredients, the original composition of which has been changed, and other newly developed food raw materials are now included in novel food conceptualisations. And third, the changes continue to exclude specific health foods and food additives. For example, health foods have been specifically regulated by administrative policies.

With the revisions to the Food Safety Law, pre-market permission is required if claims are to be made regarding the health benefits of any novel food. To apply for approval of a novel food material, the applicant needs to submit a safety assessment document that clearly indicates the involved chemical substances, the composition, the labelling and other relevant information. Whether these statements comply with the mandatory national food safety standards are further reviewed by scientific experts. If the substantial equivalence principle is met, safety assessment may cease with no further requirement for assessment. However, approval is not infinite. Granted approvals can be subjected to follow-up assessments in light of newly emerged scientific information or safety issues related to the approved food material in question, in order to avoid health risks. Therefore, both science-based obligation and precaution in the case of scientific uncertainty have been integrated into novel food regulation in China. Part of such regulation involves a publicised novel food material catalogue listing all substances that can be legally used in food products and production practices.

Overall, the regulation of novel food in China can be characterised by three distinct points. First, the modernisation of food safety regulation is a context driving the update of novel food regulation. The restructuring of the Food Safety Law, in place of the Food Hygiene Law, has shifted the focus more toward the interests of public health. As far as a legal framework is concerned, vertical legislation has been completed on the basis of Food Safety Law to cover different food or food-related categories such as health food and food additives. This is why the initial scope of novel food sources has been narrowed down to exclude products such as food additives. It is interesting to note that genetically modified (GM) food has been excluded in novel food conceptualisation. Historically, GM food could be regarded as novel food in line with the definition provided by the Measures on the Hygiene of Food from New Resources in 1990. However, one striking change in the regulation of novel food was to exclude GM food from the regulating scope of novel food. As required in the Measures on Food from New Resources in 2007, the regulation of GM food complies with other relevant regulation. Consequently, the regulation of GM food has been placed under the regulatory framework of the Ministry of Agriculture, including the Regulations on Administration of Agricultural Genetically Modified Organism Safety. There are thus legislative gaps regarding the regulation of GM food, as the existing rules, rather than law, are at the relatively lower level of legal hierarchy. Therefore the attitude of government in the regulation of GM food is quite ambiguous (Li, 2015).

Second, experiences have indicated that material- rather than product-shaped rules can reduce the administrative workload and promote the application for novel food material. Once a food material is announced as a safe raw material, food operators can use it in a variety of food products, as long as they respect the requirements regarding its usage, quantity and labelling (Wang, 2011). So the food product that is produced with approved novel food material is then regarded as conventional food rather than novel food (Sun and Zhao, 2014).

Third, although the China Food and Drug Administration is responsible for food safety regulation, the safety review and approval of novel food is still the function of the National Health and Family Planning Commission. To carry out this work, the Commission has further provided detailed rules on the application and acceptance of novel food material as well as the procedure for safety review. In practice, the public is informed of approved novel food materials in the form of an official announcement on the Commission's website.

Legal liability in the case of non-compliance

As the revised Food Safety Law in 2015 requires safety assessment and pre-market approval, failure to comply may constitute an obstacle to bringing novel food into the domestic market in China. As part of the control system, this law also provides administrative sanctions in the case of non-compliance. Accordingly,

> ... if it is not criminally punishable, the food and drug administrative department of the people's government at or above the county level shall confiscate its illegal income and the food or food additives illegally produced or dealt in, and may also confiscate the tools, equipment, raw materials, and other items used for illegal production or distribution; shall impose a fine of not less than 50,000 yuan but not more than 100,000 yuan on it if the goods value of the food or food additives illegally produced or dealt in is less than 10,000 yuan or a fine of not less than ten times but not more than 20 times of the goods value if the goods value is 10,000 yuan or more; and if the circumstances are serious, shall revoke its permit. (Food Safety Law, 2015, Article 124)

In addition to official controls and administrative sanctions, it is interesting to note the role of public engagement in the fight against non-compliance regarding novel food. As a specialty in China, consumers are entitled to claim an indemnity of ten times the price paid or three times the loss if the food at issue has failed to meet the food safety standards, including the misbranded food if it involves a safety concern. Such practices are meant to deter malpractice in food systems, but also encourage consumers to be involved in the fight against illegal food production and distribution. These goals are often met, as the one-time price paid is quite low, especially in comparison to the high resource commitment in litigation. As mentioned, an approved novel material would be listed in the catalogue for novel food material and announced to the public with the requirement on the amount and labelling.

If a consumer finds a food product contained a novel material not listed in the catalogue, that consumer may claim an indemnity of ten times the cost of that food product, and report the incident to the local competent authority, who may pose a fine. For example, aloe vera gel is approved as a novel food material in China, pending that package labelling informs consumers – especially pregnant women – of using this product with caution. However, a food product imported from South Korea was found to contain another kind of aloe and failed to label this material or provide the required information. As a result, consumers were successful in claiming compensation at ten times the product cost. If many consumers buy this kind of product and claim an indemnity of ten times the price paid, this could mean a considerable loss for the producer.

It is interesting to note a rise in so-called professional consumers or anti-counterfeiting professionals who buy misbranded food on purpose and claim compensation as a way of making money, although this does provide some pressure to improve compliance by food operators in order to avoid the excessive fines. It can also be regarded as consumers' engagement and power in improving the food system, perhaps as a form of food democracy (see Chapter 22, this volume), or what is called social governance or co-governance in China. Other current debates point out that certain misbranding issues have nothing to do with food safety, but cause heavy burdens on food operators while wasting administrative and judicial resources. With continuing discussion on this phenomenon, it may be important to consider exemptions if the misinformation neither impairs food safety nor misleads consumers.

When administrative sanctions are provided in China as part of a food law enforcement system, the use of forbidden non-edible substances can be criminally punishable. However, it is important to keep in mind that food is characterised by national specialty, since it is a complex issue that should be addressed by taking into account the geography, history, culture, economy and technology in a given place. The difference in legal systems can also lead to disparities in what should be eaten as food and how to control its supply by law enforcement agencies. For example, known as 'lean meat powder', Clenbuterol is forbidden in China and its use in meat products is subject to criminal sanction. But it is legal in other countries, even though it often requires a prescription and there are limits on the quantity that can be used, and may enter China through various channels of trade and movement. Due to the hazard it presents to human health, China is seeking to reinforce its regulation despite the geographic and political differences in criminalisation.

Conclusion

Food supply and regulation have long been strongly influenced by the application of science and technology, although countries differ in the purpose and manner in which they choose to carry out regulations. As in the case of novel food regulation, the application of technological innovation in the food domain is of value while regulation is a subject of dispute. With technological and scientific innovation, food and potential opportunities for food crime continually evolve. What is needed is legislative and regulatory cooperation among a variety of stakeholders across a multitude of spaces.

The complexity of food crime stems in part from its intertwining with issues of food fraud and food safety, which requires a network-level regulatory consideration of the role of governments, food industries and consumers with respect to public health and interests (see Chapter 14, this volume). Responding to food crimes and harms requires governance involving different stakeholders, harmonising food safety regulation both in public sanitary measures and private food standards, and facilitating cooperation in the fight against international food fraud, especially economically motivated adulteration. With the continual advancement of science and technology, it is wise to take advantage of new technologies to widen efforts aiming to maximise its benefits and prevent associated risks.

References

Alemanno, A. (2012) 'Public perception of risk under WTO law: A normative perspective', in G. van Calster and D. Prévost (eds) *Research handbook on environment, health, and the WTO*, Cheltenham: Edward Elgar, pp 270–303.

Andrew, S. (2011) 'Tests show most store honey isn't honey', *Food Safety News*, 7 November (www.foodsafetynews.com/2011/11/tests-show-most-store-honey-isnt-honey/#.WJqk3fl97IU).

Arcuri, A. (2011) *Risk regulation*, Rotterdam Institute of Law and Economics, pp 7–8.

Bee, W. (2008) *Swindled: The dark history of food fraud, from poisoned candy to counterfeit coffee*, Princeton, NJ: Princeton University Press.

Beck, U. (1992) *Risk society: Towards a new modernity* (translated by M. Ritter), London: Sage Publications.

Chris, D. (2013) 'The rise and fall of the new EU novel food regulation: The complex influence of the WTO SPS Agreement', *Asian Journal of WTO & International Health Law and Policy*, vol 8, p 249.

Committee on Science, Engineering, and Public Policy (1993) *Science, technology, and the Federal government: National goals for a new era*, Washington, DC: National Academy Press.

David, L. (2006) 'FDA's regulation of genetically engineered foods: Scientific, legal and political dimensions', *Food Policy*, vol 31, pp 570–91.

Economist, The (2014) 'Organized gangs have a growing appetite for food crime', 15 March (www.economist.com/news/britain/21599028-organised-gangs-have-growing-appetite-food-crime-la-cartel).

Fergus, W. (2013) 'Horsemeat – food fraud, not food safety', BBC News, 15 February (www.bbc.com/news/health-21482127).

Gamer, B. (2004) *Black's law dictionary* (8th edn), Eagan, MN: Thomson West.

Joachim, S. (2005) 'The GM foods debate in Europe: History, regulatory solutions, and consumer response research', *Journal of Public Affairs*, vol 5, pp 263–74.

Li, X. (2015) 'The predicament and outlet of genetically modified foods regulation in China', *Journal of South China Normal University*, vol 1, pp 140–1.

Manning, L. and Soon, J.M. (2016) 'Food safety, food fraud, and food defence: A fast evolving literature', *Journal of Food Science*, vol 81, no 4, pp 823–34.

McGuire, M. (2012) *Technology, crime and justice, the question concerning technormia*, Abingdon: Routledge.

News (2007) 'The establishment of measures on food from new resources by Ministry of Health (卫生部发布《新资源食品管理办法》)', *China Pharmacy (中国药房)*, vol 21, p 1627.

OECD (Organisation for Economic Co-operation and Development) (1993) *Safety evaluation of foods derived by modern biotechnology*, Paris: OECD.

Renee, J. (2014) 'Food fraud and "economically motivated adulteration" of food and food ingredients', *Congressional Research Service*, 10 January.

Reece, W. (2007) 'Food crime, regulation and biotech harvest', *European Journal of Criminology*, vol 4, no 2, pp 217–18.

Ruckelshaus, W. (1984) 'Risk in a free society', *Risk Analysis*, vol 4, no 3, pp 157–62.

Sarantis, M. (2015) 'Parliament vote on novel food heats up cloned animals debate', 4 November (www.euractiv.com/section/agriculture-food/news/parliament-vote-on-novel-foods-heats-up-cloned-animals-debate/).

Sun, J. (2012) 'The evoling appreciation of food safety', *European Food and Feed Law Review*, vol 7, no 2, pp 84–5.

Sun, J. (2015) 'The regulation of "novel food" in China: The tendency of deregulation', *European Food and Feed Law Review*, vol 6, pp 442–8.

Sun, C. and Zhao, G. (2014) 'The systematic changes from novel food towards novel food material and respond (从新资源食品到新食品原料的制度变迁与应对)', *Science and Technology of Food Industry (食品工业科技)*, vol 1, p 19.

Ulrich, S. (2016) 'The paradigm shift in the global risk society: From criminal law to global security law, an analysis of the changing limits of crime control', *Journal of Eastern-European Criminal Law*, vol 14, pp 13–26.

Wang, Y. (2011) 'The status-quo of novel food regulation in China and its analysis (我国新资源食品管理现状与分析)', *Chinese Journal of Health Inspection (中国卫生监督杂志)*, vol 1, pp 20–3.

18

Food crimes, harms and carnist technologies

Linnea Laestadius, Jan Deckers and Stephanie Baran

Introduction

The number of animals raised for food has increased dramatically over the past half-century. In the US alone, almost 9 billion chickens were slaughtered for food in 2015, an increase of over 100 million from just the year before (USDA, 2016). The weight of farmed animals at the time of slaughter has also grown, with the average weight of cows and buffalo in developed nations increasing by over 100kg per animal between the 1960s and mid-2000s (Alexandratos and Bruinsma, 2012). Thanks to the development and adoption of novel agricultural and food technologies, the world is producing more food from non-human animals (hereafter 'animals') than ever before. Unfortunately, this comes at the expense of the health of animals, humans and the environment. This chapter explores some of the key ways in which technologies designed to meet human demand for animal-based food, which this chapter terms *carnist technologies*, serve to facilitate or remedy food crimes in the 21st century.

Carnism is the largely invisible belief system in which eating certain animals is considered ethical and appropriate, representing a counter-point to vegetarian and vegan beliefs about the role of animals (Joy, 2011, p 30). Accordingly, carnist technologies are technologies that facilitate, enact or reinforce the normative belief that animals are a source of food. The term highlights the ideological underpinning of these technologies. Carnism also results in a policy environment in which most of the harms caused to animals by the application of food technology are not only legal, but recognised as an inherent part of 'legitimate food production' (Nurse, 2016, p 36).

In conjunction with carnism, neoliberalism must also be recognised as a dominant ideology shaping the modern Western food system. As per Croall's (2013) foundational work on food crime, the current economic context of the food system is criminogenic since it creates a culture where profits are prioritised to the extent of normalising deviant corporate behaviours. Harms become seen as part of the cost of doing business. In short, government policies are unlikely to fully address even the human and environmental harms from carnist technologies, and many practices remain 'lawful but awful' (Passas, 2005; Gray and Hinch, 2015; see also Chapter 1, this volume). A legalistic definition of crime is thus likely to overlook many of the ways these technologies cause serious harms to the marginalised and powerless, particularly when those harms are caused by corporations or governments (Passas, 2005; Dorling et al, 2008). With this in mind, it is important to embrace the field's emphasis on 'negative or harmful consequences on a variety of both human and nonhuman victims', regardless of formal legality (Gray and Hinch, 2015, p 97).

What follows is an exploration of the licit and illicit harms caused by carnist technologies, including both first-generation technologies focused on industrialising animal agriculture to maximise efficiency and agribusiness profits and second-generation technologies that were developed in response to the growing recognition of harms from industrial animal agriculture. Within this, we also consider the extent to which these newer technologies may alleviate the problems posed by first-generation carnist technologies.

Technologies for the industrialisation of animal agriculture

Humans have raised animals for food for thousands of years, but industrial techniques for animal farming first gained widespread popularity in the 1930s (Walker et al, 2005). Cheap grain prices from green revolution technologies and crop subsidies, the expansion of transportation systems and novel animal rearing technologies all contributed to large efficiency gains in animal agriculture (Pew

Commission, 2008). Paired with growing demand for animal-based food, farmers had clear incentives to expand operations. Some of these technological innovations included animal feed with added antibiotics and hormones and the use of selective breeding to increase production (Pew Commission, 2008). In the name of efficiency and profit, animals are now growing faster and larger in increasingly small allotments of space, while farms are increasingly consolidated and mechanised (Fitzgerald, 2015). The application of these technologies to facilitate industrial animal agriculture creates a broad spectrum of harms and food crimes. While a full consideration is beyond the scope of this chapter and covered in existing literature, a brief review of key harms from first-generation carnist technologies is offered.

Most harms to animals are not technically illegal due to animals' status as agricultural commodities used for food production. This is particularly true in the US, where only the transportation and slaughter of animals is regulated with welfare in mind at federal level (Pew Commission, 2008; see also Chapter 13, this volume), although such policies remain ineffective. Harms, however, are exceptionally common. Close confinement leads to the spread of infectious disease and prevents animals from engaging in natural behaviours, resulting in intentional mutilation by farmers to prevent negative behaviours associated with stress (Pew Commission, 2008). The increased growth rate of animals has been linked to physical ailments and chronic pain, while the rapid pace of slaughter lines has occasionally resulted in animals having their throats cut or being boiled while still conscious (McLeod-Kilmurray, 2012). These harms are often not inflicted out of ill will, but rather for farmers to survive in a competitive market. It is also important to note that these technologies have facilitated increased animal consumption, resulting in billions of animal lives being taken each year.

Environmental harms and crimes are also common despite ostensibly being regulated by environmental protection agencies. Production practices facilitated by first-generation carnist technologies contribute to climate change, increased water and land use, and water and air pollution (Pew Commission, 2008). Managing the large volume of manure created by thousands of animals in a single location is a particular challenge, resulting in the spread of nutrient and chemical contaminants, as well as pathogens (Walker et al, 2005). An increasingly pressing concern is the spread of antibiotic-resistant bacteria from the use of sub-therapeutic levels of antibiotics to prevent disease and promote growth (Pew Commission, 2008). Farmworkers and communities surrounding facilities are all put at risk (Walker et al,

2005). Consumers also suffer from the risk of foodborne illness from food contaminated with pathogens from manure (Pew Commission, 2008). Almost all of the costs of these externalities are borne by the public rather than by producers, serving as a subsidy for animal products.

Since these facilities are frequently located in marginalised communities, industrial animal agriculture also contributes to environmental injustices (Mirabelli et al, 2006). Slaughterhouse work, a dangerous and emotionally taxing profession, has long suffered from similar justice concerns (Sinclair, 1906). Many facilities have moved to states with fewer protections for workers and are known to hire undocumented individuals with limited labour rights (Nibert, 2014). Large animal agriculture corporations have also been known to take advantage of smaller farmers who raise their animals, offering exploitative contracts that may not pay enough to cover operating and clean-up expenses. Having taken out large loans to pay for equipment and land, farmers become trapped in unfavourable arrangements until they can pay off their loans (Pew Commission, 2008).

Despite evidence of serious food crimes and harms, major corporations continue to cast the expansion of efficiency-focused first-generation carnist technologies as the solution for meeting the needs of a growing global population. The industrial agriculture lobby also routinely applies political pressure in defence of its current practices. For example, several US states have passed or attempted to pass 'ag-gag' laws that ban undercover photography or filming of animal farms and worked to block reforms recommended by public health advocates (Kim et al, 2013). While fines are occasionally brought against corporations and farms for poor behaviour, these have little impact on overall operations. Multinational animal processor Tyson Foods, for example, has been fined by multiple US agencies for environmental and labour violations (some of which included human fatalities) (US EPA, 2013), but continues to operate and engage in new violations. The legal protection of industrial agriculture and first-generation carnist technologies represents a clear example of governments and businesses working together to promote profits at the expense of the wellbeing of animals, humans and the environment (Gray and Hinch, 2015).

'Humane' technologies

Given growing public concern with the harms experienced by animals, a whole discipline of animal welfare science has emerged to advocate for 'humane farming'. Many of these efforts take a techno-fix model where rearing and slaughtering processes, as well as the *animals themselves*, are re-engineered in an attempt to minimise pain and suffering. The idea of humanely farmed 'happy meat' falls soundly within the realm of carnist technologies by failing to question the practice of consuming animals (Cole and Morgan, 2013, p 205), only the fact that pain and suffering is inflicted on them in the process.

Humane technologies receive significant popular support, particularly in Europe. For example, Compassion in World Farming (2013, pp 9–10), which defines itself as 'not a vegetarian organisation' (instead, aiming to end factory farming), lists European Union (EU) bans on first-generation carnist technologies used to keep calves, pigs and hens among its campaigning successes. In each case, the aim of these legal developments was to replace first-generation technologies with either more humane existing technologies, such as extensive farming systems, or novel second-generation technologies. An example of the latter is the use of the so-called 'enriched cages', supported by European Council Directive 1999/74/EC. In these cages, chickens have slightly more space to move around, litter for pecking and scratching, perches that allow at least 15cm per hen, and claw-shortening devices. Slaughterhouses have also been re-engineered to cause animals less stress. In the US, many slaughterhouses integrated principles developed by Temple Grandin. Among other techniques, she developed a restrainer system to hold cows and bulls during stunning in order to provide 'more efficient and humane systems for rapidly handling large numbers of' animals (Grandin, 1988, p 327). She also sought to reduce prodding of animals by removing visual and sound distractors, air drafts, inappropriate lighting arrangements and slick floors.

An alternative approach to 'humane technologies' is to change the animals themselves. Farmers have long sought to obtain benefits through the internal transformation of animals, for example, by using selective breeding. In recent years, scientists have engaged in the genetic engineering of animals for the same purpose. While only one modified animal had been approved as food in the US at the time of writing – the 'AquAdvantage salmon' (US FDA, 2015) – work in this area continues to grow and push regulatory boundaries. In the US, genetically modified (GM) animals are regulated primarily under provisions for new animal drugs, requiring human safety to be taken into account. EU law takes a similarly shallow, anthropocentric focus, for example, in Directive 2001/18/EC, which is concerned primarily about human safety in relation to the release of new products into the environment.

One example of such a technology is a new variety of pigs created to contain bovine α-lactalbumin in the mammary gland that boosts milk production and results in fewer deaths among piglets (Wheeler et al, 2001). Recent developments in gene editing are also likely to result in significant growth in this sector. At present, scientists and research firms are pushing back against applying current US regulations to animals modified using more precise gene editing techniques. For example, the start-up company Recombinetics (2016) argues that its painless 'genetic dehorning' of cows raised for dairy production should be exempt from regulations for other modified animals since 'genome editing can be used to produce precise analogues of the naturally occurring mutations we routinely consume'. In light of growing consumer interest in animal welfare, they also tout that their productivity and welfare-enhancing traits 'could be rapidly commercialized'.

While animal welfare might be improved through the insertion of new genes, scientists can also select against the inclusion of genes that might negatively affect animal welfare. This is why the topic of 'animal disenhancement', which aims to enhance animal welfare by the removal of a basic trait, has come to the fore in recent years. Early discussion on this topic stems from the accidental creation of a blind strain of chickens who might be less aggressive with each other in close confinement, which is what led some to suggest that it might be a good idea to replace conventional strains with this blind alternative (Varner, 2012, pp 277–8). Strict animal welfarists might argue that this technique ought to be embraced as it reduces harm. A similar argument could be made for supporting 'genetic dehorning', to avoid the widely practised disbudding and dehorning of animals. It is of note that the problems these technologies seek to address are almost entirely human-created and driven by first-generation carnist technologies that confine large numbers of animals to increasingly small spaces.

Taking the engineering of animals for welfare to its logical conclusion, farmed animals with reduced capacities to feel pain and suffering might also be created. Shriver (2009, p 118), for example, commented on research where scientists were able to genetically 'knock out' enzymes in mice to reduce their capacity to suffer, and suggested that it might be possible to replicate this in other mammals. Similarly, it might one day be possible to create micro-encephalic animals with just enough consciousness to be alive (Streiffer and Basl, 2014), but not enough to feel much pain or suffering.

Clearly, these technologies are limited in that they work only to address one specific set of harms from animal production. However, they fall short even on the measure of reducing harms to animals. Modifying animal rearing and slaughter may reduce trauma experienced by animals, but does nothing to address their status as objects for human consumption and the moral harms that follow from casually making such a judgement (Deckers, 2016). The engineering of animals causes even further harm by reinforcing carnist norms. Through such projects, people not only objectify animals by using them as food, but also through re-designing them from within to be nothing but food.

Cultured meat and cellular agriculture technologies

Another approach to addressing the broader spectrum of harms and food crimes arising from animal production is to instead engineer animals out of the production process. Starting from a biopsy of cells from an animal, scientists are now able to produce animal muscle tissue in a lab setting (Datar and Betti, 2010). While the process continues to be improved on in order to scale up production and bring down costs, it builds on the culturing of cells in bioreactors containing a growth medium (Datar and Betti, 2010). The resulting product, known as cultured meat, in-vitro meat, or more recently, clean meat, is essentially identical to tissue from conventionally raised animals at the cellular level. While work by Mark Post at Maastricht University is perhaps the best-known effort to date, start-ups such as Memphis Meats are also working to develop and eventually commercialise cultured meat. Others, such as Clara Foods and Perfect Day Foods, are focusing on the creation and commercialisation of cultured eggs and milk. To create these, scientists reprogramme yeast by inserting genes for milk or egg proteins rather than relying on animal cells. Collectively, both of these production methods have become known as cellular agriculture (New Harvest, 2016). At the time of writing, none of these products are available for purchase by the general public, but estimates suggest that milk from cellular agriculture will be commercially available in late 2017 and cultured meat sometime within the next two decades (Bonny et al, 2015; Hocquette, 2016; Perfect Day Foods, 2016).

By largely breaking the link between living animals and food derived from animals, cultured products should hypothetically reduce consumer demand for farmed animals without necessitating public willingness to change diets. This is one of the key benefits of reframing social problems as technological problems (Scott, 2010), and of cultured products in particular. The more people who switch from conventional to cultured products, the greater the potential for reducing some of the harms and food crimes tied to producing animal-based foods. Since these products are not yet available, benefits remain purely speculative, but have been predicted to include the following:

- Reduction in the number of animals raised for food, which would also eliminate issues tied to manure handling and labour concerns associated with animal rearing and slaughter.
- Reduction in water and land use as compared to conventional production, as well as reduced global warming potential as compared to ruminants (Tuomisto and Teixeira de Mattos, 2011; Mattick et al, 2015).
- Reduction in the incidence of epidemic zoonoses due to fewer interactions between farmed animals and humans (Datar and Betti, 2010).
- Reduction in foodborne illnesses due to the use of aseptic techniques (Datar and Betti, 2010).
- Improved nutritional profile and fewer allergens relative to conventional animal products due to the ability to precisely engineer outputs (Datar and Betti, 2010; Perfect Day Foods, 2016).

Cultured meat, however, leaves the idea that animal flesh is appropriate for human consumption unchallenged and, arguably, validated. The Good Food Institute, a non-profit focused on promoting alternatives to animal products, notes that cultured meat is '100-percent real meat' (Good Food Institute, 2016). This is a pragmatic asset, but also one that may complicate efforts seeking to reshape the social role of animals (Milburn, 2016). Cellular agriculture for the production of animal products can then be cast as a second-generation carnist technology, albeit one that abandons first-generation technologies and may eliminate direct harms to animals.

Cultured products currently fail to challenge the food system's neoliberal ideology. In and of itself, the technology does not impact overall labour relations or food justice, and many of the initial cultured animal product start-ups are funded by venture capitalists who will expect businesses to maximise return on their investments (Kolodny, 2017). Cultured animal products also hold the potential for creating new harms. Effects remain entirely speculative at this point, and unanticipated harms can potentially arise from any complex technology, but predictions include harmful epigenetic modifications that could arise in the production process (Bonny et al, 2015). Some raise concerns that cultured products would further strengthen the power of the large food corporations at the expense of low-income consumers, farmers and developing nations (Laestadius and Caldwell, 2015; Hocquette, 2016). Additionally, a recent anticipatory lifecycle analysis indicates that cultured meat may have a higher global warming potential than the rearing of some animals due to the high volume of industrial energy needed for production (Mattick et al, 2015).

With regard to the regulatory environment and the potential for formal food crimes, these technologies are so novel that regulatory frameworks have yet to catch up. Regulation of animal-based foods is currently designed with animal rearing and slaughter in focus. This makes current regulations for the production of animal products almost entirely irrelevant to cultured products. This chapter does not allow for an exploration of the complex set of regulatory structures that may or may not come into play once products are ready for commercialisation, but there is a lot of uncertainty at present, particularly for cultured meat. For egg and milk products, it seems more likely that the US Food & Drug Administration (FDA) will waive pre-market review and allow the products to come to market as Generally Recognised as Safe (GRAS), since outputs would be deemed substantially equivalent to egg white and milk proteins already considered to be safe (Devitt, 2016). This would be consistent with the FDA's approach to GM plant foods, which focuses on objective food characteristics rather than the methods by which they were produced (US FDA, 1992).

Given the potential for benefits from cultured products, it is also important to consider the extent to which current policies may hamper their development and perpetuate existing food crimes. One of the primary barriers to the development of cultured products has been the lack of funding for research on cellular agriculture (Datar, 2013). Additionally, government subsidisation of first-generation carnist technologies through price supports and allowing environmental externalities to go unaddressed will make it difficult for cultured products to compete based on price (Bonny et al, 2015). Rethinking these subsidies and increasing government research support would greatly increase the viability of cultured products (Bonny et al, 2015). A clearer regulatory framework, both to protect the public from harms and to build public trust, is also essential for successful commercialisation (Laestadius and Caldwell, 2015).

Technologies for transforming plants into analogues of animal products

Modifying animals, the slaughter process and the relationship between animals and animal products all take a harm reduction approach to the consumption of animal-based foods. An alternative approach is to not improve the profile of animal products, but instead to bring innovation to plants with the hope that they can take the place of animals. While not a new development, a novel high-tech approach to analogues has emerged within the past decade. For example, Hampton Creek worked to develop a database of 'botanical, molecular, and functional data across more than 100,000 plant species and varieties' in their efforts to create plant-based alternatives to dairy and egg ingredients (Tetrick, 2015), while Impossible Foods have developed a veggie burger that contains plant-derived heme to recreate 'the precise flavors, textures, aromas, and nutrition of ground beef' (Impossible Foods, 2016).

These companies aspire to make analogues appeal both to ethically minded consumers and everyday consumers (Pacelle, 2016). Unlike cultured products, analogues are already available to consumers and represent markets worth billions of dollars (Nkwocha, 2016). While technically not promoting animal consumption, some argue that replicating foods from animals may be ethically questionable due to a lack of reverence for animals or because it would represent the enjoyment of something harmful, even if by proxy (Fischer and Ozturk, 2016). For example, Beyond Meat's newest product, the Beast Burger, is engineered to bleed beet juice (Chamlee, 2016). Additionally, in at least once instance, the effort to engineer foods that offer 'the sensory experience meat lovers crave' has involved animal testing (Impossible Foods, 2017). Others suggest that while analogues are not morally wrong, they perpetuate the normative nature of animal consumption. Francione (as cited in Milburn, 2016), for example, argues that analogues contribute to the notion that 'a diet of vegetables, fruits, grain, beans, and nuts/seeds' is in some way insufficient. To the extent that analogues try to mimic animal products and to the extent that they are sought out because of it, these arguments may be correct. Accordingly, analogue technologies are grouped together with second-generation carnist technologies, but may fall into something of a grey area given that they are often made entirely of plants despite resembling animal products.

The widespread adoption of analogues would significantly reduce the number of animals raised for food, yielding reductions in many animal, environmental and human health harms. Initial estimates suggest that analogues have smaller environmental footprints than cultured products (Smetana et al, 2015). As with cultured products, however, analogues function primarily as a techno-fix reliant on free market logic. By engineering plant-based foods to taste, feel and look like animal products, the hope is to seamlessly fit products into mainstream Western diets and ideologies. As long as consumers can be swayed by desire and taste, firms profit and consumers are never inconvenienced by ethical obligations (Pacelle, 2016). The techno-fix avoids 'the troubling problem of trying to make people morally better' (Scott, 2010, p 223). This holds appeal from both a pragmatic and profit-driven perspective, and analogues have received significant funding from venture capitalists (Pacelle, 2016). Yet relying on the profit motive to create positive change inevitably runs into the issue that 'doing good' is not always profitable. More specifically, using plants rather than animals does not make companies immune from causing harms or engaging in food crimes in other areas.

Since analogues are already available, one can take a more concrete look at some of the food crimes and harms associated with them. While it is possible that analogues may create novel harms, there is little evidence of this to date with the exception of allergies to mycoprotein-based analogues (Limbach, 2010). To date, the most tangible food crime specific to analogues relates to product labelling. While courts have dismissed similar cases in the past, advocates of conventional animal products continue to point out that plant-based milks do not technically meet the US identity standard for milk, which is defined as the 'lacteal secretion' obtained from milking a cow (Watson, 2016b). Additionally, the FDA threatened to 'revoke [Hampton Creek's] use of the term "mayo"' for its Just Mayo product on account of not using eggs' (Pacelle, 2016). This was eventually resolved through minor changes to the product's label, but the suggestion that conventional carnist labels cannot be used to name alternatives, or even to criminalise such labels, appears to be another instance of food policy working to preserve the status quo at the expense of harm-reducing technologies.

More problematic are the harms and food crimes arising from current business practices. Hampton Creek, for example, was probed by the US Securities and Exchange Commission in 2016 for possible 'securities violations and criminal fraud' after being in a scheme in which the company was accused of sending undercover contractors into stores to buy back its own products (Zaleski et al, 2016). The company has also been accused of misleading investors, and recently settled a lawsuit in which it was accused of violating the Fair Labor Standards Act and the New York Labor Law by misclassifying employees as contractors (Watson, 2016a). All of these developments offer support for the notion that the neoliberal context of the food system is inherently criminogenic, no matter how well intentioned companies aim to be (Croall, 2013).

Hampton Creek was also recently celebrated by many animal advocates for getting its products into Walmart stores (Pacelle, 2016). While Hampton Creek's push against 'food elitism' is laudable (Kaye, 2015), working with a company known to be a repeat offender of crimes against workers does not necessarily speak toward a commitment to food justice. The growing number of analogue companies purchased by major corporations, such as Gardein and Silk, also raises questions about the trade-offs between expanding market access and pushing for more significant food systems reform. Tyson Foods, one of the largest processor of animal flesh in the world and a repeat offender of crimes against workers, animals and the environment, recently purchased a 5 per cent stake in Beyond Meat (Strom, 2016). Analogues may eliminate many of the harms of animal production, but they still fall squarely within the confines of the current criminogenic food system. Similar to cultured products, the underlying technologies of analogue products are valuable, but in and of themselves they are not sufficient for creating a just food system.

Conclusion

In this chapter, some of the known harms associated with first-generation carnist technologies have been documented, and the stage is set for needed discussion about the role of second-generation carnist technologies in addressing these harms and crimes. These novel technologies include 'humane' technologies, cellular agriculture technologies and plant-based analogues. While some of these technologies may stem from unease with carnism, and may, on balance, reduce its harms, none fully challenge carnist ideology. Given the manner in which they have been developed and promoted, all three second-generation technologies also fail to question neoliberal thinking in which consumers can theoretically buy their way to a better world despite economic actors prioritising the acquisition of money rather than the promotion of 'physical, mental, social, and planetary wellbeing' (Hastings, 2012).

There may well be an important role for these technologies in addressing harms from the large-scale rearing of animals for food. Indeed, it would be foolish to reject them for failing to solve *all* possible harms and food crimes. However, it is also clear that these technologies alone are insufficient to address the full scope of harms tied to demand for animal-based foods, and may perpetuate or even compound more systemic food crimes. Given growing public interest in the food system, the opportunity for even greater changes may be present and should not be overlooked. At a minimum, firms using these technologies must still be held accountable if they exploit workers or work against food justice. To create meaningful change, technological solutions must be accompanied by concrete social policies informed by critical thinking about both current and novel harms experienced by the full range of actors in the food system.

References

Alexandratos, N. and Bruinsma, J. (2012) *World agriculture towards 2030/2050: The 2012 revision*, ESA Working Paper No 12-03, Rome: Agricultural Development Economics Division, Food and Agriculture Organization of the United Nations (FAO) (www.fao.org/docrep/016/ap106e/ap106e.pdf).

Bonny, S., Gardner, G.E. and Pethick, D.W. (2015) 'What is artificial meat and what does it mean for the future of the meat industry?', *Journal of Integrative Agriculture*, vol 14, no 2, pp 255–63.

Chamlee, V. (2016) 'Why do people want veggie burgers that bleed?' (www.eater.com/2016/7/25/12270698/lab-grown-meat-beyond-burger-impossible-foods).

Cole, M. and Morgan, K. (2013) 'Engineering freedom? A critique of biotechnological routes to animal liberation', *Configurations*, vol 21, no 2, pp 201–29.

Compassion in World Farming (2013) *Strategic plan 2013–2017 for kinder, fairer farming worldwide* (www.ciwf.org.uk/media/3640540/ciwf_strategic_plan_20132017.pdf).

Croall, H. (2013) 'Food crime. A green criminology perspective', in N. South and A. Brisman (eds) *Routledge international handbook of green criminology*, New York: International Handbook of Green Criminology, pp 167–83.

Datar, I. (2013) 'Opinion: Why your burger should be grown in a lab', CNN, 9 August (www.cnn.com/2013/08/08/opinion/datar-lab-burger/index.html).

Datar, I. and Betti, M. (2010) 'Possibilities for an in vitro meat production system', *Innovative Food Science & Emerging Technologies*, vol 11, no 1, pp 13–22.

Deckers, J. (2016) *Animal (de)liberation: Should the consumption of animal products be banned?*, London: Ubiquity Press.

Devitt, E. (2016) 'As lab-grown meat and milk inch closer to U.S. market, industry wonders who will regulate?', *Science*, 15 March (www.sciencemag.org/news/2016/08/lab-grown-meat-inches-closer-us-market-industry-wonders-who-will-regulate).

Dorling, D., Gordon, D., Hillyard, P., Pantazis, C., Pemberton, S. and Tombs, S. (2008) *Criminal obsessions: Why harm matters more than crime* (2nd edn), London: Centre for Crime and Justice Studies.

Fischer, B. and Ozturk, B. (2016) 'Facsimiles of flesh', *Journal of Applied Philosophy*, doi: 10.1111/japp.12223.

Fitzgerald, A. (2015) *Animals as food: (Re)connecting production, processing, consumption, and impacts*, East Lansing, MI: Michigan State University Press.

Good Food Institute (2016) 'Why good food?' (www.gfi.org/why).

Grandin, T. (1988) 'Double rail restrainer conveyor for livestock handling', *Journal of Agricultural Engineering Research*, vol 41, no 4, pp 327–38.

Gray, A. and Hinch, R. (2015) 'Agribusiness, governments and food crime: A critical perspective', in R.A. Sollund (ed) *Green harms and crimes*, New York: Palgrave Macmillan, pp 97–116.

Hastings, G. (2012) 'Why corporate power is a public health priority', *British Medical Journal*, vol345, 21 August, e5124.

Hocquette, J.F. (2016) 'Is in vitro meat the solution for the future?', *Meat Science*, vol 120, October, pp 167–76.

Impossible Foods (2016) 'The impossible burger' (https://impossiblefoods.com/).

Impossible Foods (2017) 'The agonizing dilemma of animal testing' (https://impossiblefoods.app.box.com/s/27skctwxb3jbyu7dxqfnxa3srji2jevv).

Joy, M. (2011) *Why we love dogs, eat pigs, and wear cows*, San Francisco, CA: Conari Press.

Kaye, K. (2015) 'Presidential candidates respond to food CEO's quirky campaign' (http://adage.com/article/media/2016-candidates-respond-food-ceo-s-quirky-campaign/299822/).

Kim, B., Laestadius, L., Lawrence, R., Martin, R., McKenzie, S., Nachman, K., Smith, T. and Truant, P. (2013) *Industrial food animal production in America: Examining the impact of the Pew Commission's priority recommendations*, Baltimore, MD: Johns Hopkins Center for a Livable Future.

Kolodny, L. (2017) 'SOSV, "the accelerator VC," closes third fund at $150 million' (http://social.techcrunch.com/2017/01/03/sosv-the-accelerator-vc-closes-third-fund-at-150-million/).

Laestadius, L.I. and Caldwell, M.A. (2015) 'Is the future of meat palatable? Perceptions of in vitro meat as evidenced by online news comments', *Public Health Nutrition*, vol 18, no 13, pp 2457–67.

Limbach, J. (2010) 'Food allergy danger seen in Quorn fungus foods' (www.consumeraffairs.com/news04/2010/09/food-allergy-danger-seen-in-quorn-fungus-foods.html).

Mattick, C., Landis, A., Allenby, B. and Genovese, N. (2015) 'Anticipatory life cycle analysis of in vitro biomass cultivation for cultured meat production in the United States', *Environmental Science & Technology*, vol 49, no 19, pp 11941–9.

McLeod-Kilmurray, H. (2012) 'Commoditizing nonhuman animals and their consumers: Industrial livestock production, animal welfare, and ecological justice', *Bulletin of Science*, vol 32, no 1, pp 71–85.

Milburn, J. (2016) 'Chewing over in vitro meat: Animal ethics, cannibalism and social progress', *Res Publica*, vol 22, no 3, pp 249–65.

Mirabelli, M., Wing, S., Marshall, S. and Wilcosky, T. (2006) 'Race, poverty, and potential exposure of middle-school students to air emissions from confined swine feeding operations', *Environmental Health Perspectives*, vol 114, no 4, pp 591–6.

New Harvest (2016) 'About' (www.new-harvest.org/about).

Nibert, D. (2014) 'Animals, immigrants, and profits: Slaughterhouses and the political economy of oppression', in J. Sorenson (ed) *Critical animal studies*, Toronto: Canadian Scholars' Press Inc, pp 3–17.

Nkwocha, K. (2016) 'Meat substitutes market set to top €3.57 billion by 2016' (www.foodnavigator.com/Market-Trends/Meat-substitutes-market-set-to-top-3.57-billion-by-2016).

Nurse, A. (2016) *Animal harm: Perspectives on why people harm and kill animals*, New York: Routledge.

Pacelle, W. (2016) *The humane economy*, New York: William Morrow.

Passas, N. (2005) 'Lawful but awful: "Legal corporate crimes"', *The Journal of Socio-Economics*, vol 34, no 6, pp 771–86.

Perfect Day Foods (2016) 'FAQs' (www.perfectdayfoods.com/faq/).

Pew Commission (2008) *Putting meat on the table: Industrial farm animal production in America*, Baltimore, MD: The Pew Charitable Trusts and the Johns Hopkins Bloomberg School of Public Health.

Recombinetics (2016) 'Leading scientists assert GRAS status for gene-edited livestock is safe for human consumption; Pre-market approval by the FDA should not be required' (www.recombinetics.com/2016/05/16/leading-scientists-assert-gras-status-gene-edited-livestock-gene-edited-livestock-safe-human-consumption-pre-market-approval-fda-not-required/).

Scott, D. (2010) 'The technological fix criticisms and the agricultural biotechnology debate', *Journal of Agricultural and Environmental Ethics*, vol 24, no 3, pp 207–26.

Shriver, A. (2009) 'Knocking out pain in livestock: Can technology succeed where morality has stalled?', *Neuroethics*, vol 2, no 3, pp 115–24.

Sinclair, L. (1906) *The jungle*, New York: Doubleday.

Smetana, S., Mathys, A., Knoch, A. and Heinz, V. (2015) 'Meat alternatives: life cycle assessment of most known meat substitutes', *The International Journal of Life Cycle Assessment*, vol 20, no 9, pp 1254–67.

Streiffer, R. and Basl, J. (2014) 'The ethics of agricultural animal biotechnology', in R. Sandler, (ed) *Ethics and emerging technologies*, London: Palgrave Macmillan, pp 501–15.

Strom, S. (2016) 'Tyson Foods, a meat leader, invests in protein alternatives', *The New York Times*, 10 October (www.nytimes. com/2016/10/11/business/tyson-foods-a-meat-leader-invests-in-protein-alternatives.html).

Tetrick, J. (2015) 'My response' (https://medium.com/@hcfoods/on-the-record-9baff4ffabd9).

Tuomisto, H.L. and Teixeira de Mattos, M.J. (2011) 'Environmental impacts of cultured meat production', *Environmental Science & Technology*, vol 45, no 14, pp 6117–23.

USDA (United States Department of Agriculture) (2016) 'Poultry slaughter 2015 summary' (http://usda.mannlib.cornell.edu/usda/nass/PoulSlauSu//2010s/2016/PoulSlauSu-02-25-2016.pdf).

US EPA (United States Environmental Protection Agency) (2013) *Tyson Foods, Inc. Clean Air Act (CAA) settlement* (www.epa.gov/enforcement/tyson-foods-inc).

US FDA (United States Food and Drug Administration) (1992) 'Statement of policy: Foods derived from new plant varieties', Notice 57 Fed Reg 22984 (www.fda.gov/Food/GuidanceRegulation/GuidanceDocumentsRegulatoryInformation/Biotechnology/ucm096095.htm).

US FDA (2015) 'FDA has determined that the AquAdvantage salmon is as safe to eat as non-GE salmon' (www.fda.gov/ForConsumers/ConsumerUpdates/ucm472487.htm).

Varner, G. (2012) *Personhood, ethics, and animal cognition*, Oxford: Oxford University Press.

Walker, P., Rhubart-Berg, P., McKenzie, S., Kelling, K. and Lawrence, R.S. (2005) 'Public health implications of meat production and consumption', *Public Health Nutrition*, vol 8, no 4, pp 348–56.

Watson, E. (2016a) 'Hampton Creek to settle worker classification lawsuit' (www.foodnavigator-usa.com/Regulation/Hampton-Creek-to-settle-worker-classification-lawsuit).

Watson, E. (2016b) 'Is it legal to call plant-based beverages from nuts, seeds and legumes, "milk?"' (www.foodnavigator-usa.com/Manufacturers/Is-it-legal-to-call-plant-based-beverages-milk).

Wheeler, M.B., Bleck, G.T. and Donovan, S.M. (2001) 'Transgenic alteration of sow milk to improve piglet growth and health', *Reproduction Supplement*, vol 58, December, pp 313–24.

Zaleski, O., Waldman, P. and Huet, E. (2016) 'How Hampton Creek sold Silicon Valley on a fake-mayo miracle' (www.bloomberg.com/features/2016-hampton-creek-just-mayo/).

Section VII
Green food

19

Farming and climate change

Rob White and Jasmine Yeates

Introduction

Global temperatures are changing quickly, and it is human activity that is the main cause (IPCC, 2013, 2014). This is part of a longer-term and rapidly acce lerating trend toward even greater warming. Farming practices are implicated in both mitigation (stopping and/or curbing of the drivers of climate change) and adaptation (adjusting to the impacts of climate change) in regards to global warming. Indeed, farming of various kinds (that include non-food purposes) and food production specifically (including its transportation and consumption) are inextricably intertwined with climate change issues.

This chapter provides a summary of the links and issues pertaining to farming, climate change and criminality. It does this by first, exploring contemporary farming practices in relation to the causes of climate change. The key drivers of global warming are greenhouse gases (including and especially carbon dioxide emissions) and deforestation (McGarrell and Gibbs, 2014). Yet, as demonstrated throughout the chapter, foreknowledge of the harm is no guarantee that harmful activities will be stopped. This is followed by consideration of the consequences of climate change for farming and food production. These involve profound shifts in the availability of water through to the climate-induced migration of humans and non-human species. The third section discusses emerging conflicts associated with the scarcities generated by localised, long-term changes in climate and weather patterns. The origins of climate-related crime are embedded in and an outcome of the existing political economy – the anthropocentric causes of global warming are simultaneously inseparable from the dominant mode of production, global capitalism.

The impacts of farming on climate change

The profound impact of human activity on the global environment, especially over the last couple of centuries, has been said to denote a new geological era, the 'Anthropocene' (Shearing, 2015). This development, originating with the industrial revolution in Europe, has been driven and underpinned by powerful forces (nation-states, companies, armies) as they have pursued specific class and state interests. It has been achieved through global imperialism, colonialism and militarism that have served to entrench a dominant capitalist worldview and the material basis for producing and utilising natural resources in a consumerist manner (Greig and van der Velden, 2015). As part of these transitions and impositions, people who, for thousands of years, had lived in harmony with nature (that is, through adopting intrinsically ecologically sustainable practices), including in some of the most humanly inhospitable places in the world (such as Arctic tundra and sand deserts), were subjected to the dispossession, displacement and destruction of their communities (Robyn, 2002). These processes are mirrored in the contemporary exploitation of natural resources worldwide (Gedicks, 2005; Klare, 2012; Le Billon, 2012), many of which directly contribute to the causes of global warming.

For instance, profit-oriented systems of food production – frequently reliant on mass production techniques and genetically modified organisms (GMOs) – increase carbon emissions (for example, via animal flatulence and deforestation) while simultaneously undermining the resilience of natural systems to withstand the effects of climate-related changes (for example, through reduction in biodiversity). Why and how this is occurring is worth elaboration. Changes in climatic conditions, for example, are putting new and additional pressures on existing global food stocks. One response by governments and agribusiness has been to foster ever-greater reliance on large-scale agricultural techniques and methods, and on new technologies such as the use of GMOs (Robin, 2010; Walters, 2011). This has involved converting land to industrial forms of agricultural production, and the application of practical restrictions on what is being grown and how. These, in turn, have implications for both climate change and human wellbeing.

Intensive farming practices

The rise of transnational agro-industrial food systems is manifest at the ground level in the form of large-scale commercial agriculture and intensive farming practices, frequently based on monocultures and specialisation (Larkins et al, 2013). Globally, both the scale and content of farm practices have been radically altered in the last century. The specific dollar value of certain types of farming is also driving the intensification of farming practices, as is population density in rural areas, which contributes to pressures to produce more on less land (Jayne et al, 2014).

For example, in New Zealand, the economy is heavily dependent on natural resource-based exports (White, 2008). Intensified farming has seen an increase in the outputs of farming per unit of an area by increasing inputs such as the use of fertilisers, feed and water in addition to an increase in livestock. This has resulted from a substantial increase in global dairy prices over the last few decades. Dairy is New Zealand's biggest export product and dairy products now fetch 460 per cent more than they did in 1990 (Foote et al, 2015). Farmers have capitalised on this trend and substantially increased the number of cows they have per unit of land.

It has been estimated that livestock production contributes to an estimated 14.5 per cent of global anthropogenic greenhouse gas emissions. It has been observed that enteric fermentation (that is, cow and other ruminant animal farts) is the single largest livestock contribution to climate change (29 per cent), followed by manure (26 per cent), feed crop production (24 per cent) and deforestation for feed crops and pastures (9 per cent) (Kim et al, 2015). Expanding meat and dairy production therefore increases contributions to global warming. The overarching consequences are thus known, but business as usual continues in the face of the factual certainties provided by the agricultural and climate sciences.

The emphasis and reliance on certain types of export earnings has a number of consequences. For instance, pollution and degradation is directly linked to the economically productive use of land. Just over 39 per cent of New Zealand's total land cover is pasture, for example, and it is from within the pastoral industry that we see the main environmental problems surfacing (New Zealand Ministry for the Environment, 2007;

Foote et al, 2015). The combination of the sheer number of animals and the use of nitrogen fertilisers is having a major negative impact on the surrounding environment. Indeed, dairy farming has been identified as the single largest cause of environmental decline in New Zealand, due to fertiliser and animal waste run-off from farms, and the use of water itself. It has also been noted that 'in contrast to many OECD countries, GHG [greenhouse gas] emissions from agriculture (e.g., methane and nitrous oxide) account for some 50% of the national total, and are rising. Changes in agricultural production have led to increased intensity of inputs, including fertiliser and irrigation water, with consequent increases in environmental pressures' (OECD, 2007, p 7).

Legal and illegal deforestation

Every year millions of hectares of forest are destroyed through legal logging of forest plantations and old growth forests as well as illegal logging (Bisschop, 2015). Deforestation is not the sole outcome of logging, however. Land clearance is also due to agricultural exploitation, cattle farming, urbanisation, mining, oil and gas installations, and hydroelectric dams (Khagram, 2004; Boekhout van Solinge and Kuijpers, 2013; Kavitha et al, 2015). There is also the phenomenon of 'conflict timber', associated with West Africa, for example, in which deforestation is linked to the funding of civil wars and armed conflicts (Boekhout van Solinge, 2008; Brisman et al, 2015). In these contexts, the ecological impact of logging and land clearance transcends the legal–illegal divide insofar as vast amounts of forest are destroyed in many different locations worldwide. The motivations, objectives and practices may vary depending on the social context and specific industry interests, but the result is further depletion of many different kinds of trees and variety of forests.

Cutting down trees has a direct bearing on global warming. For instance, it has been estimated that by 2022, biofuel plantations could destroy 98 per cent of Indonesia's rainforests, and that 'every ton of palm oil used as biofuel releases 30 tons of CO_2 into the atmosphere, ten times as much as petroleum does' (Shiva, 2008, p 79). Overall, it has been estimated that deforestation accounts globally for about 12 per cent of total human-caused greenhouse gas emissions (IPCC, 2013). This deforestation not only involves the cutting down of trees, but also frequently the burning of forests as part of converting land for other uses such as agriculture and biofuel plantations.

Moreover, deforestation associated with the planting of flex crops (see below) is linked to fires started in order to cheaply clear land for palm oil and pulp and paper plantations (ABC, 2015a). The subsequent smoke haze now regularly negatively affects people living in Malaysia, Singapore, Brunei, Cambodia, the Philippines, Vietnam and Thailand (Varkkey, 2013). According to some estimates, Indonesian forest and agricultural fires that regularly cloak South-East Asia in an acrid haze spew more greenhouse gases into the atmosphere each day than all US economic activity (ABC, 2015b). For example, according to the World Resources Institute, over several months in 2015 carbon emissions from the fires had exceeded average US daily output on 26 out of 44 days (ABC, 2015b). A major reason for this is that the fires involve the burning of tropical peatlands that store some of the highest quantities of carbon on the planet.

Flex crops

The rise of 'flex crops' is having a major impact on biodiversity (Borras et al, 2013), and this, too, has implications for climate change. Flex crops refer to a single crop or commodity that is highly valuable precisely because of its multiple characteristics and uses. Typically, a flex crop straddles multiple commodity sectors (food, feed, fuel and other industrial commodities), geographical spaces and international political economy categories. The four key flex crops today are maize, oil palm, soybean and sugarcane. Important producers and exporters of flex crops and commodities include, for example, Argentina for soya, Malaysia and Indonesia for palm oil, and Vietnam for fast-growing trees (Borras et al, 2013). One type of crop, such as fast-growing trees, can be sold as a commodity in respect to diverse markets, including in this case timber products, biofuel and/or carbon offsets.

Indeed, another reason for deforestation and biodiversity reduction is the increasing reliance on energy from organic sources, especially in the Global North, using flex crops (Timilsina et al, 2011; Burrell et al, 2012; Charles et al, 2013). For example, the profitability of biofuel production, based on flex crops such as palm oil, is leading to large-scale plantations in places such as Indonesia, Brazil and Colombia. This has resulted in the clearing of rainforests and in some instances forcing Indigenous people off their lands, as well as widespread contamination of soils and groundwater (Mol, 2013).

The use of flex crops is also associated with intensified pastoral industries, for example, the importing of palm kernel expeller (PKE), a product left over in the palm oil production process, as feed. Significantly, New Zealand is the largest global importer of PKE (Foote et al, 2015).

Consequences of climate change for farming

The degradation of natural resources associated with climatic change further perpetuates the demise of existing agricultural and pastoral systems in ways that will continue to generate famine and climate-induced migrations, for human and non-human species. This section looks specifically at three consequences involving water, heat and migration.

Water scarcity

The amount of fresh water on earth (from both surface and groundwater sources) is limited. Drought, high temperatures leading to increased rates of evaporation and the world's exponential population growth have all contributed to its increasing scarcity. It is estimated that around 85 per cent of the world's population live in the world's driest regions, and that by 2025, 3.5 billion of the earth's inhabitants will be living in water-stressed conditions. In Africa alone, over 300 million people live in arid areas, which cover approximately 66 per cent of the continent (GI, 2014).

Only 2.5 per cent of the planet's water is fresh water and of use to human and animal life on earth (Panjabi, 2014). Restricted quantities of clean water make it a particularly valuable property for those who own and control it. The securitisation and theft of water (GI, 2014), water-related corruption and violence, and water market price fixing (KWAHO, 2009) are emerging as important issues. Global warming will only make the existing situation worse.

A recent Australian study on the perspectives of farmers provides an insight into how fresh water is being stolen through diversion, despoiling and depletion (Barclay and Bartel, 2015). Water theft includes the pumping, impoundment or diversion of water from irrigation channels, river systems, dams or ground water bores without a license or in contravention of license conditions that cause changes to flows and reduce water access to neighbouring farms, livestock and riparian zone management (Barclay and Bartel, 2015). On the other hand, contamination of water may be a consequence of intensive farming practices involving use of chemical fertilisers and sizeable effluent run-off.

The cumulative impact of water theft has the potential to jeopardise the sustainability of water resources. For example, over-extraction of coastal groundwater can have detrimental effects for terrestrial, fresh water and coastal marine ecosystems that rely on water flows through creeks and rivers (Poff and Zimmerman, 2010; Vörösmarty et al, 2010). It can also cause seawater intrusion into coastal aquifers and render these aquifers unsuitable for irrigation, therefore impacting land productivity and farmers' viability, as experienced in parts of coastal Queensland (Narayan et al, 2007; Werner, 2010; Greiner et al, 2016).

Heat-related stresses and resilience

Sudden changes in temperature as well as longer-term shifts in climatic conditions have enormous implications for animals and plants at the heart of the farming enterprise (Sundström et al, 2014). Heat stress increases mortality in animals raised for food, and can make them less able to withstand disease. Temperature changes will simultaneously change the composition of grass species, thereby affecting food sources for grazing animals. The dearth of adequate supplies of fresh water also has ramifications for the spread of disease and general health and wellbeing.

Reductions in biodiversity in the field and the paddock also threaten crops and livestock populations alike. Food production is increasingly influenced by localised changes in biodiversity, and by the overarching effect of global warming. Climate change is altering the physical and biological world in many ways. For instance, two-thirds of the North Sea's fish species have shifted in both latitude and depth, and worldwide movements are occurring in respect to mobile species (Macauley, 2016). Simultaneously, local species may be placed under threat due to changes in temperature, moisture, wind and carbon dioxide that may diminish their ability to withstand hitherto familiar pathogens, much less competing species newly invading their spaces.

The threats to biodiversity are many and profound, including reliance on GMOs and monocultures, a situation likely to be made worse by the consequences of climate change (SCBD, 2010). These trends also affect resilience. For instance, 'over the ages farmers have relied upon diverse crop varieties as protection from pests, blights and other forms of crop failure' (French, 2000, p 61). Reducing this diversity affects the inbuilt mechanisms that helped to protect the soil and the vitality of the overall agricultural process. Moreover, intensive use of land and soils that rely on chemical additives to ensure productivity, rather than, for example, traditional methods of crop rotation, further diminishes longer-term agricultural viability. Contemporary farming practices that feature biodiverse fields (based on many different types of seed crops) have not only been found to be more resilient to frost, drought and variations in rainfall, but also to produce more food and cash earnings than that of corn monoculture (Shiva, 2008). Diversity is strength.

Climate-induced migrations

In the light of climate change, consideration also has to be given to matters such as systemic crop failure, and resultant survival and migration strategies. Changes in local weather conditions affect how people behave psychologically and socially, including participation in activities that may involve poaching and illegal harvesting (Mares, 2010). Climate change-induced migration may lead people to either fight over diminished resources in one area (Barnett and Adger, 2007) or leave affected areas, with possible conflict arising in the receiving areas (Barnett and Adger, 2007; Reuveny, 2007). When subsistence fishing, farming and hunting withers due to overexploitation and climate change, then great shifts in human populations and resources are likely to occur (Refugee Studies Centre, 2008). This is not a new problem; such migrations have been experienced in Southern Africa (Singh, 1996), and are presently at the top of the agenda for many Islanders living in the South Pacific.

As environmental conditions deteriorate due to global warming, the size and extent of migration will be shaped by geography, global power relations and the defence of human rights. It can be anticipated that various crimes tied to climate-related events, such as food riots and climate-induced migration, will become more prevalent. Examples include looting and blackmarketeering in relation to food stuffs, illegal fishing and killing of birds and land animals, and trafficking in valued commodities such as water and food. A bifurcation of crime will occur. The rich and powerful will use their resources to secure food advantages; those without the means will do whatever they can to survive.

Global warming will radically change present 'settings' when it comes to the relationship between particular kinds of habitat and particular species of animal and plant. It is not only humans who are migrating, but non-human species as well (Macaulay, 2016). The phenomenon of assisted colonisation, which involves the moving of species to sites where they do not currently occur or have not been known to occur in recent history, also signals the nature of the dilemma. This is happening in response to climate change, and is usually directed at species in the wild (see, for example, Sutherland et al, 2009).

The movement of non-native species into new ecosystems is already recognised as a major conservation problem (SCBD, 2010). This is evidenced, for example, by the rapid expansion in the numbers of Indo-Pacific lionfish along the east coast of the US and in the Caribbean to the detriment of native coral reef fish, and the devastating impact of the introduction of the cane toad in Australia. The effect of such migrations on food production and farming efforts is considerable.

Emergent conflicts over scarcity

While climate change has global consequences, the extent of the impact varies depending on the vulnerability of particular locales, social groups and livelihoods. Diverse circumstances give rise to a range of responses, from the continuation of unsustainable production practices and the systematic hoarding of food, through to widespread social unrest linked to food scarcity and criminality such as individual theft and pilfering.

Securitisation of natural resources

Environmental security refers to the idea that natural resources such as fresh water, fish and trees need to be protected and secured for the public benefit of those living within nation-states. At a concrete level, the social construction of 'security' in an environmental context frequently privileges the rights and interests of the powerful over the public interest (White, 2014). In pursuit of the ownership and control over natural resources, and to exploit these for particular purposes, governments and companies have singularly and in conjunction with each other worked to break laws, bend rules and undermine participatory decision-making processes. Sometimes this takes the form of direct state-corporate collusion (state-corporate crime); in other instances, it involves manoeuvring by government officials or company executives to evade the normal operating rules of planning, development and environmental impact assessment.

Demand is escalating worldwide for commodities of all types, and increasingly there are scarcities of specific resources, leading to a proliferation of ownership contests. Meanwhile, to guard against immediate food shortages, government-backed agricultural firms in China, South Korea, Saudi Arabia and the United Arab Emirates are already buying vast tracts of arable land in Africa and elsewhere to provide food for consumption at home (Brisman, 2013). Security is being sought through the appropriation of resources in specific biosocial locations.

Food scarcity

The exploitation of the world's natural resources by major transnational corporations occurs through the direct appropriation of lands, plants and animals as 'property' (including intellectual property, as in the case of patents). It also occurs through the displacement of existing systems of production and consumption by those that require insertion into the cash–buyer nexus, in other words, the purchase of goods and services as commodities. This has happened in the food production area as it has in other spheres of human life. For example, Africa was virtually self-sufficient in grain production in 1950; by 1988 it was heavily reliant on outside Western producers of corporate supplied food (French, 2000).

Scarcity is tied both to the over-exploitation of natural resources and to the consequences of global warming. Sustainable use occurs when the underlying stock is not depleted in quantity or degraded in quality; but this is rarely the case today. Scarcity can arise from the depletion or degradation of the resource (supply), an increased demand for it and its unequal distribution and/or resource capture. As Homer-Dixon (1999, p 47) comments, these three factors are interrelated: 'deforestation increases the scarcity of forest resources, water pollution increases the scarcity of clean water, and climate change increases the scarcity of the regular patterns of rainfall and temperature on which farmers rely.' Scarcity on a world scale is intentional and consequential. It has little to do with universal human interests (such as food security, air security and water security for all) or the intrinsic worth of animals, plants and specific eco-systems as such.

Social inequality, desperation and radicalisation

The rich and powerful will use their resources to secure productive lands, restrict access to food and water, exploit the financial hardships of others and impose their own coercive rule (private security and private armies is a contemporary growth industry worldwide). Crimes of the less powerful will be crimes of desperation, and child soldiers and armed gangs will flourish in conditions of welfare collapse or non-existent government support. Vulnerable people will flee and be criminalised for seeking asylum; others will stay, to fight for dwindling resources in their part of the world. Communities will be pitted against each other, and industries against communities. Law and order will be increasingly more difficult to maintain, much less enforce in other than repressive ways.

Nowhere is this more evident than in present-day Syria (Gleick, 2014). Between 2003–09 the Tigris-Euphrates Basin – comprising Turkey, Syria, Iraq and western Iran – lost water faster than any other place in the world except northern India. Frictions started to emerge as different groups and rural clans lay claim to water resources, and the dictatorship, imposed rule and corruption was met by growing dissent. Meanwhile, Syria's population grew from 3 million in 1950 to 22 million in 2012, further decreasing the country's total per capita renewable water availability. In the period 2006–11 Syria experienced multi-season, multi-year periods of extreme drought, contributing to agricultural failures, and further economic and population displacements. The trend toward privatisation of agricultural lands corroded customary law over boundary rights, and more than 1.5 million people, mostly agricultural workers and family farmers, moved from rural lands to cities and camps on the outskirts of major cities (Gleick, 2014). Civil war eventually erupted, reducing many cities to rubble, further undermining food production.

Social inequality and social exclusion can simultaneously foster the drift toward radicalisation on the part of desperate people. It is also very much linked to large-scale transformations such as climate change. According to Mary Robinson, former Irish President and United Nations Commissioner for Human Rights, 'climate change is a threat multiplier – it exacerbates poverty and water scarcity, it compounds food and nutrition insecurity and it makes it even harder for poor households to secure their rights', and moreover, 'In a world where climate change exacerbates the stresses of daily life on people already disenfranchised by poverty or social standing, radicalisation is very likely' (Robinson, 2015). The links between inequality, radicalisation and climate change are real and pressing.

Conclusion

Mitigation and adaptation to climate change are heavily influenced by how and where humanity farms, and for what purposes. As this chapter has illustrated, certain types of farming practices are directly linked to the causes of global warming. The flipside of this is that climate change, in turn, has negative consequences for humanity's ability to farm due to shortages of water and the effects of shifts in weather patterns. The net result of present inequalities and short-sightedness is the prospect of enduring social hardship and universal threats to human and non-human wellbeing. Regardless of belief to the contrary, climate change is one reality from which there is no escape, and from which no one will be left untouched.

References

ABC (Australian Broadcasting Corporation) (2015a) 'Southeast Asia's haze: Find out what is behind the choking smoke covering Indonesia, Malaysia and Singapore', *ABC News*, 19 October.

ABC (2015b) 'South-East Asian haze strikes the Pacific as fires exceed greenhouse gas output of the US', *ABC News*, 22 October.

Barclay, E. and Bartel R. (2015) 'Defining environmental crime: The perspective of farmers', *Journal of Rural Studies*, vol 39, pp 188–98.

Barnett, J. and Adger, W. (2007) 'Climate change, human security and violent conflict', *Political Geography*, vol 26, pp 639–55.

Bisschop, L. (2015) *Governance of the illegal trade in e-waste and tropical timber: Case studies on transnational environmental crime*, Farnham: Ashgate.

Boekhout van Solinge, T. (2008) 'Crime, conflicts and ecology in Africa', in R. Sullund (ed) *Global harms: Ecological crime and speciesism*, New York: Nova Science Publishers, pp 13–24.

Boekhout van Solinge, T. and Kuijpers, K. (2013) 'The Amazon rainforest: A green criminological perspective', in N. South and A. Brisman (eds) *Routledge international handbook of green criminology*, New York: Routledge, pp 199–213.

Borras Jr, S., Franco, J. and Wang, C. (2013) 'The challenge of global governance of land grabbing: Changing international agricultural context and competing political views and strategies', *Globalizations*, vol 10, no 1, pp 161–79.

Brisman, A. (2013) 'Not a bedtime story: Climate change, neoliberalism, and the future of the arctic', *Michigan State International Law Review*, vol 22, no 1, pp 241–89.

Brisman, A., South, N. and White, R. (eds) (2015) *Environmental crime and social conflict: Contemporary and emerging issues*, Farnham: Ashgate.

Burrell, A., Gay, S. and Kavallari, A. (2012) 'The compatibility of EU biofuel policies with global sustainability and the WTO', *The World Economy*, vol 35, no 6, pp 784–98.

Charles, C., Gerasimchuk, I., Birdle, R., Moerenhout, T., Asmelash, E. and Laan, T. (2013) *Biofuels – At what cost? A review of costs and benefits of EU biofuels policies*, Manitoba: International Institute for Sustainable Development.

Foote, K.J., Joy, M.K. and Death, R.G. (2015) 'New Zealand dairy farming: Milking our environment for all its worth', *Environmental Management*, vol 56, no 3, pp 709–20.

French, H. (2000) *Vanishing borders: Protecting the planet in the age of globalization*, New York: Norton.

Gedicks, A. (2005) 'Resource wars against native peoples', in R. Bullard (ed) *The quest for environmental justice: Human rights and the politics of pollution*, San Francisco, CA: Sierra Club Books, pp 85–111.

GI (Global Initiative Against Transnational Organized Crime, The) (2014) 'Water, water everywhere: Charting the growth of organized water theft', *Analysing Organised Crime*, p 4e5 (www.globalinitiative. net).

Gleick, P. (2014) 'Water, drought, climate change, and conflict in Syria', *Weather, Climate, and Society*, vol 6, pp 331–40.

Greig, A. and van der Velden, J. (2015) 'Earth hour approaches', *Overland*, 25 March (https://overland.org.au/2015/03/earth-hour-approaches/).

Greiner, R., Fernandes, L., McCartney, F. and Durante, J. (2016) 'Reasons why some irrigation water users fail to comply with water use regulations: A case study from Queensland', *Land Use Policy*, vol 51, pp 26–40.

Homer-Dixon, T. (1999) *Environment, scarcity, and violence*, Princeton, NJ: Princeton University Press.

IPCC (Intergovernmental Panel on Climate Change) (2013) *Working group I contribution to the IPCC fifth assessment report climate change 2013: The physical science basis: summary for policymakers*, 27 September.

IPCC (2014) *Climate change 2014 synthesis report, Approved summary for policymakers* (www.ipcc.ch/pdf/assessment-report/ar5/syr/AR5_SYR_FINAL_SPM.pdf).

Jayne, T., Chamberlin, J. and Headley, D. (2014) 'Land pressures, the evolution of farming systems, and development strategies in Africa: A synthesis', *Food Policy*, vol 48, pp 1–17.

Kavitha, A., Somashekar, R. and Nagaraja, B. (2015) 'Urban expansion and loss of Agricultural land – A case of Bengaluru city', *International Journal of Geomatics and Geosciences*, vol 5, no 3, pp 492–8.

Khagram, S. (2004) *Dams and development: Transnational struggles for water and power*, New York: Cornell University Press.

Kim, B., Neff, R., Santo, R. and Vigorito, J. (2015) 'The importance of reducing animal product consumption and wasted food in mitigating catastrophic climate change', *John Hopkins Center for a Livable Future*, doi: 10.13140/RG.2.1.3385.7362.

Klare, M. (2012) *The race for what's left: The global scramble for the world's last resources*, New York: Metropolitan Books, Henry Holt & Company.

KWAHO (Kenya Water for Health Organization) (2012) *Enhancing water and sanitation governance in Kenya: Human rights-based approach for reforms in the Kenya water sector*, Nairobi, Kenya: KWAHO.

Larkins, M., Gibbs, C. and Rivers III, L. (2013) 'Toward advancing research on the social and environmental impacts of confined animal feeding operations', *CRIMSOC: Journal of Social Criminology*, vol 4, pp 10–63.

Le Billon, P. (2012) *Wars of plunder: Conflicts, profits and the politics of resources*, New York: Columbia University Press.

Mares, D. (2010) 'Criminalizing ecological harm: Crimes against carrying capacity and the criminalization of eco-sinners', *Critical Criminology*, vol 18, pp 279–93.

Macaulay, C. (2016) 'Species on the move worldwide', *The Mercury*, pp 14–15.

McGarrell, E. and Gibbs, C. (2014) 'Conservation criminology, environmental crime, and risk: An application to climate change', *Oxford Handbooks Online: Criminology and Criminal Justice, Criminological Theories*, doi: 10.1093/oxfordhb/9780199935383.54.

Mol, H. (2013) '"A gift from the tropics to the world": Power, harm, and palm oil', in R. Walters, D. Westerhuis and T. Wyatt (eds) *Emerging issues in green criminology*, Basingstoke: Palgrave Macmillan, pp 242–60.

Narayan, K., Schleeberger, C. and Bristol, K. (2007) 'Modelling seawater intrusion in the Burdekin Delta irrigation area, North Queensland, Australia', *Agriculture Water Management*, vol 89, pp 217–28.

New Zealand Ministry for the Environment (2007) *Environment New Zealand 2007: Summary*, Wellington: Ministry for the Environment.

OECD (Organisation for Economic Co-operation and Development) (2007) 'Conclusions and recommendations', *OECD Environmental Performance Review of New Zealand*, Paris: OECD.

Panjabi, R.K.L. (2014) 'Not a drop to spare: The global water crisis of the twenty-first century', *Georgia Journal of International and Comparative Law*, vol 42, no 2, pp 277–424.

Poff, N. and Zimmerman, J. (2010) 'Ecological responses to altered flow regimes: A literature review to inform the science and management of environmental flows', *Freshwater Biology*, vol 55, pp 194–205.

Refugee Studies Centre (2008) *Forced migration review: Climate change and displacement*, Issue 31, Oxford: University of Oxford, Refugee Studies Centre.

Reuveny, R. (2007) 'Climate change-induced migration and violent conflict', *Political Geography*, vol 26, pp 656–73.

Robin, M.M. (2010) *The world according to Monsanto: Pollution, corruption and the control of our food supply*, New York: The New Press.

Robinson, M. (2015) 'Mary Robinson: climate change "very likely" to increase radicalisation', *The Conversation*, 7 December (http://theconversation.com/mary-robinson-climate-change-very-likely-to-increase-radicalisation-51508).

Robyn, L. (2002) 'Indigenous knowledge and technology', *American Indian Quarterly*, vol 26, no 2, pp 198–220.

SCBD (Secretariat of the Convention on Biological Diversity) (2010) *Global biodiversity outlook 3*, Montreal: SCBD.

Shearing, C. (2015) 'Criminology and the anthropocene', *Criminology & Criminal Justice*, vol 15, no 3, pp 255–69.

Shiva, V. (2008) *Soil not oil: Environmental justice in an age of climate crisis*, Brooklyn, NY: South End Press.

Singh, M. (1996) 'Environmental security and displaced people in Southern Africa', *Social Justice*, vol 23, no 4, pp 125–33.

Sundström, J.F., Albihn, A., Boqvist, S., Ljungvall, K., Marstorp, H., Martiin, C., et al (2014) 'Future threats to agricultural food production posed by environmental degradation, climate change, and animal and plant diseases – A risk analysis in three economic and climate settings', *Food Security*, vol 6, pp 201–15.

Sutherland, W.J., Clout, M., Cote, I., Daszak, P., Depledges, M.H., Fellman, L., et al (2009) 'A horizon scan of global conservation issues for 2010', *Trends in Ecology and Evolution*, vol 25, no 1, pp 1–7.

Timilsina, G., Mevel, S. and Shrestha, A. (2011) 'Oil prices, biofuels and food supply', *Energy Policy*, vol 39, pp 8098–105.

Varkkey, H. (2013) 'Oil palm plantations and transboundary haze: Patronage networks and land licensing in Indonesia's peatlands', *Wetland*, vol 33, pp 679–90.

Vörösmarty, C., McIntyre, P., Gessner, M., Dudgeon, D., Prusevich, A., Green, P., et al (2010) 'Global threats to human water security and river biodiversity', *Nature*, vol 467, pp 555–61.

Walters, R. (2011) *Eco crime and genetically modified food*, New York: Routledge.

Werner, A. (2010) 'A review of seawater intrusion and its management in Australia', *Hydrogeological Journal*, vol 18, pp 281–5.

White, R. (2008) 'The transnational context of local environmental harm', *New Zealand Sociology*, vol 23, no 7, pp 119–34.

White, R. (2014) 'Environmental insecurity and fortress mentality', *International Affairs*, vol 90, no 4, pp 835–51.

20

Food waste (non)regulation

Michael A. Long and Michael J. Lynch

Introduction

Food waste is ubiquitous. With a world population of over 6 million people that needs to be fed, waste from the production, transport and consumption of food is inevitable. However, the current scale of food waste is so large that it appears unsustainable. According to one of the more conservative estimates, almost 30 per cent of food is wasted throughout the supply chain (REFRESH, 2017). Others have suggested that up to half of all food grown is wasted (Lundqvist et al, 2008; Parfitt et al, 2010). This is an incredible amount of waste, at least some of which could go to the millions of people in the world who go hungry every day. To put the level of food loss into perspective, roughly 100 million tons of food is wasted annually in the European Union (EU), which is enough food to feed the hungry people throughout the world – twice (European Commission, 2017).

There are differing opinions regarding what qualifies as food waste, and therefore there are numerous definitions of food waste. For example, in an overview of food waste definitions, Parfitt and colleagues (2010, p 3065) focus on a definition provided by the Food and Agriculture Organization (FAO, 1981), which suggests that food waste includes, '[w]holesome edible material intended for human consumption, arising at any point in the food supply chain that is instead discarded, lost, degraded or consumed by pests.' This definition has been broadened by Stuart (2009) who argues that in addition to what the FAO classifies as food waste, it should also include, 'edible material that is intentionally fed to animals or is a by-product of food processing diverted away from the human food' (Parfitt et al, 2010, p 3065). This chapter adopts this more inclusive definition of food waste.

All conceptualisations of food waste stress that it occurs throughout the food supply chain. Interestingly, however, food waste occurs more often during the earlier stages of the supply chain in low-income countries. The most common reasons for this include: poor storage facilities that cause spoilage and give rodents, other pests and fungus access to the food; poor infrastructure and transportation; lack of refrigeration; unsanitary market facilities; and poor packaging (Gustavsson, 2011). Food waste in high-income countries most often occurs later in the food supply chain due primarily to: quality standards (for example, aesthetic defects); food lost to the manufacturing process (for example, trimming scraps, transportation losses during processing); poor conditions during display (for example, food kept at incorrect temperatures); best-used-before dates; and leftovers (Gustavsson, 2011). Clearly, there are many opportunities for food to be wasted throughout the supply chain, making the problem of food waste amenable to interventions that might reduce waste. At the same time, however, the current structure of the food marketplace itself is an impediment to food waste reduction efforts, and makes it difficult to substantially reduce food waste.

While the social science literature on food production, distribution and consumption is robust, until recently, the study of food waste has been relatively neglected by social scientists (Evans et al, 2013). In some ways, this recent interest in food waste scholarship parallels the perception and understanding of food waste in wider society. Evans and colleagues (2013) demonstrate how wasting food was a concern during the mid-18th to mid-20th century due to the high cost of food relative to wages during this time, and the effects of rationing during both World Wars. However, food waste became invisible after the Second World War as a result of rising incomes, food surpluses generated from US and European agricultural subsidies, high employment and refrigerator ownership. In short, it was no longer economically necessary for individuals and governments to care about food waste. However, the global food crisis (see Rosin et al, 2012) that resulted from the Great Recession of 2008–09 increased the cost of food, and consequently the need to reduce food waste became 'visible' once again (Evans et al, 2013). It was during this most recent period of food waste history that social science scholarship focusing on food waste dramatically increased.

Recent scholarship on the broader category of waste has included work on second-hand consumption (Gregson and Crewe, 2003), ethics and waste (Hawkins, 2006), and demolition (Gregson et al, 2010a), among other issues (see, for example, Scanlan, 2005; Gregson, 2007; Gregson et al, 2007; Gregson et al, 2010b). Food waste scholarship includes a suggestion to develop a 'rubbish imagination' akin to the sociological imagination, to help people understand the role of food waste in our lives (O'Brien, 2007). Other work has unpacked the role of food waste regimes (Gille, 2007, 2013), consuming leftovers (Cappellini, 2009; Cappellini and Parsons, 2013), the relationship between materialism and food waste (Evans, 2011), waste from food packaging (Hawkins, 2013), date labelling (Milne, 2013), geographic differences in food waste definitions (Coles and Hallett IV, 2013), and freeganism (scavenging; Edwards and Mercer, 2013). Thus, the social science food waste scholarship is beginning to tackle numerous important issues. This chapter continues this trend by examining how the current level of food waste can be considered a crime.

The remainder of this chapter is organised as follows. First, a description of how food waste and its consequences fit within this volume's definition of food crime is provided, including a discussion of the social, ethical and ecological consequences of food waste. Next, an overview of responses and potential solutions to the problem of food waste are discussed. Finally, the relationship between global capitalism and food waste is highlighted, with a particular focus on the structural factors that impact the level of food waste throughout the world.

Food waste and its consequences

Processes of food production, distribution and consumption are highly regulated. Food waste, however, is not. For example, the EU has very detailed rules and regulations for food, such as the appropriate curvature of bananas, but substantially fewer rules about the level and amount of food waste that is acceptable. Government regulation involving food waste usually focuses on what gets classified as waste and what does not. In the EU this sorting process is detailed in the *European Waste Catalogue* (EWC), which categorises all types of waste, including food waste (Sustainability Exchange, 2017). Consequently, the main regulations for food waste are technocratic measures that suggest guidelines for when food becomes waste and should not be eaten (for example, best-before dates) or cosmetic guidelines that retailers impose on producers to help with the saleability of food products (for example, the banana regulations mentioned earlier). Unfortunately, these regulations actually increase rather than decrease food waste, and therefore exacerbate rather than reduce problems caused by food waste.

Research has documented numerous ethical, social and ecological consequences of food waste. The United Nations (UN) has stated that access to a sufficient quantity of nutritious food is a basic human right, 'which is critical to adequate health and wellbeing, and central to human dignity' (Graham et al, 2016, p 1; see also UN, 1948, 1999). If access to food is a basic human right, wasting food in the quantities detailed earlier is ethically problematic and perhaps a human rights violation. The UN World Food Programme (WFP) estimates that there are 795 million hungry people in the world (UN WFP, 2017). It is therefore unethical to waste food that is still edible for cosmetic reasons, is slightly past the best-before date, or is just not consumed and consequently discarded.

Denying hundreds of millions of people their basic human right to sufficient food while others discard somewhere between one-third and one-half of all food produced contributes to the widespread social issue of food poverty. According to the Food Standards Agency (FSA, 2017), 'food poverty is the inability of individuals and households to obtain an adequate and nutritious diet, often because they cannot afford healthy food or there is a lack of shops in their area that are easy to reach.' Food poverty causes a myriad of social, educational and health problems for children and adults (see Graham et al, forthcoming, for a review). Therefore, crafting regulations and social practices that promote – rather than reduce – food waste can, in this view, be understood as criminal.

In addition to the ethical and social implications of food waste, there are also ecological consequences. For instance, biologists have calculated that in the US, food waste accounts for over 25 per cent of the country's total freshwater consumption, which has implications for global climate change (Hall et al, 2009). As Wang (2014) notes, food production generates large quantities of food waste-based waste water with high concentrations of solids that must be treated before they can be released back into the environment without generating other deleterious effects (for example, waterway eutrophication). Others have documented how food waste also wastes energy. Cuellar and Webber (2010) suggest that food waste accounts for 2 per cent of energy consumption in the US. Energy production, predominately through fossil fuel extraction, has many documented negative environmental consequences, and anything that increases energy use, increases energy consumption and therefore increases the associated environmental destructive outcomes. For these reasons, the ecological consequences of food waste can be conceptualised as a crime against nature (see Lynch et al, 2013, for an extended discussion of environmental destruction as a crime).

Given the ethical, social and ecological consequences of food waste detailed above, this chapter argues that the current state of food waste, production and (non)regulation is a crime, against both poor people and the environment. The next section includes a discussion of responses and potential solutions to the problem of food waste that have arisen throughout the world.

Responses and potential solutions

The current scale of food waste is ethically, socially and environmentally problematic, and as this chapter suggests, criminal. This latter argument is in regards to both UN human rights definitions and ethical considerations, but not from the legal perspective of criminal or regulatory law. Efforts to address these problems associated with the global food waste crisis have centred on strategies for reduction. First, and most importantly, are attempts to prevent food losses and waste from occurring. This is a paramount concern as the vast majority of food waste ends up as landfill. For example, current estimates suggest that over 97 per cent of food waste in the US is deposited in landfills (Levis et al, 2010). Gustavsson (2011) recommends that low-income countries increase local investments and education, use refrigeration where possible, and improve packaging and market facilities to reduce food that gets lost early in the food supply chain. To prevent food waste in high-income countries, Gustavsson (2011) notes that countries should improve communication in supply chains, improve purchase and consumption planning, and increase education around best-before dates. There are clearly a number of ways to reduce food waste throughout the entirety of the food supply chain that producers, retailers and consumers need to implement.

Prevention is not always possible. When food is transformed into food waste there are several options for either recycling the food (that is, reclaim it as food and consume it), harvest materials from the food waste, or convert it into energy. These options are often conceptualised in a hierarchy according to how much of the food waste is used, or the amount of energy needed to convert the waste into energy. The top of this hierarchy is to reclaim the food waste as food and to consume it. Almost all food sold in supermarkets and other shops is regulated by national governments for health and safety reasons. This has resulted in overly cautious use of best-before dates, a date where the food item is no longer 'safe' to eat based on government regulations. Retailers are forced to discard food items that are past this date as they are not legally permitted to sell it. However, this food is often completely safe to eat. This has given rise to the phenomenon of 'freeganism'. Freegans collect and redistribute food that has been discarded by supermarkets to people who are hungry and who live in food poverty (Edwards and Mercer, 2013). The majority of freegans do not need to live off of discarded food, but rather do so to make a political statement about food waste and food poverty, while also helping to feed those who are hungry.

It is important to note that this process of reclassifying food into food waste is often influenced by powerful actors in the capitalist marketplace. Decisions to label food products as food waste are not always made for consumer health reasons. Rather, capitalist systems have created opportunities to profit from food waste, including the reduction of incentives to reclaim the food for consumption. To exemplify this, and what represents an example of the next step down the food waste hierarchy, is the sending of food waste to biorefineries. A biorefinery is a facility that converts biomass (food waste is classified as biomass) into fuels, energy and value-added chemicals, in a low carbon process that is less detrimental for climate change than oil refining (Smith, 2007; Cherubini, 2010). Biorefineries are able to turn food waste into energy and chemicals that can be reused in the manufacture of future products.

Moving down the hierarchy further, and currently one of the most popular approaches for reducing food waste, is the transformation of food waste into energy via methane production. Producing energy from food waste is below biorefinery use on the food waste hierarchy because it usually requires larger amounts of energy than biorefineries to produce the energy that is created through methane production. This approach for turning food waste into energy uses anaerobic digestion – a process where microorganisms are used in different stages to break down biodegradable matter – to generate 'biogas', primarily composed of methane, as a renewable energy resource with a small carbon footprint. In terms of climate change, the production of biogas, unlike other gases and fossil fuels used as energy resources, is neutral in its effect, since growing materials used to create biogases consumes as much carbon dioxide from the atmosphere as is released from burning biogases. Like other gases, biogas can be compressed for storage and use. Bagher and colleagues (2015) estimate that in some countries like the

UK, biogases could replace 17 per cent of fossil fuels used to operate vehicles, thus lowering carbon pollution generated from fossil fuel consumption (for estimates related to Ireland, see O'Shea et al, 2016).

Studies have also addressed the economic costs and efficiency of biogas conversion, examining how long it takes to recover initial investments in biogas production. Such studies are important to the extent that these can impact the willingness of private investors to build biogas production facilities. For example, Balaman and Selim (2014) studied biogas conversion in Turkey, and found that it takes about five years of operation of a biogas facility to return the initial investment. In China, the government has recognised that biogas conversion can be utilised to address a variety of problems related to the disposal of food waste and related ecological contamination from food waste disposal. Wen and colleagues (2016) reported that the Chinese government has created 100 food waste treatment projects in cities across China to address these concerns. In their economic analysis of one of these facilities, they found that the plant can generate significant quantities of biogas along with biodiesel, and that the plant's daily net profit is equivalent to about US$12,196 per day.

Recently, the US, led by the Department of Agriculture and the Environmental Protection Agency (EPA), have become more involved in food waste reduction and recycling efforts. According to the American Biogas Council (2017), the volume of food waste in the US (34 million tons) is sufficient to cover Manhattan, one of the boroughs of New York City, in six feet of food waste annually. In 2015, the US announced the Food Loss & Waste 2030 reduction goal of 50 per cent by 2030. This is an important issue in the US, where there is extensive food waste. In an effort to stimulate increased biogas production, the EPA added definitions of renewable biogas to US environmental protection statutes in 2014 (40 CFR § 80.1401). That definition, however, limits the application of this statute to 'pipeline quality' biogases and their injection into the existing US natural gas pipeline system. The EPA also encourages voluntary participation in biogas generation from livestock waste through the AgSTAR programme, due to its estimates that the use of anaerobic digesters on livestock farms in the US has reduced greenhouse gas emissions by about 3 million metric tons. However, since the US produces about 6 billion metric tons of greenhouses gases, the voluntary use of anaerobic digesters on livestock farms has been an ineffective mechanism for reducing total greenhouse gas emissions, which amount to only 0.05 per cent from livestock farm waste conversion. But this is still a significant improvement over 2010 figures for the US, when only about

1.6 million metric tons of livestock waste was saved from entering the atmosphere as greenhouse gases. Clearly, these figures and the limited effort of the US government to encourage the transformation of food waste into biogas indicate a very different policy position on this issue in comparison to the EU and China.

In the EU, the story is very different due to more stringent government policies encouraging the expansion of food waste to biogas. In comparison to the 1,800 estimated biogas plants in the US, the European Biogas Association (2017) estimates that Germany has 10,786 and Italy has 1,491 of these facilities. Germany, with its population of 80.6 million people, has a concentration of one biogas facility per every 7,472 people. In Italy, where the population is 59.83 million, there is one biogas facility for every 40,000 people. In the US, the same ratio is one biogas facility for every 177,166 people. The US ranks well behind Switzerland (1:12,766), Denmark (1:36,219), Belgium (1:60,870); Finland (1:61,112), the Netherlands (1:66,666), the UK (1:78,840) and France (1:89,714) in terms of biogas facilities per person. The US biogas per person ratio is less than those found in somewhat lesser developed or rather small EU nations such as Bulgaria (1:660,500), Estonia (1:73,500) and Ireland (1:164,107). Clearly, on this front the US could do much more to encourage the use of biogas conversion from food waste. In China, for example, more than 30 million homes are now equipped with biogas digesters, and these small units produce 1.2 per cent of energy used in China (Behera and Varma, 2016).

Although the adoption of policies that encourage biomass conversion in biorefineries and biogas production from food waste vary across countries, it is encouraging that governments and policy-makers are thinking proactively about food waste. However, more research regarding the structural causes of the creation of food waste is necessary to dramatically reduce food waste throughout the supply chain. The relationship between global capitalism and food waste is now briefly examined with particular emphasis paid to how political economic conditions encourage the creation of food waste.

Global capitalism and food waste

While the technological solutions discussed above hold promise for reducing some food waste, it is doubtful that real meaningful reductions in food waste can occur under the current neoliberal global economic system, which is based on continuous economic growth and capital accumulation. For example, O'Brien (2013) points out that under capitalism everything is a commodity to exploit for surplus value – including food waste (see also Shukin, 2009). Food waste that is transformed in biorefineries or into biogas becomes a commodity that can be traded and sold. O'Brien (2013, p 206) notes that government regulations on food waste (in documents such as the EWC) include not just a list of what is and what is not food waste, but in addition, he suggests that, 'waste policy defines who can and who cannot profit from the surplus that capitalism produces. The EWC and its surrounding labyrinth is not merely a "list" of wastes, rather, it is a flowchart of allowances and permissions for waste's exploitation.' This leads to an interesting question: will conversion of food waste into profitable commodities lead to the production of more food waste (or at least discourage the reduction of food waste)? The answer to this question is currently unknown. This question, however, should be of interest to criminologists, because if regulations are created by states that tacitly accept the current level of food waste, supported and backed by members of industry, this could qualify as a state-corporate crime (Michalowski and Kramer, 2006). In other words, governments would be facilitating capitalist interests over feeding vulnerable populations and protecting the environment. Or, as O'Brien (2013, p 207) puts it, '[t]here's gold (or, at least, fuel) in them-there waste receptacles – and where there's gold there's a state-supported structure of exploitation that marginalises, criminalises and demonises alternative solutions to capital accumulation.'

It is also important to understand the role of food in the global capitalist economy. The majority of food produced in the world is not consumed by the producer(s) nations; rather, it is produced and turned into a commodity with the purpose of being traded or sold. Typically, that chain of food supply moves higher-value foods from less developed to more developed nations, and from places where food is needed and in short supply (that is, a larger proportion of the population is hungry or malnourished), to where it is less needed and becomes part of luxury consumption. This process contributes to the unequal distribution of consumed calories across nations (Hawkes, 2006; Carr et al, 2016). The growth imperative of capitalism requires larger and larger quantities of goods (food) to be produced in order to encourage economic growth. This results in overproduction, extensive processing and overconsumption of food, and therefore increases the amount of food waste.

Finally, it is important to understand the geopolitical causes of food waste. Gille (2007, 2013) introduces the concept of 'food waste regimes', which is similar to the work of Friedmann and McMichael (1987) and their notion of 'food regimes'. Both perspectives highlight how food – or food waste – are not only commodities, but also social relations. For example, Gille (2013) recounts the story of Ethiopian agriculture during the late 20th century. Ethiopians face some of the highest rates of food poverty in the world. The presence of food aid, primarily from the US, has created disincentives for Ethiopians to grow their own food because it would be more expensive than the food aid from the US. Furthermore, much of the food that is grown locally in Ethiopia is wasted because people can receive food aid for free. The US provides food aid to Ethiopia and other less developed countries, not out of benevolence, but rather to provide a market for the surpluses produced by US farmers who are subsidised by the government. The US, then, is simultaneously displacing its own food by-products and creating food waste in other countries in order to prop up its own domestic food industry.

This discussion is not meant to discourage technological solutions to food waste, such as biorefinery and biogas production. These are important partial solutions for some amount of food waste that is produced. However, it is also important to recognise how structural factors tolerate and in some cases may encourage food waste. In other words, the technological approaches described above are treating food waste in reactive ways, while prevention of waste is not targeted because capitalism has found ways to commodify and profit from it. Consequently, stricter regulations alone may not be a panacea for food waste, as many of these regulations often reclassify food that is still edible into waste that can then be turned into profit by capitalists.

Conclusion

This chapter has outlined the current state of social science scholarship on food waste production and regulation, and noted that in recent years, scholars have started to pay greater attention to this important issue. Next, the numerous ethical, social and ecological consequences have been outlined, arguing how the current state of food waste non(regulation) could be considered criminal for three main reasons. First, estimates put the amount of food waste somewhere between one-third and one-half of all food produced globally. Much of this food is still edible, yet there are hundreds of millions of people throughout the world who are currently being denied their basic human right of access to sufficient food. Second, the negative environmental impacts of food waste are substantial, which can be conceptualised as a crime against nature. And third, the structure of the global world food market generates conditions that contribute to food waste, and in this sense, can also be considered criminal by denying people their food rights as defined by the UN. The chapter then reviewed several responses and solutions to food waste, including reclaiming food waste for consumption, sending it for conversion into energy and value-added chemicals in a biorefinery facility, and using anaerobic digestion of methane gas to produce biogas. While these technological solutions to food waste have provided some optimism regarding the reduction of food waste, it is argued that without paying sufficient attention to the effects of global capitalism on food waste, significant reductions in food waste are unlikely. While generating some food waste is unavoidable, this chapter has argued that the current level and lack of regulation of food waste is criminal.

The introduction noted that food waste is ubiquitous, making potential solutions to this problem seem unrealistic. In some ways, real solutions to the problem *are* unrealistic unless global capitalism's effect on food waste is recognised and directly dealt with. Global food production transforms the vast majority of food into commodities to sell for profit. This creates unnecessary cosmetic restrictions on food products, a global demand for specialised products, overly cautious best-before dates and most importantly, consistent over-production of food. This is where most unnecessary food waste originates. Reorganising global food production to a system where feeding the citizens of the world is the goal, rather than constant economic growth, has the potential to dramatically reduce food waste throughout the world.

References

American Biogas Council (2017) 'Food waste' (www. americanbiogascouncil.org/biogas_foodWaste.asp).

Bagher, A.M., Fatemeh, G., Saman, M. and Leili, M. (2015) 'Advantages and disadvantages of biogas', *Bulletin of Advanced Scientific Research*, vol 1, no 5 (www.asdpub.com/index.php/basr/article/view/265).

Balaman, Ş.Y. and Selim, H. (2014) 'A network design model for biomass to energy supply chains with anaerobic digestion systems', *Applied Energy*, vol 130, pp 289–304.

Behera, B.K. and Varma, A. (2016) *Microbial resources for sustainable energy*, Geneva, Switzerland: Springer.

Cappellini, B. (2009) 'The sacrifice of re-use: The travels of leftovers and family relations', *Journal of Consumer Behaviour*, vol 8, pp 365–75.

Cappellini, B. and Parsons, E. (2013) 'Practising thrift at dinnertime: Mealtime leftovers, sacrifice and family membership', *The Sociological Review*, vol 60, no S2, pp 121–34.

Carr, J.A., D'Odorico, P., Suweis, S. and Seekell, D.A. (2016) 'What commodities and countries impact inequality in the global food system?', *Environmental Research Letters*, vol 11, no 9, pp 095013.

Cherubini, F. (2010) 'The biorefinery concept: Using biomass instead of oil for producing energy demands', *Energy Conversion and Management*, vol 51, no 7, pp 1412–21.

Coles, B. and Hallett IV, L. (2013) 'Eating from the bin: Salmon heads, waste and the markets that make them', *The Sociological Review*, vol 60, no S2, pp 156–73.

Cuellar, A.D. and Webber, M.E. (2010) 'Wasted food, wasted energy: The embedded energy in food waste in the United States', *Environmental Science & Technology*, vol 44, no 16, pp 6464–9.

Edwards, F. and Mercer, D. (2013) 'Food waste in Australia: The freegan response', *The Sociological Review*, vol 60, no S2, pp 174–91.

European Biogas Association (2017) 'Biomethane & biogas report 2015' (http://european-biogas.eu/2015/12/16/biogasreport2015/).

European Commission (2017) 'Food waste' (http://ec.europa.eu/food/safety/food_waste_en).

Evans, D. (2011) 'Blaming the consumer – once again: The social and material contexts of everyday food waste practices in some English households', *Critical Public Health*, vol 21, no 4, pp 429–40.

Evans, D., Campbell, H. and Murcott, A. (2013) 'A brief pre-history of food waste and the social sciences', *The Sociological Review*, vol 60, no S2, pp 5–26.

FAO (Food and Agriculture Organization) (1981) 'Food loss prevention in perishable crops', FAO Agricultural Service Bulletin, no 43, FAO Statistics Division.

Friedmann, H. and McMichael, P. (1987) 'Agriculture and the state system: The rise and fall of national agricultures, 1870 to present', *Sociologia Ruralis*, vol 29, no 2, pp 93–117.

FSA (Food Standards Agency) (2017) 'Food poverty' (www.food.gov.uk/northern-ireland/nutritionni/ninutritionhomeless).

Gille, Z. (2007) *From the cult of waste to the trash heap of history: The politics of waste in socialist and postsocialist Hungary*, Bloomington, IN: University of Indiana Press.

Gille, Z. (2013) 'From risk to waste: Global food waste regimes', *The Sociological Review*, vol 60, no S2, pp 27–46.

Graham, P.L., Crilley, E., Stretesky, P.B., Long, M.A., Palmer, K.J., Steinbock, E. and Defeyter, M.A. (2016) 'School holiday food provision in the UK: A qualitative investigation of needs, benefits, and potential for development', *Frontiers in Public Health*, vol 4, doi: 10.3389/fpubh.2016.00172.

Gregson, N. (2007) *Living with things: Ridding, accommodation, dwelling*, Oxford: Sean Kingston.

Gregson, N. and Crewe, L. (2003) *Second hand cultures*, Oxford: Berg.

Gregson, N., Metcalfe, A. and Crewe, L. (2007) 'Identity, mobility, and the throwaway society', *Environment and Planning D: Society and Space*, vol 25, pp 682–700.

Gregson, N., Watkins, H. and Calestani, M. (2010a) 'Inextinguishable fibres: Demolition and the vital materialisms of asbestos', *Environment and Planning A*, vol 42, pp 1065–83.

Gregson, N., Crang, M., Ahamed, F., Akter, N. and Ferdous, R. (2010b) 'Following things of rubbish value: End-of-life ships, "chock-chocky" furniture and the Bangladeshi middle class consumer', *Geoforum*, vol 41, pp 846–54.

Gustavsson, J. (2011) 'Global food losses and food waste', Save Food Congress, Dusseldorf, 16 May.

Hall, K.D., Guo, J., Dore, M. and Chow, C.C. (2009) 'The progressive increase of food waste in America and its environmental impact', *PLoS One*, vol 4, no 11, e7940, doi: 10.1371/journal.pone.0007940.

Hawkes, C. (2006) 'Uneven dietary development: linking the policies and processes of globalization with the nutrition transition, obesity and diet-related chronic diseases', *Globalization and Health*, vol 2, no 1, p 4.

Hawkins, G. (2006) *The ethics of waste: How we relate to rubbish*, Lanham, MD: Rowman & Littlefield.

Hawkins, G. (2013) 'The performativity of food packaging: Market devices, waste crisis and recycling', *The Sociological Review*, vol 60, no S2, pp 66–83.

Levis, J.W., Barlaz, M.A., Themelis, N.J. and Ulloa, P. (2010) 'Assessment of the state of food waste treatment in the United States and Canada', *Waste Management*, vol30, pp 1486–94.

Lundqvist, J., de Fraiture, C. and Molden, D. (2008) 'Saving water: From field to fork – Curbing losses and wastage in the food chain', SIWI Policy Brief, Stockholm, Sweden: SIWI.

Lynch, M.J., Long, M.A., Barrett, K.L. and Stretesky, P.B. (2013) 'Is it a crime to produce ecological disorganization? Why green criminology and political economy matter in the analysis of global ecological harms', *British Journal of Criminology*, vol 53, no 6, pp 997–1016.

Michalowski, R.J. and Kramer, R.C. (2006) *State-corporate crime: Wrongdoing at the intersection of business and government*, New Brunswick, NJ: Rutgers University Press.

Milne, R. (2013) 'Arbiters of waste: Date labels, the consumer and knowing good, safe food', *The Sociological Review*, vol 60, no S2, pp 84–101.

O'Brien, M. (2007) 'A "lasting transformation" of capitalist surplus: From food stocks to feedstocks', *The Sociological Review*, vol 60, no S2, pp 192–211.

O'Brien, M. (2013) 'A "lasting transformation" of capitalist surplus: From food stocks to feedstocks', *The Sociological Review*, vol 60, no S2, pp 192–211.

O'Shea, R., Kilgallon, I., Wall, D. and Murphy, J. D. (2016) 'Quantification and location of a renewable gas industry based on digestion of wastes in Ireland', *Applied Energy*, vol 175, pp 229–39.

Parfitt, J., Barthel, M. and Macnaughton, S. (2010) 'Food waste within food supply chains: Quantification and potential for change to 2050', *Philosophical Transactions of the Royal Society B*, vol 365, pp 3065–81.

REFRESH (Resource Efficient Food and dRink for the Entire Supply cHain) (2017) 'Background' (http://eu-refresh.org/about-refresh#about-the-project).

Rosin, C., Stock, P. and Campbell, H. (eds) (2012) *Food systems failure: The global food crisis and the future of agriculture*, London: Earthscan.

Scanlan, J. (2005) *On garbage*, London: Reaktion Books.

Shukin, N. (2009) *Animal capital: Rendering life in biopolitical times*, Minneapolis, MN: University of Minnesota Press.

Smith, W.J. (2007) *Mapping the development of UK biorefinery complexes*, Tamutech Consultancy NNFCC, 20/6/2007.

Stuart, T. (2009) *Waste, uncovering the global food scandal*, London: Penguin.

Sustainability Exchange (2017) *The European Waste Catalogue* (www.sustainabilityexchange.ac.uk/the_european_waste_catalogue_ewc).

UN (United Nations) (1948) *Universal Declaration of Human Rights* (www.un.org/en/documents/udhr/index.shtml#a14).

UN (1999) *Substantive issues arising in the implementation of the international covenant on economic, social and cultural rights: General comment 12* (http://data.unaids.org/publications/external-documents/ecosoc_cescr-gc14_en.pdf).

UN WFP (United Nations World Food Programme) (2017) 'Hunger statistics' (www.wfp.org/hunger/stats).

Wang, L. (2014) 'Food processing waste as an energy feedstock: Availability and sustainability', in L. Wang (ed) *Sustainable bioenergy production*, Boca Raton, FL: CRC Press.

Wen, Z., Wang, Y. and de Clercq, D. (2016) 'What is the true value of food waste? A case study of technology integration in urban food waste treatment in Suzhou City, China', *Journal of Cleaner Production*, vol 118, pp 88–96.

21

Responding to neoliberal diets: School meal programmes in Brazil and Canada

Estevan Leopoldo de Freitas Coca and
Ricardo César Barbosa Júnior

Introduction

Food is a tool of power that has permitted capitalism to be established as the dominant mode of production (McMichael, 2001). Within capitalism, cheap food from the 'Green Revolution' sought to prevent the 'Red Revolution' (Patel, 2013), or so-called 'communist threat'. Even though it is recognised as a fundamental human right (UN, 2013), food is increasingly mercantilised as a commodity (Murphy, 2009). This term refers to the perversion of food from a social good into merchandise, produced and sold as any other. As this volume demonstrates, this process in connected with many harms associated with food and agriculture (Gray and Hinch, 2015).

Although for some time global agriculture has produced enough for every person in the world to have access to 2,850 calories – enough to live healthily (The World Bank, 2008) – about 795 million people are still subject to hunger (FAO, 2015). Concurrently, the World Health Organization (WHO, 2016) indicates that more than 1.9 billion people are overweight due to unbalanced diets. This is not simply because they eat too much, but because they consume industrialised foods of low nutritional value (Guthman, 2011).

Children and youth are among the most vulnerable to the consequences of such discordance in the agri-food system (Gunson et al, 2016). For instance, in many poor countries malnutrition starts in utero when a mother's precarious nutritional intake affects the formation of a foetus's biological structures (Ziegler, 2011). Additionally, due to a powerful process of 'conquering minds' through advertising, millions are persuaded to partake in a low-nutrient diet model, exemplified by fast foods (Azuma and Fisher, 2001; Schlosser, 2001; Nestle, 2002; Pollan, 2007). Hunger and obesity are not episodic manifestations; on the contrary, they have biological, economic and social determinations, to the extent where one can even inherit its detriment. This chapter discusses the standardisation of diets as the result of neoliberal capitalism, as well as the forms of resistance and countermeasures in schools.

The school-aged demographic of Western countries have largely adopted food habits based primarily on processed goods of low nutritional value (Winson, 2010). Changes in school meal programmes are seen as a form of reverting this process (Poppendieck, 2010). In this chapter, resistance to the standardisation of diets is assessed through a qualitative analysis of two school food programmes: the newest version of the National School Feeding Programme (PNAE), established by the Brazilian federal government, and the Farm to School British Columbia (F2S BC) network, part of the non-governmental organisation (NGO) Public Health Association of BC. PNAE's objective is to introduce local family farmers' products into the menus of public schools. F2S BC seeks to increase consumption of local products in public education institutions by adopting food as a pedagogical resource and promoting school gardens. While other Canadian provinces have similar programmes, British Columbia (BC) has been chosen primarily because it has one of the most consolidated Farm to School experiences, and we both undertook research as interns at the University of British Columbia.

This chapter draws on research carried out over the last three years that seeks to understand the emergence of short circuits of food production, commercialisation and consumption as an alternative to the hegemonic agri-food system in regions of Brazil and Canada. First, the characteristics of food processes in the context of neoliberal globalisation are explored. Next, school meal initiatives are introduced as alternatives to the hegemonic agri-food system in Brazil and Canada. This assessment suggests that although both initiatives are innovative, they also have limitations such as not taking advantage of the pedagogical dimension of food (in the Brazilian example) and limited reach (in the Canadian example).

Neoliberalism and the perverse effects of standardising the global diet

Since the late 1980s, capitalism has generated a new pattern of accumulation characterised by a more flexible model of organising space (Harvey, 2005), marking the emergence of large corporations as important players in global geopolitics (Stopford et al, 1991). Given this, productive spatial circuits have emerged that denote the global dynamics of large corporations, operating beyond a regional logic (Santos, 1988). The state's role has been less emphatic while societies are faced with structural unemployment, expansion of the tertiary sector and financialisation of the economy (Harvey, 2001).

In the agri-food system, this has resulted in the mercantilisation of food, placing the food sovereignty of nation-states at risk (Barbosa Junior and Coca, 2015). That is, large agri-food corporations control the flow of food in space internationally, with profit growth as the primary objective. Therefore, production does not directly meet the populational food demands, but rather, operates in search of better market opportunities. The consolidation of agribusiness as the main model of agricultural production has led millions of peasant production units to become economically unfeasible (McMichael, 2009). Peasants become dissociated from labour on the land, while mechanisation and the use of chemical inputs advance as a norm to grow agri-food. Large corporations begin to control the various stages of agri-food systems, ranging from the selection of seeds, through intellectual property agreements (Pfrimer and Barbosa Junior, 2017), to consumption. Conglomerates that operate in the retail sector, many of which are controlled through holdings, become increasingly influential (Monteiro and Cannon, 2012).

Due to this, Dixon (2009) emphasises that the current technological control exercised by large corporations in the agri-food system manifests itself as a true class struggle across the countryside and in cities. As a result, the global population goes through a nutritional transition, evident by the decrease in the variety of foods that comprise the human diet (Popkin, 2002). Foods that were traditionally cultivated by specific populations, engaged in their hereditarily transmitted production techniques, have been replaced by processed goods to the extent that this designates a global standardisation of taste (Lotti, 2010). Such an approach allows us to recognise the extent of large corporations' capacity to determine the energy, proteins and calories obtained by human beings through food – a level of control that is intensely delineated by business interests.

To understand food mercantilisation and the resulting resistances, class-based struggles need to be approached as responses to corporate food crimes through a political economy perspective. An agri-food system heavily influenced by corporations has both individual and structural consequences. Collective scale examples include endemic and epidemic cases of hunger, the extent to which the quest for profit diminishes the quality of food (illustrated in the recent case of expired beef being sold in Brazil) and the exaggerated use of agrochemicals. On an individual scale, examples include diseases such as type 1 diabetes, hypertension and cancer. Under these conditions, the effects of the food crimes have repercussions on the individual and collective scales dialectically, which draws attention to how the mercantilisation of food brings about a range of public health problems.

With regard to the individual dimension, we draw on Crawford and Beveridge's (2013) concept of 'everyday security', which manifests not only in processes external to each person, but also in the decisions they make about themselves (that is, consumer relations). Pertaining to the food process, as food mercantilisation advances, the ability to choose what to eat becomes limited, due to the lack of variety and limited income. In other words, because low-income people cannot afford agri-food in sufficient quantity and quality to live in good health, millions of people around the world find themselves in a state of individual insecurity (Nunes, 2014). Thus, while mercantilisation is located at the macro-structural level, and individuals themselves do not go through these processes, they are significantly affected by them.

In Brazil, for example, families spend an average of 19.8 per cent of their monthly income on food, leading 75.2 per cent of Brazilians to feel unsure of whether their monthly income will be enough to satisfy basic living expenses (IBGE, 2011). In such circumstances, the choice of what foods families consume is restricted by price, with lesser consideration given to nutritional quality (Chen, 2016). In contexts such as this, school meals contribute to mitigating the nutritional insecurity of children and youth (Smith, 2016). These state-level policies promote general food-related wellbeing. Yet, each beneficiary directly experiences the consequences. Conversely, in places where there are no national school meal policies such as Canada, educational institutions are not obliged to create nutritional arrangements in favour of their students (Siqueira, 2014; Coca, 2016). The lack of policy can be harmful to the population's health, in particular, children of food-insecure households. This may even contribute negatively to their performance in school, as children are more vulnerable to learning problems due to malnutrition (Sawaya, 2006).

In regards to the collective scale, factors such as hunger and obesity are, above all, social constructions that denote the inequalities of the hegemonic economic system (de Castro, 1984). This means that the nutritional and dietary problems that affect a large part of the global population have, in fact, a systemic origin as they are a consequence of the dominant mode of production (Clapp and Scrinis, 2017). This was evident in the 2007–08 food crisis, when collective looting erupted in multiple Latin American, African and Southeast Asian countries as a result of the desperate situation of those affected (Tokar and Magdoff, 2009). In high-income countries, although drastic events such as these have not been witnessed, food insecurity among the low-income population, such as groups of immigrants, black and indigenous communities, have also increased (Clapp and Helleiner, 2012). In Canada, for example, 19.6 per cent of recent immigrant households reported food insecurity in comparison to 12.4 per cent of Canadian-born respondents; likewise, rates for black (27.8 per cent) and aboriginal (28.2 per cent) households are almost two-and-a-half times that of all Canadian households (12.6 per cent) (Tarasuk et al, 2014). Nevertheless, in the same period, the leading agri-food corporations have seen their profits rise (Murphy et al, 2012). This characterises a contradiction between the promotion of the human right to adequate food and power-wielding large corporations' control over the various stages of the global agri-food system (Claeys, 2015).

The food crimes accompanying food mercantilisation take on dissimilar forms. Individuals are directly harmed (for example, malnutrition, obesity, poor health, death), yet this cannot be dissociated from systems and structures that indirectly do harm to specific groups by enabling certain production–consumption patterns. From a political economy perspective, this is a consequence of prioritising the market above environmental, social and health concerns. To sum up, there are multiple mechanisms that work in favour of the market and not the general population, characterising food as merchandise rather than a resource available to all. In sequence, school meal initiatives in Brazil and Canada are assessed, demonstrating specific responses to overcoming food crimes.

PNAE and the Brazilian example

Within the first two decades of the 21st century, Brazil made significant progress towards combating hunger and poverty (Maluf et al, 2015). As a result, in 2014, the country was no longer listed on the Hunger Map released annually by the United Nations (UN) Food and Agriculture Organization (FAO). This was primarily due to the rise of the Workers Party (PT) to the Presidency, with Lula da Silva (2003–10) and Dilma Rousseff (2011–16). Within this period, social policies were implemented that played a large role in reducing hunger and poverty. Two examples include Bolsa Família (Family Grant), with the central objective of guaranteeing a minimum household income (in particular, for those families that have school-age children) and its expansion through the *Brazil Without Poverty Plan*, that supplemented the income of families living on less than R$70 per person per month.

Although they did not go beyond the limits of capitalism, such changes in policy were possible because the PT governments were responsive to some of the propositions presented by representatives of the subaltern forces in society. In relation to food policies, rural social movements have been prominent, such as the Landless Rural Workers' Movements (MST), the Movements of Small Farmers (MPA), the Movements of those Affected by Dams (MAB) and the Peasant Women's Movement (MMC), all members of the international coalition La Via Campesina. Social movements are invited to discuss large corporations' control over public policies, with resulting changes that are not only institutional, but also reflected in the socioeconomic structure of the country's population.

With direct regard to the agri-food system, it is essential to discuss the implementation of the 2003 Zero Hunger Programme (PFZ) (Wittman and Blesh, 2017). Through a series of structural and more immediate measures, PFZ had the goal of guaranteeing all Brazilians at least three meals a day (Kilpatrick and Beghin, 2010). Among these measures, territorial development policies – which directed specific investments to regions with low economic and social indicators – generated greater participation of civil society through advisory and deliberative councils. In addition, the Food Acquisition Programme (Programa de Aquisição de Alimentos, PAA) sought to insert family farming into the institutional market, while also providing people in conditions of social vulnerability with good food, through a purchase-and-donate model (Schneider et al, 2016). This chapter focuses primarily on the newest version of PNAE, established by Law No 11.947 of 16 June 2009. The nation-wide implementation of PNAE was possible in Brazil because of the shared collaboration structure between the federal government, federative units and municipalities that manage the educational system.

PNAE originated in 1955 as a response to the hunger and poverty depicted in the works carried out by Josué de Castro – doctor, geographer and former head of FAO (Leão and Maluf, 2012). His book, *The geography of hunger*, drew attention to the political construction of hunger in Brazil. In 2009, PNAE was altered to focus not only on students who receive food served at school, but also local family farmers (FNDE, 2014). The change stipulates that family farmers should produce at least 30 per cent of the food purchased with resources from the National Education Development Fund (FNDE). In addition, family farmers providing organic or agro-ecological products are to be paid 30 per cent more than the price for conventional products (Triches et al, 2016), favouring not only a particular type of farmer, but also of farming. Changes in PNAE's legislation resulted in a significant increase in resources invested in school food programmes. According to FNDE (2014), the amounts (in millions) were as follows: R$2,013 in 2009, R$3,024 in 2010, R$3,051 in 2011, R$3,306 in 2012, R$3,542 in 2013 and R$3,693 in 2014. These characteristics make PNAE an innovative public policy (de Schutter, 2014), that has become an example for measures implemented in other countries in Latin America (FAO, 2015) and Africa (Clements, 2015).

PNAE seeks to diversify the diet of school-age children and youth. The products acquired by the state are not standardised but seasonal (da Cunha et al, 2014). Despite the fact that it is a national-level policy, multiple community-level food cultures are respected, in accordance with a food sovereignty perspective (Forum for Food Sovereignty, 2007). This is evident in the case of the Association of Parents and Friends of the Exceptional (APAE), a programme in the municipality of Candói, in the state of Paraná, which assists 150 people. In this programme, student meals are overseen by the director of Candói's APAE, who explains how the quality and freshness of the food also impacts other meals: "We also serve breakfast, for those coming from afar and the afternoon snack. We use PNAE's food at school events, for example, at special lunches for parents, on commemorative dates."

PNAE has an even greater impact on the nutritional benefit for children and youth of groups in conditions of social vulnerability who are mostly able to access nutritious food at school (Smith, 2016). The Coronel Nestor da Silva Indigenous State School, located in the Rio das Cobras Reserve, has about 250 students that benefit from PNAE, from children attending elementary school to students from the Youth and Adult Education (EJA) programme. The school's director indicates that, "in this school, the meals are essential for indigenous children. The culture here is not so much to plant. They are hunters. We realize that their diet has improved a great deal, they have the opportunity to consume things that they would not usually have access to." A greater variety of foods make up school meals (Soares et al, 2017), especially through the novel inclusion of natural products exemplified in the case of the indigenous school by the director's statements: "It is very diverse! It varies from green spices, lettuce ... everything seasonally planted in the region; then comes honey, meat.... We no longer receive canned meat, we get everything natural, every 10 days it comes ... it's really great!."

Accordingly, it becomes evident that PNAE has directly contributed to mitigating some of the harmful consequences of the hegemonic agri-food system for the school-aged public, as it guarantees less dependence on processed goods and those of low nutritional value, which are among the main causes of child and youth health problems (WHO, 2016). Triches (2015) corroborates this idea, explaining that PNAE has the capacity to contribute to healthy eating while also promoting sustainable development. In other words, the programme's beneficiaries receive foods rich in proteins, vitamins, minerals, carbohydrates and fibre – unlike the standardised products from agribusiness that do not support local farmers. PNAE simultaneously addresses lacking social policies by contributing to the regional economy and encouraging the adoption of healthier production methods (Sonnino et al, 2014).

PNAE's implementation by the Brazilian federal government is recognised as one of the main examples of institutionalising of food sovereignty (Wittman, 2015). PNAE feeds 43 million school students, some of them three meals a day, and provides a secure market for many family farmers (Osava, 2017). This public policy represents the establishment of short circuits of food, bringing producers and consumers closer with strategies that value environmentally friendly agriculture. Consequently, PNAE represents one of the most significant efforts undertaken in Brazil to eradicate hunger. It goes beyond the top-down premises of multilateral institutions, concentrating on structural mechanisms to move past the agribusiness production model (Leão and Maluf, 2012). For instance, despite relying on governmental resources, this public policy is continually and equally evaluated and directed by public and civil society organisations.

However, PNAE is limited for not including local food in official teaching programmes. This is evident in the Guidelines and Bases of Education (Law 9,394 of 20 December 1996, and its updates), which stipulate the content of the various stages of teaching in Brazil. At no point does this document identify food as a pedagogical resource. Albeit on a smaller scale and with limited state presence, the experience of the F2S BC network advances this practice, beyond what is taking place in Brazil, as shown in the following section.

The F2S BC network and the Canadian example

Canada is the only country among the G8 that does not have a national school meal programme (Siqueira, 2014; Coca, 2016). This is primarily due to the autonomy granted to each province. It is estimated that 70 per cent of Canadian school children and youth do not eat at least four servings of fruits and/or vegetable a day (F2CC, 2012). Furthermore, the processed food and drinks industries spend more than $2 billion CAD annually on advertisements to attract children, which has stimulated the consumption of products of low nutritional value (F2CC, 2012). As a response, the F2S BC network came together in 2007 seeking to promote healthy, local, sustainable and environmentally friendly food. Despite being restricted to the province of British Columbia (BC), F2S BC belongs to a collective of other initiatives called Farm to School in countries such as Canada – where it is called Farm to Cafeteria Canada (F2CC) on a national level – as well as others, for instance, the US and the UK (Winson, 2010). F2S BC asserts that 'Farm to School empowers students and school communities to make informed food choices while contributing to vibrant, sustainable regional food systems that support the health of people, place and planet' (F2S BC, 2016).

The F2S BC network began as a Salad Bar project funded by the BC Living Health Alliance, which aimed to diversify the nutrition of students from selected schools. Subsequently, a series of developments furthered the initiative: an advisory committee that includes members of civil society and the government was established; the web page was created; various marketing initiatives and new methods of implementing its policies were advanced (Public Health Association of BC, 2012). Accordingly, the F2S BC (2016) network proposes the following goals:

- supporting the development of sustainable regional food systems in BC by bringing more healthy, local and sustainable food into BC schools;

- promoting healthy eating in schools by supporting the development of healthy school food environments;
- advancing experiential, hands-on learning opportunities related to food systems and the development of student food literacy;
- advancing school and community connectedness; and
- developing promising Farm to School practice models that are sustainable, self-financing, eco-friendly and have the potential to be implemented elsewhere.

In addition, the network operates through three regional hubs: Kamloops Region, Vancouver Region and a Regional Capital. Through these hubs, hundreds of initiatives are articulated at the provincial level, which seek to propose policy as well as to implement productive practices and conscious consumption in the school itself and with food more generally. To help frame the scope of the F2S BC network, three key activities are examined: Learning Labs, cooking classes and school gardens.

Learning Labs are spaces for stakeholders to articulate among themselves with the aim of promoting strategies that support local agri-food systems through sustainable practices (F2CC, 2014a). In the Metro Vancouver region, the F2S BC network has held a Learning Lab in partnership with the non-profit organisation Farm Folk City Folk. The central goal is to work with the Vancouver School Board "to determine the ways in which they can buy more local, healthy and sustainable food in their schools", as stated by Farm Folk City Folk's Manager of Strategic Partnerships and Development. In this sense, Learning Labs are geared toward directing government and other stakeholders' activities towards better school food. Granting what 'good food' means can vary, contingent to actor or organisation; it generally refers to quality of food, the process of production and distribution, as well as its significance in the regional dynamics.

Additionally, the F2S BC network holds culinary courses where food is introduced as part of learning. BC's Ministry of Education incorporates food into the public school curriculums, recognising that the study of food has interdisciplinary value (BC Ministry of Education, 2015). Project CHEF's Founder and Executive Director (part of the F2S BC network) explains that: "what we have done is gone forward with the whole curriculum and linked what we do with the different learning outcomes in the different curriculum guides of British Columbia." This way, the FS2 BC network not only acts to improve students' nutrition, but also educates them through active learning, using food as a pedagogical resource.

Moreover, the F2S BC network promotes the incorporation of school gardens into public schools. Hence, as a result of investing in and nurturing school gardens and greenhouses, schools also become spaces for growing food (F2CC, 2014b). The school's community consumes the products grown on site, inviting students behind the veil of food production, distribution and consumption.

Despite the contributions that the F2S BC network has offered towards inserting food into provincial curriculums and school food programmes, there are some limitations. First, it is not legally mandated, which means school boards can decide whether to implement it or not on a voluntary basis. Second, there are no financial resources exclusively allocated for such projects in the provincial governments' annual budget, meaning that these efforts develop mainly through private donations. And third, relations with local family farmers are still weak. In most cases, it is more financially beneficial for farmers to sell their goods to private food establishments rather than to schools. Notwithstanding these limitations, F2S BC has yielded empirically validated qualitative changes in the ways the school-age public, their parents and the school community more broadly relate to food.

Conclusion

In neoliberal times, food functions as merchandise. The commodification of food has negative implications concerning public health, especially among school-age children and youth. We insist that the mercantilisation of food is an authentic crime, especially problematic for the poorest among us. Nevertheless, while globalisation homogenises social relations, it also allows for the emergence of resistance (Massey, 1999). Food policies designed for schools in Brazil and Canada validate this argument.

In the case of Brazil, analysis indicates that PNAE is an innovative measure that enables family farmers to contribute to the food security of schools' populations, and that behind such a policy is the intention to contribute towards an alternative agricultural model. However, this public policy is limited in that it treats schools as spaces where food is solely a product of consumption, not a pedagogical resource. In contrast, the F2S BC network in Canada has a greater scope of objectives insofar as it envisions schools as a space of food consumption, production and education in addition to contributing towards the implementation of sustainable agri-food systems. However, the fact that schools adhere to this practice on their own accord limits large-scale change to a potential, but not an enforceable, actionable plan. These cases demonstrate how food strategies may be established to counter those of the hegemonic corporate agri-food system, responsible for numerous social, political, public health and environmental harms – that is, food crimes.

References

Azuma, A.M. and Fisher, A. (2001) *Healthy farms, healthy kids: Evaluating the barriers and opportunities for farm-to-school programs*, Venice, CA: Community Food Security Coalition (http://alivebynature.com/pub/HealthyFarmsHealthyKids.pdf).

Barbosa Junior, R.C. and Coca, E.L. de F. (2015) 'The WTO 's international multilateral trade system and its effects on the production and consumption of food', *Boletim Meridiano 47*, vol 16, no 150, pp 42–9.

BC Ministry of Education (2015) 'Curriculum packages by grade' (www.bced.gov.bc.ca/irp/gc.php?lang=en).

Chen, W. (2016) 'From "junk food " to "treats". How poverty shapes family food practices', *Food, Culture & Society*, vol 19, no 1, pp 151–70.

Claeys, P. (2015) 'The right to food: Many developments, more challenges', *Canadian Food Studies*, vol 2, no 2, pp 60–67.

Clapp, J. and Helleiner, E. (2012) 'Troubled futures? The global food crisis and the politics of agricultural derivatives regulation', *Review of International Political Economy*, vol 19, no 2, pp 181–207.

Clapp, J. and Scrinis, G. (2017) 'Big food, nutritionism, and corporate power', *Globalizations*, vol 14, no 4, pp 578–95.

Clements, E.A. (2015) 'Addressing rural poverty and food insecurity through local food purchasing and school lunch programs: PAA Africa, PRONAE and the creation of institutional markets in Mozambique', *Revista NERA*, vol 18, no 26, pp 28–50.

Coca, E.L. de F. (2016) 'A soberania alimentar através do Estado e da sociedade civil: O Programa de Aquisição de Alimentos (PAA), no Brasil e a rede Farm to Cafeteria Canada (F2CC), no Canadá', Presidente Prudente: Unesp (PhD Thesis).

Crawford, E. and Beveridge, R. (2013) *Strengthening BC's agriculture sector in the face of climate change*, Victoria: The Pacific Institute for Climate Solutions (http://pics.uvic.ca/sites/default/files/uploads/publications/Strengthening%20BC%27s%20Agriculture%20Sector_0.pdf).

da Cunha, D.T., Gonçalves, H.V.B. de Lima, A.F.A., Martins, P.A., de Rosso, V.V. and Stedefeldt, E. (2014) 'Regional food dishes in the Brazilian national school food program: Acceptability and nutritional composition', *Revista de Nutrição*, vol 27, no 4, pp 423–34.

de Castro, J. (1984) *Geografia da fome* (10th edn), Rio de Janeiro: Edições Antares.

de Schutter, O. (2014) *The power of procurement: Public purchasing in the service of realizing the right to food*, Geneva: UN (www.srfood. org/images/stories/pdf/otherdocuments/20140514_procurement_ en.pdf).

Dixon, J. (2009) 'From the imperial to the empty calorie: How nutrition relations underpin food regime transitions', *Agriculture and Human Values*, vol 26, no 4, pp 321–33.

F2CC (Farm to Cafeteria Canada) (2012) *Farm to cafeteria: BC communitties share paths to success*, Vancouver: F2CC (https:// foodsecurecanada.org/sites/foodsecurecanada.org/files/f2c-pathstosuccess-singles-web.pdf).

F2CC (2014a) *Learning labs*, Vancouver: F2CC (www. farmtocafeteriacanada.ca/wp-content/uploads/2014/08/Learning_ Lab_EN.pdf).

F2CC (2014b) *Farm to school: Dig in!*, Vancouver: F2CC (www. farmtocafeteriacanada.ca/wp-content/uploads/2014/08/ GettingStartedF2S_EN.pdf).

F2S BC (Farm to School BC) (2016) *About us*, Victoria: PHABC (http://farmtoschoolbc.ca/about-us/what-is-farm-to-school/).

FAO (Food and Agriculture Organization) (2012) *The state of food insecurity in the world: Economic growth is necessary but not suficient to accelerate reduction of hunger and malnutrition*, Rome: FAO (www.fao. org/docrep/016/i3027e/i3027e.pdf).

FAO (2015) *Las compras públicas a la agricultura familiar y la seguridad alimentaria y nutricional en América Latina y el Caribe: Lecciones aprendidas y experiencias*, Santiago: FAO (www.fao.org/3/a-i4902s.pdf).

FNDE (Fundo Nacional de Desenvolvimento da Educação) (2014) *Aquisição de produtos da agricultura familiar para a alimentação escolar*, Brasilia: FNDE (www.fnde.gov.br/programas/alimentacao-escolar/ agricultura-familiar).

Forum for Food Sovereignty (2007) *Declaration of Nyéléni*, Nyéléni: La Vía Campesina (https://nyeleni.org/IMG/pdf/DeclNyeleni-en.pdf).

Gray, A. and Hinch, R. (2015) 'Agribusiness, governments and food crime: A critical perspective', in R.A. Sollund (ed) *Green harms and crimes: Critical criminology in a changing world*, New York: Palgrave Macmillan, pp 97–116.

Gunson, J.S., Warin, M. and Moore, V. (2016) 'Visceral politics: Obesity and children's embodied experiences of food and hunger', *Critical Public Health*, pp 1–12.

Guthman, J. (2011) 'Excess consumption or over-production? US farm policy, global warming, and the bizarre attribution of obesity', in R. Peet, P. Robbins and M. Watts (eds) *Global political ecology*, London and New York: Routledge, pp 51–67.

Harvey, D. (2001) 'Globalization and the "spatial fix"', *Geographische Revue*, vol 2, no 3, pp 23–31.

Harvey, D. (2005) *A brief history of neoliberalism*, New York: Oxford.

IGBE (Instituto Brasileiro de Geografia e Estatatística) (2011) *Pesquisa de orçamentos familiares 2008–2009: Antropometria e estado nutricional de crianças, adolescentes e adultos no Brasil*, Rio de Janeiro: IGBE (www.abeso.org.br/uploads/downloads/71/553a23f27da68.pdf).

Kilpatrick, K. and Beghin, N. (2010) *Fighting hunger in Brazil: Much achieved, more to do*, London: Oxfam (www.oxfam.org/sites/www.oxfam.org/files/cs-fighting-hunger-brazil-090611-en.pdf).

Leão, M. and Maluf, R.S. (2012) *A construção social de um sistema público de segurança alimentar e nutricional: A experiência brasileira*, Brasília: ABRANDH.

Lotti, A. (2010) 'The commoditization of products and taste: Slow food and the conservation of agrobiodiversity', *Agriculture and Human Values*, vol 27, no 1, pp 71–83.

Maluf, R.S., Burlandy, L., Santarelli, M., Schottz, V. and Speranza, J.S. (2015) 'Nutrition-sensitive agriculture and the promotion of food and nutrition sovereignty and security in Brazil', *Ciência & Saúde Coletiva*, vol 20, no 8, pp 2303–12.

Massey, D. (1999) 'Space-time, "science" and the relationship between physical geography and human geography', *Human Geography*, vol 24, no 3, pp 261–76.

McMichael, P. (2001) 'The impact of globalisation, free trade and technology on food and nutrition in the new millennium', *The Proceedings of the Nutrition Society*, vol 60, no 2, pp 215–20.

McMichael, P. (2009) 'A food regime analysis of the "world food crisis"', *Agriculture and Human Values*, vol 26, no 4, pp 281–95.

Monteiro, C.A. and Cannon, G. (2012) 'The impact of transnational "big food" companies on the South: A view from Brazil', *PLOS Medicine*, vol 9, no 7, pp 1–5.

Murphy, S. (2009) 'Free trade in agriculture: A bad idea whose time is done', *Monthly Review*, vol 61, no 3, pp 78–91.

Murphy, S., Burch, D. and Clapp, J. (2012) *Cereal secrets: The world's largest grain traders and global agriculture*, London: Oxfam (www.oxfam. org/sites/www.oxfam.org/files/rr-cereal-secrets-grain-traders-agriculture-30082012-en.pdf).

Nestle, M. (2002) *Food politcs: How the food industry influences nutrition and health*, Los Angeles, CA: University of California Press.

Nunes, J. (2014) 'Questioning health security: Insecurity and domination in world politics', *Review of International Studies*, vol 40, no 5, pp 939–60.

Osava, M. (2017) 'Brazil drives new school feeding model in the region', Rome: IPS (www.ipsnews.net/2017/05/brazil-drives-new-school-feeding-model-in-the-region/).

Patel, R. (2013) 'The long green revolution', *Journal of Peasant Studies*, vol 40, no 1, pp 1–63.

Pfrimer, M.H. and Barbosa Junior, R.C. (2017) 'Neo-agro-colonialism, control over life, and imposed spatio-temporalities', *Contexto Internacional*, vol 39, no 1, pp 9–33.

Pollan, M. (2007) *The omnivore's dilemma*, New York: Large Print Press.

Popkin, B.M. (2002) 'An overview of the nutrition transition and its health implications: The Bellagio meeting', *Public Health Nutrition*, vol 5, no 1, pp 93–103.

Poppendieck, J. (2010) *Free food for all: Fixing school food in America*, Berkeley, CA: University of California Press.

Public Health Association of BC (2012) *A fresh crunch in school lunch: The BC Farm to School guide* (2nd edn), Victoria: PHABC (http://farmtoschool.phabc.org/wp-content/uploads/sites/3/2015/10/F2Sguide-2nd-edition-singles.pdf).

Santos, M. (1988) *Metamorfoses do espaço habitado*, São Paulo: Hucitec.

Sawaya, S.M. (2006) 'Malnutrition and poor academic performance: Critical contributions', *Estudos Avançados*, vol 20, no 58, pp 133–46.

Schlosser, E. (2001) *Fast food nation: What the all-American meal is doing to the world*, London: Penguin.

Schneider, S., Thies, V.F., Grisa, C. and Belik, W. (2016) 'Potential of public purchases as markets for family farming', in D. Barling (ed) *Advances in food security and sustainability*. Burlington, VA: Academic Press, pp 69–95.

Siqueira, W.V. (2014) *The school system in Canada: Comprehensions toward the implementation of a national program*, Vancouver: Food Sovereignty Research Group.

Smith, T.A. (2016) 'Do school food programs improve child dietary quality?', *American Journal of Agricultural Economics*, vol 99, no 2, pp 339–56.

Soares, P., Davó-Blanes, M.C., Martinelli, S.S., Melgarejo, L. and Cavalli, S.B. (2017) 'The effect of new purchase criteria on food procurement for the Brazilian school feeding program', *Appetite*, vol 108, pp 288–94.

Sonnino, R., Lozano Torres, C. and Schneider, S. (2014) 'Reflexive governance for food security: The example of school feeding in Brazil', *Journal of Rural Studies*, vol 36, pp 1–12.

Stopford, J., Strange, S. and Henley, J. (1991) *Rival states, rival firms. Competition for world market shares*, London: Cambridge University Press.

Tarasuk, V., Mitchell, A. and Dachner, N, (2014) *Household food insecurity in Canada, 2012*, Toronto: PROOF (http://nutritionalsciences.lamp. utoronto.ca/wp-content/uploads/2014/05/Household_Food_ Insecurity_in_Canada-2012_ENG.pdf).

Tokar, B., and Magdoff, F. (2009) 'An overview of the food and agriculture crisis', *Monthly Review*, vol 61, no 3, pp 1–10.

Triches, R.M. (2015) 'Promoção do consumo alimentar sustentável do contexto da alimentação escolar', *Trabalho, Educação e Saúde*, vol 13, no 3, pp 757–71.

Triches, R.M., Schabarum, J.C. and Giombelli, G.P. (2016) 'Demanda de produtos da agricultura familiar e condicionantes para a aquisição de produtos orgânicos e agroecológicos pela alimentação escolar no sudoeste do Paraná', *Revista NERA*, vol 19, no 31, pp 91–110.

UN (United Nations) (2013) *The millennium development goals report*, New York: UN (www.un.org/millenniumgoals/pdf/report-2013/ mdg-report-2013-english.pdf).

WHO (World Health Organization) (2016) 'Obesity and overweight: Fact sheet', Geneva: WHO (www.who.int/mediacentre/factsheets/ fs311/en/).

Winson, A. (2010) 'The demand for healthy eating: Supporting a transformative food "movement"', *Rural Sociology*, vol 75, no 4, pp 584–600.

Wittman, H. (2015) 'From protest to policy: The challenges of institutionalizing food sovereignty', *Canadian Food Studies*, vol 2, no 2, pp 174–82.

Wittman, H. and Blesh, J. (2017) 'Food sovereignty and fome zero: Connecting public food procurement programmes to sustainable rural development in Brazil', *Journal of Agrarian Change*, vol 17, no 1, pp 81–105.

World Bank, The (2008) *Agriculture for development: World development report 2008*, Washington, DC: The World Bank (https://siteresources. worldbank.org/INTWDR2008/Resources/WDR_00_book.pdf).

Ziegler, J. (2011) *Destruction massive: Géopolitique de la faim*, Paris: Seuil.

Section VIII
Questioning and consuming food

22

Counter crimes and food democracy: Suspects and citizens remaking the food system

Sue Booth, John Coveney and Dominique Paturel

Introduction

There can be no doubt that the current industrial food system is broken. Examples of large-scale disease outbreaks such as bovine spongiform encephalopathy (BSE), and scandals such as melamine-tainted powdered milk and horsemeat in frozen beef lasagne still linger in the public consciousness. As previous chapters have illustrated, perhaps a more fitting descriptor of the global food system would be that of a system of 'organised crime'. Organised crime refers to illegal activities or harmful offences at transnational or national level undertaken purely for profit. The charge sheet for organised crime by the global food system documents a litany of harmful or illegal activities against the environment, consumers, food producers and agricultural workers, public health and animal welfare. Against this background consumers are increasingly seeking truth and transparency as to the provenance of their food.

This chapter explores 'counter crime', namely, activities that prevent or defend against criminal actions. These actions, some underpinned by democratic principles, constitute a participatory movement whereby citizens exert some modicum of control over their food system. Collectively known as food democracy, it offers a quantum of hope in what Hinrichs (2007, pp 5–6) calls 're-making' the food system. Hinrichs argues that 'remaking shifts us from a paralysing focus on what is worrying, wrong, destructive and oppressive about our current food system to a wide-angle view that takes in the broader landscape whose troubling contours we begin to notice, are punctuated by encouraging signs of change.' Starting with an investigation of food consumption crimes, this chapter explores examples of citizen 'counter crime' movements using oppositional politics to galvanise action, then focusing on food democracy and constructivist approaches to remake the food system.

Crimes of consumption

Crime in this context does not relate to activities that are law-breaking as such, but rather to those who use their powers to subvert standards of decency and fair play. Use of these powers, especially when turned on those who have no ability to fight back, can be considered criminal in a broad sense. In Chapter 1 of this volume, Gray suggests a food crime perspective is one that may include 'situations of law-making or law-breaking, suspect or ineffective enforcement or lack thereof, harms resulting from insufficient or absent regulation, or philosophical and pragmatic questions of corruption, deviance, justice and erroneousness.' Three examples are explored below.

Supermarket power, control and lack of choice

Australia, and many similar economies, support free trade and a market economy. This sociopolitical economic system is predicated on the ability of consumers to have free choice so that the market 'decides' by virtue of popularity and appeal. Yet, Australia has one of the most concentrated grocery markets in the world (Caraher and Coveney, 2004) The so-called 'duopoly' of the Coles and Woolworths chains (Tonkin, 2016) dominates the supermarket landscape, and essentially robs people of choice and freedom. Similarly, the power of the 'duopoly' allows supermarkets to treat suppliers poorly, and unjustly (Devin and Richards, 2016). Essentially, farmers in this system are price-takers not price-makers, as they have little control of the price paid to them.

Food waste

The volume of food wasted has long been regarded as scandalous. Much research (Bartl, 2011) has focused on domestic food waste and the volume of uneaten food that ends up in landfill; however, in Western jurisdictions, the culprits are mostly retailers (Devin and Richards, 2016). Again, powerful supermarkets play a major role in generating food waste, for example, supermarket cosmetic specifications for fruit and vegetables often result in rejected produce (Richards and Devin 2016). Processed food waste including unpopular product lines are being donated to food banks, thus some food manufacturers are using food banks as an alternative waste stream to landfill dumping. Why is it acceptable to use waste food to feed vulnerable people? Food banks are not an emergency response – a report from Perth, Western Australia, indicated the average length of use for individuals was 7.5 years (Campbell and Mackintosh, 2015). In South Australia, processed food made up nearly 60 per cent of total foodbank donations in 2016 (Mr G. Pattinson, personal communication, 16 January 2017). This raises concerns as evidence from the US (Saint Louis, 2016) shows that a long-term diet based predominantly on processed foods donated to food banks exacerbates chronic conditions, for example, diabetes.

Food advertising to children

There are surely no greater crimes than those directed to the most vulnerable. On that basis, the exploitation of children's gullibility and credulity through promotion of unhealthy food products can be seen as dastardly and indefensible. Much research has shown that the supposed self-regulation by food and media industries to rein in aggressive marketing of junk foods to children has simply not worked. In some jurisdictions such as Canada and Sweden, government regulation has prohibited advertising at particular timeslots to protect children from the effects of promotion of unhealthy food products (Mehta et al, 2014). Nevertheless these prohibitions have been undermined as junk food advertising moves to another timeslot where children still form a large part of the viewing audience. Alternatively advertisers may adopt subversive tactics and mask promotions as targeting adults, and are thus not counted as breaching government ruling by advertising to children. Some food industries even run programmes within educational systems to cleverly promote certain food products disguised as learning about health and wellbeing (for example, the Ontario dairy industry). Clearly, the promotion of unhealthy food products to children is vulnerable when industry seeks to obey the letter of the law rather than the spirit of the law. While not technically a crime, there is a moral charge of 'foul play' that can justifiably be directed at the perpetrators.

'Counter crimes'

Widespread food crime within the global food system affects many food system actors, and has prompted acts of resistance against corporate injustices. These acts of resistance are, in effect, 'counter crimes', undertaken by individuals, citizen groups and consumer movements. Examples include guerrilla gardening, movements against genetically modified (GM) foods and anti-globalisation protests.

One of the most famous counter crimes was committed by José Bové, a French sheep's milk cheese producer. In 1999, Bové led a number of fellow farmers in an attack against a nearby McDonald's restaurant under construction. The attack resulted in the virtual dismantling of the building and simultaneous worldwide media coverage. Consequently, Bové was convicted and spent three months in prison. His book, *Le monde n'est pas une marchandise* [*The world is not a commodity*] (2000), co-authored by Francois Dufour, provides an account of the steps required to resist the industrialisation of the food supply, and the inevitable domination by transnational companies that exploit both people and the environment (Bové and Dufour, 2000).

Further acts of disobedience can be seen emanating from other actions. For example, during the late 1980s an Australian campaign against the promotion and advertising of tobacco products gained national and international attention. The movement was called Billboard Utilising Graffitists Against Unhealthy Promotions, or BUGA-UP. The BUGA-UP movement (Chapman, 1996) defaced billboards and other advertising that promoted tobacco, often reshaping, ironically, the advertisement text to much public amusement. These acts of civil disobedience led to the arrest of BUGA-UP supporters, and in so doing, provided publicity of the blatant strategies in tobacco advertising.

Civil disobedience has long been used to publicise causes deemed worthy, thus, the advent of guerrilla gardening is unsurprising as a more recent food-centred act. Guerrilla gardening is an act of defiance since public land or private property is appropriated for growing food. While not overtly reactionary, David Tracey's book, *Guerrilla gardening: A manifesto* (2007), calls citizens to get 'dirty' and subversive by growing food in public for the public.

Since the promotion of genetically modified organisms (GMOs) in the late 1980s there has been widespread resistance from scientific and public communities (Lockie et al, 2005). One example of the latter is the group amassing under the banner MAdGE (Mothers Against Genetic Engineering in Food and the Environment). MAdGE has been most active in Australia, where it has harassed the government of the state of Victoria, especially when a moratorium on banning the growing of GM canola for commercial purposes was lifted. MAdGE has also engaged in acts of civil disobedience in supermarkets where members have targeted and relabelled food products suspected of harbouring GM ingredients with stickers proclaiming 'Contaminated – Genetically Modified'. The ensuring publicity has given greater voice to MAdGE, which now sees itself as a campaign where 'Mothers Are Demystifying Genetic Engineering'.

'Counter crimes' can therefore be seen as a spectrum of acts of crime or disobedience that have used food to make public statements. Collectively, 'counter crimes' are an oppositional force against the current malpractices of the industrial food system.

The politics of alternative agri-food movements

Notably, some examples of 'counter crime', such as anti-globalisation protests led by Jose Bové mentioned earlier, constitute criminal damage *themselves*. Others, such as guerilla gardening, are more about contested spaces and the use of space without permission, yet this, too, may constitute illegal activity – namely, trespassing (Hardman and Larkham, 2014).

Collectively, spaces of resistance constitute alternative agri-food movements. These movements aim to use protests to invite government and consumer scrutiny to the policies and practices of what Neil Hamilton calls 'Big Food' (Hamilton, 2004). 'Big Food' refers to the transnational food and beverage industry that is powerful, profit-driven and focused on the production of cheap, nutrient-poor food, with serious consequences for public health and the environment.

Alternative agri-food movements are divided into two categories of political activity: oppositional and constructivist. Examples such as guerilla gardening and activities opposing animal treatment in industrial feedlots constitute forms of oppositional politics. Oppositional activities are 'primarily aimed at directly opposing and challenging existing institutions or structures/practices in an attempt to reform/transform aspects of the dominant agri-food system' (Scrinis, 2007, p 123).

In their analysis of how alternative food movements may stimulate change, Stevenson and colleagues (2007) proposes the 'Warrior, Builder, Weaver' framework as change agents. 'Warriors' are alternative food system actors who work to transform the food system through resistance activities. These may include efforts that are confrontational or draw attention to issues, such as public protests. 'Builders' seek to create new food systems or collaborative structures that strive for goals of sustainability, equity and health. 'Weavers' are responsible for creating civil society coalitions and fostering participation as well as creating linkages between 'Warriors' and 'Builders' (Stevenson et al, 2007). These orientations are not mutually exclusive, but in considering this framing with respect to counter crime, some food movement actors may use oppositional politics, and thus predominantly function as 'Warriors'.

A good example of the effectiveness of oppositional politics is the ban on the international export of live Australian cattle. Animals Australia (2011) is an organisation dedicated to preventing animal cruelty, especially with respect to the factory farming of chickens, pigs and the live cattle export trade. In 2011, Animals Australia publicly released damning video footage of the mistreatment of Australian live cattle exported to Indonesia. The resulting political furore forced an international live cattle export trade ban, while investigations were conducted in abattoirs and more humane slaughter techniques implemented (Animals Australia, 2011).

Food movements undertaking constructivist politics differ from oppositional activities in that they involve new ways of operating as a form of 'resistance' to 'Big Food'. Constructivist activities are incubators for the emergence of *new* food systems, whereas oppositional activities focus on the *current* food system. Constructivist efforts involve fostering and building different food systems for consumers, underpinned by democratic processes. Examples include farmers' markets and community gardens. In terms of Stevenson and colleagues' (2007) framework, such constructivist activities involve actors functioning as 'Builders' and 'Weavers', with minimal 'Warrior' activities.

'Counter crimes' using oppositional politics or resistance activities can be newsworthy and attract a high profile (such as the live cattle export example above), but may be intermittent. The sporadic nature of, and effort involved in, oppositional activities may mean these activities fade from the public consciousness more quickly than constructivist approaches. However, a more sustained counter crime comes from food democracy, as a coordinated alternative that uses constructivist politics to build new food systems such as farmers' markets. Food democracy in action, such as farmers' markets, is a case in point. The rise and expansion of farmers' markets in Australia and similar countries are well entrenched public displays of constructivist politics in action. The next section explores the nature of food democracy, its underlying principles and examples.

Food democracy

Food democracy is a movement that uses fundamental principles of democracy to make a stand against food crime and 'Big Food'. In comparison to the 'counter crimes' explored in the previous section, food democracy activities are broader in focus and seek to operate within the bounds of the law. Also called food citizenship, food democracy is a social movement based on the idea that individuals can and should participate more actively in the food system, thus transforming individuals from passive food consumers to active food citizens. Small but consistent efforts by concerned citizens at individual, household and community level can be fruitful in achieving a more equitable and just food system.

The nature and importance of democracy

Composed of the Greek words *demos* meaning 'the people' and *kratos* meaning 'power', democracy's root meaning is 'power of the people' (Ober, 2008). Ober's critical analysis of the meaning of democracy in ancient Greece argues that the 'power' inherent in democracy is not about the authority to decide matters by majority rule such as a voting; rather, it is power in the sense of the 'capacity to do things' (Ober, 2008). In terms of the global food system, power is concentrated among a few multinational corporations, so Ober's 'capacity to do things' involves people having the locus of control and power over food production, thus reclaiming it from 'Big Food'. Barber (1984) calls this 'strong democracy' whereby people use democratic principles to actively engage and participate in actions that re-shape the food system for the better.

Key dimensions of food democracy proposed by Hassanein (2008) include citizens collaborating towards food system sustainability by building coalitions to direct power and effect change. In addition to collaborative action, food democracy involves participatory democracy or meaningful participation. Hassanein (2008) proposes meaningful participation involves citizens: becoming knowledgeable about food and the food system; sharing ideas about the food system with others; developing efficacy with respect to the food system; and acquiring an orientation towards community good. Food democracy, then, uses principles of openness and transparency, freedom of information and exchange and participatory dialogue. It is these principles that transform passive consumers into active food citizens.

Hassanein's dimensions align with 'deep democracy' as described by Carlson and Chappell (2015). 'Deep democracy' is a tool to create sustainable food systems that place citizens at the centre of decision-making processes via participatory governance. In 'deep democracy', actively listening and discussing issues with others informs citizens' values. An example of 'deep democracy' is citizens' juries, whereby a sample of citizens are briefed on complex issues such as GM food or biotechnology, and discuss possible issues in order to foster better decision-making (Carlson and Chappell, 2015).

Food democracy in action

In practice, food democracy operates at several loci – individual, community and national levels – each offering citizens different levels of control and influence on 'Big Food', as illustrated below. The multiplicity of entry points, voices, organisations and interests to participate in food democracy provides invaluable diversity. Diversity is a key feature of social movements, and Hassanein (2003) notes three positive aspects with respect to community and national levels of action. First, different social movement organisations address specific problems and thereby fulfil different functions of the movement. Second, a diversity of organisational approaches gives their members an opportunity to participate in different ways. And finally, different organisational approaches foster vitality that can lead to new insights and practices.

Food democracy at individual/household level

Urban agriculture underpins the wider food democracy movement and can be defined as 'growing fruits, herbs and vegetables, and raising animals in cities, a process that is accompanied by many supplementary activities such as processing and distributing food, collecting and re-using food waste and rainwater, and educating, organising and employing local residents' (Cohen et al, 2012, p 13). Implicit in urban agriculture is the role of individuals and families exerting control and participating meaningfully to build resilient local food systems. Urban agriculture activities include backyard food production, school and restaurant gardens, street gardens and verge plantings, urban beehives, and vertical and rooftop gardens (Burton et al, 2013). Urban agriculture is not new. Historically, backyard food production galvanised the nation during wartime (Gaynor, 2016). It remains relevant today as a buffer against the disruption of global food supply chains due to extreme weather events, strikes or oil shortages, which can leave local communities vulnerable (Gertel, 2005).

Urban agriculture in Australian cities is motivated by consumer concerns about food provenance and a desire to reconnect with nature and seasonality by growing more of their own food (Burton et al, 2013). Backyard food production is popular with 52 per cent of all households growing some of their food, and a further 13 per cent planning to (Wise, 2014). The food potential of suburban home garden production is considerable, with modelling in Western Sydney estimating 800–1100 kilograms per year (Ghosh, 2011).

Urban agriculture offers significant health, social and community benefits. These include stronger social connections, increased awareness and consumption of fresh produce, increased physical activity and food security and greater awareness of food provenance. This results in a higher degree of control of the food system for consumers, decreased reliance on 'Big Food' and improved health outcomes (Edwards, 2011; Kortright and Wakefield, 2011; Burton et al, 2013).

Food democracy at community level

Farmers' markets are defined as 'a predominantly fresh food market that operates regularly within a community at a focal public location that provides a suitable environment for farmers and specialty food producers to sell farm origin and associated value-added specialty foods for human consumption' (Australian Farmers' Markets Association, 2016). Consumer drive for food provenance, high-quality fresh produce and connection with those who grow food has fuelled the expansion of farmers' markets. Well-established farmers' markets exist in North America (Lowery et al, 2016), Canada (Dodds et al, 2014), the UK and Australia (Fielke and Bardsley, 2013), with emerging markets in Czechoslovakia (Spilkova et al, 2013) and Italy (Lanfranchi and Gianetto, 2014).

Hassanein's (2008) key principles of food democracy are evident at farmers' markets. Customers are provided with quality produce, authenticity, transparency, reliability and a sense of trustworthiness – the latter lacking from 'Big Food' in recent times. Markets offer consumers direct contact and communication with farmers and growers where information and learning occurs (Woodburn, 2014). Scottish consumer research suggests the growth of farmers' markets is related to consumer demand for fresh food, direct from growers, and offers a means to express consumer values associated with food choices (Carey et al, 2011).

Farmers supplying supermarkets are paid low prices and required to meet unreasonable cosmetic standards for produce (Booth and Coveney, 2015). In contrast, farmers' market sales allow farmers to regain control from supermarkets, access direct customer feedback and gain economic benefit (Woodburn, 2014). Other advantages for farmers include diversifying distribution channels, creating sufficient demand and business growth opportunities (Woodburn, 2014). Local communities also reap economic benefits from farmers' markets in terms of community wellbeing, tourism and employment (Woodburn, 2014). In Australia, the Victorian farmers' markets contribute an estimated $227 million to the economy (Parliament of Victoria Outer Suburban/Interface Services and Development Committee, 2010). Indeed, farmers' markets have been considered a 'win-win' for all (Coster and Kennedy, 2005).

Food democracy at national/state level

At state and national level, food democracy has the potential to galvanise citizens via alliances, networks and campaigns. In the absence of a current Australian food and nutrition policy or related leadership, the actions of food democrats building multi-stakeholder alliances at these levels are critically important. Examples, such as the Australian Food Sovereignty Alliance (AFSA), Sydney Food Fairness Alliance (SFFA) and Sustain: The Australian Food Network, are helping to build the food democracy momentum by providing a higher-level focus for topical food system issues and building consumer awareness and participation. State and national networks such as these have been shown to increase the success of movements in several ways, such as by stimulating social mobilisation, building alliances, facilitating the diffusion of ideas and practices, contributing to a more sustained level of activity and establishing legitimate and political forms of organisation

(Levcoe, 2014). Networks strengthen food movements, such as food democracy, and are an important catalyst for food system transformation at state and national levels.

Food democracy and food aid: a case study in France

Food aid in France transformed itself through a process of exploiting the current culprits of food waste. Based on the notion of participation in systems of food aid, movements in France undermined conventional food aid programmes and radically shaped how food was made available to those populations with a history of food insecurity.

Although the French state recognises food as a basic need, there is no right to food in France. Only the Universal Declaration of Human Rights of 1948 in its Article 25 mentions the right to food access. France is largely sufficient in food quantity and quality, and few in France die of hunger. However, there is a population in France (about 4.2 million people) that is unable to access adequate and sufficient food on a regular basis. This intermittent supply of food can be described as 'food precariousness' and represents a state known as 'food insecurity'.

From distribution to participation

In response to such food precariousness or insecurity, the French food aid system defied existing models of food relief and radicalised food insecurity within principles of food democracy. In the 1980s, a significant increase in the number of people requesting food aid required a rethinking of the food distribution system (Paturel, 2013). In 1984, several charities gathered to create the first French food bank in Paris. These were based on the US model of food distribution to the needy. In December 1985, a French actor, Michel Coluche, created the Restos du Cœur – or the Restaurant of Love, a French charity distributing food packages and hot meals to people in need – and developed the principle of taxation called Coluche. This law, which continues to this day, allows a tax reduction of 75 per cent of the amount of a donation if it is made in favour of an association or a foundation whose object is the free provision of meals, care or accommodation to people in difficulty.

From the onset of the economic crisis, the types of food aid recipients became more complex. Initially, recipients consisted of people represented as excluded and marginalised and to whom 'food was to be fed'. This eventually broadened to include other groups such as low-income single-parent families, unemployed people, migrants and asylum-seekers, and families awaiting examination of their application for financial assistance. Some recipients were not experiencing 'food precariousness', but their plight was deemed to be in need of redress.

Gradually a practice and discourse emerged based on 'food donation with counterpart', that is, the necessity of food aid recipients to be an integral element of participation (as financial counterpart) in the initiative. Consequently, the concept of the active participation of food aid recipients was placed at the heart of projects addressing food insecurity – which was counter to conventional thinking and practice.

From passive distribution to participation as a goal

Gradually, food aid in parts of France diversified, by adding actions such as Restos du Coeur and food gardens, food banks and various workshops, kitchens and budgets. In this way, food aid resisted being mortgaged to emergency interventions only, and sought to address long-term actions needed to address food insecurity. In March 2003, a plan to strengthen the prevention and fight against poverty defined priority areas for the prevention of exclusion and marginalisation. For the first time, nutritional support for the most disadvantaged became a priority.

Out of a number of initiatives, social grocery stores developed as radical alternatives to conventional food banking, and the National Association for the Development of Solidarity Grocery Stores (ANDES) emerged as a peak body for this sector. This Association speaks of a food divide and, as such, raises concerns about the presence of food insecurity in disadvantaged populations. However, in so doing it has adopted a different discourse. Rather than assuming a position of product choice constrained by supply – a food aid recipient paradigm – the discourse starts with an assumption of a freedom of choice of products – a consumer-focused paradigm.

The Uniterres project

Food security in France took one step further in 2012, when one of the employees of ANDES created the Uniterres project. The aim of Uniterres is to create links between producers and consumers of solidarity grocery stores, and to participate in the development and maintenance of local and regional primary horticulture and agriculture. However, a fundamental aspect of this is making fresh and quality products available to people in precarious situations via the network of solidarity or social grocery stores (noting that farmers use food aid as a beneficiary). Three main principles underpin the project. The first principle involves the direct supply of food to social and solidarity grocery stores. Thanks to a one-year pre-order system by solidarity grocery stores, negotiated at 'fair' prices each year for the season, producers can count on the security of finding a ready market for their products. Products are offered on a self-service basis at prices less than 30 per cent below normal. A second principle involves participatory actions such as cooking workshops and farm visits, while a third principle posits individual support for vulnerable producers by the rural coordinator, Uniterres.

The principles of Uniterres aligns with Stevenson and colleagues' three goals for changing the food system: including the poorest, beneficiaries and producers, changing the rules of food aid supply, and developing a food transition through coaching (such as Atelier Parents/ Enfants, Producer's table, visit to farms). The success of solidarity grocery stores lies in the exploitation of a productionist food system of excess in which food aid acts to distribute surpluses. In contrast, solidarity stores use food aid to encourage interaction with the food supply, by participating in production. In so doing, it is working within the current food system to modernise food aid in the current neoliberal context.

Conclusion

Food crimes, those involving illegal, criminal, harmful, unjust or unethical food-related issues, are rife within a global food system that sees food primarily as a commodity. Acts of resistance or counter crimes have emerged in response to the harms done, through both oppositional and constructivist politics. Food democracy is a method of organised counter crime against the malpractices of 'Big Food'. Food democracy goes beyond a single issue focus and is advantageous because it does not rely on oppositional politics; rather, it is a sophisticated and systemic method of organised counter crime that uses constructivist approaches to positively shape new or improved food systems. According to Stevenson and colleagues' (2007) framework, constructivist approaches can be distinguished from oppositional approaches as they involve mainly 'Builder' and 'Weaver' activities with minimal 'Warrior' roles. In and of itself, food democracy activities will never replace or seriously contest the current food system; however, it offers citizens *some* control, choice and freedom. The food democracy movement (also known as 'Small Food') sits alongside 'Big Food' and helps create a quiet revolution, acting as a constant reminder of ways in which citizens can actively participate in remaking the food system.

References

Animals Australia (2011) 'Ban on live cattle trade to Indonesia', 8 June (www.animalsaustralia.org/media/in_the_news.php?article=2420).

Australian Farmers' Markets Association (2016) Home page (www. farmersmarkets.org.au).

Barber, B. (1984) 'Strong democracy: Politics as a way of living', in B. Barber (ed) *Strong democracy: Participatory politics for a new age*, Berkeley, CA: University of California Press, pp 117–38.

Bartl, A. (2011) 'Barriers towards achieving a zero waste society', *Waste Management*, vol 31, no 12, pp 2369–70.

Booth, S. and Coveney, J. (2015) *Food democracy – From consumer to food citizen*, Singapore: Springer.

Bové, J. and Dufour, F. (2000) *Le monde n'est pas une merchandise*, Paris: Éditions la Découverte.

Burton, P., Lyons, K., Ricahrds, C., Amati, M., Rose, N., Du Fours, L. and Barclay, R. (2013) *Urban food security, urban resilience and climate change*, Gold Coast, QLD: National Climate Change Adaptation Research Facility.

Campbell, C. and Macintosh, B. (2015) *Report on mapping of the charitable food sector*, Preliminary draft report, Health Promotion Special Initiative, Perth, WA: Curtin University.

Caraher, M. and Coveney, J. (2004) 'Public health nutrition and food policy', *Public Health Nutrition*, vol 7, no 5, pp 591–8.

Carey, L., Bell, P., Duff, A., Sheridan, M. and Shield, M. (2011) 'Farmers' market consumers: A Scottish perspective', *International Journal of Consumer Studies*, vol 35, no 3, pp 300–6.

Carlson, J. and Chappell, M. (2015) *Deepening food democracy*, Minneapolis, MN: Institute for Agriculture and Trade Policy.

Chapman, S. (1996) 'Civil disobedience and tobacco control: The case of BUGA UP – Billboard Utilising Graffitists Against Unhealthy Promotions', *Tobacco Control*, vol 5, no 3, pp 179–85.

Cohen, N., Reynolds, K. and Sanghvi, R. (2012) *Five Borough Farm: Seeding the future of urban agriculture in New York City*, New York: Design Trust for Public Space in partnership with Added Value.

Coster, M. and Kennedy, N. (2005) *New generation farmer's markets in rural communities*, Camberra, ACT: Rural Industries Research and Development Corporation, Australian Government.

Devin, B. and Richards, C. (2016) 'Food waste, power and corporate responsibility in the Australian food chain', *Journal of Business Ethics*, April, doi: 10.1007/s10551-016-3181-z.

Dodds, R., Holmes, M., Arunsopha, V., Chin, N., Le, T., Maung, S. and Shum, M. (2014) 'Consumer choice and farmers' markets', *Journal of Agriculture and Environmental Ethics*, vol 27, no 3, pp 397–416.

Edwards, F. (2011) 'Small, slow and shared: Emerging social innovations in Australian landscapes', *Australian Humanities Review*, vol 51, pp 115–34.

Fielke, J. and Bardsley, D. (2013) 'South Australian farmers' markets: Tools for enhancing the multifunctionality of Australian agriculture', *GeoJournal*, vol 78, no 5, pp 759–76.

Gaynor, A. (2016) 'Is it time to resurrect the wartime "Grow Your Own" campaign', *The Conversation*, 28 October (https://theconversation.com/is-it-time-to-resurrect-the-wartime-grow-your-own-campaign-66337).

Gertel, J. (2005) 'Inscribed bodies within commodity chains', in N. Fold and B. Pritchard (eds) *Cross continental food chains*, London: Routledge, pp 109–24.

Ghosh, S. (2011) *Growing healthy local food: Sustainability potential and household production in home gardens*, Melbourne.

Hamilton, N. (2004) 'Food democracy and the future of American values', *Drake Journal of Agriculture*, vol 9, no 1, pp 9–31.

Hardman, M. and Larkham, P. (2014) 'Guerrilla urban agriculture: Unearthing the hidden movement', in M. Hardman and P. Larkham (eds) *Informal urban agriculture – The secret lives of guerrilla gardeners*, Switzerland: Springer International, pp 1–7.

Hassanein, N. (2003) 'Practising food democracy: A pragmatic politics of transformation', *Journal of Rural Studies*, vol 19, no 1, pp 77–86.

Hassanein, N. (2008) 'Locating food democracy: Theoretical and practical ingredients', *Journal of Hunger & Nutrition*, vol 3, no 2-3, pp 286–308.

Hinrichs, C. (2007) 'Practice and place in remaking the food system', in C.C. Hinriches and T.A. Lyson (eds) *Remaking the North American food system – Strategies for sustainability*, Lincoln, NE: University of Nebraska Press, pp 1–15.

Kortright, R., and Wakefield, S. (2011) 'Edible backyards: A qualitative study of household food growing and contribution to food security', *Journal of Agriculture and Human Values*, vol 28, no 1, pp 39–53.

Lanfranchi, M. and Gianetto, C. (2014) 'Analysis of producers knowledge of farmers' markets', *Italian Journal of Food Science*, vol 26, no 3, pp 335–40.

Levcoe, C.Z. (2014) 'The food movement in Canada: A social movement network perspective', *The Journal of Peasant Studies*, vol 41, no 3, pp 385–403.

Lockie, S., Lawrence, G., Lyons, K. and Grice, J. (2005) 'Factors underlying support or opposition to biotechnology among Australian food consumers and implications for retailer-led food regulation', *Food Policy*, vol 30, no 4, pp 399–418.

Lowery, B., Sloan, D., Payán, D., Illum, J. and Lewis, L. (2016) 'Do farmers' markets increase access to healthy foods for all communities? Comparing markets in 24 neighbourhoods in Los Angeles', *Journal of the American Planning Association*, vol 82, no 3, pp 252–66.

Mehta, K., Handsley, E., Ward, P. and Coveney, J. (2014) 'Parents' and children's perceptions of the ethics of food marketing on the Internet: Implications for policy to restrict children's exposure', *Public Health Ethics*, vol 7, no 1, pp 21–34.

Ober, J. (2008) 'The original meaning of "democracy": Capacity to do things, not majority rule', *Constellations*, vol 15, no 1, pp 3–9.

Paturel, D. (2013) *Aide alimentaire et accès à l'alimentation en France [Food aid and access to food in France]* (www.academia.edu/19835962/Aide_alimentaire_et_acc%C3%A8s_%C3%A0_lalimentation_en_France).

Parliament of Victoria Outer Suburban/Interface Services and Development Committee (2010) *Inquiry into farmers' markets*, Melbourne.

Richards, C. and Devin, B. (2016) 'Powerful supermarkets push the cost of food waste onto suppliers, charities', *The Conversation*, 29 February (http://theconversation.com/powerful-supermarkets-push-the-cost-of-food-waste-onto-suppliers-charities-54654).

Saint Louis, C. (2016) 'Foodbanks take on a Contributor to diabetes: Themselves', *The New York Times*, 17 June (www.nytimes.org).

Scrinis, G. (2007) 'From techno-corporate food to alternative agri-food movements', *Local Global: Identity, Security, Community*, vol 4, pp 112–40.

Spilkova, J., Fendrychova, L. and Syrovatkova, M. (2013) 'Farmers' markets in Prague: New challenges within urban shoppingscapes', *Agriculture and Human Values*, vol 30, no 2, pp 179–91.

Stevenson, G.W., Ruhf, K., Lezberg, S. and Clancy, K. (2007) 'Warrior, builder and weaver work – Strategies for changing the food system', in C.C. Hinrichs and T. Lyson (eds) *Remaking the North American food system – Strategies for sustainability*, Lincoln, NE: University of Nebraska Press, pp 33–61.

Tonkin, B. (2016) *Supermarkets and grocery stores in Australia*, IBIS World Industry report, G411.

Tracey, D. (2007) *Guerrilla gardening: A manifesto*, Gabriola Island, BC: New Society Publishers.

Wise, P. (2014) 'Grow your own: The potential value and impact of residential and community food gardening', Policy Brief No 59, Canberra, ACT: The Australia Institute.

Woodburn, V. (2014) *Understanding the characteristics of Australian farmers' markets*, Canberra, ACT: Rural Industries Research and Development Corporation.

23

Consumer reactions to food safety scandals: A research model and moderating effects

Camilla Barbarossa

Introduction

Food safety scandals are defined as well-known events related to food safety issues or harms associated with some food brands or products (Röhr et al, 2005). Perrier's chemical benzene-contaminated mineral water (James, 1990), Coca-Cola's fungicide-contaminated soft-drinks (BBC News, 1999), the *E. coli* outbreak in Taco Bell's lettuce (CNN, 2006), Sanlu's melamine-contaminated baby formula (BBC News, 2008), the European horsemeat adulteration (BBC News, 2013), KFC and Pizza Hut's sale of expired meat (Bora, 2014), Caraga candy poisonings (ABS-CBN, 2015), the listeriosis outbreak involving contaminated beef in Ontario (Weatherill, 2009), and Mars product recall after plastics were found in Snickers chocolate bars (Quinn et al, 2016) represent a few examples of food safety incidents.

While minor food product imperfections may mildly inconvenience consumers, food safety issues can conversely result in serious injuries for consumers' health. For instance, due to Sanlu's melamine-contaminated baby formula, four infants died from kidney damage and 54,000 babies were hospitalised (NBC News, 2008). Furthermore, food safety scandals may represent striking threats to food companies. For example, food safety scandals can generate negative consumer responses toward a food company deemed accountable of commercialising harmful products (Verbeke, 2001), affect competing food brands' sales, even if the latter were not involved in the scandal (Bakhtavoryan et al, 2014), and even damage consumer confidence in the safety and quality of the whole food industry (Berg, 2004). Food safety issues therefore have severe implications for individual wellbeing, public welfare and environmental health (see Chapter 1, this volume).

Due to the concern that food safety issues generate, it is quite easy to justify concern for food and food systems, and it is of the utmost importance to investigate how consumers respond to food safety scandals and the companies deemed accountable for these incidents. To this end, scholars and marketers are now calling for more research into the psychological mechanisms through which consumers form attributions of responsibility toward food companies involved in food safety scandals, the psychological processes through which attributions of blame drive negative consumer responses toward the food brand at fault, and the variables that may influence judgements of blame and subsequent responses in the context of a food safety scandal (Regan et al, 2015).

This chapter attempts to address these issues. In so doing, it has three aims. First, it aims to provide theoretical bases for the psychological mechanisms through which consumers form judgements of blame toward food brands involved in food safety scandals. Second, it aims to clarify how attributions of blame negatively affect relevant consumer non-behavioural responses (emotions and attitude) and behavioural responses (purchase intention, word-of-mouth and boycott) toward faulty food brands. And third, it aims to provide a literature review of the most relevant consumer-, brand- and context-related variables, which may influence the psychological mechanisms of blame attribution, and subsequent non-behavioural and behavioural responses, in the context of a food safety incident.

This work provides scholars researching in the field of (ethical) food consumption, product harm crises and food safety scandals, as well as brand managers and policy-makers operating in the food industry, with important answers to the following questions: What reactions do consumers have toward brands involved in food safety scandals? What are the psychological mechanisms behind these responses? How do consumer-, brand- and context-related variables influence these processes? To practitioners operating in the food industry, knowledge gained from this work is also essential because it sheds light on the variables that they could use to reduce consumer perceptions of brand culpability and therefore obtain more favourable responses toward the faulty food brand.

The rest of the chapter is organised as follows. First, the chapter presents theoretical work on the psychological mechanisms through which consumers form an attribution of blame. Second, the literature on the non-behavioural and behavioural consequences of blame attribution is reviewed. Third, the most significant consumer-, brand- and context-related variables that impact the psychological mechanisms described above are analysed. Finally, the chapter concludes with implications for food brand managers and practitioners operating in the food industry.

Consumer attributions of blame and the causal variables of attributions

Consumer evaluations of brands involved in a food safety scandal are partly based on attributions of *blame* (Folkes, 1984), that is, the extent to which consumers perceive the food brand as being responsible, accountable and blameworthy for the food harm (Berg, 2004; Bánáti, 2011; Yamoah and Yawson, 2014; Barnett et al, 2016). In this regard, Weiner's (2000) causal variables of attributions represent a meaningful framework to understand how consumers spontaneously construct attributions of responsibility toward faulty food brands, based on their appraisal of a food scandal (Weiner, 2010; Regan et al, 2015).

When applied to food harm crises, Weiner's model conceptualises three causal dimensions of attributions that lead to an overall judgement of blame: the locus, stability and controllability of the harmful behaviour. *Locus* refers to the extent to which consumers perceive the company ('internal locus'), rather than other parties such as suppliers, trade associations, governments or consumers ('external locus') to be the source of a crisis. *Stability* refers to the extent to which consumers perceive the negative event as recurrent in the company's life (that is, consumers recognise the negative event as an enduring and repetitive company occurrence) or occasional (that is, consumers recognise the negative event as an occasional, provisional company occurrence). Finally, *controllability* refers to the extent to which consumers believe the brand has control over the negative event. The negative event can be perceived to be within the brand's control (that is, the company could have predicted the negative event) or outside the brand's control (that is, the company was unable to predict the negative event). Hence, the more consumers perceive that the food company is directly responsible for the food crime, is recurrently involved in a series of food safety incidents, and could have controlled the negative event, the more they attribute responsibility to the agent food company and blame it for the food safety scandal (Klein and Dawar, 2004; Gupta, 2009). Figure 23.1 represents this conceptual model.

Empirical evidence corroborates this causal flow. In the context of consumer reactions to the 2013 horsemeat scandal, Barbarossa and colleagues (2016) analysed how Weiner's (2000) causal variables of attributions led consumers to form attributions of responsibility toward food brands involved in that incident. They found that the more consumers perceive the locus of the horsemeat scandal as internal and the company's harmful behaviour as stable and controllable, the more they attribute higher responsibility to the agent food company and direct their negative reactions against it.

Figure 23.1: Appraisal of food harms, attributions of blame, non-behavioural and behavioural responses toward a faulty food brand, and moderating variables

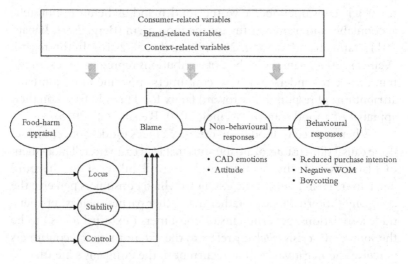

Non-behavioural responses: negative moral emotions and unfavourable attitudes

Ascription of responsibility by consumers directly or indirectly exposed to the food safety scandal engenders both negative moral emotions and unfavourable attitudes toward a faulty food brand. With reference to negative moral emotions, Haidt (2003, p 853) defines moral emotions as those 'that are linked to the interests or welfare either of society as a whole or at least of persons other than the judge or agent.' Among 'other-focused' moral emotions with negative valence, righteous anger, disgust and contempt (also known in the moral emotion literature as the 'CAD triad') play a pivotal role in understanding consumer reactions to food safety scandals (Tse et al, 2016). *Righteous anger* (hereafter defined as anger) is a retrospective emotion of painful feelings, describing a desire or impulse for revenge elicited when an individual becomes aware that freedom or human dignity has been violated (Haidt, 2003). *Disgust* describes something 'revolting', an affective reaction experienced when the human respect is violated (Tangney et al, 2007). *Contempt* refers to the negative evaluation of others in terms of their social or ethical conduct, and is considered a blend of anger and disgust.

Early research considered contempt, anger and disgust as distinct emotions elicited by partially different moral violations, which lead to partially different consequent actions. However, recent research in consumer behaviour has emphasised that in real situations of corporate social irresponsibility, such as food safety scandals, the likelihood is great that these negative emotions jointly occur together to drive punitive actions against the wrongdoing food company. As will be discussed in the next section, CAD emotions may indeed drive consumers to avoid purchasing the food company's products, engage in negative word-of-mouth and boycott the food company's products (Xie et al, 2015). Chiu (2016) investigated consumer reactions to companies involved in the food safety problem of the adulteration of edible oil with 'recycled waste oil' in Taiwan in September 2014, to find that anger, contempt and umbrage jointly drove consumers to participate in boycotting activities.

Besides the development of negative moral emotions toward the faulty food brand, consumer attributions of blame also affect consumer *attitudes* toward the faulty food company. The theory of cognitive dissonance (Festinger, 1957) corroborates this notion. Individuals seek to maintain congruity between thoughts, evaluations and actions, because they strive for internal consistency. An individual who experiences inconsistency tends to become psychologically uncomfortable, and is motivated to try to reduce this dissonance through his or her behaviour. Hence, when individuals perceive that a company is responsible and blameworthy for a food scandal, they tend to develop negative predispositions towards the faulty food company. Empirical findings in the domain of product harm crises provide compelling evidence that judgement of culpability increases perceptions of a company as being bad, unfavourable and negative. Jorgensen (1994) applied Weiner's (2000) model of consumer attributions in the context of serious company disasters, such as an airline crash or a food poisoning incident, and found that consumer attributions of blame diminish positive attitudes toward the company.

Behavioural responses: unwillingness to buy, negative word-of-mouth and boycotting

Attribution of blame leads consumers to develop negative consumption behaviours, such as consumers' avoidance (or reduction) in purchasing the food company's products in the aftermath of a scandal, their engagement in actions of negative word-of-mouth against the food company, and the boycotting of the company's harmful food products (Braunsberger and Buckler, 2011). Consumer-reduced purchase intentions, negative word-of-mouth and boycotting result from the direct effect of attribution of blame, as well as from its indirect effects through negative emotions of CAD and unfavourable attitudes toward the faulty food brand. The more consumers blame the food company for a food scandal, the more they develop negative emotions of CAD and unfavourable attitudes toward the faulty food company, and the more likely they are to reduce their purchase intentions, engage in negative word-of-mouth and boycott the food company's products (see Figure 23.1).

Consumer *unwillingness* (or reduced intention) to purchase the faulty brand in the aftermath of a food scandal can be defined as consumers' stated beliefs that they will not purchase (or that they will purchase to a lower extent) from the food company at fault at some future date (Barbarossa et al, 2016). Deciding not to purchase from the wrongdoing food company is an evaluative-driven behaviour, a deliberate problem-focused coping strategy through which the consumer eliminates the potential chance of future harmful experiences. It is also an emotion-focused coping strategy, through which the consumer aims to reduce their emotional discomfort and restore control (Bánáti, 2011). Verbeke (2001) analysed consumer beliefs, attitude and behaviour toward fresh meat consumption in Belgium, after the BSE crisis. Findings show that consumer appraisal of the BSE crisis significantly impacts the attitude toward consuming fresh meat, which, in turn, influences the actual consumption of fresh meat.

Negative word-of-mouth can be defined as interpersonal communication concerning a food company that is aimed at denigrating the food company and its products. This is considered an emotion-driven behaviour, because it is commonly less considered, more spontaneous and thus more likely to reflect instant emotional states. 'Easing anger' is a key motivator of negative word-of-mouth, because consumers tend to voice their negative emotions, and therefore obtain emotional release, through engaging in this behaviour. In the context of severe service failures in high-class hotels, Xie and Heung (2012) analysed the effects of perceived stability and controllability on consumers' negative emotional responses, such as anger, resentment and disappointment. They found that the more consumers perceive the service failure as stable and controllable by the company, the more they develop negative emotions of anger, resentment and disappointment, which, in turn, drive consumers to engage in punitive actions, such as reducing their purchase intentions and engaging in negative word-of-mouth.

Boycotting is an attempt by one or more parties to achieve certain objectives by urging individual consumers to refrain from making selected purchases in the marketplace. The 'urging' of a boycott normally comes from a non-governmental organisation (NGO) that is protesting corporate practices (Klein et al, 2004). NGOs may use denunciatory tactics to accuse food brands of misconduct, demand remedial actions and invite consumers to make a 'green, ethical, and/ or conscious choice' when making buying decisions by evaluating (and reacting to) the food company's behaviour (Braunsberger and Buckler, 2011; Grappi et al, 2017). For instance, in 2011 Greenpeace publicly reported John West's use of 'destructive' fishing methods to catch tuna fish, and offered the food brand at fault a chance to accept its requests and eliminate the source of the problem (Greenpeace, 2011). Later in 2016, the NGO again claimed that the food company was still using fish aggregation devices in its fishing fleet despite a promise in 2011 that 100 per cent of its tuna would have been sustainable by 2016, and invited consumers to boycott the brand (*The Guardian*, 2016).

Overall, the literature reviewed maintains that consumer appraisal of a food safety scandal leads consumers to make inferences about the causal variables of attributions, that is, locus, stability and controllability. These variables, in turn, form overall judgements of blame toward the faulty food company. Overall judgements of blame then lead consumers to develop both negative emotional reactions (for example, contempt, anger and disgust) and unfavourable attitudes toward the faulty food company. Finally, negative moral emotions and unfavourable attitudes motivate consumers to engage in punitive actions against the wrongdoing company, such as to reduce their purchase intentions, engage in negative word-of-mouth and boycotting the company's products.

However, past research shows that this process is not straightforward. Consumers may have different reactions to the same negative event. These differences may be ascribed to the effects of moderating variables that influence the effects of a food safety scandal on relevant consumer outcomes. The next section addresses these issues.

Moderating responses toward faulty food brands

A moderator can be defined as a variable that alters the direction or strength of the relationship between an antecedent and a dependent variable. Research in the literature of product harm crises found that moderators may refer to three categories: *consumer-*, *brand-* or *context-related* variables (see Figure 23.1). These categories are not exhaustive, but are the three on which this chapter focuses.

Consumer-related moderators are moderating variables pertaining to a consumer's individual characteristics or traits. In this regard, the roles of gender, age, ethical beliefs, consumer-perceived risk and attitude toward risk are investigated in the context of food safety scandals. Previous research has shown that women, more often than men, blame companies for product harm crises, and that older adults focus less on the negative information associated with a crisis, and are thus less likely to incorporate this negative information into their attitudes and preferences (Laufer and Gillespie, 2004; Silvera et al, 2012). Furthermore, consumers with strong ethical beliefs tend to attribute higher levels of responsibility to the company involved in the crisis, express high levels of anger and purchase a product from the faulty company to a lesser extent (Vassilikopoulou et al, 2011).

Furthermore, research in the context of risk perceptions related to bovine spongiform encephalopathy – commonly known as mad cow disease (or BSE) – showed that consumer-perceived risk (that is, a consumer's perceived likelihood of being exposed to harmful food products) and consumer attitude toward risk (that is, a consumer's general predisposition toward taking risks while consuming food products) play pivotal roles in affecting consumer responses to food safety scandals (Pennings et al, 2001; Fuentes and Fuentes, 2015). The combination of these two variables leads to the development of four different consumer segments (Wansink, 2004): 'accountable' (low risk aversion–low risk perception); 'concerned' (low risk aversion–high risk perception); 'conservative' (high risk aversion–low risk perception); and 'alarmist' (high risk aversion–high risk perception). 'Accountable' consumers see themselves as responsible for their own food consumption and what results from it. They ignore any available information on risk and keep their habits, even though some risk may be involved in their food consumption. They show less negative responses toward the food company, and are likely to give the food company a second chance during a food safety scandal. 'Concerned' consumers' behaviour is mainly dictated by the perceived risk associated with consuming a certain food. As perceived risk increases, they finally get to a point where they avoid consuming the food. They show severe reactions toward the faulty food company only when they are directly exposed to the food harm. 'Conservative' consumers do not take unnecessary risks about food consumption. They strongly rely on elements such as brand trust and brand familiarity to form their responses during a food safety scandal. Finally, 'alarmist' consumers exhibit the most severe reactions against a faulty food company. They also avoid consuming the products of competing food brands operating in the same industry ('negative spillover effect').

Brand-related moderators are moderating variables pertaining to the brand or the relationship between a consumer and the brand. In this regard, a food brand's post-crisis communication strategy, country-of-origin and familiarity are analysed in the context of food safety scandals. Faulty food brands' *post-crisis communication strategies* fall into two main categories (Coombs, 2007). Food brands may choose to adopt a reconciliatory orientation, by accepting the accusation of misconduct, apologising for the harmful behaviour and promising to remedy the food incident. Conversely, they may decide to adopt a defensive orientation, by ignoring, denying or even disputing the misconduct charge. Previous research showed that confessions and reconciliatory actions are more effective than defensive actions in lessening consumer negative emotional and behavioural reactions. In the fashion industry, Grappi and colleagues (2017) analysed brands' responses to Greenpeace's Detox campaign, a campaign that sought to persuade major clothing brands to eliminate all releases of hazardous chemicals from their supply chains and products. In response to this activism, some brands committed themselves to detoxify their productions (for example, Burberry and Valentino), while other brands did not (for example, Armani and Versace). The authors found that the strategic decision of the companies involved to comply with the Detox campaign was the most effective way to minimise negative consumer responses.

A food brand's *country-of-origin*, that is, the country that a consumer associates a certain food product or brand as being its source, may also impact consumer responses to a food safety scandal (Xu et al, 2013). A food company's country-of-origin associated with a highly competent (well developed) country is perceived by consumers as a diagnostic cue that the food company offers high-quality and reliable food products (Verbeke and Ward, 2006). Berry and colleagues (2015) found that consumers' inferences about the safety and quality of food products were higher for products from competent countries because of these countries' comparatively high health standards. When the food company originates from a country with a positive country image, consumers transfer the positive country image onto the food company, and are more likely to believe that the food company is able to deliver safe and high-quality products, despite its involvement in the food incident. In the context of the 2013 horsemeat scandal, Barbarossa and colleagues (2016) found that, under conditions of high country-of-origin competence, consumers perceive the product harm crisis as an occasional, rare incident, which only marginally affects the company's ability to deliver high-quality goods. Conversely, under conditions of low country-of-origin competence, consumers perceive the scandal as a potentially recurrent event in the company's life, which exacerbates their negative evaluations toward the harmful products.

Brand familiarity is defined as a consumer's direct and indirect experience with a brand, which is based on previous product usage or exposure to advertising (Laufer et al, 2009). Su and Tippins (1998) found that consumers attribute more blame to the manufacturer of a little-known brand than that of a well-known brand for product harm crisis. They claimed that this effect is due to well-recognised customers' tendency to infer high product quality from high levels of brand familiarity, thereby giving the benefit of the doubt to a well-known brand for the product harm crisis. Similarly, Dawar and Pillutla (2000) examined whether consumers' prior expectations about a brand – that are based on consumers' prior direct and indirect experience with a brand – may play a role in the impact of a product harm crisis on consumer responses. They found that consumers' strong positive prior expectations about a brand caused them to selectively seek and process confirmatory – rather than disconfirmatory – information, thereby lessening the negative impact of the crisis on their evaluations of the company.

Finally, *contextual-related factors* are moderating variables pertaining to consumer perceptions about the environment in which the faulty company operates. In this regard, the reasons consumers have for justifying a food company's unethical behaviour in the market are analysed in the context of food safety scandals. Based on d'Astous and

Legendre's (2009) work, consumers may have three main reasons for justifying food companies' unethical behaviour in the market: *reality of economic development, government dependency* and *economic rationalisation.* The *economic development* argument includes the rationalisation that economic development can only happen with a certain degree of unethical corporate behaviour. Based on this rationale, consumers believe that the negative environmental-related externalities (for example, air pollution, water contamination, antibiotic-resistant insects, diminished soil quality) and the health-related externalities (for example, outbreaks of foodborne diseases, increased overweight and obesity rates, the poor nutritional quality of food) of the large-scale food industry are the price to pay for mass-produced food (Brownell and Horgen, 2004). The *government dependency* argument refers to the beliefs that institutions, such as the government and national food safety authorities, and not companies, are responsible for legally and ethically regulating how food products should be produced and sold. Consumers believe that if there are no laws regulating food companies' misconduct, their behaviour is legal, and thus it is not justifiable to blame them for it. For example, in 2013 many consumers claimed that European Union (EU) policy, not food companies, was to blame for the horsemeat adulteration scandal, due to a lack of detailed regulation aimed at controlling the production of beef meat in Europe (Meade, 2013). Finally, the *economic rationalisation* argument claims that price and other material attributes are more important in economic exchanges than other attributes of safety and ethics, because consumers demand for cheap food, regardless of how it is manufactured (Heilig, 2003). Hence, the more consumers justify companies' unethical behaviour in the food industry – through their considerations of the reality of economic development, government dependency and economic rationalisation – the less they blame the food company for misconduct (Grappi et al, 2017), and the less they reduce their purchase intentions in the aftermath of a scandal, engage in negative word-of-mouth and boycott the food company's harmful products.

Conclusion

Food safety scandals are recurring occurrences in the food industry worldwide. Neither consumers nor food companies are immune to the highly negative consequences of these events. A deep understanding of how consumers perceive, evaluate and respond to food harm crises is of pivotal importance for scholars and practitioners. This chapter has offered a contribution toward reaching this goal. First, it has provided the theoretical bases for analysing the psychological mechanisms through which consumers form attributions of blame toward food brands involved in food safety scandals. Second, it has clarified how attributions of culpability affect relevant consumer outcomes. Finally, it has provided an overview of the most relevant variables that moderate consumer responses toward faulty food companies.

To practitioners operating in the food industry, knowledge gained from this work is essential because it clarifies the presence of different consumer segments (for example, men and women, young and adult consumers, and 'accountable', 'concerned', 'conservative' and 'alarmist' consumers, low versus high brand familiarity consumers), which are based on relevant consumer- and brand-related factors. In this regard, this chapter has clarified how practitioners should develop different post-crisis communication strategies tailored for different consumer segments. Some food safety scandals are criminally defined illegal events, others are defined as harmful, while others are defined as unethical, immoral or unjust. Many are a mixture of all of such constructions (see Chapter 1, this volume). Regardless of these different constructions, this chapter has emphasised how food companies and brands involved in food safety scandals should adopt conciliatory post-crisis communication strategies, to mitigate consumers' negative responses. The strategic decision of the companies involved in the food safety scandal to adopt a reconciliatory orientation (for example, to comply with the requests of an NGO campaign) is the most effective way to minimise negative consumer responses. From a broader perspective, this action can be compared to a confession post-crisis communication strategy, which can decrease losses and preserve the relationship with consumers and customers. Food brand managers and practitioners operating in the food industry could address the risk of a public NGO campaign by adopting the most effective strategy available; that is, they could accept responsibility, apologise and promise not to engage in such unethical (harmful or illegal) actions in the future. This commitment could stimulate virtuous initiatives focused on new, more ethical approaches. For example, Greenpeace recently lauded Nestlé and Ferrero's palm oil pledges to reduce deforestation (GreenBiz, 2016), after the recent 'Stop palm oil' campaign. Similarly, after the 'Not just tuna' Greenpeace campaign, the NGO publicly recognised brands such as Wild Planet, American Tuna and Ocean Naturals, which abandoned destructive and irresponsible practices in favour of more sustainable, ethical and fair ones (Greenpeace, 2015).

References

ABS-CBN (2015) 'Candies down over 1,600; poisoning outbreak declared', 12 July (www.abs-cbnnews.com/nation/regions/07/11/15/food-poison-outbreak-declared-caraga-region).

Bakhtavoryan, R., Capps Jr, O. and Salin, V. (2014) 'The impact of food safety incidents across brands: The case of the Peter Pan peanut butter recall', *Journal of Agricultural and Applied Economics*, vol 46, no 4, pp 559-73.

Bánáti, D. (2011) 'Consumer response to food scandals and scares', *Trends in Food Science & Technology*, vol 22, no 2, pp 56-60.

Barbarossa, C., de Pelsmacker, P., Moons, I. and Marcati, A. (2016) 'The influence of country-of-origin stereotypes on consumer responses to food safety scandals: The case of the horsemeat adulteration', *Food Quality and Preference*, vol 53, pp 71-83.

Barnett, J., Begen, F., Howes, S., Regan, A., McConnon, A., Marcu, A., Rowntree, W. and Verbeke, W. (2016) 'Consumers' confidence, reflections and response strategies following the horsemeat incident', *Food Control*, vol 59, pp 721-30.

BBC News (1999) 'Contaminated coke threatens UK', 16 June (http://news.bbc.co.uk/1/hi/uk/370517.stm).

BBC News (2008) 'Timeline: China milk scandal' (http://news.bbc.co.uk/2/hi/7720404.stm).

BBC News (2013) 'Q&A: Horsemeat scandal', 10 April (www.bbc.com/news/uk-21335872).

Berg, L. (2004) 'Trust in food in the age of mad cow disease: A comparative study of consumers' evaluation of food safety in Belgium, Britain and Norway', *Appetite*, vol 42, no 1, pp 21-32.

Berry, C., Mukherjee, A., Burton, S. and Howlett, E. (2015) 'A COOL effect: The direct and indirect impact of country-of-origin disclosures on purchase intentions for retail food products', *Journal of Retailing*, vol 91, no 3, pp 533–42.

Bora, K. (2014) 'Yum! Brands says China food scandal hurting KFC, Pizza Hut sales', *International Business Times*, 31 July (www.ibtimes.com/yum-brands-says-china-food-scandal-hurting-kfc-pizza-hut-sales-1644416).

Braunsberger, K. and Buckler, B. (2011) 'What motivates consumers to participate in boycotts: Lessons from the ongoing Canadian seafood boycott', *Journal of Business Research*, vol 64, no 1, pp 96-102.

Brownell K.D. and Horgen, K.B. (2004) *Food fight: The inside story of the food industry, America's obesity crisis, and what we can do about it*, New York: McGraw-Hill.

Chiu, H.K. (2016) 'Exploring the factors affecting consumer boycott behaviour in Taiwan: Food oil incidents and the resulting crisis of brand trust', *International Journal of Business and Information*, vol 11, no 1, pp 49-66.

CNN (2006) 'Taco Bell lettuce suspected in *E. coli* outbreak', 13 December (http://money.cnn.com/2006/12/13/news/tacobell_lettuce/index.htm?postversion=2006121322).

Coombs, W.T. (2007) 'Protecting organization reputations during a crisis: The development and application of situational crisis communication theory', *Corporate Reputation Review*, vol 10, no 3, pp 163-76.

d'Astous, A. and Legendre, A. (2009) 'Understanding consumers' ethical justifications: A scale for appraising consumers' reasons for not behaving ethically', *Journal of Business Ethics*, vol 87, no 2, pp 255-68.

Dawar, N. and Lei, J. (2009) 'Brand crises: the role of brand familiarity and crisis relevance in determining the impact on brand evaluations', *Journal of Business Research*, vol 62, no 4, pp 509-16.

Dawar, N. and Pillutla, M.M. (2000) 'Impact of product-harm crises on brand equity: The moderating role of consumer expectations', *Journal of Marketing Research*, vol 37, no 2, pp 215-26.

Festinger, L. (1957) *A theory of cognitive dissonance*, New York: Row Peterson.

Folkes, V.S. (1984) 'Consumer reactions to product failure: An attributional approach', *Journal of Consumer Research*, vol 10, no 4, pp 398-409.

Fuentes, M. and Fuentes, C. (2015) 'Risk stories in the media: Food consumption, risk and anxiety', *Food, Culture & Society*, vol 18, no 1, pp 71-87.

Grappi, S., Romani, S. and Barbarossa, C. (2017) 'Fashion without pollution: How consumers evaluate brands after an NGO campaign aimed at reducing toxic chemicals in the fashion industry', *Journal of Cleaner Production*, vol 149, April, pp 1164-73.

GreenBiz (2016) 'Greenpeace lauds Nestle and Ferrero palm oil pledges, slams others' (www.greenbiz.com/article/greenpeace-slams-lack-business-progress-palm-oil-deforestation).

Greenpeace (2011) 'And then there were none: John West changes its tuna to drop FADs' (http://web1.greenpeace.org.uk/node/226904).

Greenpeace (2015) 'Tuna shopping guide' (www.greenpeace.org/usa/oceans/tuna-guide/).

Guardian, The (2016) 'John West accused of breaking tuna pledge to end "destructive" fishing methods', 6 October (www.theguardian.com/environment/2015/oct/06/john-west-accused-of-breaking-tuna-pledge-to-end-destructive-fishing-methods).

Gupta, S. (2009) 'How do consumers judge celebrities' irresponsible behaviour? An attribution theory perspective', *Journal of Applied Business and Economics*, vol 10, no 3, pp 1-14.

Haidt, J. (2003) 'The moral emotions', in R.J. Davidson, K.R. Scherer and H.H. Goldsmith (eds) *Handbook of affective sciences*, Oxford: Oxford University Press, pp 852–70.

Heilig, G.K. (2003) 'Do we really care about food safety? Facts and myths about consumers' preferences', Proceedings of the International Symposium Food Safety: Consumer, Trade, and Regulation, Hangzhou, Zhejiang.

James, G. (1990) 'Perrier recalls its water in US after benzene is found in bottles', *The New York Times*, 10 February (www.nytimes.com/1990/02/10/us/perrier-recalls-its-water-in-us-after-benzene-is-found-in-bottles.html).

Jorgensen, B. (1994) 'Consumer reaction to company-related disasters: The effect of multiple versus single explanations', *Advances in Consumer Research*, vol 21, no 1, pp 348–52.

Klein, J.G. and Dawar, N. (2004) 'Corporate social responsibility and consumers' attributions and brand evaluations in a product-harm crisis', *International Journal of Research in Marketing*, vol 21, no 3, pp 203-17.

Klein, J.G., Smith, N.C. and John, A. (2004) 'Why we boycott: Consumer motivations for boycott participation', *Journal of Marketing*, vol 68, no 3, pp 92-109.

Laufer, D. and Gillespie, K. (2004) 'Who's to blame? Differences in consumer attributions of blame between men and women: The role of perceived vulnerability and empathic concern', *Psychology and Marketing*, vol 21, no 2, pp 209-22.

Laufer, D., Gillespie, K. and Silvera, D.H. (2009) 'The role of country of manufacture in consumers' attributions of blame in an ambiguous product-harm crisis', *Journal of International Consumer Marketing*, vol 21, no 3, pp 189-201.

Meade, G. (2013) 'Don't blame us for horsemeat scandal, says EU consumer chief', *Independent*, 13 February (www.independent.co.uk/news/world/europe/dont-blame-us-for-horsemeat-scandal-says-eu-consumer-chief-8493234.html).

NBC News (2008) 'Nearly 53,000 Chinese children sick from milk' (www.nbcnews.com/id/26827110/#.WHpc2lPhCpo).

Pennings, J.M., Wansink, B. and Meulenberg, M.T. (2002) 'A note on modeling consumer reactions to a crisis: The case of the mad cow disease', *International Journal of Research in Marketing*, vol 19, no 1, pp 91-100.

Quinn, B., Butler, S. and Smithers, R. (2016a) 'Mars recalls chocolate bars in 55 countries after plastic found in product', *The Guardian*, 23 February (www.theguardian.com/lifeandstyle/2016/feb/23/mars-chocolate-product-recalls-snickers-milky-way-celebrations-germany-netherlands).

Regan, Á., Marcu, A., Shan, L.C., Wall, P., Barnett, J. and McConnon, Á. (2015) 'Conceptualising responsibility in the aftermath of the horsemeat adulteration incident: An online study with Irish and UK consumers', *Health, Risk & Society*, vol 17, no 2, pp 149-67.

Röhr, A., Lüddecke, K., Drusch, S., Müller, M.J. and Alvensleben, R.V. (2005) 'Food quality and safety: Consumer perception and public health concern', *Food Control*, vol 16, no 8, pp 649-55.

Silvera, D.H., Meyer, T.M. and Laufer, D. (2012) 'Age-related reactions to a product harm crisis', *Journal of Consumer Marketing*, vol 29, no 4, pp 302-9.

Su, W. and Tippins, M.J. (1998) 'Consumer attributions of product failure to channel members and self: The impact of situational cues', in T.K. Srull (ed) *Advances in consumer research*, Provo, UT: Association for Consumer Research, pp 139–45.

Tangney, J.P., Stuewig, J. and Mashek, D.J. (2007) 'Moral emotions and moral behaviour', *Annual Review of Psychology*, vol 58, pp 345–72.

Tse, Y.K., Zhang, M., Doherty, B., Chappell, P. and Garnett, P. (2016) 'Insight from the horsemeat scandal: Exploring the consumers' opinion of tweets toward Tesco', *Industrial Management & Data Systems*, vol 116, no 6, pp 1178-200.

Vassilikopoulou, A., Chatzipanagiotou, K., Siomkos, G. and Triantafillidou, A. (2011) 'The role of consumer ethical beliefs in product-harm crises', *Journal of Consumer Behaviour*, vol 10, no 5, pp 279–89.

Verbeke, W. (2001) 'Beliefs, attitude and behaviour towards fresh meat revisited after the Belgian dioxin crisis', *Food Quality and Preference*, vol 12, no 8, pp 489-98.

Verbeke, W. and Ward, R.W. (2006) 'Consumer interest in information cues denoting quality, traceability and origin: An application of ordered probit models to beef labels', *Food Quality and Preference*, vol 17, no 6, pp 453-67.

Wansink, B. (2004) 'Consumer reactions to food safety crises', *Advances in Nutrition Research*, vol 48, pp 103-50.

Weiner, B. (2000) 'Attributional thoughts about consumer behaviour', *Journal of Consumer Research*, vol 27, no 3, pp 382-7.

Weiner, B. (2010) 'The development of an attribution-based theory of motivation: A history of ideas', *Educational Psychologist*, vol 45, no 1, pp 28-36.

Xie, C., Bagozzi, R.P. and Grønhaug, K. (2015) 'The role of moral emotions and individual differences in consumer responses to corporate green and non-green actions', *Journal of the Academy of Marketing Science*, vol 43, no 3, pp 333-56.

Xie, D. and Heung, V.C. (2012) 'The effects of brand relationship quality on responses to service failure of hotel consumers', *International Journal of Hospitality Management*, vol 31, no 3, pp 735-44.

Xu, H., Leung, A. and Yan, R.N.T. (2013) 'It is nice to be important, but it is more important to be nice: Country-of-origin's perceived warmth in product failures', *Journal of Consumer Behaviour*, vol 12, no 4, pp 285-92.

Weatherill, S. (2009) *Report of the independent investigator into the 2008 listeriosis outbreak*, Government of Canada.

Yamoah, F.A. and Yawson, D.E. (2014) 'Assessing supermarket food shopper reaction to horsemeat scandal in the UK', *International Review of Management and Marketing*, vol 4, no 2, pp 98-107.

24

Responding to food crime and the threat of the 'food police'

Allison Gray

Introduction

It is no accident that many published articles about food, food processing and food distribution fail to reference the crimes and harms committed by the food industry – that is, the darker side of food (see Holtzman, 2013). Nonetheless, as this volume outlines, there are a myriad of ways in which foodstuffs and food processes are entwined with immoral, unjust, harmful and illegal (in)actions. This chapter focuses on the forms of activism and food movements that react to these crimes and harms, including retort and backlash by food corporations. The first part of the chapter conceptualises the contemporary global food system as the 'risky food regime' and outlines its role in the production of food crimes and harms, and the consequences on foodstuffs and consumers. Grounded in this context, the chapter then includes a sketch of how various agents and organisations respond to these problems, including how food corporations counter these food movements and food activism through specific defence strategies. The chapter closes with a discussion of how the 'food police' are mitigating – that is, threatening – food choice, and argues that food corporations are simultaneously (and ironically) key facilitators of food crime *and* the food police.

A risky food regime

The way humanity relates to food has shifted over time, across cultures, and continues to be a largely heterogeneous personal experience for individuals. However, many researchers analysing the structural patterns of production and consumption argue that the current food system can be broadly characterised as a corporate-industrial food regime or era. Based on the work of Friedmann and McMichael (1989), McMichael (2009) defines the contemporary food system, which originated in the 1970s and gained traction in the 1980s, as being global in scope and expressed by trends of national deregulation of production systems. Termed the 'corporate food regime', it is characterised by food companies and agribusinesses holding and wielding increasing power across food chains (McMichael, 2009; Clendenning et al, 2016), where 'agrofood corporations are the major agents attempting to regulate agrofood conditions' (Friedmann, 2003, p 52). Such corporate organisation is maintained by what Pechlaner and Otero (2010) call 'neoregulation', where states actively facilitate the self-regulating mechanism of the economic market, producing a 'neoliberal food regime' encompassing both private and public sectors. Research supports this classification, with particular attention to the increasing role of retailers. For instance, while food policy is increasingly directed at processes of consumption, these middle stages of food systems become more and more powerful (Lang and Heasman, 2004). This concentration of the food industry is forming an hourglass figure, where food is funnelled between production and consumption processes, essentially making food retailers the gatekeepers of the food industry (Howard, 2016).

There are many effects of this corporatisation and concentration within the food industry. A key theme involves how the nutritional quality of foodstuffs is impacted by changing production practices. Winson (2013) has termed the current state of the global food system as the 'industrial dietary regime'. This highlights the ways that processes of industrialisation have significantly degraded food quality while producing ever greater arrays of 'nutrient-poor edible commodities' (Winson, 2013; Winson and Choi, 2016). This has instigated a 'nutrition transition' (Dixon, 2009), which involves an emphasis on nutritional discourses – or 'nutritionism' – actively constructed and maintained by food industries. In this 'functional nutritional era' the food industry uses and projects a 'nutritional gaze' where food is decontextualised and reduced to its nutrients at the expense of understanding its means of production, processing and broader quality (Scrinis, 2013). This connotes a particular interpretation at the consumption level, too. Foods are comprehended as inherently neutral: there are no good or bad foods, only good or bad diets (Lang and Heasman, 2004). Consumers are individualised and responsibilised. They are required to use rational decision-making in the form of self-help to work toward goals of personal transformation – and not to rely on, or expect, guaranteed entitlements involving food and health from regulatory bodies or public policies (Alkon and Mares, 2012). Although it seems bizarre, consumers are given the right to be *un*healthy (Lang and Heasman, 2004).

This responsibilisation of individual consumers is, in part, disseminated through forms of a crisis discourse involving food systems. For example, the so-called 'food crisis' during 2007–08 of peak food prices (see Department of Economic and Social Affairs, 2011) exemplifies a specific framing of an event as a crisis through its labelling as such – where crisis discourse functions as a technique of government (Lawrence, 2014). Crisis events, as constructed, operate as the means to desired ends. For example, certain food industry agents actively advocated for the role of the technology involved with genetically modified (GM) foods as the solution to food shortages and elevated food prices. This position, argues Stone and Glover (2011), originated from goals of marketing or public relations, rather than public interest, as the claims were very generic without specific details or scientific claims as to how exactly GM technology is a practical response.

Crisis discourse as a technique of government produces an atmosphere of uncertainty (Lawrence, 2014), and consumers develop a natural anxiety about food (Levenstein, 2012). Further bombarded with ideas and messages in the media about food risks, scares and scandals, consumers are swiftly overwhelmed about food safety (Halkier, 2001). Such anxiety and fear is compounded by the ontological assumptions of the neoliberal sociopolitical environment. Consumers are burdened to engage with, and change, the global food system through making 'good choices' (Guthman, 2008; Goodman et al, 2010). The idea is that 'consumers are key actors in the security and safety of "modern" food systems, and that they have a moral responsibility to make "good" food decisions' (Abbots and Coles, 2015, p 542). Crisis and risk narratives involving food construct this specific responsibilised 'risk handler' identity for consumers, where they are not completely blamed for food crimes and harms, but are also not pure victims (Fuentes and Fuentes, 2015). In other words, consumers are expected to choose what to eat based on rational ideations of the least risky choices in an inherently *risky food regime*.[1] Abbots and Coles (2013, p 536) argue that food crisis discourses are used to '(dis)place blame onto an (ir)responsible "other" located on social, economic, cultural and discursive margins.' Rather than bringing attention to systemic causes of food crimes and harms, this facilitates within-consumer blame, giving momentum to the 'dangers of eating cheap meat' impression that condemns consumers making poor food choices while making invisible their often vulnerable status (Abbots and Coles, 2013). The contemporary food system is encompassed by uncertainty and risk – defining food crime as a normal occurrence – and expects consumers to secure themselves against resulting harm. Unfortunately, responding to food concerns by enacting risk management strategies (such as being educated about food choices or practicing safe food handling) in a risky food regime only makes eating a more manageable practice, but does not eliminate food anxiety or solve food crimes and harms (Halkier, 2001; Milne et al, 2011; Meah and Watson, 2013). Within this perspective, the solution to food crimes and harms is 'right type of consumption – by the right type of people' (Abbots and Cole, 2013, p 546).

Responding to food crime

Due to the influence of the risky food regime, individualised responsibilised consumer-based food movements are common responses to food crimes and harms. Even food movements that are seemingly oppositional often possess elements that incorporate the centrality of the role of consumer choice. Many of the food crimes and harms outlined within this book have obvious and easy solutions framed within this perspective. Don't want to support the child slave labour in the cocoa industry? Buy fairtrade chocolate! Worried about the global obesity epidemic? Make dietary changes! Concerned about consuming horsemeat in products labelled 'beef'? Strategically purchase meats! While the contributors to this book do not solely advocate for such personal choices as solutions, these ideas are, to some extent, often embraced within many food movements in practice, from anti-GM food, to organics, to local food, to animal welfare, to veganism and more, despite being theoretically opposed to the neoliberal responsibilised consumer narrative (Guthman, 2008; Winson, 2010). This is not due to chance, as the effect of food activism is constrained by neoliberal structures that limit the possibilities of changing the food system (Alkon and Mares, 2012).

A food regime framework posits that food systems are built on – and thus are transformed through – a series of contradictions and crises (Friedmann and McMichael, 1989; McMichael, 2009; Levidow, 2015). From this perspective, food movements will be successful if tensions in the food system are dealt with in certain ways. Arguably, in the contemporary neoliberal (risky) food regime, the significant majority of food crises are denied existence (Paarlberg, 2010). Thus, there is little possibility for regime transition and restricted roles for food movements in eliciting broader structural change. Nonetheless, food movements do exist.

The key contradiction within the contemporary food regime, for Winson (2010), is the tension between the corporate-controlled food system's goal of profit maximisation and food as a basic human need. Thus, the most fundamental food movement involves efforts to ensure healthy eating in society (Winson, 2010). Virtually all food-based social movements can fall under this broad description. Food security, or the condition of accessing adequate food, food justice or the mitigation of injustices disproportionately impacting vulnerable populations, and food sovereignty, or the right to food and its production, are key examples of food movements that attempt to enhance the health of both individuals and societies, albeit in different ways. It is easy to point to the dissimilarities – and oppositions – between food movements. For instance, a food sovereignty perspective advocates for people-provided alternatives to global capitalist food systems beyond market approaches, and often criticises food justice perspectives for enabling the market and seeking assistance from the state (Clendenning et al, 2016). Similarly, a food sovereignty perspective critiques food security discourses for neglecting the structural issues involving how food is produced while using individual-focused activism such as purchasing power (Clapp, 2014).

Therefore, while the means by which food movements operate vary, their goals overlap around this idea of 'ensuring healthy eating in society'. But not all methods are equally effective. Holt-Giménez and Shattuck (2011) argue that there are two current trends in global food movements. One is labelled progressive, which is characterised by actions that work within capitalist food systems, often through advancing practical alternatives. The other is labelled radical, which is characterised by working to change systems of rights to land and food, including class-based redistribution of these resources. A key example in line with the former trend is the use of individualised consumer-based activism – a product of the risky food regime. Increasingly common, largely due to its populist scope, it tends to undermine citizenship responsibilities and state regulation and thus (partially) supports neoliberal culture (Johnston and Szabo, 2011). The most well known example of the latter trend is practised through the activism of La Via Campensina (2011), an international movement advocating, through the voices of peasants, for food and land rights for people – not corporations. While individuals are more likely to be successful in using consumer-based activism, the effect of their practices is significantly lower in terms of fundamentally impacting the foundations of food systems. Radical movements, such as La Via Campensina, seeking to change the deep structures of food production, would be very influential, yet have a very difficult time achieving these goals due to the comprehensive power of the neoliberal risky food regime.

While the risky food regime is dominant and robust, both materially and discursively, the existence of food movements and forms of resistance, no matter their effect, is evidence that the food regime is not invincible. These messages of discontent are not just originating from humans. Nature itself is showing a backlash to the environmentally damaging practices of intensive industrialised food production, including the challenges climate change, crop failures and drought have on future food production (see Chapter 19, this volume). In reaction to the unjust and harmful conditions of factory farms and concentrated animal feeding operations, farmed animals themselves are actively resisting the dominant food regime by physically escaping their confinement (Gillespie, 2015). These forms of resistance exemplify Polanyi's (1944) double-movement, when capitalist expansion produces negative effects provoking defensive reactions. The presence of these food movements move to denaturalise and historicise the capitalist market economy, allowing attentiveness to its tensions and enabling regime change. The risky food regime, however, fights back.

Countering responses to food crime

Food corporations and agribusiness actively practise various defence strategies in reaction to food movements and 'counter crimes' (see Chapter 22, this volume). One of the most common reactions involves the idea of 'corporate social responsibility' (CSR), which characterises food agents and companies that adhere to societal expectations encompassing economic, legal and ethical principles in particular contexts (Carroll, 1979, 1999). Although CSR is thoroughly voluntary, governments are often keen to encourage its acceptance and adherence by food production companies (Marotta et al, 2014). For instance, in the early 2000s, Starbucks introduced fairtrade coffee and McDonald's changed its requirements of its egg suppliers – voluntary actions that they both advertised as ways in which their companies were striving for social justice goals, but more so as ways to entice the socially just consumer to buy their products (Lang and Heasman, 2004). While these practices are seemingly good developments with benefits for (human) animal and environmental health, they are more often marketing gimmicks that make the companies appear responsible, but fail to materialise any significant improvements or changes.

The limitations of CSR centre on its voluntary use. The logic behind CSR states that 'ought implies can' but not 'ought implies will' (Hartmann, 2011). Food companies, even if they argue they utilise a CSR model, are not obliged to act on its principles. Its use in food systems is particularly problematic, as responsibility along food chains depends on the agent or member of the organisation that is the least responsible (Heikkurinen and Forsman-Huggs, 2011). But perhaps most importantly, as hinted at, CSR is more about building brand image through marketing techniques (Lang and Heasman, 2004; Richards et al, 2015). As Richards and colleagues (2015) argue, there is a very fine line between food corporations being responsible citizens, and being deceptive profit-seeking organisations neglecting public health interests. The remainder of this section outlines three themes of defence strategies used by food corporations: profit potential, blame shifting and cooptation.

The role of profit making in the food system is an unfortunate reality. Food is predominately industrial and produced by the private sector. It is well documented that corporations are able to transform dissatisfaction and rebellion into marketing opportunities (Frank, 1998; Heath and Potter, 2004; Johnston, 2008). The concepts 'greenwashing' and 'nutriwashing' have been constructed to help explain corporate reaction to food movements. Greenwashing is the 'practice of making unwarranted or overblown claims of sustainability or environmental friendliness in an attempt to gain market share' (Dahl, 2010, A234). The use of green-coloured labels and words such as 'green' or 'natural' suggest that these foodstuffs are environmentally friendly, although these claims are (often) unfounded. Nutriwashing results from food industries realising the commercial potential of advertising using nutrient-level messages, and exploiting them as such (Simon, 2006; Scrinis, 2013). For example, this occurs in beef packaging emphasising the red meat's high iron content, despite its otherwise low nutrient profile. Another example involves the labelling of yogurt products containing specific probiotic strains – an issue that Rijkers and colleagues (2011) argue represents a discrepancy as to where food science ends and business begins.

Compounded by a lack of or insufficient regulation of marketing and advertising practices, these techniques enable food companies and supermarkets to become 'cultural authorities' by creating new products to sell and building consumer preferences (Parker and Scrinis, 2014; see also Lang and Heasman, 2004; Richards et al, 2015). This has facilitated the growth of niche markets selling 'yuppie chow' or specialty food items, which are not fundamental antidotes to the agri-food system (Guthman, 2003). The nutritionism ideology is similarly problematic, as 'nutrient-focused labeling may inherently favor the interests of food manufacturing companies, as these companies are able to modify the nutrient composition of foods, and focus their marketing on particular nutrients, thereby distracting attention from the type and quality of the ingredients used in the production of their foods' (Scrinis and Parker, 2016, p 242). Thus, food corporations embrace the commercial potential of food and aim to utilise defence strategies such as greenwashing and nutriwashing through profit avenues.

Another defence strategy involves how food corporations shift blame for food crimes and harms away from themselves. Some of the same techniques can be used here. For example, Dahl (2010) argues that food corporations engage in 'deep greenwash' – a political strategy advocating for corporate voluntary self-policing using substantial greenwashing practices – at the expense of more authoritative government policies. Without public regulation, there is no formal process to punish any harmful practices of food corporations, and the responsibilisation of the consumer escalates. Part of this blame-shifting strategy involves food corporations positioning themselves as beyond the law. Companies try to pre-empt food policy, including production regulations, marketing laws and specific food taxes, by constructing their own policy initiatives (Lang and Heasman, 2004). Parker and Scrinis (2014) argue that such practices allow food businesses, and supermarkets in particular, to become 'regulatory authorities', sometimes even displacing governmental standards. This means that the interests of food industries prevail, potentially at the expense of the wellbeing of (human) animals and the environment. In other ways, food retailers embrace CSR ideas in order to tactically retreat from some forms of blame. For instance, rather than contribute to the problem of food waste, supermarkets and grocery retailers 'practise CSR' by donating unsellable food to charitable organisations (Devin and Richards, 2016). This largely shifts responsibility for food waste from food retailers on to other parts of the food system, rather than dealing with such food crime directly.

Perhaps the most extreme defence strategy food corporations utilise involves forms of cooptation of food movement practices and/or ideologies. This is especially witnessed in association with the organic food movement where – often large – conventional food companies (producing non-organic foodstuffs) are acquiring (buying out) smaller organic food companies, and continuing to produce an organic line of commodities. Friedmann (2005) terms this a modification of the corporate food regime into the 'corporate-environmental food regime', where the result is less full corporate cooptation than a hybrid of food commodification and food democracy (Johnston et al, 2009). Nonetheless, the ownership details of many organic products are concealed, thus it is very difficult for consumers to know if a specific organic food product is produced, processed and marketed by a largely non-organic mainstream firm. Concealing 'big food' ownership is valuable to such food corporations, as knowledge that purchasing organic food is profitable for a predominately conventional company would cause significant customer loss (Howard, 2016). This veil is furthered through what Scanlan (2013) terms 'grainwashing' – or what the industry and its allies call CSR – where food corporations use 'feeding the world' rhetoric to distract the public from the political economic perspective of food and agriculture and recognition of the food crime and harms that occur. Even the growing argument that 'we need all solutions' is a broad deflection of the role of the corporate food regime in undermining all forms of solutions (Holt-Giménez and Shattuck, 2011; see Chapter 2, this volume).

These types of techniques work to reproduce the current risky food regime, and negate the goals of food movements and activists. Consider the case of food labels. The idea is that food labels display information for consumers to influence their rational decision whether to purchase any given product, thus maintaining the consumer responsibilisation ideology. However, critical researchers, such as Knezevic (2012, p 11), argue that labels actually serve the industry, assuring consumers that it is acceptable to *not* know where food comes from, further 'separating people from the sources of their food and nutrition with as many interventions as possible.' This is accompanied with other problems, including power imbalances in standards and certification processes (Jaffee and Howard, 2010), and within-group disputes resulting in the use and promotion of eco labels to defy the bureaucratic realities of organic label criteria (Howard and Allen, 2010). This all distracts from food crimes and harms, and continues to reproduce the structures of the risky food regime and responsibilise consumers. While these CSR-based defence strategies have negative influences on contemporary food movements, it is the contradictions surrounding the idea of responsibility – and choice – that prove most problematic.

The food police

The success of neoliberal politics, the risky food regime and the defence strategies of food industries has prioritised a culture and environment of choice – food choice. This is part of the 'reformist trend' within the corporate food regime, where food movements and food activism are defined as 'consumption-as-politics' (Holt-Giménez and Shattuck, 2011). The idea is that change can happen without jeopardising consumer choice. This is embodied through movements advocating for the use of brand boycotts – or 'buycotts' – or purchasing organic or fairtrade products, which produce this idea that one can vote with one's fork.

Food corporations are keen to keep food choice as a paramount value, as it continues to responsibilise individuals while enabling food industries to produce, market and profit from more and more foodstuffs. To do this, food corporations align themselves with consumers, congratulating themselves for offering consumers so many great options, and target regulatory bodies or governments as their enemies – the evil 'food police' (Simon, 2006). This clash goes beyond formal policy-makers and enforcers, to involve various forms of informal governance of food choice. Food industries argue that any type of 'liberal' intervention is condescending because it deems individuals as unintelligent and irrational victims (Lang and Heasman, 2004). The perpetrators involve anyone 'bent on taking away the rights of consumers – even children – to freely decide which foods are best for them' (Simon, 2006, p 36), from certified nutritionists and government food guides, to preachy environmentalists or hippy vegans. These 'food cops' are projected as undesirable and unconstructive: 'if you believe the blandishments of the self-styled food police, every food science innovation further contributes to obesity, chronic diseases, and even addiction to fat and sugar' (Stier and Miller, 2013, p 8). It is fathomable that the majority of the contributors to this book would be characterised as food police. This creates quite the paradox, as food corporations are (in)directly involved in facilitating and causing a variety of food crimes and harms, but shift the criminal language to those agents whom seek to mitigate or prevent such problems.

The reality, however, is that food choice is less about freedom and more about options. Choices are often the product of industry marketing and environmental impositions, such as allocation of pseudo-foods – as key profit-makers – on privileged retail spaces on supermarket shelves (Winson, 2004). Even retailers following CSR principles, such as Whole Foods Market, prioritise consumers' choice of products at the expense of citizenship duties (Johnston, 2008). The food system embodies complex and multiple economic, political, social and cultural processes operating beyond individual control, impacting food access and selection, yet responsibilising individual consumers for their choices, even when they have little to no control over them (Simon, 2006; Martin, 2012).

Recognising this context, Thaler and Sunstein (2008) argue that in order to avoid formal regulations, food industries utilise 'nudges'. Nudges are non-commanding architectures of choice, or the way in which options are presented to suggest choices without limiting or penalising other choices (Scrinis and Parker, 2016): 'putting the fruit at eye level counts as a nudge. Banning junk food does not' (Thaler and Sunstein, 2008, p 6). Labels are common examples, which somewhat inform consumers but more so obscure food production conditions, fail to empower consumers, and further nutricentric dependence on expert advice (Parker, 2013; Scrinis and Parker, 2016), while being ineffective in tackling major health improvements in populations (Rayner and Lang, 2011). This confinement of choices parallels a deskilling of consumerism where food industries aim to 'save consumers from themselves' (Simon, 2006; Howard, 2016), through offering 100 calorie snack packs rather than unrationed portions, or microwaveable oatmeal so individuals no longer have to worry about boiling water for instant oatmeal.

In the risky food regime, the food police are problematic. Agents seeking to intervene in consumers' food choices are perceived as threatening market freedom, and by proxy, threatening the responsibilised consumer discourse. Meanwhile, food corporations actively interfere in the food supply and mediate consumer choice through a variety of CSR-driven defence strategies in reaction to food activist movements seeking to prevent food crimes and harms. Food industries are arguably the most deserving of the food police label, and through the perpetuation of food choice discourse, are also the key facilitators of food crime.

Conclusion

The contemporary global food system is a 'risky food regime', where the array of food crimes and harms are conceptualised as normal probability-based outcomes of chance. A variety of food activist movements have developed in response to these problems, but food industries actively work to resist or coopt these reactions through several types of defence strategies. Largely controlled by industrial food corporations, and maintained by neoliberal cultural-politics, food has become a tool to characterise individuals as consumers and circumscribe their power in the food system to their food choices. Every bite taken symbolises a political vote for how the food system operates and what it produces, but it also marks individuals with responsibility for the consequences of the food system, regardless of the limited control individuals have over their dietary decisions.

The extent of the varied examples of food crime documented in this book point to an uncomfortable reality that the transition to a safer and/or less harmful food regime will be difficult at best. Food corporations have coopted the individual responsibility discourse, leaving individuals with a false belief that they are able to – and must – make good food choices, and a false sense that 'buycotts' and 'voting with forks' can change corporate behaviour. The system is harmful itself, and rather than continue this cycle, no matter how difficult it will be to accomplish substantial structural and discursive change, it is time for a food regime change.

Note

[1] It makes sense to me that links to food industries or food corporations are omitted from the title of the contemporary food regime, as the purpose of the neoliberal food system is to deflect blame from them, and to responsibilise the consumer. Thus the concept: risky food regime.

References

Abbots, E. and Coles, B. (2015) 'Horsemeat-gate: The discursive production of a neoliberal food scandal', *Food, Culture & Society: An International Journal of Multidisciplinary Research*, vol 16, no 4, pp 535–50.

Alkon, A. and Mares, T. (2012) 'Food sovereignty in US food movements: Radical visions and neoliberal constraints', *Agriculture and Human Values*, vol 29, no 3, pp 347–59.

Carroll, A.B. (1979) 'A three-dimensional conceptual model of corporate performance', *The Academy of Management Review*, vol 4, no 4, pp 497–505.

Carroll, A.B. (1999) 'The pyramid of corporate social responsibility: Towards the moral management of organization stakeholders', *Business Horizon*, vol 34, no 4, pp 39–48.

Clapp, J. (2014) 'Food security and food sovereignty', *Dialogues in Human Geography*, vol 4, no 2, pp 206–11.

Clendenning, J., Dressler, W. and Richards, C. (2016) 'Food justice or food sovereignty? Understanding the rise of urban food movements in the USA', *Agriculture and Human Values*, vol 33, no 1, pp 165-77.

Dahl, R. (2010) 'Green washing: Do you know what you're buying?', *Environmental Health Perspectives*, vol 118, no 6, A234.

Department of Economic and Social Affairs (2011) *The global social crisis: Report on the world social situation 2011*, United Nations (www.un.org/esa/socdev/rwss/docs/2011/rwss2011.pdf).

Devin, B. and Richards, C. (2016) 'Food waste, power, and corporate social responsibility in the Australian food supply chain', *Journal of Business Ethics*, doi: 10.1007/s10551-016-3181-z.

Dixon, J. (2009) 'From the imperial to the empty calorie: How nutrition relations underpin food regime transitions', *Agriculture and Human Values*, vol 26, pp 321–33.

Frank, T. (1998) *The conquest of cool: Business culture, counterculture, and the rise of hip consumerism*, Chicago, IL: University of Chicago Press.

Friedmann, H. (2003) 'The political economy of food: A global crisis', *New Left Review*, vol 197, pp 29–57.

Friedmann, H. (2005) 'From colonialism to green capitalism: Social movements and the emergence of food regimes', in F.H. Buttel and P. McMichael (eds) *New directions in the sociology of international development: Research in rural sociology and developments* (vol 11), Amsterdam: Elsevier, pp 227–64.

Friedmann, H., and McMichael, P. (1989) 'Agriculture and the state system: The rise and decline of national agricultures, 1870 to the present', *Sociologia Ruralis*, vol 29, pp 93–117.

Fuentes, M. and Fuentes, C. (2015) 'Risk stories in the media: Food consumption, risk and anxiety', *Food, Culture & Society*, vol 18, no 1, pp 71–87.

Gillespie, K. (2015) 'Nonhuman animal resistance and the improprieties of live property', in I. Braveman (ed) *Animals, biopolitics, law: Lively legalities* (edited by I. Braveman), New York: Routledge, pp 115–32.

Goodman, M.K., Maye, D. and Holloway, L. (2010) 'Ethical foodscapes? Premises, promises, and possibilities', *Environment and Planning A*, vol 42, pp 1782–96.

Guthman, J. (2003) 'Fast food/organic food: Reflexive tastes and the making of "yuppie chow"', *Social and Cultural Geography*, vol 4, no 1, pp 45–58.

Guthman, J. (2008) 'Bringing good food to others: Investigating the subjects of alternative food practice', *Cultural Geographies*, vol 15, no 4, pp 431–47.

Halkier, B. (2001) 'Consuming ambivalences: Consumer handling of environmentally related risks in food', *Journal of Consumer Culture*, vol 1, no 2, pp 205–24.

Hartmann, M. (2011) 'Corporate social responsibility in the food sector', *European Review of Agricultural Economics*, vol 38, no 3, pp 297–324.

Heath, J. and Potter, A. (2004) *Rebel sell: Why the culture can't be jammed*, Toronto: Harper Collins.

Heikkurinen, P. and Forsman-Huggs, S. (2011) 'Strategic corporate social responsibility in the food chain', *Corporate Social Responsibility and Environmental Management*, vol 18, pp 306–16.

Holt-Giménez, E. and Shattuck, A. (2011) 'Food crises, food regimes and food movements: Rumblings of reform or tides of transformation?', *Journal of Peasant Studies*, vol 38, no 1, pp 109–44.

Holtzman, J. (2013) 'Reflections on fraught food', in E.J. Abbots and A. Lavis (eds) *Why we eat, how we eat: Contemporary encounters between foods and bodies*, Aldershot: Ashgate, pp 139–43.

Howard, P.H. (2016) *Concentration and power in the food system: Who controls what we eat?*, London: Bloomsbury Publishing.

Howard, P.H. and Allen, P. (2010) 'Beyond organic and fair trade? An analysis of ecolabel preferences in the United States,' *Rural Sociology*, vol 75, no 2, pp 244–69.

Jaffee, D. and Howard, P. (2010) 'Corporate cooptation of organic and fair trade standards', *Agriculture and Human Values*, vol 27, no 4, pp 387–99.

Johnston, J. (2008) 'The citizen–consumer hybrid: Ideological tensions and the case of Whole Foods Market', *Theory and Society*, vol 37, no 3, pp 229–70.

Johnston, J. and Szabo, M. (2011) 'Reflexivity and the Whole Foods Market consumer: The lived experience of shopping for change', *Agriculture and Human Values*, vol 28, no 3, pp 303–19.

Johnston, J., Biro, A. and Mackendrick, N. (2009) 'Lost in the supermarket: The corporate-organic foodscape and the struggle for food democracy', *Antipode*, vol 41, no 3, pp 509–32.

Knezevic, I. (2012) 'Labels and governance: Promises, failures, and deceptions of food labelling', in M. Koç, J. Sumner, and A. Winson (eds) *Critical perspectives in food studies*, Ontario: Oxford University Press, pp 247–59.

La Via Campensina (2011) *The international peasant's voice* (www.viacampesina.org/en/index.php/organisation-mainmenu-44).

Lang, T.M. and Heasman, A. (2004) *Food wars: The global battle for mouths, minds and markets*, London: Earthscan.

Lawrence, J.C. (2014) 'The EU in crisis: Crisis discourse as a technique of government', *Netherlands Yearbook of International Law*, vol 44, pp 187–202.

Levenstein, H.A. (2012) *Fear of food: A history of why we worry about what we eat*, Chicago, IL: University of Chicago Press.

Levidow, L. (2015) 'European transitions towards a corporate-environmental food regime: Agroecological incorporation or contestation?', *Journal of Rural Studies*, vol 40, pp 76–89.

Marotta, G., Simeone, M. and Nazzaro, C. (2014) 'Product reformulation in the food system to improve food safety. Evaluation of policy interventions', *Appetite*, vol 74, pp107–15.

Martin, D. (2012) 'Nutrition transition and the public-health crisis', in M. Koç, J. Sumner and A. Winson (eds) *Critical perspectives in food studies*, Ontario: Oxford University Press, pp 208–22.

McMichael, P. (2009) 'A food regime genealogy', *The Journal of Peasant Studies*, vol 36, pp 139–69.

Meah, A. and Watson, M. (2013) 'Cooking up consumer anxieties about "provenance" and "ethics": Why it sometimes matter where foods come from in domestic provisioning', *Food, Culture and Society*, vol 16, no 3, pp 495–512.

Milne, R., Wenzer, J., Brembeck, H. and Brodin, M. (2011) 'Fraught cuisine: Food scares and the modulation of anxieties', *Distinction: Scandinavian Journal of Social Theory*, vol 12, no 2, pp 177–92.

Paarlberg, R. (2010) *Food politics: What everyone needs to know*, New York: Oxford University Press.

Parker, C. (2013) 'Voting with your fork? Industrial free-range eggs and the regulatory construction of consumer choice', *The ANNALS of the American Academy of Political and Social Science*, vol 629, no 1, pp 52–73.

Parker, C. and Scrinis, G. (2014) 'Out of the cage and into the barn: Supermarket power food system governance and the regulation of free range eggs', *Griffith Law Review*, vol 23, no 2, pp 318–47.

Pechlaner, G., and Otero, G. (2010). 'The neoliberal food regime: Neoregulation and the new division of labor in North America', *Rural Sociology*, vol 75, no 2, pp 179–208.

Polanyi, K. (1957 [1944]) *The great transformation: The political and economic origins of our time*, Boston, MA: Beacon Press.

Rayner, G. and Lang, T. (2011) 'Is nudge an effective public health strategy to tackle obesity? "No"', *British Medical Journal*, vol 342, pp 898–9.

Richards, Z., Thomas, S.L., Randle, M. and Pettigrew, S. (2015) 'Corporate social responsibility programs of big food in Australia: A content analysis of industry documents', *Australian and New Zealand Journal of Public Health*, vol 39, no 6, pp 550–6.

Rijkers, G.T., de Vos, W.M., Brummer, R., Morelli, L., Corthier, G. and Marteau, P. (2011) 'Health benefits and health claims of probiotics: Bridging science and marketing', *British Journal of Nutrition*, vol 106, no 9, pp 1291–6.

Scanlan, S.J. (2013) 'Feeding the planet or feeding us a line? Agribusiness, "grainwashing" and hunger in the world food system', *International Journal of Sociology of Agriculture and Food*, vol 20, no 3, pp 357–82.

Scrinis, G. (2013) *Nutritionism: The science and politics of dietary advice*, New York: Columbia University Press.

Scrinis, G. and Parker, C. (2016) 'Front-of-pack labeling and the politics of nutritional nudges', *Law & Policy*, vol 38, no 3, pp 234–49.

Simon, M. (2006) *Appetite and profit: How the food industry undermines our health and how to fight back*, New York: Nation Books.

Stier, J. and Miller, H. (2013) 'How much of food activism is nonsense', *Regulation*, vol 36, no 2, pp 8–10.

Stone, G.D. and Glover, D. (2011) 'Genetically modified crops and the "food crisis": Discourse and material impacts', *Development in Practice*, vol 21, nos 4–5, pp 509–16.

Thaler, R. and Sunstein, C. (2008) *Nudge: Improving decisions about health, wealth and happiness*, New York: Penguin Books.

Winson, A. (2004) 'Bringing political economy into the debate on the obesity epidemic', *Agriculture and Human Values*, vol 21, no 4, pp 299–312.

Winson, A. (2013) *The industrial diet: The degradation of food and the struggle for healthy eating*, New York: New York University Press.

Winson, A. and Choi, J.Y. (2016) 'Dietary regimes and the nutrition transition: Bridging disciplinary domains', *Agriculture and Human Values*, doi: 10.1007/s10460-016-9746-8.

Index

Note: the following abbreviations are used – f = figure; n = note; t = table